RÉGION ET DÉVELOPPEMENT

n° 39-2014

The regional dimension of economic crisis in Greece

L'Harmattan

REVUE RÉGION ET DÉVELOPPEMENT

Revue fondée en 1995 par Gilbert Benhayoun et Maurice Catin

Revue semestrielle référencée dans ECONLIT et dans IDEAS (REPEC)

Site web : www.regionetdeveloppement.org
ISSN 2117-0843

5-7, rue de l'Ecole polytechnique, 75005 Paris

http://www.harmattan.fr
diffusion.harmattan@wanadoo.fr
harmattan1@wanadoo.fr
ISBN : 978-2-343-05132-1
EAN : 9782343051321

Région et Développement

n° 39 - 2014

The regional dimension of economic crisis in Greece

Guest edited by
Yannis PSYCHARIS, Michel DIMOU, George PETRAKOS

INTRODUCTION TO THE SPECIAL ISSUE:

ECONOMIC CRISIS IN GREECE - LOOKING AT THE GEOGRAPHICAL IMPACTS

Yannis PSYCHARIS[*], **Michel DIMOU**[**], **George PETRAKOS**[***]

This special issue focuses on the geographical impact of economic crisis in Greece. During the years 2008-2014 Greece has experienced the most severe economic crisis in its modern history with an unprecedented 26 % shrinkage of GDP, 16% reduction in declared income (2009-2012) and a rocketed in 27% of labor force unemployment rate. These trends have made Greece one of the countries most affected by the recent Great Recession. While aspects of the Greek economic crisis have been discussed within different contexts in economics literature, the regional dimension of the crisis is still a relatively less debated issue. However, the geographical dimension of economic crisis is of particular importance for economic analysis and policy and Greece is offering a representative example that may go beyond the peculiarities of the Greek case.

The links between economic crisis and geography are ever stronger today for quite a few reasons. First, geography is an integral part of European integration. Economic crisis which is widening the asymmetry in the levels of economic development within Europe questions the functioning of the European economy as a whole. Second, economic crisis put a threat on the returns of the cohesion policy which has been an explicit policy goal for the European Union over a long period of time and for which there has been invested a great amount of structural assistance/funding from the E.U. budget. Finally, the social impacts of crisis and the degradation of urban environment questions the pace and limits of urbanization that has been under process in many countries across the globe in recent years.

The idea for this special issue on the Greek economic crisis started in September 2013, following the interesting debates that took place during the special session that was organized in Florence within the GDRI-DREEM (Développement des Recherches Economiques Euro-Méditerranéenes) conference. The positive feedback from the conference along with the awareness that there has been a gap in the literature regarding the regional dimension of economic crisis

[*] Panteion University of Social and Political Sciences, Department of Economic and Regional Development. psycharis@panteion.gr
[**] LEAD, University of Toulon. dimou@univ-tln.fr
[***] Department of Planning and Regional Development, University of Thessaly. petrakos@uth.gr

The editors of the special issue would like to thank the GDRI CNRS DREEM for the setting up of a special seminar on the Greek crisis during the Conference in Firenze on September 2013. This seminar has been the starting point for this special issue.

made the preparation of a special issue on this theme a very tempting task. This selection of papers is a representative example of the research that is recently being carried out by Greek academics and prominent researchers in this field.

The papers that are included in this special session look at the impacts of economic crisis at different geographical scales such as regions, cities, urban space. They cover a variety of issues on the geography of crisis impact such as employment and unemployment, regional development, poverty, housing market, construction, tourism and agriculture. These attempts are supported by recent key statistical data and sources that have been collected to fulfill the requirements of this issue. In sum, this issue is providing unique evidence on the relationship between economic crisis and geography that could go beyond the peculiarities of Greece.

The paper by **George Petrakos** is an introductory paper and provides a chronicle of the economic crisis in Greece along with a detailed account of the underlying causes and drivers. The author argues that policy deficits and the mismanagement of the crisis at the European and the national level jointly reinforced a negative spiral that after some point accelerated and had snow-ball effects for the Greek economy. It also discusses the lessons learned and makes some useful policy recommendations to finding the ways out of the crisis.

The next five papers are making an attempt to modeling economic crisis regional effects. The first paper by **Vassilis Monastiriotis** deals with the regional unemployment incidence and regional labor markets. The key issue under consideration is to examine whether the crisis led to convergence in the way the country's regional labor markets reward different labor characteristics. Descriptive evidence from aggregate data suggests that regional wages show signs of accelerated convergence during the crisis. Underneath this aggregate pattern of 'convergence through crisis', however, it finds significant heterogeneity, implying that regional responses to the crisis have been far from uniform.

The paper by **Yannis Psycharis, Antonis Rovolis, Vassilis Tselios and Panayotis Pantazis** sets out to examine the determinants of regional development in Greece before and during the economic crisis. By proposing an econometric model with spatial effects for the years 2005-2008 and 2009-2011, which represent the sub-periods of growth and decline of the Greek economy respectively, they make it possible to capture the different factors that affect the regional economic development of the NUTS III regions in the country. Results highlight that the most urbanized and high income level regions are more affected by the economic crisis.

The paper by **Alexandra Schaffar and Sotiris Pavleas** aims to study the evolution of urban hierarchies and the nature of urban growth processes in Greece from 1951 to 2011. The main results are that the Greek cities converge towards a middle city-size population throughout the study period, while the preeminence of the Athens agglomeration slowly decreases. In addition the paper delivers evidence concerning the changes that affect urban demographical trends in Greece over the last decade. These changes can be related to the economic crisis and the profound socioeconomic upheaval that Greece has undergone since the beginning of the 21st century.

The paper by **Aggeliki Anagnostou and Stephanos Papadamos** employs a Bayesian PVAR model to measure the impact of monetary policy shocks on regional output of 58 regions of four South Euro-Zone countries: Greece, Spain, Italy and Portugal over the period 1980-2009. The results provide evidence of different regional responses of regional GDP on monetary policy shocks. The policy's asymmetric effects are explained by employing the Optimal Currency Area which provides a good framework for understanding the asymmetric effects of the monetary policy shocks in the South European Regions.

The paper by **Panagiotis Artelaris and George Kandylis** deals with poverty. The aim of this paper is to assess and map, the distribution of poverty at the NUTS III level in Greece, as well as to evaluate and map the regional impact of the ongoing economic crisis on poverty, by comparing the poverty rates before and during the crisis (in 2005 and 2011). Analysis that is based on Small Area Estimation technique shows that the significant increase in the national anchored at-risk-of-poverty (AROP) rate in a period of severe recession is reflected in every single NUTS III region, especially in the vast and relatively prosperous metropolitan regions where the highest increase in AROP rates takes place.

The next two papers deal with the impact of crisis on housing, urban segregation and real estate market and focus more specifically on the Athens agglomeration. The paper by **Dimitris Emmanuel** examines the impact of the economic crisis on the home ownership pattern with a specific reference to Athens. Home ownership is very high in Greece and very common feature in Southern European countries. The paper argues that the most important consequence of the crisis on home ownership is a radical change in the system of small housing production, widespread property ownership and familist support. These trends constitute a shift to a sharply modified "southern" housing regime rather than simply a prolonged economic shock.

The paper by **Thomas Maloutas** also deals with Athens the capital city of Greece and discusses how economic crisis has impacted on the socio-spatial restructuring of the city. The discussion focuses on the rather weak social polarization and segregation resulting from global forces until the mid-2000s, and on the subsequent change of socioeconomic and demographic conditions forming a new social and political environment in which the socially dividing impact of the current crisis is potentially becoming deep.

Finally, the last two papers deal feature more empirical analysis concerning the resilience of the Greek regions, the impacts of the crisis over tourism, which is an important sector of the Greek economy and the locational behavior of urban Greek households during the crisis.

The paper from **Andreas Papatheodorou and Pavlos Arvanitis** concerns tourism. Tourism has been considered as one of resilient factors that would potentially help the country to counter-balance (at least in part) the income loses as a subsequent result of economic crisis. Based on different spatial indexes, analysis shows that a new geography of tourism seems to emerge in Greece during the economic crisis where the clear losers are those regions, which had specialized predominantly in domestic tourism. From a policy perspective, this stresses the need to expedite the internationalization of the tourism profile of the regions in question to overcome the adverse effects of the economic crisis.

The last paper by **Marie-Noëlle Duquenne** analyses how economic crisis has impacted on agricultural sector and whether there has been a return of people from cities to homeland places and the extent to which they age engaged in agricultural activities. Results show that some rural territories in Greece seem to follow a dynamic demographical trend during the crisis thanks to migration from urban households.

Summing up, this selection of papers explicitly relates the impact of economic crisis on the spatial economy and provides unique evidence from Greece. However, the economic variables under consideration, the analytical techniques that have been applied and the variety of issues covered give to this attempt a novelty that can communicate with the international literature and make a contribution to the scientific discussions in this field.

ECONOMIC CRISIS IN GREECE. EUROPEAN AND DOMESTIC MARKET AND POLICY FAILURES

George PETRAKOS*

Abstract **-** *This paper provides a detailed account of the drivers behind the economic crisis in Greece, which has destroyed one quarter of the GDP of the economy and has led more than a quarter of labour force to unemployment in a period of five years. The paper claims that a mix of background factors at the European and the national level and the policy reaction to the crisis jointly reinforced a negative spiral that after some point accelerated and had snowball effects for the Greek economy. At the European level the background factor is the unbalanced European economic architecture, while at the national level the background factors include the structural weaknesses of the economy and the operation of the political system and the public sector. These factors, along with a number of serious policy deficits and the mismanagement of the crisis at the European and domestic level have transformed quickly Greece from a celebrated success story to a disappointing failure and the EU economy for a first time to an unsecure landscape with many slippery spaces in its periphery.*

Key words **-** ECONOMIC CRISIS, AUSTERITY PROGRAMS, GREECE, EUROPEAN ECONOMY

JEL Classification **-** A1, B2

---

* Department of Planning and Regional Development, University of Thessaly.
petrakos@uth.gr

1. INTRODUCTION

Taking a broader perspective in the understanding of the economic crisis in Greece, a critical and somehow uncomfortable question arises: How is it possible for an economy, member of the Eurozone, that was considered to be a 'success story' of convergence in Europe for more than a decade (in the period 1995-2009) to turn out to be considered as a profound case of failure in the early 2010 and beyond and subsequently suffer a deep and unprecedented economic crisis, in which it lost almost 25% of its GDP in a period of 5 years? This dramatic change in the perception of the Greek economy by international policy makers and markets in a period of a few months is a rare event in economic history that deserves a closer examination and a better understanding in the hope to avoid similar situations in the future.

This paper intends to discuss a number of important questions related to the Greek economic crisis taking a critical perspective and putting on the discussion table all these elements that have affected it, either as background factors, or as accelerators during its evolution. Although the discussion is highly diverse, there are clear interdependencies: The understanding or the perceptions about the causes of the crisis determine to a large extent the policy response to the crisis. The discussion about the policy mix becomes a more complicated issue when the causes of the crisis are both domestic and European.

We need to learn something concrete about the causes of the crisis, the policies that were applied in order to confront it and especially about the strength of the relationship between the causes of the crisis and the policy reaction mix. Finally, we would definitely like to know if there was an alternative policy reaction path and what is the eventual assessment of the effectiveness of the current 'austerity plus reforms' policy mix.

2. THE CHRONICLE AND THE EFFECTS OF THE CRISIS

After an audit ordered by the newly elected Socialist government, public deficit for 2009 was reported to be 12.7% and later 15.4% of GDP instead of roughly 6% stated by the previous government. The cost of borrowing started to increase dramatically (Table 1) and financial markets closed for Greece in a period of a few months (Bank of Greece 2011a). An *ad hoc* rescue mechanism[1] was decided by the EC, the ECB and the IMF (the Troika), according to which a €110 billion loan (and later a debt haircut) was provided in combination with an austerity program and a reform program (Monastiriotis 2013). The austerity measures were supposed to eliminate the public deficit in a period of 2-3 years,

[1] This rescue mechanism was not foreseen in the EU Treaties and was against their spirit, as they include a number of conditions that (in theory) prevent the accumulation of excess debt in the Eurozone countries. The mechanism was based on lending provided primarily by the other Eurozone countries in proportion to their size and after receiving permit from their national parliaments. IMF had a relatively small financial contribution and participated in the program because of its experience and expertise with austerity and reforms in over-debted countries.

mainly through wage and pension cuts and tax increases. In addition, a long list of structural reforms, including deregulation of markets, reorganization of the state and privatization were included in a Memorandum of Understanding that was signed between the Greek government and the EU, the IMF and the ECB. The austerity program was implemented according to schedule in a climate of severe political conflict and social protest with cross-the-board reduction in public spending, including wages, pensions and public investment and severe increases in taxation. On the other hand, the reform program and the privatization program were delayed in its implementation due to the indecisiveness of the government, the inability of the public sector to support the reforms and the strong public and political reaction. These programs were periodically evaluated, but also updated, with typically new conditions or goals being added after every review.

Table 1. Yields of Greek Government Bonds (Oct. 2009 - Dec. 2010)

		3-yrs	5-yrs	10-yrs
2009	October	2.26	3.37	4.57
2009	November	2.45	3.63	4.84
2009	December	3.72	4.67	5.49
2010	January	4.72	5.40	6.04
2010	February	5.92	6.30	6.46
2010	March	5.51	5.84	6.24
2010	April	7.91	7.87	7.83
2010	May	8.28	8.59	7.97
2010	June	9.41	9.50	9.10
2010	July	11.17	10.85	10.34
2010	August	11.65	11.33	10.70
2010	September	11.63	11.65	11.34
2010	October	9.64	9.64	9.57
2010	November	13.08	12.27	11.52
2010	December	13.75	12.89	12.01

Source: Bank of Greece (2011a).

The impact of the crisis and the austerity programs was severe and beyond any projection. Greece experienced a deep recession and lost in a period of five years 25% of its GDP and about one million employment positions. Unemployment jumped in 2013 to 27% and youth unemployment reached 50% (INE, 2013). An undermining, for the long-term prospects of the country, process of brain-drain takes place during the crisis, where the young and educated Greek population leaves massively the country in search of employment and security in the advanced EU economies. The crisis resulted in a severe social polarization and poverty, as about one-fourth of the population lives below the poverty line and thousands of homeless people and beggars plunder the centers of large cities[2]. The housing market collapsed, causing a severe reduction in the net wealth of the households, while hundreds of thousands of home owners are

[2] According to ELSTAT in 2011 24.8% of population lived in poverty (ELSTAT 2013). In the city of Athens alone, it is estimated that 20 thousand people live in the streets (Klimaka, 2013).

faced with the threat to lose their property because of their inability to serve their loans[3]. This will lead to a further polarization and an unprecedented in peace-time income redistribution at the expense of the weaker and more vulnerable groups. The inability of the two main center-left and center-right political parties to come up with a reasonable and sustainable 'national rescue' or 'national development plan' that will negotiate with the lenders has led to a serious political crisis, the undermining of democratic values and the rise of the extreme right[4].

One of the striking characteristics of the period was the failure of the Troika and especially the IMF to predict or estimate the impact of the austerity program on the economy. The drop in output is much higher than initially expected because of a gross underestimation of the government spending multiplier in Greece. As a result, the debt to GDP ratio continues to be very high (Figure 1), despite the billions of euros of the bailout programs, questioning the sustainability of the debt and the effectiveness of the whole program (Christodoulakis 2011, 2013).

Figure 1. Public Debt and the Debt-to-GDP ratio of Greece, 1990-2014

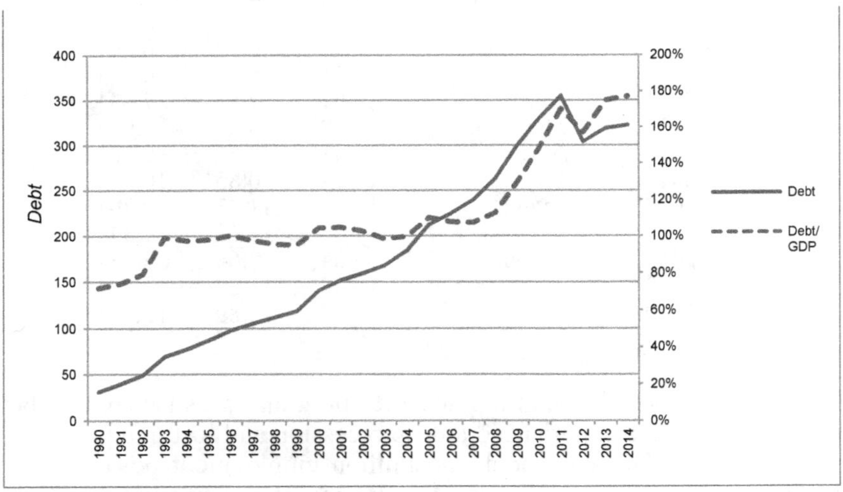

Source: AMECO (2014).

Because of the reduction in public investment[5], the only possible source of growth was the increase in private domestic and foreign investment. This, how-

[3] Non-performing loans reached 31% of total loans in 2013 (World Bank 2014).

[4] The neo-Nazi party of 'Chrisi Avgi' received in the 2012 parliamentary elections 7% of the vote and in the 2014 elections for Regional Governors 9.3% of the vote, taking the third place in the preferences of the voters. Its support was much stronger in poor inner city areas with high presence of illegal immigrants and in the social groups that were hit harder by the crisis (unemployed, home owners, elderly).

[5] From 9.5 billion in 2009 to 6.11 billion in 2012, that is a decline of 36% (Bank of Greece 2011b, 2014).

ever, did not happen. Private investment declined throughout the period[6] despite the serious reductions in labor cost and despite the reduction in State bureaucracy, because of the uncertainty that surrounds the future of the economy and the dramatic increase in taxation. FDI has been limited, declining and well below the EU average level (Figure 2), while in most cases they take the form of acquisitions of obsolete public enterprises or buy-outs of over-debted firms, especially in the service sector. This type of FDI is not really associated with new investment and new capital formation in the economy, but with a transfer of productive resources from domestic to foreign hands.

Figure 2. FDI stock per capita, 1995-2011

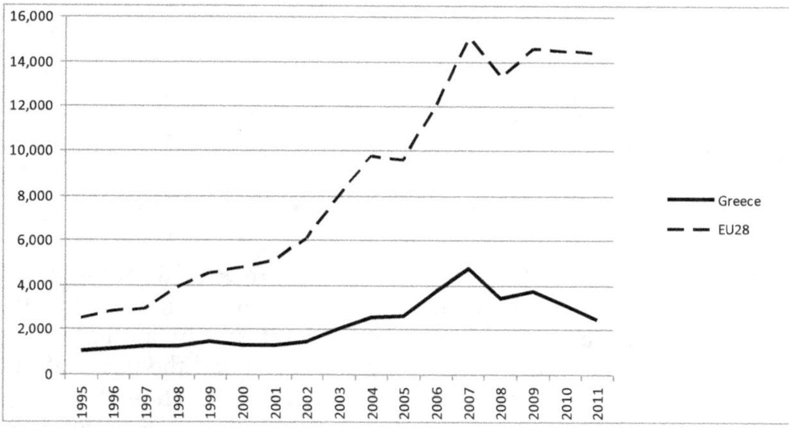

Source: UNCTAD (2013).

As a result, the recovery process of the economy is expected to be slow, even with the official IMF projections (Figure 3). This means that it may take Greece more than a decade to return to the GDP per capita ratio that it had before the crisis.

So, this is where we stand now: Dramatic losses in income and employment, an international rescue mechanism and a government with limited authority and under international supervision, continuous legislative reforms in nearly all aspects of economic life, but very little and slow progress in terms of recovery and for many people the wrong recipe. What has caused this 'sudden death' in the fastest converging Eurozone Member State in the pre-2010 decade (Arghyrou and Tsoukalas, 2011)? What went so wrong and an excess deficit situation evolved to the largest economic, political and humanitarian crisis that the country has lived after the WWII? Answering this question is a requirement in order to discuss policy options and in order to prevent the next crisis in the European landscape.

[6] In the period 2001-2008 average private investment was equal to 19.6% of GDP, while in 2012 it was only 11.2% of GDP. This accounts for a drop of 43% during the period of the crisis (Bank of Greece 2011b, 2014).

Figure 3. IMF projections of GDP: EU, EU>100 and Greece (2008=100)

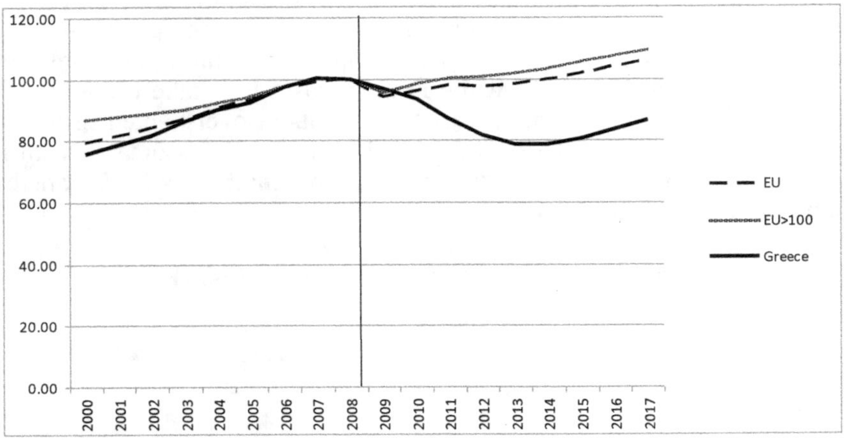

Source: IMF (2014).

3. THE DETERMINANTS OF THE CRISIS

We are going to argue in this section that the Greek crisis is the outcome of the combination and the accumulated impact of several developments at the domestic and the European level and not the outcome of a single overriding factor. A mix of background factors at the European and the national level and the policy reaction to the crisis jointly reinforced a negative spiral that after some point accelerated and had snow-ball effects. At the European level the background factor is the unbalanced European economic architecture, which generates more competition and more deficits than the South and the East can take, while at the national level the background factors include the structural weaknesses of the economy and the operation of the public sector. These factors, along with a number of serious policy deficits and the mismanagement of the crisis at the European and domestic level have transformed quickly Greece from a celebrated success story to a disappointing failure and the EU economy (for a first time) to an unsecure landscape with many slippery spaces in its periphery.

3.1. Unbalanced European economic architecture

There is plenty of evidence now that the progress made in the European economic space has been highly selective. Growth has been driven by scale effects, agglomeration economies, knowledge embedded in the quality of human resources, an integration process that was particularly friendly to forerunners and initial conditions with respect to place, market size and development levels. These drivers typically favor more the larger, central, advanced and with better economic structure areas, triggering mixed processes of inclusion – exclusion that make the European economy as heterogeneous as ever (Figure 4) (Petrakos 2008, Petrakos et al 2011). As a result, in relative terms, the economic picture of Europe looks very similar from decade to decade. Persistent North-South,

East-West and Core-Periphery patterns, associated with increasing inequalities at the regional level raise the question to what extent the celebrated convergence of the East and the South has been based on technological progress or on the accumulation of public and private debt (Petrakos et al 2014).

Figure 4. GDP per capita in NUTS II regions of EU, 2008

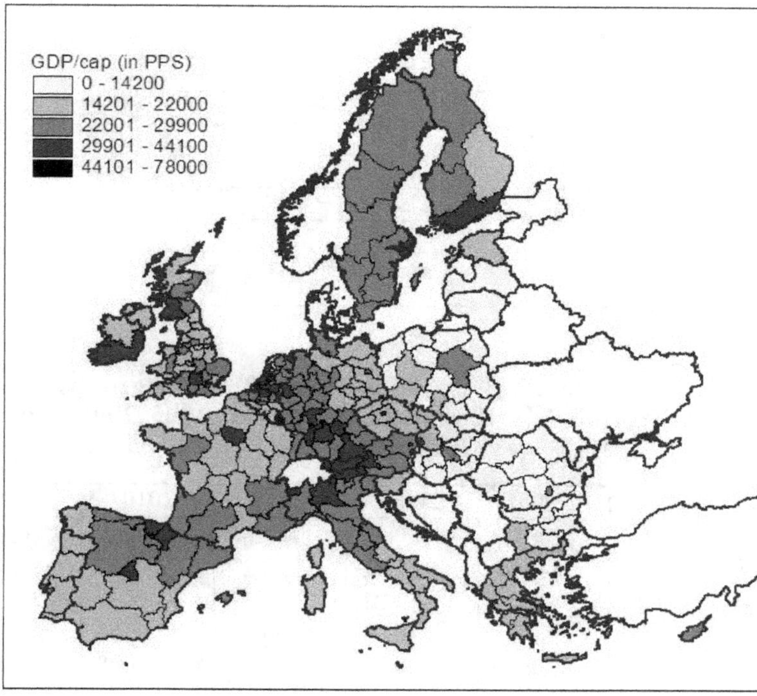

Source: Eurostat (2014).

These developments indicate that the European economic architecture, as it is presently shaped by the Single European Market, the Economic and Monetary Union, the Regulations and the Treaties produces more competition than the EU South (and East) could face. Serious and persistent differences in performances among the EU areas that were partially hidden in debt (Figures 5, Table 2) generated unsustainable trade and FDI imbalances.

It is clear that this particular type of integration is not a space neutral process. It is highly unbalanced and has combined open markets with increasing trade deficits and public deficits in the periphery, leading to a serious redistribution of income, wealth and resources at the expense of the less attractive or less productive places[7].

[7] A number of studies in the regional growth literature have provided evidence that the process of integration in the EU may increase inequalities and may have adverse effects in the less advanced regions that are mostly concentrated in the EU South and East (Petrakos et al. 2011; Fotopoulos et al. 2010; Petrakos et al. 2005; Petrakos 2003).

Figure 5. GDP per capita of top-20 and bottom-20 in NUTS II regions in EU-27, 1995-2009

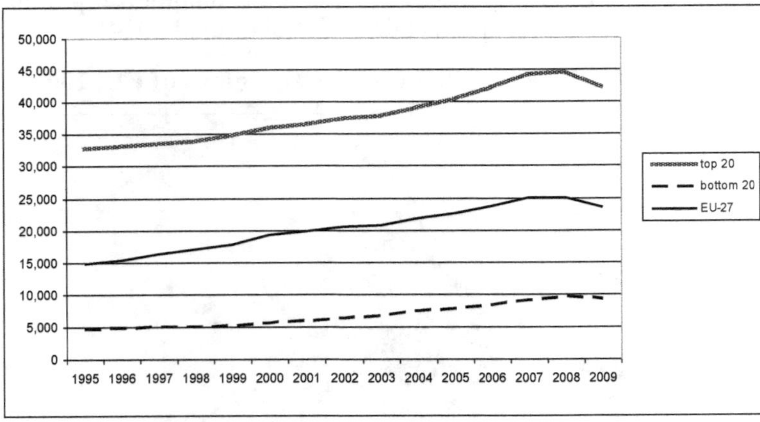

Source: Eurostat (2014).

Table 2. GDP per capita (EU=100) in the EU28 & subgroups EU<50, EU<75, EU<100, EU>100 for the years 1990, 1995, 2000, 2005, 2010 and 2013

	1995	2000	2005	2010	2013
EU-28	100.00	100.00	100.00	100.00	100.00
EU<50	21.30	24.32	28.27	32.34	34.01
EU<75	29.10	32.21	36.11	39.39	39.29
EU<100	42.95	46.65	50.70	52.68	51.74
EU>100	129.50	128.71	126.33	124.98	125.19
σ-convergence in EU-28	0.56	0.52	0.47	0.45	0.46

Source: Eurostat (2014).

Figure 6. Share of exports to EU and non-EU countries, 2001-2012

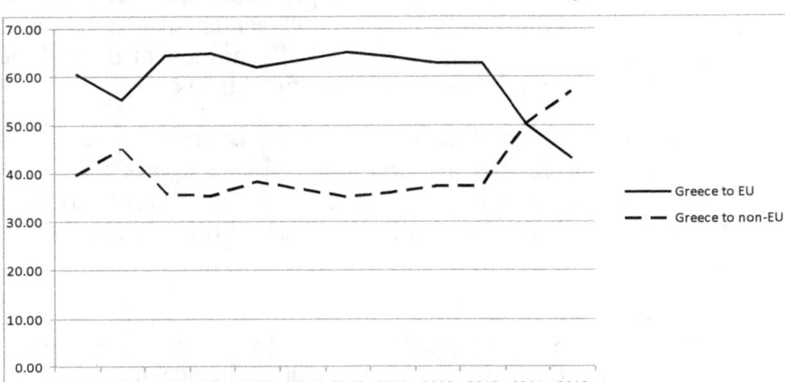

Source: World Bank (2014).

Figure 7. Trade deficit and public deficit as a share of GDP, 2009

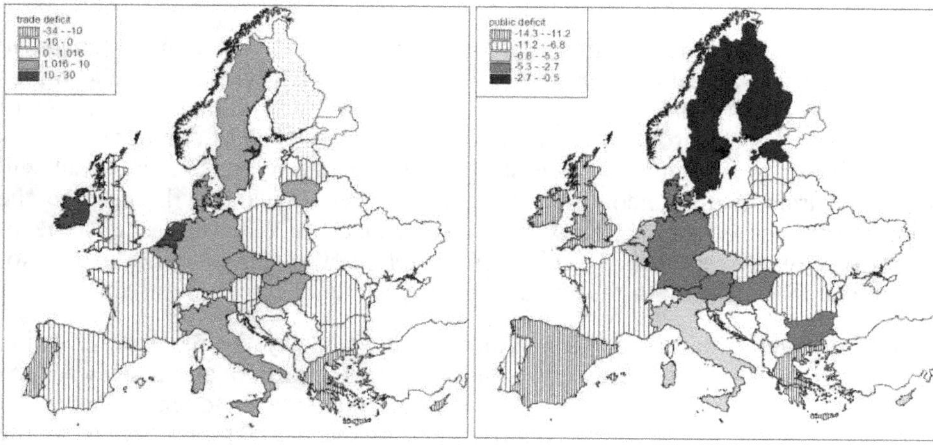

Source: World Bank (2014).

This unbalanced economic architecture has generated an interacting triple deficit of Europe. A high core-periphery competitiveness gap that has been based on serious differences in the availability, strength and quality of the drivers of growth among countries and regions triggers a serious core-periphery trade deficit that has been largely the outcome of a process of integration among unequal partners, where the more advanced run trade surpluses and the less advanced run trade deficits. Figure 7 shows that in 2009 only 9 (mostly advanced) EU countries were running a trade surplus. The remaining 19 countries were experiencing a trade deficit, while 10 of them were experiencing a trade deficit higher than 10% of GDP. These trade deficits imply excessive import penetration and lead to the contraction of the production base of the country and eventually to budget deficits, which depict to a large extent the inability of the private sector to generate enough employment and enough income and services in the less competitive Southern and Eastern economies[8]. There is a clear interdependence among the three deficits that in the absence of corrective policies takes a spiral form in the periphery: a continuous competitiveness gap leads to an increasing trade deficit, which in turn implies a higher import penetration and a contraction of the tradable part of the private sector. This results to a contraction in income (and tax revenues) and an increase in unemployment, which in turn leads to lower public revenues and higher public spending in terms of unemployment benefits and social protection measures. Therefore, an increasing competitiveness gap based on technological, institutional or geographical advantages quickly transforms to an increasing trade deficit and sooner or later to an increasing public deficit. Any attempt to stop this vicious cycle needs to understand the way of the causality and focus its attention on the deficiencies in the drivers of productivity growth (scale effects, agglomeration economies, the

[8] Figure 6 depicts the 'paradoxical' type of EU integration for Greece, which exports less to the EU than to the non-EU countries, indicating an increasing difficulty of the Greek products to penetrate the EU markets.

quality of human resources, type of integration, technology and institutions) if it wants to have long-term effects.

Any attempt to reduce deficits by corrective measures alone (like increase in taxes or cuts in spending) foreseen in the EU Treaties will only make things worse, as contractionary policies deal with the symptoms and not the causes of the competitiveness problem[9]. In addition, in Western type of democracies, it is very unlikely to implement successfully a self-corrective mechanism that will suppress dramatically incomes, wages, social benefits and will increase the competitiveness of the economy, simply because the effects of such type of austerity violates established social contracts and arrangements and lead to social unrest that increase instability and kill investment and competitiveness.

Unfortunately, the Eurozone architecture did not pay the required attention to the huge North-South deficiencies in the drivers of growth and considered the Treaty provisions for public deficits (which are however endogenous) as a sufficient condition for systemic stability[10]. However, the participation of the weaker EU members in Eurozone removed the ability to exercise national monetary policy (Kotios 2011) and intervene in the exchange rate market (Konhler 2012). At the same time, the Eurozone imposed excessive budgetary discipline, practically removing fiscal policy from the policy options of the weaker states (De Grauwe and Ji 2013). Therefore, the crisis in Greece simply revealed in the most dramatic way the weaknesses of the European economic architecture and especially the restrictions of the Stability and Growth Pact and the Lisbon Strategy (Ioannou and Stracca 2014) that did not include any offsetting mechanisms aiming to reduce major imbalances in growth potential among countries.

The European economic architecture did not also include any provision of synchronization in economic policy among the member states. When Germany imposed restrictions in wage rises during the decade before the crisis in order to keep labor unit cost more or less stable, the Southern European economies experienced an increase in unit labor cost of about one-third. This was due to a spiral of higher prices and higher wages that accrued from a model of growth in these economies that had a higher consumption component[11]. A decade later (in

---

[9] To a large extent the North-South competitiveness gap in the Eurozone was fuelled by suppressed wages in Germany and increased consumption in the South (Monastiriotis 2011), which was – however – a necessary condition for the production surplus of the North to be absorbed (Lapavitsas et al. 2010). Without the deficits of the southern countries, surplus countries would put in danger their growth rates since domestic demand was lower than total supply (Tsakalotos 2010).

[10] The EU architecture was based on the assumption that major economic shocks endogenous to the system are unlikely to come up considering unnecessary any mechanism for that kind of events (Tsakalotos 2010).

[11] Due to a complex set of transformations in the pre-crisis European division of labour the South was slowly replaced as a production space for traditional or labour-intensive products by the Eastern Europe and Asia) and was partly transformed to a consumption space intended to absorb the excess supply of the European North. To some extent, its function to prevent an over-production crisis in the North resulted to a debt-crisis in the South.

2011), the German economy had increased its competitiveness in the European and international market, while the South experienced a significant decline in international competitiveness and an equally significant increase in its trade deficit, which, to a large extent was the mirror-image of the German trade surplus (Miller and Sciacchitano 2012). If the economic policies of the EU member states were better synchronized at the European level in order to avoid undesirable side effects, if Germany had allowed for higher wages in order to support its economic expansion by an increase in domestic demand and not exports and if the Southern member states (and especially Greece) were more concerned about their cost base, Europe would have probably been a more balanced place and the crisis could have been avoided.

Finally, we have to notice that despite the high and recently increasing North-South and East-West inequalities in terms of development levels, the EU does not have yet an active fiscal policy that will_complement monetary policy and pursue the provision of equal quality of infrastructure and public services to its citizen. In the current arrangement fiscal policy is the responsibility of the member states, which means that the more affluent states with better infrastructure, better universities and better public services can continue to spend more to improve them, while the less affluent with serious deficiencies in all the above must do anything they can with their own limited resources, without borrowing very much from the markets because there is a ceiling in the Stability and Growth Pact and because all types of financial analysts, rating agencies and speculators are waiting in the corner. The lack of fiscal policy at the EU level and the absence of policy-led redistribution mechanisms that would (partially) counterbalance the intense market-led redistribution that took place mainly through trade flows in the EU is an important deficit in the European economic architecture that has contributed to the rising imbalances and the eventual outbreak of the crisis. The fact that Europe ended up during the crisis with both low total investment and an even more uneven distribution of that investment between its surplus and deficit regions is a clear indication of the absence of reliable fiscal policy with a clear counter-cyclical orientation (Torres 2013, Varoufakis et al. 2013).

The institutional setting of the European financial markets has also contributed to the outbreak and the acceleration of the crisis in two important ways. The first one is related to the unequal_borrowing conditions taking place for the European core and the European periphery in the early stages of the crisis. Typically, the weaker States in the South and the East borrow from the financial markets at a much higher interest rate than the advanced Western and Northern States. These differences are based on accreditation ratings provided by 'independent' rating agencies. The advanced EU countries have very high ratings allowing them to borrow at a very low interest rate and finance their budget in a more effective way, while the less advanced countries usually borrow at a higher or a much higher rate, with all the consequences that this may have in the formation of their debt. Apart from the discussions related to speculative games and the self-fulfilled prophecies of the rating agencies, a more fundamental problem arises here for the European economic architecture. How is it possible to expect convergence in the European economic landscape if the countries that need investment funds the most are either excluded from funding or pay a much higher interest rate? Also, how is it possible for the countries with the higher debt to reduce it, if serving the debt cost significantly more to those that are less able to pay? Would it be acceptable for the weakest German Lander to borrow in order to maintain its public sector at a rate that is 2, 3 or 5 times higher than that of Munich, Frankfurt or the Federal State? Clearly, the idea that each EU country is at each own when faced with the international financial markets produces not only inequality, but also inefficiency, as it increases the average borrowing rate of the European economy and therefore its growth prospects. In the case of Greece, the rapid deterioration of the borrowing conditions and the final cut off from the financial markets was the major factor that triggered the debt crisis.

The second way that the architecture of the financial system has contributed to the Greek crisis is related to the absence of an EU-wide guarantee of the bank deposits. This has made the guarantee of the Greek State for the deposits in the Greek banks to look unreliable during the crisis and has contributed to a fly of deposits even from healthy banks. This was one of the main mechanisms that transformed a debt crisis to a banking sector crisis and reduced dramatically the ability of the banks to finance investment activity[12]. When the discussion about default of Grexit among European policy makers, economic analysts and speculators took a critical momentum, about 80 billion euros fled the Greek banks because their owners did not want to risk waking up one day with (dramatically devalued) drachmas instead of euros[13]. The largest share of that money ended up in German and Swiss banks (Bank of Greece 2014)[14]. Therefore, the absence of a truly European banking system where the supervision of the banks will be the responsibility of the ECB and were deposits will be equally guaranteed in all countries has had a major role in transmitting the debt crisis to the banking sector and set in motion a negative spiral of deposit-fly, lack of liquidity in the economy and deeper recession.

It is clear that the mainstream economic model expectation that existing institutional arrangements were sufficient for the market forces to correct serious

---

[12] The banking sector in Greece suffered also from two more major negative developments: (a) the haircut of the Greek debt as it was holding a significant amount of Greek bonds and (b) the red loans that are related to the inability of households that lost their income and near bankrupt business to serve their loans. The recapitalization of the banking system by the ESF has increased the debt of Greece by 41 billion so far (Bank of Greece 2014).

[13] The total deposits in the Greek banks in 2009 were 237 billion. During the crisis (and until 2012) the banks lost about 80 billion (one-third of the deposits) of which 60 billion were transferred abroad (Bank of Greece 2014).

[14] As strange and unjust it may sound, the evidence shows that the German banks benefited from the Greek crisis by attracting deposits from Greece, but also from the rest of the European periphery, appearing as a 'safe haven' in a highly speculative and unstable environment for the deposits of the more affluent people in these countries. Therefore, the liquidity drought in the European South that made the exodus from the crisis more difficult was associated with an excess liquidity in the North that financed with very favorable terms the expansion of the economy.

imbalances was unrealistic. On the contrary, the market mechanisms revealed that the existing type of unfinished financial and economic integration was incapable to maintain the stability of the system for very long when the common currency was introduced (Mayer et al. 2012).

To summarize the argument, the economic crisis in Greece was simply the expression of an unavoidable Eurozone crisis, as the European economic architecture is ill-designed and generates imbalances that are very likely to lead to a debt crisis, typically by triggering speculation in the financial markets.

3.2. European and international policy failures: The response to the crisis

Judging from a distance, the most striking characteristic of the period was the slow reaction of the EU authorities to the rapid isolation of Greece from bond markets in late 2009 early 2010 (Christodoulakis 2011). This delay in decision making and the absence of a robust response resulted to a credibility crisis, attracted the attention of speculators and lead to the rise of spreads and eventually the fiscal crisis (Monastiriotis 2011). The existing EU mechanisms (Excessive Deficit Procedure and Stability and Growth Pact) failed to predict and prevent the crisis because they were too loose before and too strict after, producing a pro-cyclical bias (Collignon 2012).

This lack of reflex was often accompanied by negative rhetoric, changing positions and conflicting messages from the EC and some high level government officials from a number of advanced member states, who were mostly responding to the populist media in their countries and addressing domestic electorates. However, their views had high coverage in the media and were in line with the inclination of part of the political elites in some core EU countries to resort to punitive policies and actions.[15] Although this rhetoric was progressively abandoned as the crisis was escalating and spreading to other countries, it played an important role in increasing uncertainty about the future of Greece in the Eurozone and in turning the debt problem of a tiny economy (with less than 2% of European GDP and debt) to a systemic risk for the Eurozone.

The early slowness was replaced by an overreaction and unrealistic and hasty rescue programs that reduced severely aggregate demand and jeopardized the credibility of the banking sector. The program was strongly pro-cyclical and included excessive cuts in public spending that had strong recessionary effects. The program was based on a gross misunderstanding of the realities of the Greek economy and a serious underestimation of the government spending multiplier. Troika (in fact the IMF) was expecting in the early 2010 that the first program will cause a limited recession that would be followed by strong growth by the end of 2010 (Christodoulakis 2013). All the subsequent estimates of the impact of the program on the economy were also far away from the reality be-

[15] It seems that the view of severe punishment of Greece (including the exodus from Eurozone) was considered attractive in the early period of the crisis in some Ministries of Finance and some conservative cycles, as it would include a very strong message that the EU will not tolerate any “irresponsible” behavior in the future.

cause of their basic failure to assess correctly the size of the multiplier (Blanchard and Leigh 2013, Petralias et al. 2013)[16].

Table 3. Predictions for GDP change made by the EC, the IMF and the OECD for the 2011-2012 period

	EC	IMF	OECD	Actual figure
Prediction date for 2011	January 2011	October 2010	December 2010	
GDP percentage change in constant prices for 2011	-3.5	-2.6	-2.7	-7.1
Prediction date for 2012 figure	January 2012	September 2011	December 2011	
GDP percentage change in constant prices for 2012	-4.7	-2.0	-3.0	-6.4

Source: Petralias et al. (2013).

There is no doubt that a multiplier of 0.50 was very convenient for the designers of the austerity programs, as it implies a limited impact of cuts on GDP. However, it is not realistic to assume that an economy with a weak productive base and a dominant for years role of the public sector in stimulating aggregate demand will have such a low multiplier. Independent estimates have shown that the investment multiplier in Greece was greater than 1.00[17]. Continuous reviews of the austerity programs revealed the unrealistic calculation of fiscal multipliers on spending cuts and taxes (Papadimitriou et al., 2013). Although it is widely accepted now that the fiscal shock therapy caused more problems than it solved and that the reduction of the debt is infeasible in a period of a couple of years (Wysploz 2013), IMF in its 2013 report on Greece addresses the failure in the multiplier calculation as a matter of secondary importance regarding the magnitude of the recession (IMF 2013). As Table 3 shows, the forecast made by the EC, the IMF and the OECD for the 2011 and 2012 decline in GDP was far away from the actual decline, implying that the rescue program was based on unrealistic assumptions and therefore it was almost impossible to meet its targets.

Despite the fact that some learning has taken place and some change in the rhetoric and the direction of policy has taken place since mid-2012, the initial reaction of the EU and the International Organizations to the crisis was damaging for the economy, while the timing and mix of policy continuous to receive serious criticism. The frontloaded character of the austerity program was ac-

---

[16] According to the IMF estimates the size of the government spending multipliers was close to 0.50, while in reality it was close to 1.50 (IMF 2014).

[17] Coenen et al. (2012) has found that the multiplier effect of government investments in Greece was equal to 0.95 and 1,13 in the long-run. Rendahl (2013) has indicated that government spending generates fiscal multipliers greater than 1 because the economy was in liquidity trap, with high and persistent unemployment; while Van Reenen (2013) claims that in crisis fiscal multipliers are much higher than in normal times, making contraction policies more damaging.

companied by a reform program that was delayed (Christodoulakis 2013) and also questioned for the reasoning of many of its provisions[18]. The reform program was criticized for favoring special interests[19] and for removing all forms of social protection for the weaker, while in many cases it ignored the realities of the market structure in Greece.

In general, the implementation of the reform program has been under a continuous evaluation process by the Troika, through which its targets were reset in a way that attracted the attention of the public and was a constant source of uncertainty and social unrest. Although several measures and reforms modernized the public sector, the Program as a whole has been perceived in a negative way by the general public for its excessive taxation and for its impact on the labour market. Continuous labour market reforms adopted in the midst of the crisis that removed protection and cut wages led to more unemployment and failed to boost new recruitment as it was envisaged by the Troika (Torres 2013). As a result, the strategy of domestic devaluation was discredited in the eyes of the average citizen as it caused enormous social and economic cost (Weisbrot and Modecino, 2012).

3.3. Domestic market failures

One of the reasons that the crisis was so severe and its duration so long is unquestionably related to the characteristics of the productive system of Greece. The production base of the country is dominated by small and very small enterprises that enjoy practically no scale effects and has limited competitiveness (Petrakos et al 2012, Doxiadis 2013, Giannitsis 2013, Petrakos et al. 2008, Petrakos and Pitelis 2001). The average firm size in terms of employment in Greece is 4 employees, while in the EU is 15 and the advanced EU countries 17 employees per firm.

This fragmented economic base is mostly inward-looking and dominated by the non-tradable sectors of the economy, such as the public sector, retail, construction and consumer services (Doxiadis 2013). The manufacturing sector has shrunk dramatically during the last 2-3 decades from about 25% to 8% of GDP in 2012 (Figure 8) and specializes mainly in consumer, labor intensive and resource intensive products serving mainly domestic market. The tradable sector

---

[18] It is difficult to explain why the reform of central government with new organizations for the ministries has not been completed five years after the first Memorandum. On the contrary, laws of minor importance (like the law for the price of milk that had the opposite effects in the market) or labor market deregulation laws that have a clear class bias against unions and collective negotiations were finished in time because of the pressure of the Troika.

[19] In many negotiations between the Greek officials and the Troika it was clear that the later had some short of 'inside information', that is detailed information about the subject of the discussion that an international organization is impossible to have. This was due to the fact that the Troika office in Athens was approached by special interest groups that considered the crisis as an opportunity to change the legal basis of the economy in their favor.

of the economy is limited and includes mainly tourism (which is highly seasonal) and a small part of the manufacturing and agricultural production.

Figure 8. Share of manufacturing (%) in GDP, 1995-2008

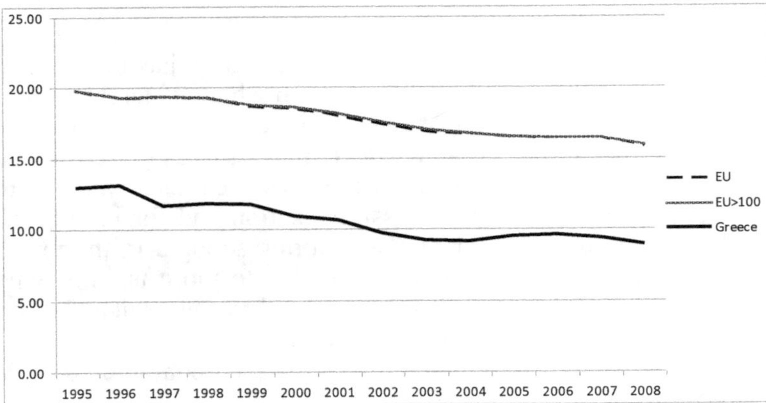

Source: World Bank (2014).

In addition to the small size and the unfavorable sectoral specialization, the economy suffers from limited forwards and backwards linkages between critical sectors, such as tourism –food industry linkages or tourism– agriculture linkages and therefore low domestic regional or sectoral output multipliers (Fotopoulos 2013).

The lack of export-orientation in the economy (Figure 9) is depicted in the trade deficit (Figure 10) and shows the low competitiveness of the economic base. Although there are significant historical factors behind the current structure of the Greek economy (Petrakos 2001), there is no doubt that the intensification of competition in the EU market, especially after the euro, generated a spiral of defensive adjustments and the concentration of economic activity in the non-tradable sectors.

Figure 9. Merchandise exports share (%) in GDP, 1995-2008

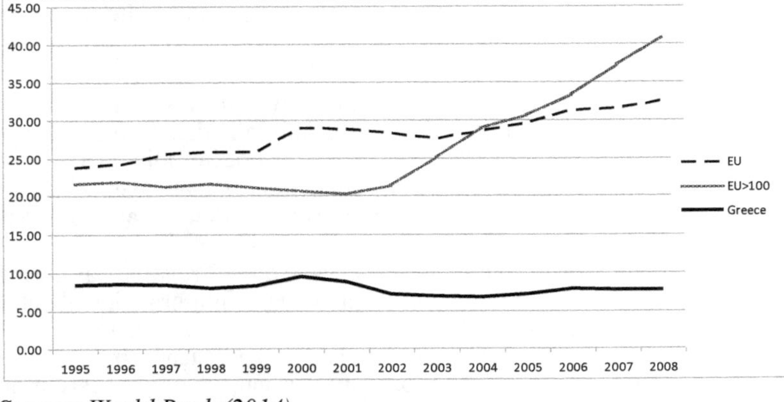

Source: World Bank (2014).

Figure 10. Merchandise trade balance share (%) in GDP, 1995-2008

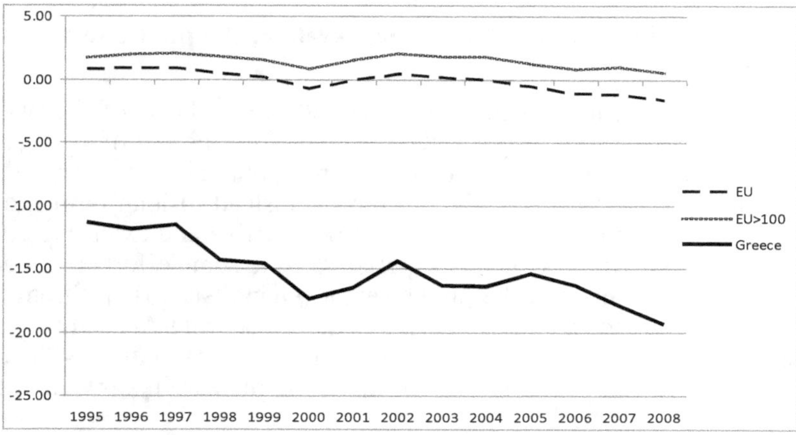

Source: World Bank (2014).

Countries or regions with unfavorable initial conditions, weak productive structure and strong pressure from international markets have no other option than to adopt a proactive policy-driven development model that will try to compensate for inherent weaknesses and build a growth strategy on the basis of existing and potential advantages. This is a difficult and perhaps unpopular long-term perspective that was never adopted systematically during the 35 years of Greek membership in the EU.

On the contrary, the development model of the country took the easier way and was based on consumption and imports instead of investment, production and exports. Lower interest rates in the post-euro period facilitated the expansion of public and private borrowing, while expanding employment in the public sector was offsetting the loss of jobs in the contracted tradable sector. Most new jobs in the private sector were in non-tradable sector like retail, consumer services and construction that were directly dependent on the level of domestic demand and indirectly on public and private borrowing. Public spending and employment were possible only because of the continuous State borrowing, as the tax revenues were typically lagging public spending by 10% of GDP due to extensive tax evasion. To the extent that the public investment funds (which included the EU Structural Funds) were considered to serve a development policy, emphasis was always placed on public infrastructure (mainly the transportation networks), while policies for the development of human capital, entrepreneurship and R&D were systematically underfunded or neglected.

This inward-looking model developed significant rent seeking activities around the public sector, the stock market and the construction sector. In times, the rewards of consultants, stock brokers and real estate agents were so high that demoralizing paid employment in either sector. This model neglected the tradable sector of the economy which is the basis of international competitiveness and eventually collapsed with the debt crisis, which to some extent was the logical outcome of its faults and weaknesses.

3.4. Domestic policy failure: The political system, the public sector and the management of the crisis

The political system in Greece has operated on the basis of the two-party system[20] that replaced each other in the elections for a period of 40 years. Despite ideological differences and at times fierce political antagonism, the two parties shared similar practices when in power. Instead of long-term economic planning they usually followed a short term perspective and extensive clientele practices that persisted throughout the period despite some efforts to modernize both the political system and the public sector (Giannitsis 2013). Strong political antagonism for power and demagogic demands from the entire political spectrum did not allow for a minimum consensus in proceeding with reforms and some measures to control public spending and increase tax revenues before the crisis.

Primarily because of the clientele practices of the political system, the state mechanism become bureaucratic, over-regulating and in some cases corrupt (Tsakalotos 2010). About 22% of the labor force of the country was employed in the public sector, which grew dramatically in terms of employment in the 2007-09 period[21]. The public sector itself is highly centralized, with limited funding and authority allowed at the regional and local level, and in most cases it discourages investment activity. Its dependence from the political system, its sluggish structure and the equally sluggish European bureaucracy did not allow the public administration to quickly adapt to the realities of the crisis and direct Structural Funds to actions and programs that would support investment and employment.

In short, the political system is considered by the majority of the population as responsible for the crisis because it increased public spending and the debt [22],

---

[20] The Center-right party of New Democracy (ND) has ruled in the periods 1974-81, 1990-93, 2004-09, while the Center-left PanHellenic Socialist Party (PASOK) has ruled in the periods 1981-1989, 1994-2004 and 2009-11. The two parties usually counted for more than 80% of the vote, with smaller parties, mainly in the left, counting for the rest. After the 2012 elections the two parties have formed a coalition government that runs the fiscal consolidation and reforms program. Their electorate basis has been reduced significantly in the 2012 elections (ND: 29.7%, PASOK: 12,3%) while the Left opposition party of SYRIZA received 26.9%.

[21] By the end of 2009 the public sector had 942,645 employees, while at the end of 2013 that figure was down to 675,530. This huge reduction (-29%) was due to the cuts in temporary staff, massive retirement of those eligible to leave in the fear of further cuts in wages or pensions and laying off of 8.500 employees from the permanent staff of the public sector (Ministry of Finance 2014).

[22] A fierce political debate has erupted among the two ruling parties for the primary responsibility of the debt. Although Greece has a long history of high public debt, the evidence seems to indicate that public primary deficits were almost eliminated by 2004 and that the debt increased dramatically in the 2007-09 period when public consumption and employment increased significantly, at the same time that public revenues collapsed

it failed to modernize the public sector and also failed to fight bureaucracy, corruption and tax evasion[23]. It is also blamed for its inability to confront more efficiently the crisis. The new socialist government that was elected in the 2009 elections was trapped in pre-election promises and was slow to realize the dangers of the rapidly changing international markets and the negative EU policy environment (Monastiriotis 2013). The new government did not come up with its own plan to deal with the crisis. Instead, it accepted the plan of Troika for deep spending cuts and reforms without negotiations, convinced by the EU and IMF assurances that the recession would be mild and of a short period[24]. Spending cuts were sharper than required, because the government failed to broaden the tax base of the economy and fight tax evasion of the more affluent social groups[25].

The Reforms agenda was also problematic. Useful reforms were delayed due to pressure by interest groups and did not have an immediate growth effect, while other reforms that were implemented caused serious opposition and dissent without having a clear justification. Similarly, the privatization goals were unrealistic and set late with no significant impact on revenues due to bureaucratic obstacles and uncertainty that discouraged investors.

Finally, the political establishment of the country is accountable because in front of the most serious crisis in the post-war period was unable or unwilling to find a minimum basis for negotiations and political consensus during the first two years of the crisis, generating more friction and conflict, but also less viable solutions than it would otherwise. For many people the crisis and the management of the crisis was a lot of pain with no gain. It was also a lot of pain without justice. The profound costs of the austerity program for the weaker social classes have been the ground for the rise of extreme populism on the one hand and ethnocentric and xenophobic sentiments on the other.

(Christodoulakis 2011). According to Eurostat (2014) government spending in 2009 reached 53.1% of GDP compared to 44.8% in 2006.

[23] The inefficient tax system that provided one of the lowest tax/GDP ratios is considered to be a crucial factor for the development of the Greek debt and the economic crisis (Kaplanoglou and Rapanos 2013, Stathakis 2010, Theodoropoulou and Watt 2012).

[24] Even before the signing of the first Memorandum with the Troika there were voices in the Papandreou Cabinet arguing that cutting public spending by 36.2 billion (the size of deficit in 2009) in 2-3 years in an economy of 231 billion (the size of GDP in 2009) would not have a mild effect and will drop the economy into a deep recession. However, Papandreou and his Minister of Finance could never imagine that the assurances of the top international organizations were entirely worthless and their estimates of the effects of the crisis completely wrong.

[25] Tax evasion is wide spread in the economy and includes all social groups except employees. Typically, professionals like doctors, lawyers or engineers and small retail and service business were typically reporting on average an annual income that was much lower than earned and in some cases lower that of the employees. As a result, even in 2011 that some reforms in the tax system were already in place, employees and pensioners were making up 70% of taxable income and paying 55% of total tax (GSIS 2012).

4. LEARNING FROM THE CRISIS: CHALLENGES FOR THE THEORY AND INTEGRATION POLICY

The experience of the European South has shown that a persistent core-periphery competitiveness gap within the Eurozone can be transformed to a serious trade deficit and that, in turn, to an unmanageable public deficit. This market imbalance combined with serious policy failures has triggered a profound economic crisis that widened the existing development gap between the EU core and the European periphery. In Greece, but also in other places, the current crisis has eliminated the progress that has taken place over the last 20 years, damaging the credibility of domestic and European institutions and undermining political stability and democracy.

Learning from failure is critical for policies of prevention, in the hope that similar situations will be avoided in the future in the EU. The first lesson from our analysis is that long-lasting imbalances in trade among EU members need to be confronted with appropriate economic policy measures. Persistent and high surpluses in the North are equally problematic with persistent deficits in the South and need to be under the scrutiny of the EC. A combination of active measures that will stimulate domestic demand in the European core, improve the productivity and the size of the tradable sector in the periphery and reduce the unit-labor cost differential among the export frontrunners and the laggards is required.

The second lesson is that once the crisis has erupted, only hard choices are available and the downwards adjustment will be unavoidable. This raises the issue of prevention that is relevant for both the European Commission and the National authorities, who did very little in the period before the crisis to avert it. It also raises the issue of speed, decisiveness and coordinated action at the EU level. It finally raises the issue of responsibility of public figures in making statements that result to negative exposure of troubled economies in the financial markets. In dealing with future crises, the EU has to make sure that it has a working plan ready, it acts quickly in order to avoid it or prevent its deepening and spreading up and that the public statements made are part of the solution and not part of the problem. Making hard choices even harder in order to satisfy domestic audiences in a number of core countries should be eliminated from the EU policy kit.

The third lesson of the analysis is that the external, higher-order, macro-level drivers of crisis are more important than internal, lower-order national-level ones. No matter how hard the domestic policies are trying to cope with the crisis, how much the deficit has been cut, how many reforms have been successful, how much the labor cost has been cut or the bureaucracy reduced, it is the decision of the European Council, the rating of Moody's, an article in the 'Financial Times' or the statements of a Finance Minister in Bloomberg that count more. Perhaps in the long-run what happens inside the country will make a difference, especially if the policy mix is consistent and leads to the same direction. During the crisis, however, the investment decisions and decisions in nervous financial or stock markets are affected primarily by the positive or negative environment and the prospects created by far more influential international actors.

The forth lesson has to do with the policy-mix applied during the crisis. It is now widely acknowledged that a slower pace of fiscal adjustment and a faster pace in reforms would have less damaging results on social, political and economic grounds. Fiscal shock therapies of the magnitude applied in Greece can be dangerous for economies with weak and inward-looking productive systems, where the public sector plays a critical role in the economy and fiscal multipliers are high. The reform program (assuming it is properly designed) will not lead to a recovery if investment activity is not well above its pre-crisis historical levels. A severe and front-loaded fiscal consolidation program that reduces public investment and spreads social unrest is very likely to discourage also foreign capital from investing in the country. The Greek economy needs currently additional investment equal to about 10% of GDP in order to return to the pre-crisis levels and this can be found only externally, in the form of a reduction of the debt-serving requirements, in the form of EU development funds, in the form of FDI or in a combination of the above. All this indicates the need for a return of development policy in the European agenda in order for depressed and crisis areas to be able to move from recession to development in a highly competitive environment. Supply side policies (reforms) will need to be decisively supported by demand side policies in order for the crisis-hit economies to assume a sustainable growth path in a reasonable time horizon.

The fifth lesson is that we need more Europe and better European institutions in order to overcome existing asymmetries and overcome the crisis. We need a more advanced, more inclusive and more balanced process of integration that will include a more coordinated economic policy, as well as financial and fiscal integration. Austerity in deficit countries should be offset by demand stimulus in the surplus countries, while macroeconomic policy should become more coordinated and more symmetric. A Fiscal Union may foresee a common liability for (part of) national debt, tighter fiscal coordination, redistribution mechanisms and Eurobonds funding for investment and development projects. A Banking Union may foresee common financial supervisory and bank resolution mechanisms and common deposit security for all EU countries.

We are not sure if the analysis offers any lessons for the improvement of the domestic political system of Greece or other countries in the South or East that is considered to be also responsible for the crisis. The interesting observation here is that the same people and the same parties that are held responsible for the accumulation of debt and the break out of the crisis are congratulated by the EC and the international organizations for the successful implementation of the austerity and reforms program. Can the same political system be both good and bad at the same time? The answer is probably not, but the observation leads to the reasonable hypothesis that the political system is an endogenous variable shaped by other factors that are related (among other things) to the condition of the economy. The political system in a country with a strong private sector and unemployment in the range of 5% receives different pressures from the electorate and behaves differently from that in a country with a weak private sector and unemployment in the range of 15%. Therefore, one may assume that the quality of the political system of a country depends on the quality of the economy and the level of social cohesion within the country. Although the causality runs both ways, more advanced and more egalitarian economies have fewer chances to end up with populist and careless politicians and a clientele political system. The other observation is that these types of political systems in the South or the East are not very likely to survive the pressures of a competitive environment. Although this may sound promising, the worrying experience of Greece has shown that the economic crisis may lead to the rise of political extremism in the extreme right and the undermining of democratic values.

The final lesson is that behind the impressive policy failure in Greece may be hiding an even more impressive theory failure. The conviction of the mainstream theories that market-led integration will generate enough product and factor flows to spread growth in space in an equilibrating way, ignoring the importance of selectivity bias, all sorts of inequality in initial conditions and the cumulative nature of development processes, is to a large extent the founding stone of the crisis. By downplaying the role of the public sector in providing equal opportunities in infrastructure, knowledge and public services and illegitimating its impact on the economy, the mainstream school has failed to understand the main causes of the crisis. Ignoring the roots of the problem or confusing causes with symptoms may end up in a situation where the medicine cures the disease but kills the patient.

REFERENCES

AMECO (2014) AMECO Database.

Arghyrou M., Tsoukalas J. (2011) The Greek Debt Crisis: Likely Causes, Mechanics and Outcomes, *The World Economy*, 34(2): 173-191.

Bank of Greece (2011a) Bulletin of Conjunctural Indicators, 136, March-April.

Bank of Greece (2011b) Bulletin of Conjunctural Indicators, 141, December.

Bank of Greece (2014) Bulletin of Conjunctural Indicators, 156, May-June.

Blanchard O. and Leigh D. (2013) Growth Forecast errors and fiscal multipliers, *IMF Working Paper*, January.

Christodoulakis N. (2011) From indecision to fast-track privatisations: Can Greece still do it? in Monastiriotis V. (ed.) *The Greek Crisis in Focus: Austerity, Recession and Paths to Recovery*, London: LSE Hellenic Observatory Papers on Greece and Southeast Europe.

Christodoulakis, N. (2013) From Grexit to Growth: On Fiscal Multipliers and how to End Recession in Greece, *National Institute Economic Review*, 224.

Coenen, G., Straub, R., Trabandt, M. (2012) Gauging the effects of fiscal stimulus packages in the euro area, *ECB-Working Paper Series*, 1483.

Collignon, S. (2012) Fiscal policy rules and the sustainability of public debt in Europe, *International Economic Review*, 53: 539–567.

De Grauwe P. and Ji Y. (2013) How much fiscal discipline in a monetary union, *Journal of Macroeconomics,* 39: 348–360.

Doxiadis A. (2013) *The invisible rift: Institutions and conducts in the Greek economy*. Athens: Ikaros (in Greek).

ELSTAT (2013) Statistical database. http://www.statistics.gr.

Eurostat (2014) Statistics. http://epp.eurostat.ec.europa.eu.

Fotopoulos G., Kallioras, D. and Petrakos, G. (2010) Spatial variations in Greek manufacturing employment growth: the effects of specialization and international trade, *Papers in Regional Science*, 89 : 109-133.

Fotopoulos G. (2013) Regional-sectoral multipliers in the Greek economy, University of the Peloponnese, Research Committee.

Giannitsis T. (2013) *Greece in Crisis*. Athens: Polis (in Greek).

GSIS (2012) Statistical Bulletin for Tax Revenues, General Secretariat of Information Systems, Ministry of Finance, 2012.

IMF (2013) Greece: Ex Post Evaluation of Exceptional Access under the 2010 Stand-By Arrangement, IMF Country Report 13/156.

IMF (2014) Data and statistics. http://www.imf.org.

INE (2013) Greek economy and employment. Annual review 2013, Institute of Labor (In Greek). http://www.inegsee.gr.

Ioannou D., Stracca L. (2014) Have the euro area and EU governance worked? Just the facts, *European Journal of Political Economy*, 34 (2014): 1–17.

Kaplanoglou G. and Rapanos V. (2013) Tax and Trust: The Fiscal Crisis Greece, *South European Society and Politics*, 18(3) : 283-304.

Klimaka (2013). http://www.klimaka.org.gr/

Konhler W. (2012) The Eurosystem in times of crises: Greece in the role of a reserve currency country?, Special Issue, CESifo Forum 2-12.

Kotios A. (2011) Greece, EMU and the crisis, University of Thessaly, Department of Planning and Regional Development, Discussion Paper, 17(1): 1-20 (In Greek).

Lapavitsas C., Kaltenbrunner A., Lindo D., Michell J, Painceira J., Pires E., Powell J., Stenfors A. Teles N. (2010) Eurozone crisis: beggar thyself and thy neighbor, *Journal of Balkan and Near Eastern Studies*, 12(4): 321-37

Mayer T., Mobert J., Weistroffer C. (2012) Macroeconomic imbalances in EMU and the euro system, CESifo Forum 2012 Special Issue.

Miller J. and Sciacchitano K. (2012) Why the United States Is *Not* Greece, *Dollars and Sense*, January.

Ministry of Finance (2014) Registry of public employment.

Monastiriotis V. (2011) The Geographical Dimension of Austerity. In: Monastiriotis, V. (ed.) *The Greek Crisis in Focus: Austerity, Recession and Paths to Recovery*, London: LSE Hellenic Observatory Papers on Greece and Southeast Europe.

Monastiriotis V. (2013) A Very Greek Crisis in Austerity Measures in Crisis Countries- Results and Impact on Mid-Term Development, *Intereconomics* 48(1): 4-32.

Papadimitriou, D., Nikiforos, M., Gennaro, Z. (2013) The Greek Economic Crisis and the Experience of Austerity: A Strategic Analysis, Levy Economics Institute of Bard College.

Petralias A., Petros S., Prodromidis P. (2013) Greece in Recession: Economic Predictions, Mispredictions and Policy Implications, *GreeSE* 75, Hellenic Observatory Papers on Greece and Southeastern Europe, September.

Petrakos G. (2003) Peripheral European Transitions: The Trade Relations of the Balkan Countries, *South-Eastern Europe Journal of Economics,* 1(1): 41-64.

Petrakos G. (2008) Regional inequalities in Europe: Evidence, theory and policy, *Town Planning Review*, Viewpoint, 79(5): i-vii.

Petrakos G., Artelaris P., Kallioras D. (2014) Debt-led convergence in Europe, submitted for publication to *Cambridge Journal of Economics*.

Petrakos G., Fotopoulos G. and Kallioras D. (2008) Economic Integration and Structural Change in Greek Regions: A Southearn Perspective, in Krieger-Boden C., Morgenroth E. and Petrakos G. (eds) *The Impact of Economic Integration on Regional Structural Change and Cohesion,* London: Routledge, 72-95.

Petrakos, G. Fotopoulos, G., Kallioras, D. (2012) Peripherality and Integration: Industrial Growth and Decline in the Greek Regions, *Environment and Planning C,* 30(2): 347-361.

Petrakos, G., Kallioras, D., Anagnostou, A. (2011) Regional convergence and growth in Europe: understanding patterns and determinants, *European Urban and Regional Studies,* 18(4): 375-391.

Petrakos, G., Rodriguez-Pose, A., Rovolis, A. (2005) Growth, Integration and Regional Inequalities in Europe, *Environment and Planning A*, 37(10): 1837-1855.

Petrakos G. and Pitelis C. (2001) Peripherality and integration: The experience of Greece as a member of the EU and its implications for the Balkan economies in Transition, in Petrakos and Totev (eds.) *The Development of the Balkan Region*, Aldershot: Ashgate, 283-316.

Rendahl P. (2013) A time to spend: New insight into the multiplier effect. In Corsetti, G. (ed.) *Austerity: Too much of a good thing?*, London : CEPR.

Stathakis G. (2010) The fiscal crisis of the Greek Economy, 2010 IIPPE annual conference, Beyond the crisis, Rethymno, Greece, September .

Theodoropoulou S. and Watt A. (2012) What did they expect? Lessons for Europe from a retrospective ex-ante evaluation of the first Greek bail-out programme, *ETUI Working Paper*.

Torres R. (2013) Introduction: European labour markets in economic crisis, *International Labour Review*, 152(2): 167-173.

Tsakalotos, E. (2010) Greek Economic Crisis, 2010 IIPPE annual conference, Beyond the crisis, Rethymno, Greece, September.

UNCTAD (2013) UNCTADSTAT. http://unctadstat.unctad.org/EN.

Van Reenen, J. (2013) Fiscal consolidation: Too much of a good thing? In Corsetti, G. (ed.) *Austerity: Too much of a good thing?* London: CEPR.

Varoufakis Y., Holland S., Galbraith J. (2013) A Modest Proposal for Resolving the Eurozone Crisis, Vol. 4.0, July.

Weisbrot M. and Modecino J., A. (2012) More Pain, No Gain for Greece: Is the Euro Worth the Costs of Pro-Cyclical Fiscal Policy and Internal Devaluation?, report CEPR.

World Bank (2014) World *Development* Indicators.

Wyplosz C. (2013) The impossible hope of an end to austerity, in Corsetti G. (ed.) *Austerity: Too much of a good thing?*, London: CEPR.

LA CRISE GRECQUE : LES ÉCHECS DES POLITIQUES NATIONALES ET EUROPÉENNES

Résumé - *Cet article retrace les étapes de la crise financière, économique et sociale de 2008 en Grèce. Le pays a connu une baisse d'un quart du PIB par habitant tandis que le chômage a augmenté de l'ordre de 25%. L'article propose une analyse détaillée de la rupture des moteurs de la croissance qui s'est manifestée depuis 2008. Il montre les faiblesses structurelles de l'économie grecque, la défaillance des politiques nationales mais aussi des politiques de stabilisation mises en place par l'Union européenne.*

Mots-clés - CRISE ÉCONOMIQUE, GRÈCE, UNION EUROPÉENNE, PROGRAMMES D'AUSTÉRITÉ

CONVERGENCE THROUGH CRISIS? THE IMPACT OF THE CRISIS ON WAGE RETURNS ACROSS THE GREEK REGIONS

Vassilis MONASTIRIOTIS[*]

Abstract - *The macroeconomic and social dimension of the Greek crisis has put to second-stage attention to its spatial manifestation and consequences. Partly because of this, the literature thus far does not seem to reach agreement about the 'regional footprint' of the crisis, i.e., whether it contributed to magnifying (Monastiriotis, 2011) or narrowing (Psycharis et al, 2014) regional disparities. In this paper we tackle one particular aspect of this question, examining whether the crisis led to convergence in the way the country's regional labour markets reward different labour characteristics – thus increasing 'spatial fairness' (defined as 'equal returns to equal characteristics, irrespective of location'). Descriptive evidence from aggregate data suggests that regional wages show signs of accelerated convergence during the crisis. To look underneath this aggregate picture, we derive region-specific shadow prices of worker and job characteristics from Mincerian wage equations and analyse their evolution following the T&I approach of Duranton and Monastiriotis (2002). Our results show that the crisis coincided with a notable acceleration of pre-existing tendencies for convergence in the returns to most characteristics. Underneath this aggregate pattern of 'convergence through crisis', however, we find significant heterogeneity, implying that regional responses to the crisis have been far from uniform.*

Key words - REGIONAL DISPARITIES, CRISIS, CONVERGENCE, WAGE RETURNS, GREECE

JEL classification - C23, J24, J31, R12, R23

Acknowledgements: I am grateful to Rebekka Christopoulou for her help with parts of the econometric analysis and to Angelo Martelli for his help with some of the illustrations. An earlier version of this paper was presented at the 4th GDRI-DREEM conference (Florence, September 2013). I am thankful to participants for their useful comments and suggestions. The useful comments of the editors and two anonymous referees are also acknowledged.

[*] European Institute, London School of Economics. v.monastiriotis@lse.ac.uk.

1. INTRODUCTION

The presence, and persistence, of regional disparities is an issue that has been at the core of regional science since its very beginnings. Research into this issue has flourished over the years and large bodies of literature exist today that examine various facets of this issue, for example the role of agglomeration and production activity, the role of local capacities and indigenous drivers to growth, the role of demand-side factors and cumulative causation forces, the role of national and regional policy, and so forth. Somewhat surprisingly, the literature has much less to say about the evolution of regional disparities in times of crisis and in relation to external shocks. Some literature exists concerning the pro-cyclicality of regional disparities (Petrakos and al, 2005) or about the impact of external developments (globalisation, trade liberalisation – Resmini, 2003; Rodríguez-Pose, 2006). But studies that address how regional disparities evolve in times of national recessions/crises are few and far between (see, for example, Blazek and Netrdová, 2012) .

Also limited is the attention in the contemporary literature on whether the evolution of disparities is related to compositional issues [1] (e.g., differences/changes in production structures, labour quality, etc) or instead to issues of functioning (e.g., production linkages within local economic systems or valuation of / demand for skills in each local economy). With regard to the latter, in a seminal contribution Duranton and Monastiriotis (2002) showed for the case of the UK that regional wage disparities are mainly driven by differences in the characteristics of the regional workforce (composition) and that observed trends of aggregate divergence (in regional wages) mask underlying trends of regional convergence in the returns (valuation) to worker and workplace characteristics across space – thus implying a process of increasing sorting across regions on the basis of these characteristics. Although numerous studies exist that examine the returns to various worker and other characteristics at the regional level, generally very few offer a systematic examination of their differences and their evolution.[2]

This paper takes up this issue and examines it for a particularly intriguing case, that of Greece in the pre-crisis period and during the recent (and ongoing) crisis. Following the eruption of the global financial crisis and the unveiling of significant fiscal imbalances in the country, Greece entered a deep crisis which destabilised it politically and pushed its economy to a deep and prolonged recession. As recent analyses have shown (Monastiriotis, 2011; Monastiriotis and Martelli, 2013; Psycharis et al, 2014), the crisis had a variable impact across the

[1] There is a long tradition in regional science employing shift-share analysis to examine issues of function-versus-composition (see Houston, 1967, Herzog and Olsen, 1977; vis-à-vis Bellini et al, 2013 and Blien et al, 2014), but this approach is less popular in the contemporary literature and in any case has rarely been employed to study issues relating directly to labour market processes.

[2] Some recent studies have looked at aspects of this at the national and supra-national levels (see, inter alia, Simon, 2012; Christofides and Michael, 2013; and Montenegro and Patrinos, 2013).

Greek regions, although unemployment increased everywhere (and economic activity declined everywhere) quite substantially. Still, regional adjustment to the crisis has not been uniform and some regions managed to contain the effects of the crisis more successfully than others (Monastiriotis and Martelli, 2013). Largely anecdotal evidence suggests that this has in part been due to migration flows – and thus to compositional changes in the local workforce. However, the extent to which the crisis has led to more uniformity, or instead to further divergence, across regions in terms of labour market functioning – and in particular in terms of the valuation of workforce characteristics – remains largely unknown.

To examine this issue we use individual level data derived from successive waves of the Greek Labour Force Survey. We estimate a large set of (extended) Mincerian wage equations for each of the 15 Greek regions[3] covering the period 2000-2012, i.e., from Greece's accession into the Eurozone to the year representing the height of the crisis. We use the derived elasticities (returns to characteristics) to implement a comparative analysis of the evolution of returns across regions before and during the crisis and examine the trends for convergence and divergence separately for the composition of workforce characteristics and for their returns. Our analysis reveals that the crisis has accelerated the pre-existing trend of convergence in the returns to key labour force characteristics across regions, thus leading on-the-aggregate to more equality in the valuation of these characteristics across the regional economies of the country. This assigns an element of 'spatial fairness' in the developments concerning (the determination of) regional wages in the country, with similar individuals (in terms of both personal and job-related characteristics) attaining increasingly similar wages irrespective of their location. Underneath this pattern of 'convergence through crisis', however, we find evidence of substantial regional heterogeneity, both in the distribution of returns and in the paths that these have followed for different (groups of) regions during the crisis.

The structure of the paper is as follows. In the next section we review the sparse literature on regional disparities in Greece and present some descriptive evidence on the evolution of regional wages and regional wage disparities in the country prior and during the crisis. Section 3 discusses our empirical strategy, including the estimating model and the method for examining regional convergence using the "trends and intercepts" approach of Duranton and Monastiriotis (2002). Section 4 presents our empirical findings concerning the evolution of regional disparities in the returns to individual and job characteristics before and during the crisis, making also some remarks about the evolution of dispari-

[3] Our sample comprises the 13 NUTS2 regions of Greece, with a separate distinction for the two main metropolitan areas of Athens and Thessaloniki, as delineated by Hellenic Statistics, the statistical service of Greece. Unfortunately, the Greek LFS does not provide more spatial detail to allow an analysis at the sub-regional level (e.g., local labour market areas – see Prodromides, 2010 and Kallioras et al, 2012). For a list of the Greek NUTS2 regions and a map showing their administrative boundaries see http://en.wikipedia.org/wiki/NUTS_of_Greece or the EUROSTAT portal at: epp.eurostat.ec.europa.eu/portal/page/portal/nuts_nomenclature/introduction.

ties in terms of the regional composition of these characteristics. Finally, the last section concludes with a summary of the results and a short discussion about the pressures on regional disparities in times of economic crises.

2. REGIONAL WAGE DISPARITIES AND PATTERNS OF CONVERGENCE IN GREECE

There are very few studies examining the geographical distribution of wages in Greece and the extent of regional disparities in labour market outcomes more generally in the country. A number of studies have examined the issue of regional income disparities following the neoclassical convergence literature and thus examining the extent of beta-convergence in labour productivity or per capita GDP. One of the first studies to do so (Siriopoulos and Asteriou, 1998) found evidence of conditional-only club convergence, with regions in the north and the south of the country converging to their own steady states, suggesting that overall the country is characterised by duality (north – south) and rather permanent differences in regional incomes. In contrast, Petrakos and Saratsis (2000) found significant evidence of beta-convergence, showing also that regional disparities in Greece appear to be pro-cyclical, i.e. rising in periods of expansion and declining in recessions. Strong evidence of beta-convergence has also been found subsequently by Tsionas (2002), Michelis et al (2004), Christopoulos and Tsionas (2004), Benos and Karagiannis (2008), and Lolos (2009).

Evidence concerning regional disparities in wages comes only indirectly, from studies examining the structure of wages (and returns to workforce characteristics) in the country.[4] For example, Christopoulou and Monastiriotis (2014a) find significant regional effects in their analysis of private and public sector wages in Greece prior to the crisis, suggesting sizeable differentials in net wages even after controlling for a large set of individual and job characteristics.[5] A similar result is implied by the study of Livanos and Pouliakas (2009) – although estimates on this are not reported directly. As is well documented (Bank of Greece, 2012; Koukiadaki and Kretsos, 2012; Monastiriotis, 2013; Daouli et al, 2013; Christopoulou and Monastiriotis, 2014b), the crisis led to a substantial decline in average wages in the country, by well over 20%. However, no study exists to date that examines in any sufficient depth – and systematically – how these changes have played out across the regions of Greece. Given this absence of systematic evidence on the geographical impact of the crisis and on the regional distribution of wages in Greece more generally (including its temporal evolution pre-crisis), a first step into our analysis is the descriptive examination of the picture of regional wage disparities. To perform this, we use data on

[4] A number of policy reports by the Institute for Employment of the General Confederation of Greek Labour occasionally document the extent of regional wage disparities in Greece, but they offer no systematic evidence on their evolution or indeed about the drivers of the observed differences.

[5] Similar regional differences have been reported in the literature with regard to unemployment (Livanos, 2007; Rodokanakis, 2010; Lolos and Papapetrou, 2011; Monastiriotis and Martelli, 2013).

monthly average wages derived from the spring waves of the Labour Force Survey of Greece for the years 2000-2012.[6]

As shown in Figure 1, nominal wages in Greece have been growing quite fast during the period from the country's accession to EMU until the eruption of the sovereign debt crisis – while with the crisis they declined substantially, reaching in 2012 levels broadly seen in 2007. The evolution seems to be broadly similar across regions – although stability seems to be much lower at the beginning and end of the period under consideration.

For most of the period, the regions of the North Aegean, South Aegean, Western Greece and Athens exhibit the highest nominal wages; while regions such as Central Macedonia (excluding Thessaloniki), Ionian and Thessaly are more often than not at the bottom. In 2006, average nominal wages ranged between 6.6968 log-points (I.e., euros expressed in natural logarithms – corresponding to €810) in Central Macedonia and 6.9164 log-points (€1,009) in the North Aegean – a max-to-min ratio of 124.5%. By 2012 this ratio had dropped to 119%, with wages ranging from €805 in the Ionian to €958 in the North Aegean. From simple inspection of Figure 1, regional disparities in average nominal wages do not appear to have been on the rise – neither prior to, nor during, the crisis. This is corroborated by a simple sigma-convergence analysis[7], as depicted in Figure 2.

---

[6] The LFS is a quarterly household survey covering information on a range of personal, household and labour market characteristics, including age, gender, marital status, education, region of residence, occupation and sector of work, regular monthly wages (excluding bonuses and overtime pay and reported in wage bundles which typically have a 100 euro range). Each wave contains 30,000 working age individuals, of which around two-fifths are wage earners. The survey includes both full-time and part-time employees but excludes the self-employed for whom incomes from employment are not reported. As this is a household survey, the data also capture the wages of salary-earners working in the informal economy. Information on wages contained in the survey is residence-based and thus individuals' wages are assigned to regions on the basis of where each individual lives. In the Greek context, where cross-regional commuting flows are minimal, this is generally not a problem; while in the case of the Athens labour market area, which extends beyond the administrative boundaries of the capital, it helps assign correctly observed wage outcomes to the relevant regional economy.

[7] This is essentially an analysis of the evolution of the standard deviation of the regional nominal wage distribution. To avoid the effect of inflation and scale effects, which tend to push towards a higher variance over time, we standardise the standard deviation by the mean of the distribution, thus deriving the corresponding coefficient of variation. By using this standardisation, we essentially deflate all wages and thus regional disparities are expressed in real terms. We do not weight our regional data by the regional population shares (as in Petrakos and Artelaris, 2009) as we are interested in the extent of disparity across the regional economies and not across the population residing in these. The small sample size (15 regions) and our focus here on the issue of convergence do not lend themselves to the use of other indices of inequality (e.g., Theil index, Gini coefficient, etc).

Figure 1. Regional nominal wages across the Greek regions

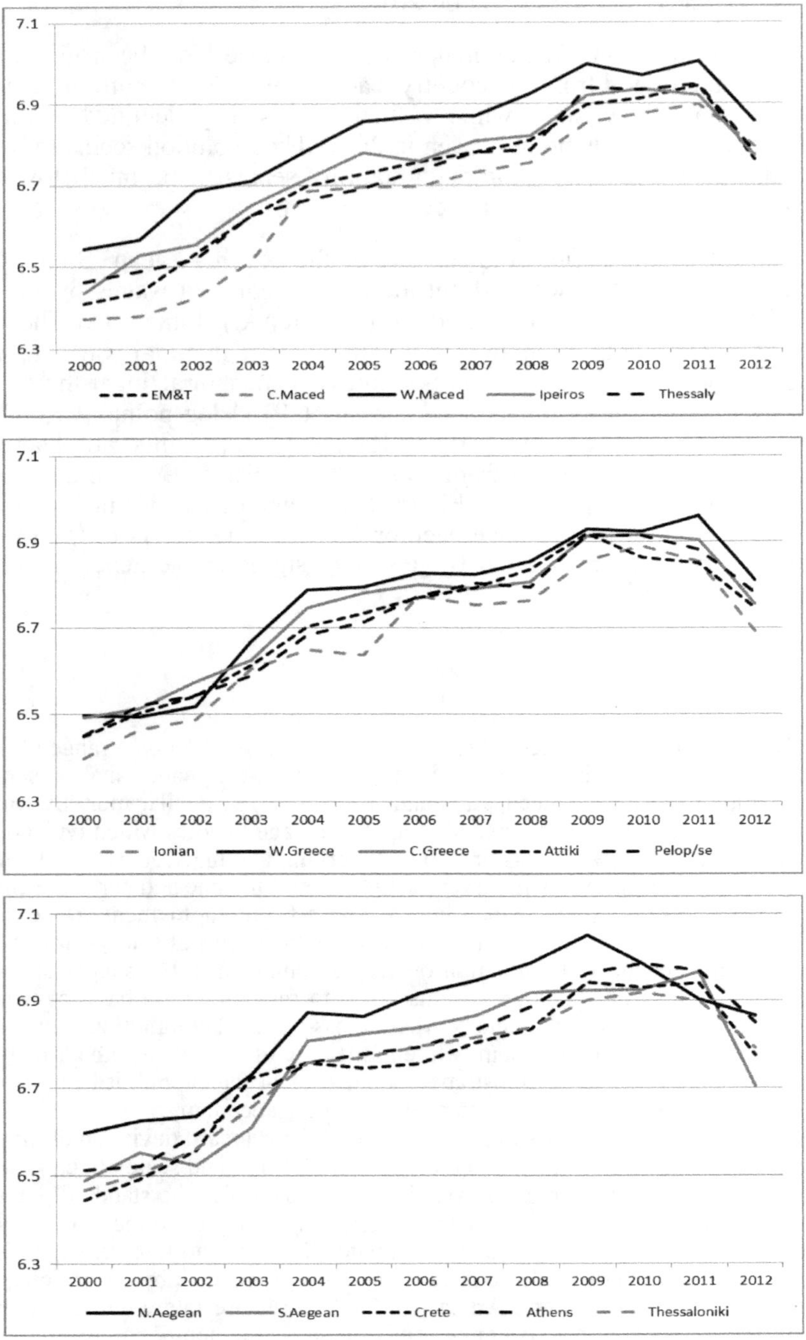

Source: Greek Labour Force Survey. Author's calculations.

As can be seen, in the pre-crisis period the coefficient of variation has been largely oscillating around a constant value, albeit with widening fluctuations as we move closer to the crisis. Some evidence of (sigma) convergence appears in 2005-2009 but with a large spike in 2008. From there, as we enter the crisis[8], we see a rather disparate evolution: a sharp decline in 2009-2010 but a subsequent rebound in 2011 and 2012. The overall trend (based on a second-order polynomial) is of declining disparities, with the drop starting near 2004 and intensifying dramatically with the crisis. But the evolution between 2009 and 2012 gives a much less conclusive picture about the evolution of regional disparities in the more recent period.

Figure 2. Regional wage disparities across the Greek regions

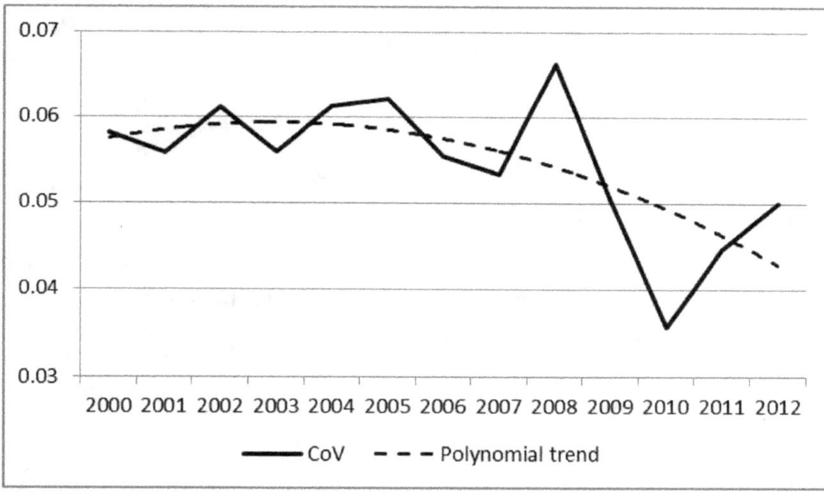

As a means for shedding more light onto this, we move on to examine the extent of beta-convergence in the country, separately for the pre-crisis and crisis periods (Figure 3) noting, however, that the sample size (15 observations) does not allow us to derive strong conclusions in a statistical sense. Evidently, the pre-crisis period is one of relative heterogeneity with no evidence of convergence. In contrast, the crisis period depicts a picture of convergence, with low-wage regions having generally slower declines in wages in the 2009-2012 period. On a close inspection, however, the picture is less clear. Removal of only two outliers (Central Macedonia, in the north-west of the graph; and North Aegean, in the south-east of the graph) suffices to turn the fitted relationship into a positive one, thus signaling divergence. Thus, the relationship appears to be neither particularly strong nor particularly robust.

This is in a way the graphical depiction of the ambiguity that surrounds the evolution of regional disparities in Greece during the recent crisis. The evidence, even at the simple level of descriptive analysis presented here, seems to

[8] Note that, as the sovereign debt crisis did not start until late in the autumn of 2009, the first crisis year in our data is essentially the year 2010.

be rather inconclusive: on the whole, regional wage evolutions seem to have been in the direction of declining disparities, consistent with the view of regional disparities as predominantly pro-cyclical; however, for sub-groups of regions (e.g., excluding outliers in Figure 3) and for specific years even inside the crisis (e.g., for 2011-2012 in Figure 2), there is as much evidence of regional divergence as there is for regional convergence.

Figure 3. Beta-convergence before and during the crisis

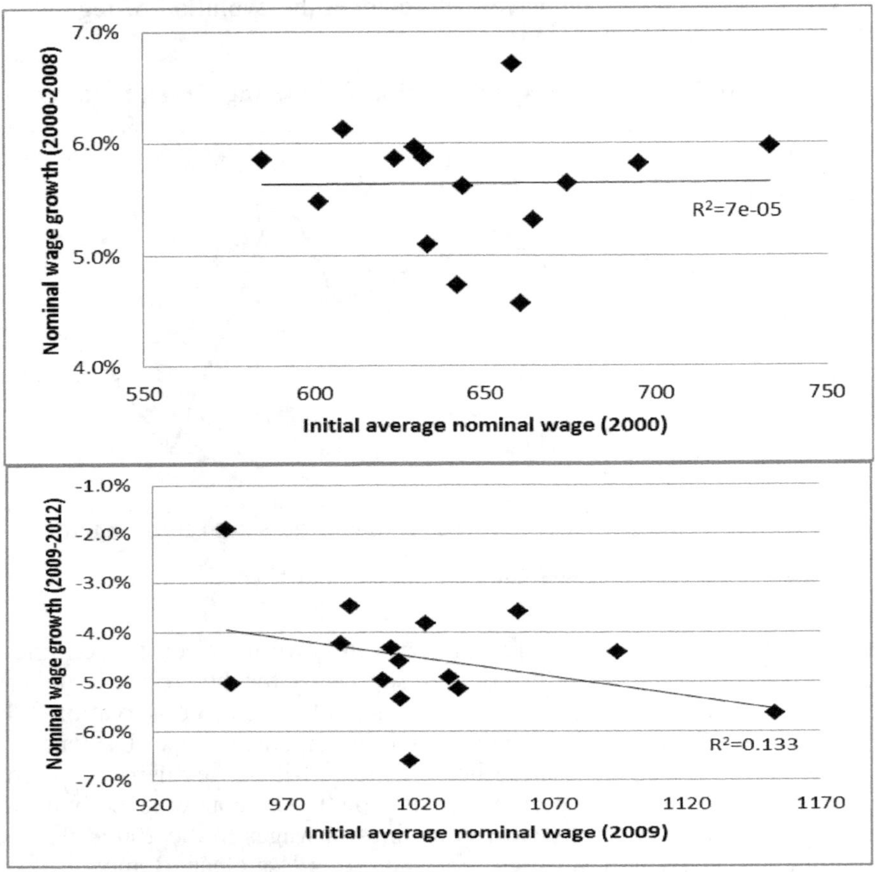

A possible explanation for this ambiguity is that, possibly, our observed wages conflate two different tendencies in the Greek regional labour markets: on the one hand a compositional movement, having to do with selective (e.g., skilled) migration and changing skill-compositions for the unemployed (i.e., employment sorting); on the other hand, a price-based movement, concerning the (shadow) prices of marketable labour force characteristics (education, experience, etc). We examine this more closely in the analysis that follows.

3. EMPIRICAL APPROACH AND METHODOLOGICAL ISSUES

To perform our analysis we estimate a large number of extended Mincerian wage equations[9], one for each year and region in our sample (15 regions, 13 years). The estimating equation makes an individual's hourly nominal wage (in logs) a function of various personal, household, and labour market characteristics, so that the derived estimates reflect the shadow prices of these characteristics and thus their contribution to the wage attained by each individual. Specifically,

$$\ln(w_{irt}) = \alpha_{rt} + b_{rt}^{G} G_{irt} + b_{rt}^{N} N_{irt} + b_{rt}^{E} E_{irt} + b_{rt}^{X} X_{irt} + b_{rt}^{M} M_{irt} + b_{rt}^{D} D_{irt} + b_{rt}^{P} P_{irt} + b_{rt}^{T} T_{irt} + b_{rt}^{F} F_{irt} + b_{rt}^{S} S_{irt} + \varepsilon_{irt} \quad (1)$$

where *i*, *r* and *t* index individuals, regions and time (years), respectively, and the right-hand-side variables are as follows: *G* is a gender dummy, equal to one if the individual is a woman; *N* is a nationality dummy, equal to one if the individual has been born abroad; *E* is years of schooling (education); *X* is years of post-education labour market experience[10]; *M* is a dummy for marital status (one if married/cohabiting); *D* is the number of under-aged dependants in the household; *P* and *T* are dummies for part-time and temporary employment, respectively; *F* is a dummy taking the value of one if the individual is employed in a small firm; *S* is a vector of sectoral dummies; and ε is an error term. Given the fact that we estimate this regression separately for each region and year, the coefficients *b* give the shadow price of the various characteristics in each location at each point in time; while α is essentially a time-varying regional fixed effect capturing 'baseline' wages (net of workforce and job characteristics) in each region-year.

As our interest is not directly on the contribution of these characteristics to individual and regional wages, but rather on the evolution of their (shadow) prices over time and across space, we do not report the estimates from these wage regressions.[11] Instead, to analyse the evolution and spatial differentiation of the valuation of the various worker and workplace characteristics we rely on an approach first developed by Duranton and Monastiriotis (2002), for a similar analysis for the case of the UK. The approach is as follows. Based on the estimated coefficients from the wage regressions we build a panel (cross-regional time-series) dataset of returns to characteristics (shadow prices). We then use the time-series dimension of this dataset to regress, for each region separately, the shadow prices of each characteristic on a simple linear time-trend. This

[9] See (Mincer, 1974) for the origins of this approach. The approach of human-capital wage equations is a literature standard with thousands of applications internationally (see Heckman et al, 2003; Hendricks, 2004; and Lemieux, 2006).

[10] In the regressions we include additionally a quadratic term of this variable, as is common in the wage regressions literature (see Heckman et al., 2003).

[11] We ran 195 regressions which produced over 3,500 coefficients. The full results can be made available upon request. Generally, our regional regressions performed very well, with the median R-square at 0.453 (ranging between 0.38 in the Ionian Islands region and 0.49 in Thessaly) and over 60% of the estimated coefficients being significant at the 0.01 level.

gives us an estimate of the annual rate of change of the shadow price of each characteristic in each region, in a similar fashion as with the calculation of a simple annualised growth rate.[12] Additionally, the intercepts from these regressions give us an estimate of the level of the shadow price of each characteristic in each region at the start of the period (base year), thus approximating, in beta-convergence terms, the 'initial level' of each shadow price. With these pieces of information (trend and intercept) we move on to produce a number of scatterplots (the so-called "Trend & Intercept plots"), one for each characteristic of interest, and derive the corresponding fitted regression line. The latter gives us an estimate of the direction and speed in the evolution of regional disparities for the returns of each characteristic.

In algebraic form the analysis is as follows. For each shadow-price estimate, b^k (with k={G,N,E,…,S} in eq.1), we estimate

$$b_{rt}^k = a_{rt}^k + \gamma_{rt}^k t_t + u_{rt}^k \tag{2}$$

separately for each region r={1,2,….,15}. We then use the cross-section of estimates a_{rt}^k and γ_{rt}^k to fit the following model, again for each parameter k separately:

$$\gamma_r^k = \delta_0^k + \delta_1^k a_r^k + \varepsilon_r^k \tag{3}$$

This set of estimates is presented in the scatterplots of the T&I analysis. This analysis resembles closely that of the (unconditional) beta-convergence, but with some important differences. As with beta-convergence, the sign of the slope of the fitted line (coefficient δ_1^k in eq.3) indicates convergence (negative slope) or divergence (upward slope); while its size is a measure of the speed of convergence or divergence. Unlike the beta-convergence approach, however, the T&I analysis captures the overall trend in the evolution of disparities and not the difference between two specific points in time; while in the T&I analysis the estimated trend is linear (and not asymptotic as in beta-convergence) – which seems more appropriate when evaluating movements in (shadow) prices than in unbounded real economic aggregates (such as labour productivity, for example).

To examine in particular how regional differences in the returns to worker and workplace characteristics evolved prior and during the crisis, we apply this analysis separately for two sub-periods – the pre-crisis period, covering the year since Greece's admission to EMU until the last year before the eruption of the crisis in Greece; and the crisis period, from the eruption of the crisis until 2012, which represents the height of the crisis in the country. We present the T&I

[12] The advantage of this approach, vis-à-vis the ad hoc calculation of a growth rate, is that it avoids the problem of relying solely on the start- and end-period data points. Given that the (shadow) prices used in this analysis are estimates, deriving from the wage regressions, and they are not directly observed, relying solely on a couple of data points may introduce too much noise in our analysis. Instead, the estimation of the annual rate of change on the basis of a linear trend makes equal use of all available data points.

plots jointly for the two sub-periods and discuss, for each characteristic, the differences observed in the context of the crisis, focusing mainly on the slope (δ_1 in eq.3) and fit of the underlying relationships. We also look comparatively at a shorter pre-crisis period (2005-2008), starting at the year after Greece hosted the 2004 Summer Olympics, and compare it to the period of the early 2000s (2000-2004) as well as to the crisis period (2009-2012).[13] To facilitate the discussion, and also bring out the analytical relevance of our results, we group the price effects of these variables into five categories, each corresponding to a particular facet of the factors underlying wage determination in the extended Mincerian model. The first category concerns shadow prices usually associated to labour market discrimination (female and foreign-born penalties). The second is related to marketable characteristics of the individual which affect productivity (returns to education and experience). The third concerns household characteristics (returns to marital status and to the number of dependants), which could be capturing either labour supply or institutional influences on wage determination (e.g., reservation wages or legally binding wage supplements). Our fourth category comprises the wage penalties associated to part-time and temporary employment, thus corresponding to characteristics related to the 'employment relationship'; while the last category groups together two employer characteristics (size and location).

For completeness, we also replicate this analysis for the regional composition of characteristics – in addition to the analysis of shadow prices, as discussed above. This in turn allows us to examine comparatively the extent to which overall (aggregate) convergence-divergence patterns are driven predominantly by trend-changes in the composition of characteristics in each region versus similar changes in the valuation (shadow prices) of these characteristics across space. Last, we implement additionally an analysis of sigma-convergence for the estimated shadow prices, which we consider as supplementary to our T&I analysis. Unlike the T&I analysis (or the traditional beta-convergence analysis), which examines the tendency of regional values to revert to a common mean, the sigma analysis examines the evolution of the spread of the distribution of these regional values over time. Thus, it allows us to get a comparative picture of whether any tendencies of convergence, in T&I terms, coincided with an actual narrowing of the cross-regional distributions of shadow prices or instead have been related more to less permanent movements around a common mean. We present and discuss the results from all these pieces of analysis in the next section.

4. EMPIRICAL RESULTS

As mentioned already, the main task of our empirical analysis is to examine the size and relative evolution of the shadow prices of a number of individual and job-related characteristics, which we group along five analytical categories capturing aspects of (i) labour market discrimination; and of the valuation of (ii) productivity-enhancing skills, (iii) household characteristics, (iv) different

[13] The corresponding T&I plots are reported in Appendix A. We make selective reference to these in the text.

forms of employment contracts, and (v) workplace-related characteristics. The summary results from the T&I analysis for all variables feeding into these five categories are presented in Table 1.

As can be seen, all shadow prices exhibit evidence of convergence, both prior to and during the crisis. Convergence, however, is much slower in the pre-crisis period (ranging for example between -0.06 for the temping penalty, which is not statistically significant, to -0.23 for the marital status premium) and seems to have speeded up significantly during the course of the crisis. In that latter period, each and every estimated slope coefficient is more negative and statistically more significant than before and all but two are over twice as large as those observed in the pre-crisis period. On this evidence, it is clear that the crisis has coincided with the emergence of a trend towards narrowing regional disparities in the returns to individual and workplace characteristics. By implication, the crisis period seems to be also a period where the valuation of characteristics became more homogenous across space and thus less disparate for similar individuals, irrespective of their location.[14] We explore this further by looking in more detail at the individual cases of the various characteristics used in our analysis.

Table 1. Trend-and-intercept analysis - summary results

Category and variable	Pre-crisis		Crisis	
	Slope (δ_1)	*Fit (R^2)*	*Slope (δ_1)*	*Fit (R^2)*
Discrimination				
Female penalty	-0.107***	0.512	-0.359***	0.616
Foreign-born penalty	-0.178***	0.675	-0.326**	0.396
Skills				
Education premium	-0.118*	0.199	-0.288***	0.440
Experience premium	-0.153***	0.793	-0.393**	0.376
Household				
Marital status premium	-0.234***	0.773	-0.402***	0.431
Dependants premium	-0.168***	0.783	-0.418**	0.341
Employment relationship				
Part-time penalty	-0.119***	0.796	-0.372***	0.680
Temping penalty	-0.069	0.155	-0.242***	0.590
Workplace characteristics				
Small-firm penalty	-0.062	0.136	-0.183***	0.573
Regional fixed-effect	-0.151***	0.469	-0.358***	0.584

*Note: The table reports slope coefficients and the overall fit (R-squared) from simple linear OLS regressions of the estimated trend-change of each shadow price on the corresponding estimate for the 'initial value' (intercept), as depicted in eq.3. *, ** and *** show significance at the 10%, 5% and 1% level, respectively.*

[14] The implication is that there is an element of increased labour market "fairness" that emerges with the crisis. We pick up on this point later in our discussion (section 5).

Starting with the discrimination variables (Figure 4), a first observation is that the speed of cross-regional convergence in the female penalty more than tripled over the period, while the increase in the speed of convergence for the foreign-born penalty was much more moderate. Importantly, in the case of the foreign-born penalty the fit of the regression line is significantly diminished, suggesting that the convergence process has been rather less homogenous across space. Indeed, as can be seen, there are two notable outliers which influence the trend for convergence (the Ionian and North Aegean island regions); while even besides these regions individual-region outcomes are rather diverse – with the South Aegean and Athens for example experiencing similar trend-changes in the foreign-born penalty (vertical axis) despite their substantially different starting positions (horizontal axis). Similar heterogeneity is observed for the case of the female penalty, with the clustering of data-points suggesting probably some sort of club-formation.

Figure 4. T-I analysis: discrimination variables

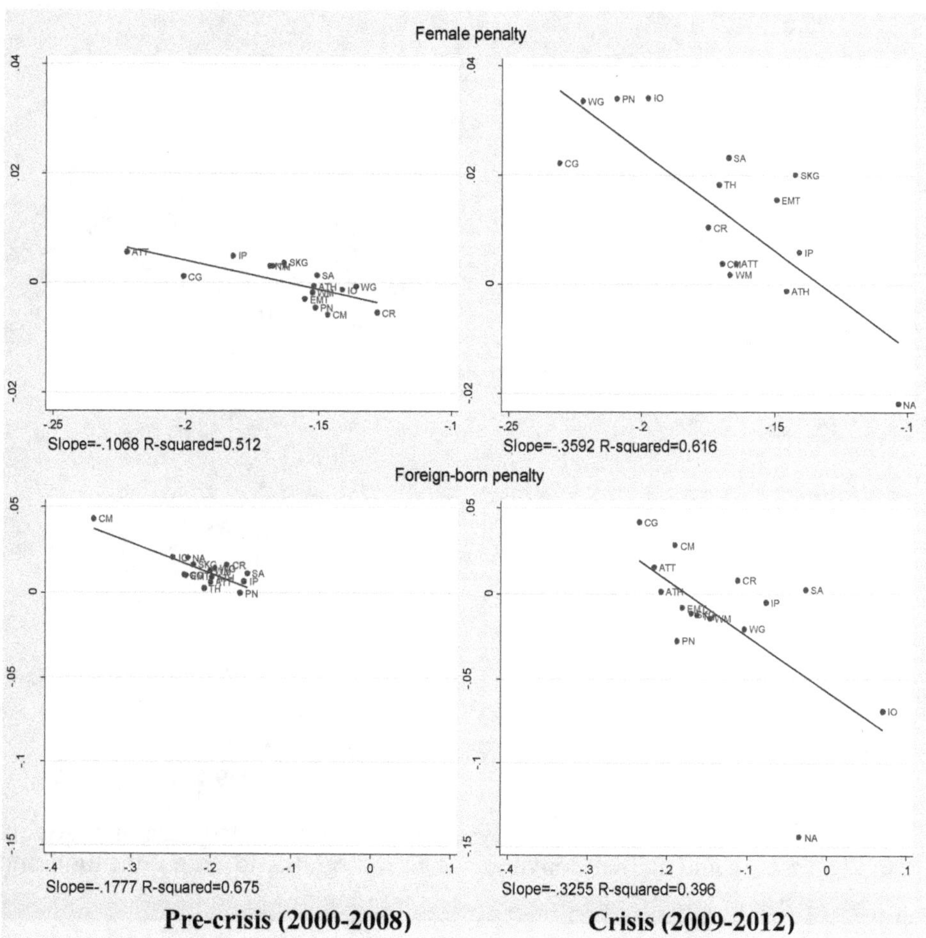

Importantly, however, when examining developments separately for the two sub-periods of the pre-crisis era (Appendix A), we find that convergence in the returns to discrimination-related characteristics was equally strong (female penalty) or stronger (foreign-born penalty) also in the period immediately preceding the crisis (2005-2008). Thus, the evidence of Figure 4 may in fact over-state the (presumed) impact of the crisis on the spatial distribution of the female and foreign-born penalties. This is consistent with the results from the sigma analysis (Appendix C), where there is little evidence of a systematic narrowing of regional disparities in the size of the two penalties. In any case, it should be noted that for almost all regions both penalties have been declining over time[15], suggesting that discrimination and 'pricing' based on pre-determined characteristics is increasingly becoming less prevalent nationally and less heterogeneous across space.

Figure 5. T-I analysis of convergence: skills-related variables

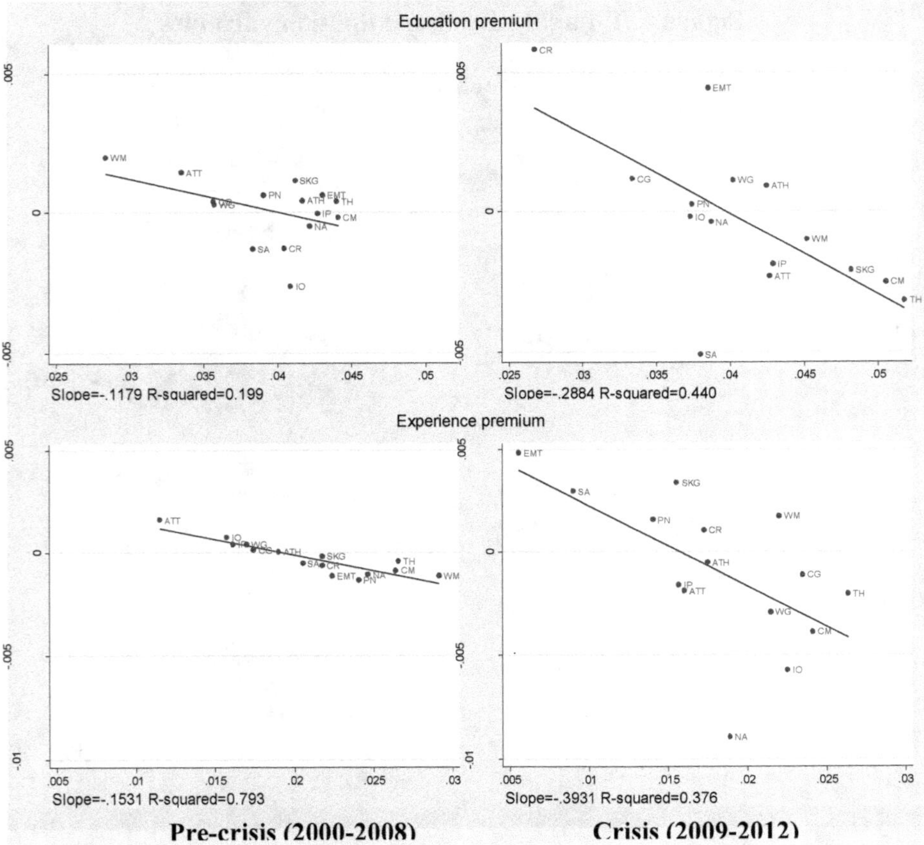

In Figure 5 we depict the T&I analysis for the skills-related variables. Again, the evidence is of intensified convergence in the returns to both education and

15 Most regions have positive trend-values (Figure 4 and Appendix A).

experience. Compared to the 2005-2008 sub-period (Appendix A), the crisis constitutes a period of 'return to convergence' for the returns to education, as in the former period convergence in these seemed to have stalled – although convergence in the returns to labour market experience seems in fact to have slowed down relative to 2005-2008. Again, the Ionian and North Aegean island regions appear as notable outliers; while some clusters of divergence (in the returns to experience) can clearly be identified (for example, a cluster comprising Central Greece, Western Greece, Thessaly, Central Macedonia, the Ionian islands and the North Aegean which seems to follow an upward-sloping pattern). This is consistent with the results from the sigma analysis (Appendix C) which suggests an absolute widening of disparities in the case of the returns to labour market experience during the crisis period. Interestingly, these evolutions were concurrent with a slow but intensifying convergence across regions in their composition of skill-related characteristics (Appendix B). This suggests that the crisis did not instigate processes of spatial sorting (e.g., selective migration of high-education individuals to high-education regions): if anything, we observe convergence in compositions, especially in the case of labour market experience.[16] By the same token, the speedier convergence in the returns to education signals a more equal valuation of formal qualifications across space, although for the majority of the regions this is combined with a trend towards declining returns (see the top-right panel of Fig.5).

As was also shown in Table 1, the results for the returns to household variables (Figure 6) are not drastically different. In both cases (marital status and number of dependants), cross-regional convergence in the associated premia accelerates with the crisis, although the fit of the regression line – and thus the extent to which the aggregate pattern of convergence describes more or less equally all regions – subsides significantly. The same applies broadly in the case of the regional compositions of these characteristics (Appendix B), although there the speed of convergence is much slower and individual regional evolutions are even more heterogeneous (especially in the case of the number of dependants). As our wage regressions control for differences in regional sectoral compositions (vector S in eq.1), it would appear that these evolutions have less to do with policy developments (e.g., universal cuts in the legislated wage supplements for spouses and children, which were originally of different relative importance to different regions due to their different sectoral compositions – see Monastiriotis, 2011) and more with changes across regions in terms of the structure and intensity of labour demand and supply.

Of more interest are perhaps the results about the part-time and temping penalties (Figure 7), as they relate to variables describing the 'employment relationship'. Here, too, penalties appear to converge faster in the crisis

[16] It seems, however, that this does not reflect any significant trend in equilibrating migration. Rather, the effect is driven by a universal rise in age-sorting, with less experienced (younger) individuals experiencing worse wage outcomes (see Christopoulou and Monastiriotis, 2014b).

period[17], albeit again with some heterogeneity across space (note the cases of Crete for the part-time penalty and of Central Macedonia and South Aegean for the temping penalty). The extent of part-timing also converged fast across regions during the crisis; while rates of temporary employment have in fact become more disparate across space in the same period (Appendix B). These evolutions in terms of composition reflect to an extent the very different nature of these two forms of flexible labour use in the Greek case. Temping, which is used extensively in the country, increased only in (three of the four) regions that specialise most in this form of flexible employment (the three island regions of Crete, Ionian and South Aegean); while it actually declined in all but one of the other regions. Temping, it seems, has not been a particular source of adjustment for most of the country during the crisis. Instead, part-timing, which stands at extremely low levels in Greece by international standards, has increased in all regions but one – and faster so in the regions that used to rely less heavily on this form of flexible employment.

Figure 6. T-I analysis of convergence: household variables

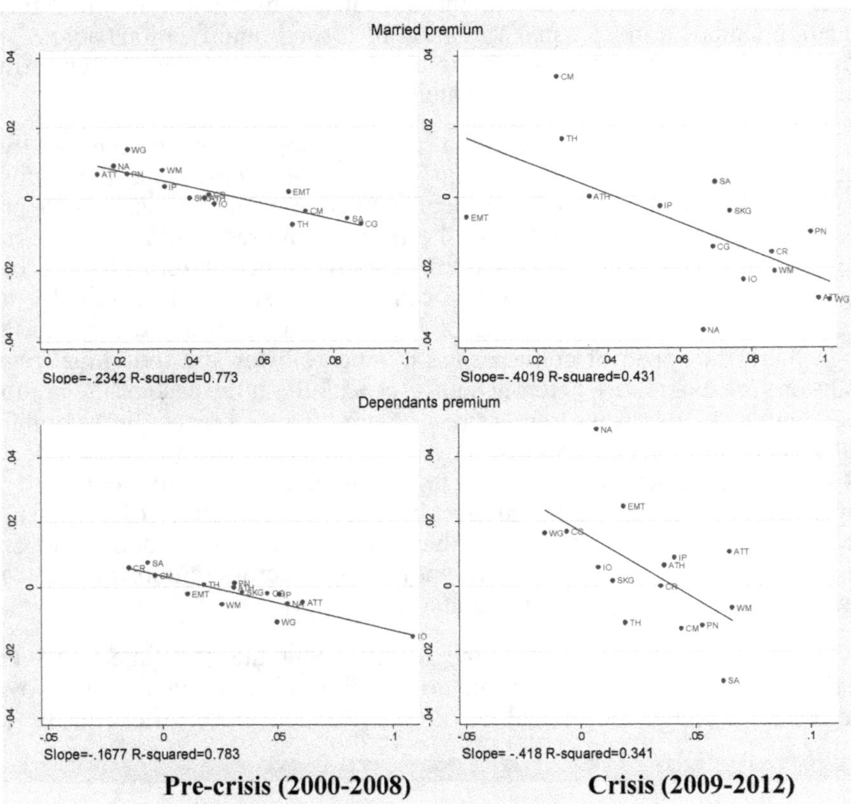

17 This time the same conclusion applies broadly to the case of sigma-convergence (Appendix C). Note for the case of the part-time penalty, the relative decline in the speed of convergence vis-à-vis the 2005-2008 period (Appendix A).

Figure 7. T-I analysis of convergence: employment relation variables

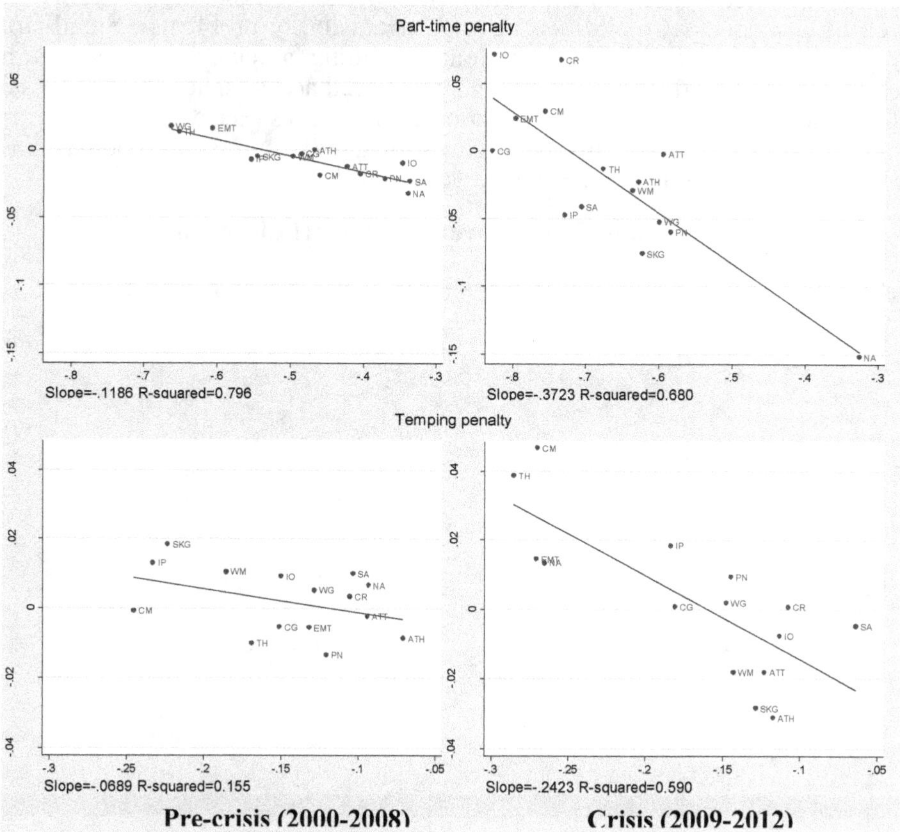

Returning to Fig.7, importantly, the observed trends in the two penalties do not show a uniform type of adjustment across regions, despite the overall evidence of convergence. For regions such as Crete, Ionian, Central Macedonia and East Macedonia & Thrace, the part-time penalty declined during the crisis; while for the majority of the other regions the part-time penalty went up – with North Aegean at the extreme having a trend-change of some 15% per year. Similarly, the temping penalty followed an increasing trend in Central Macedonia, Thessaly, East Macedonia & Thrace, Ipeiros, Peloponesse and the North Aegean; but it declined in most other regions and most emphatically in the two metropolitan regions of Athens and Thessaloniki – where this penalty was at the start of the period relatively moderate.

Figure 8 presents the T&I results for the shadow prices of the 'workplace' variables. As can be seen in the top panel, the small-firm penalty declined in most regions during the crisis and exhibited speedier cross-regional convergence relative to the pre-crisis period (but not relative to 2005-2008). Interestingly, this penalty increased in the region of the North Aegean (a remote and relatively poor region near Turkey) and in the metropolitan region of

Thessaloniki (a much more accessible and developed area at the north of Greece) – suggesting that developments with regard to this shadow price are not driven by a unique set of influences (e.g., accessibility problems). Small-firm employment also declined in most regions (including, albeit only moderately, in Thessaloniki and the North Aegean) and converged across space (Appendix B), showing to an extent the disproportionate difficulties faced by small firms during the crisis – especially in regions such as Central Macedonia, East Macedonia & Thrace, Ipeiros, South Aegean and Crete.

Figure 8. T-I analysis of convergence: workplace variables

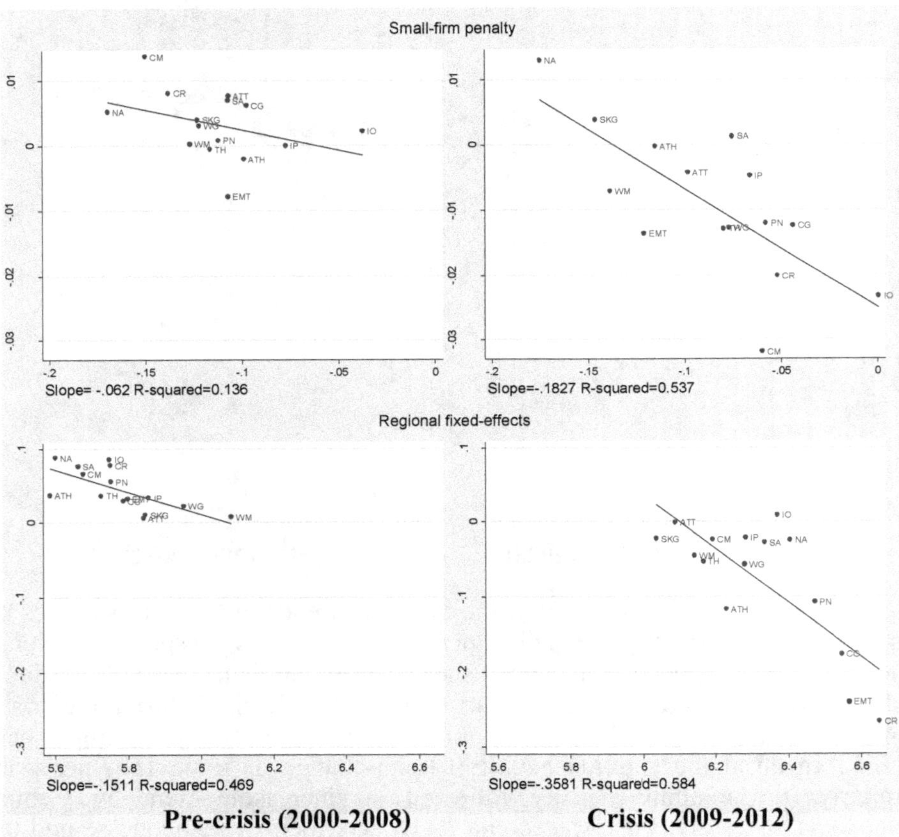

Last – but by no means least – among our variables (shadow prices) of interest is the one concerning the regional fixed effcets. As briefly mentioned earlier, these fixed effects capture the 'baseline' wages prevailing in each region – i.e., the regional wage levels net of the influences of composition (distribution of characteristics) and valuation (distribution of the returns to characteristics). In this sense, they reflect the wider demand and supply conditions in each of the regions, besides the prevailing regional distributions of skills and personal attributes or of job characteristics. As is shown in the bottom panel of Fig.8, at the start of the crisis these baseline wages were substantially larger than in the pre-crisis period (see the differences along the horizontal axis between the two graphs). At the same time, however, baseline wages followed a negative trend in almost all regions during the crisis (in the right-hand-side graph all regions but one are below the zero-mark on the vertical axis). Generally, the decline has been much more substantial in those regions that enjoyed at the start of the crisis the highest baseline wages, thus leading to a strong convergence coefficienct in the T&I analysis (slope=0.358). There is however subsantial heterogeneity in this result.[18] For a large number of regions, the trend-declines in baseline wages were rather moderate (between 0-10%) and, it appears, largely unrelated to the initial levels (intercepts) at the start of the period. In fact, the finding of convergence is almost entirely driven by four or five regions (Crete, East Macedonia & Thrace, Central Greece, Athens and, less so, the Peloponesse) , which experienced trend-decline rates of between 10-30%.

This finding raises again the issue of the substantial heterogeneity that seems to characterise the Greek regions not only in terms of structures (e.g., composition of characteristics) and outcomes (e.g., wages and returns to characteristics) but also in terms of the evolution of these structures and outcomes, both in absolute terms and relative to other regions, and both prior to and – especially – during the crisis. We move to a discussion of this issue, informed by the findings presented here, in the next section.

5. CONCLUSIONS

The starting point in our analysis has been the underlying question about how the crisis in Greece may have affected regional disparities and regional outcomes more generally and in the labour market in particular. Casual inspection of aggregate patterns in regional wage data suggests a subsiding of regional disparities during the crisis – consistent with the limited evidence in the literature about the pro-cyclicality of regional disparities (Petrakos et al, 2005). At closer inspection, however, the evidence of convergence appears less robust – with evidence for both temporal and spatial heterogeneity around the presumed aggregate trend (see our discussion vis-à-vis Figures 2 and 3). Adding to this, are questions about labour market functioning, concerning especially the question as to how (regional) labour markets adjust in times of crisis. Are tendencies of convergence driven for example by equalisation in regional prices – or are they rather driven predominantly by compositional changes (e.g., via cross-regional migration)?

Our approach to examining these questions follows the logic of the analysis of beta- and sigma-convergence. But in our empirical analysis we applied a slightly different methodology, estimating the average growth (trend) and initial level (intercept) of the shadow prices that constitute the variables of our interest through a regression analysis rather than calculating them directly from the data. This has the advantage of avoiding problems related to the definition of

[18] Note also the evidence from the sigma-convergence analysis which shows a fast narrowing of disparities in the early phase of the crisis but a substantial reversal of this trend in 2012 (Figure C.2.).

the start- and end-points for the analysis and reducing the econometric noise that unavoidably exists in our shadow prices, which are themselves estimated through a number of first-stage Mincerian wage equations.

On a first reading of our results, it appears evident that the crisis has seen a notable acceleration of the process of cross-regional convergence in the returns to individual and job-related characteristics – with the logical implication that the observed trend of aggregate convergence is at least in part driven by a process of 'price equalisation'. This is an important finding, both as a general empirical observation and in relation to our understanding of the consequences of the crisis in Greece: it implies that the valuation of labour market characteristics became more homogeneous across space during the crisis – and thus that the functioning of the Greek regional labour markets also became more similar. It also implies that in a way the valuation of labour became spatially 'fairer', in the sense that there is a trend for similar individuals (with similar characteristics and working under similar conditions) to be paid more equally across the different regions. Importantly, this 'spatial fairness' has not been found to be combined with a process of spatial sorting[19] (i.e., the separation of different types of jobs and/or workers across different locations) – which would in turn imply a competing move towards spatial 'unfairness', in the form of increased segregation. To the contrary, most characteristics examined in this paper show, too, continuing cross-regional convergence during the crisis.

On the other hand, the sigma-convergence analysis shows a rather different picture: evidence of convergence is present only for one of the shadow prices examined here (the temping penalty), while for many the evidence points instead to divergence (especially for the experience premium). Overall, however, there seems to be much volatility in the behaviour of the measures of disparity used in the sigma-convergence analysis, with no clear overall trend either prior or during the crisis. This applies not only to the shadow prices associated to individual and job characteristics, but also to the regional wages (both actual and 'baseline') at large.

Habitually, evidence of beta-convergence without sigma-convergence is taken to signal a process of 'overshooting', whereby the catching-up regions overtake the former leaders – so that the overall spread of the corresponding distribution changes little.[20] The evidence gathered from our more detailed analysis of the T&I plots suggests a set of rather different, and more nuanced, explanations. For the discrimination penalties, the prima-facie evidence of convergence is underlined by two important developments: one the one hand, a process of cross-regional convergence that pre-dated the crisis; on the other hand, a pro-

---

19 In their application of the T&I analysis in the case of the UK regions, Duranton and Monastiriotis (2002) found strong evidence of spatial sorting, which explained the presence of 'aggregate divergence' (divergence in actual regional wages) despite the underlying trend for 'disaggregate convergence' (convergence in the returns to characteristics).

20 See Young et al. (2008) for a discussion of other explanations for this discrepancy between beta- and sigma-convergence.

cess of across-the-board reduction in these penalties recently, presumably as the corresponding rewards (for males and natives) were squeezed by the crisis. This is an interesting finding that may extend well beyond the experience of the Greek case.

A similar squeeze is observed, for the majority of regions, for the case of the skills-related premia – implying possibly a job-competition or bumping-down process in these regions, whereby more educated or experienced workers 'crowd-out' from lower-paid jobs less qualified and younger ones[21] (to avoid falling into unemployment), leading to an ad hoc reduction in their private returns to education and experience. In the case of the returns to education this is combined with evidence of cross-regional convergence (returns falling faster in regions that had higher returns initially); whereas for the returns to experience there is some evidence of within-group divergence, which results in an explosive trend in sigma-divergence terms.

The penalties associated to the 'employment relationship' variables also show evidence of cross-regional equalisation, albeit with rather heterogeneous underlying developments in terms of labour market adjustment – with some regions experiencing increasing and other regions experiencing declining penalties; and with evidence showing the extent of temporary (part-time) employment to decline (increase) in most regions and to diverge (converge) across space. In a similar fashion, the estimated regional fixed effects (capturing 'baseline' wages) also exhibit evidence of convergence, but with much heterogeneity both temporally and across space. Temporally, the evidence of convergence from the T&I analysis is corroborated by the sigma-convergence analysis only for the period 2009-2011: in 2012, there is an exceptionally large peak in the dispersion of the distribution of regional baseline wages, which is not captured by the T&I analysis. Spatially, the evidence for convergence seems to be driven by only a sub-group of regions, which experienced rather sizeable declines in baseline wages (over 10% and up to 30% per year), while for the majority of regions the declines were more moderate and cross-regional differences remained rather stable. This implies perhaps important differences across space in demand pressures (and wage adjustments) during the crisis.[22]

To conclude, our analysis helped unveil a number of important facets of intra- and inter-regional wage adjustments in Greece during the crisis. On the whole, regional wage disparities seem to have declined, although more recently a trend for divergence may be (re-)emerging. Regional convergence is present, albeit not for all cases and not always equally strongly, both in the case of re-

[21] This is also consistent with the evidence of nation-wide (for all regions) increases in the average levels of education and labour market experience observed in our data, as depicted in the relevant graphs in Appendix B. Note, however, that nationally the returns to education on the whole increased during this period, driven mainly by developments in Athens and in the private sector in particular (see Christopoulou and Monastiriotis, 2014b).

[22] This is consistent with the evidence presented, for the case of unemployment, in Monastiriotis and Martelli (2013).

turns to characteristics (shadow prices) and in the case of the distribution of these characteristics (composition). Thus, the crisis does not seem to have instigated either processes of spatial sorting or processes of divergence in the valuation of worker and workplace characteristics. In that sense, perhaps rather surprisingly, there is a clear element of 'spatial fairness' that comes with the crisis in Greece. But underneath these aggregate patterns and trends is some notable variation and heterogeneity in terms of the processes and dynamics that underpin labour market adjustment, both within and across regions, in the country.

This conclusion has important implications for policy. Despite the known problems of functioning and institutional quality of the Greek labour market (or maybe because of these), the particular forms of adjustment that prevailed in the different regional economies of the country do not seem to have accentuated existing regional imbalances. Thus, within-region price adjustments have produced a more homogenous environment of wage returns while quantity adjustments (employment sorting within regions or migration across/outside regions) have also produced a less unequal landscape in terms of the composition of workforce characteristics. Although, however, on the face of it this may seem as suggesting a limited scope for regional policy, underlying our results is a large number of disparate regional evolutions (for example, the rise in the returns to education in East Macedonia & Thrace, showing increased skills-based wage sorting, and the decline in these returns in South Aegean, showing instead a more intensified job-sorting by skills) which undoubtedly call for a more careful and case-specific (place-based) regional policy that will understand the labour market weaknesses and particular needs of different areas and devise measures and policies to address them accordingly.

Last, a final note should be made about the contribution of the paper more generally, besides its relevance to labour market and regional policy questions for Greece. As was noted in the Introduction, studies on the geography and regional-temporal evolution of wage returns are rather scant in the literature and usually they offer simple descriptions of patterns but no systematic analyses of these. The T&I approach employed here, although not novel, offers a very useful guide for the systematic analysis of wage returns, and of shadow prices more generally, in a spatio-temporal framework. Especially for the case of Greece, for which no prior study of the regional distribution of wage returns exists, the implementation of this approach offers a unique insight into the working of the country's regional labour markets and their adjustment in times of crisis. But the range and informational value of our results also show the relevance of this approach more widely for the literature of labour market research within the fields of regional science and quantitative economic geography / geographical economics. The comparative study of shadow prices within a micro-econometric framework is certainly on the ascent in the literature and the T&I approach is, as we believe is manifested from our own analysis in this paper, a very useful tool in this regard.

REFERENCES

Bank of Greece (2012), Governor's Report for the Year 2011, Athens.

Bellini E., Ottaviano G. I., Pinelli D., Prarolo G., 2013, Cultural diversity and economic performance: evidence from European regions, *Geography, Institutions and Regional Economic Performance*, Springer Berlin, 109-137.

Benos N., Karagiannis S., 2008, Convergence and economic performance in Greece: evidence at regional and prefecture level, *Review of Urban and Regional Development Studies* 20, 52-69.

Blazek J., Netrdová P., 2012, Regional unemployment impacts of the global financial crisis in the new member states of the EU in Central and Eastern Europe, *European Urban and Regional Studies* 19, 42-61.

Blien U., Eigenhüller L., Promberger M., Schanne, N., 2014, The shift-share regression: an application to regional employment development in Bavaria, *Applied Regional Growth and Innovation Models*, Springer Berlin, 109-137.

Christofides L., Michael M., 2013, Exploring the public-private sector wage gap in European countries, IZA Journal of European Labor Studies, 2, 1-53.

Christopoulos D., Tsionas E., 2004, Convergence and regional productivity differences: Evidence from Greek prefectures, *Annals of Regional Science*, 38 (3), 387-396.

Christopoulou R., Monastiriotis V., 2014a, The Greek public sector wage premium before the crisis: size, selection and relative valuation of characteristics, *British Journal of Industrial Relations*, 52 (3), 579-602.

Christopoulou R., Monastiriotis V., 2014b, The public-private duality in wage reforms and adjustment during the Greek crisis, Crisis Observatory Research Paper 9, ELIAMEP,.

Daouli J., Demoussis M., Giannakopoulos N., Laliotis I., 2013, Firm-level collective bargaining and wages in Greece: a quantile decomposition analysis, *British Journal of Industrial Relations*, 51 (1), 80-103.

Duranton G., Monastiriotis V., 2002, Mind the gaps: the evolution of regional earnings inequalities in the UK, 1982–1997, *Journal of Regional Science*, 42 (2), 219-256.

Heckman J., Lochner L., Todd P., 2003, Fifty years of Mincer earnings regressions, IZA Discussion Paper No775, Institure for the Study of Labor.

Hendricks L., 2004, A Database of Mincerian Earnings Regressions, available at www.lhendricks.org/Mincer.htm.

Herzog H. W., Olsen, R., 1977, Shift-share analysis revisited: the allocation and stability of regional structure, *Journal of Regional Science*, 17(3), 441-454.

Houston d., 1967, The Shift and Share Analysis of Regional Growth: A critique, *The Southern Economic Journal*, April 1967, 577-81.

Kallioras D., Kandylis G., Kromydakis N., Pantazis P. (2012), Delineation of local labour markets in Greece on the basis of travel-to-work flows, *Geographies*, 20, 99-116.

Koukiadaki A., Kretsos L., 2012, Opening Pandora's Box: the sovereign debt crisis and labour market regulation in Greece, *Industrial Law Journal*, 41 (3), 276-304.

Lemieux T., 2006, The 'Mincer equation' thirty years after schooling, experience, and earnings, in Grossbard S. (ed), *Jacob Mincer: a pioneer of modern labour economics*, Springer, 127-145.

Livanos I., 2007, The Incidence of Long-Term Unemployment: Evidence from Greece, *Applied Economics Letters*, 14 (4), 405-408.

Livanos I., Pouliakas K., 2009, The Gender Wage Gap as a Function of Educational Degree Choices in an Occupationally Segregated EU Country, IZA Discussion Paper 4636.

Lolos S. (2009), The Greek Regions: Convergence and Cohesion, Gutenberg.

Lolos S., Papapetrou E., 2011, Unemployment disparities and persistence: assessing the evidence from Greek regions, 1981-2008, Department of Economics Discussion Reports No2011/4, University of Athens.

Michelis L., Papadopoulos A., Papanikos G., 2004, Regional convergence in Greece in the 1980s, *Applied Economics*, 36, 881-888.

Mincer J., 1974, *Schooling, Experience and Earnings*, NBER, New York.

Monastiriotis V., 2011, Making geographical sense of the Greek austerity measures: compositional effects and long-run implications, *Cambridge Journal of Regions Economy and Society*, 4 (3), 323-337.

Monastiriotis V., 2013, A very Greek crisis, *Intereconomics*, 1 (Forum), 4-9.

Monastiriotis V., Martelli A., 2013, Beyond rising unemployment unemployment risk, crisis and regional adjustments in Greece, GreeSE Paper 80, Hellenic Observatory, LSE.

Montenegro C., Patrinos H., 2013, Returns to schooling around the world, Background paper for the World Development Report.

Petrakos G. and Artelaris P. (2009), European regional convergence revisited: a weighted least squares approach", *Growth and Change,* 40 (2), 314-331.

Petrakos G., Rodríguez-Pose A., Rovolis A., 2005, Growth, integration, and regional disparities in the European Union", *Environment and Planning A*, 37 (10), 1837-1855.

Petrakos G., Saratsis Y., 2000, Regional inequalities in Greece, *Papers in Regional Science*, 79 (1), 57-74.

Prodromidis P. (2010), Identifying spatial labour markets in Greece from the 2001 travel-to-work patterns, *South-Eastern Europe Journal of Economics,* 8 (1), 111-128.

Psycharis Y., Kallioras D., Pantazis P., 2014, Economic crisis and regional resilience: detecting the 'geographical footprint' of economic crisis in Greece, *Regional Science Policy and Practice*, 6 (1), 121–141.

Resmini L., 2003, Economic integration, industry location and frontier economies in transition countries, *Economic Systems*, 27 (1), 204-221.

Rodokanakis S., 2010, Comparing the probability of unemployment in Northern Greece vis-à-vis the entire country, *Journal of Economic Asymmetries,* 7 (1), 137-174.

Rodríguez-Pose A., 2006, How does trade affect regional disparities?, *World Development*, 34(7), 1201-1222.

Simón H., 2012, The gender gap in earnings: an international comparison with European matched employer–employee data, *Applied Economics*, 44 (15), 1985-1999.

Siriopoulos C., Asteriou D., 1998, Testing for Convergence across the Greek Regions, *Regional Studies*, 32 (6), 537-546.

Tsionas E., 2002, Another Look at Regional Convergence in Greece, *Regional Studies*, 36 (6), 603-609.

Young A., Higgins M. and Levy D., 2008, Sigma Convergence versus Beta Convergence: Evidence from U.S. County-Level Data", Journal of Money Credit and Banking, 40 (5), 1083-1093.

Appendix A: T-I analysis for the pre-crisis sub-periods (2000-2004 vs 2004-2008)

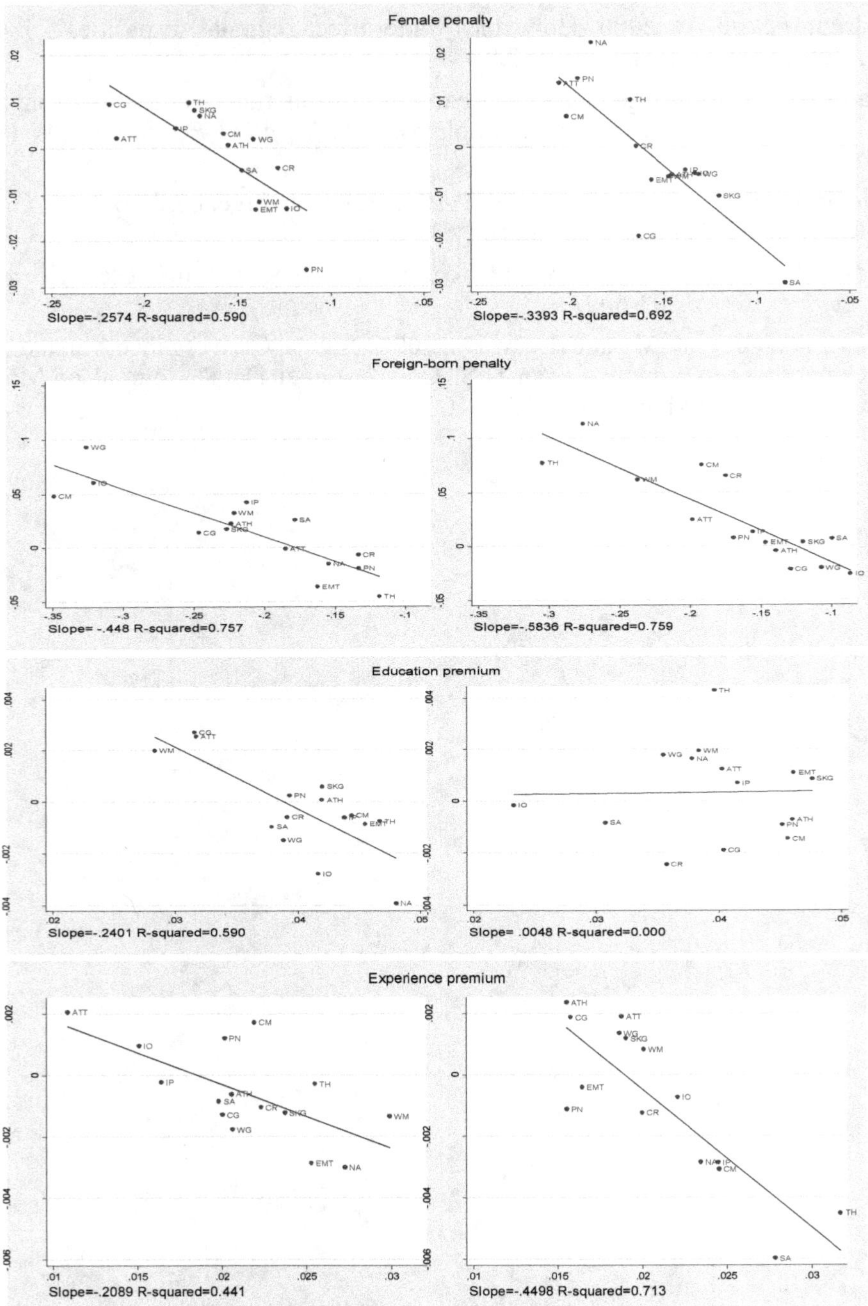

Early EMU period (2000-2004) **Pre-crisis (2005-2008)**

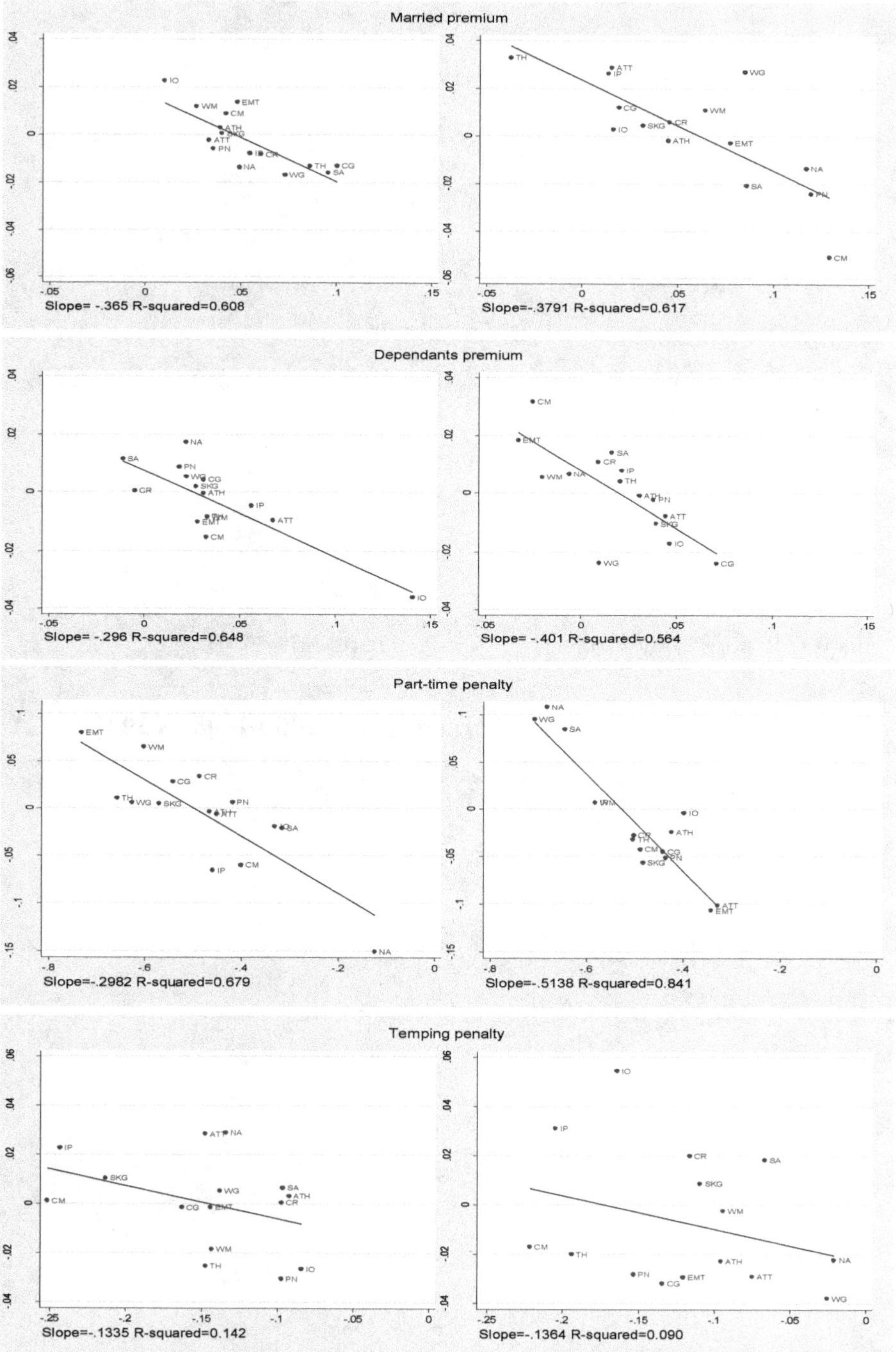

Early EMU period (2000-2004) **Pre-crisis (2005-2008)**

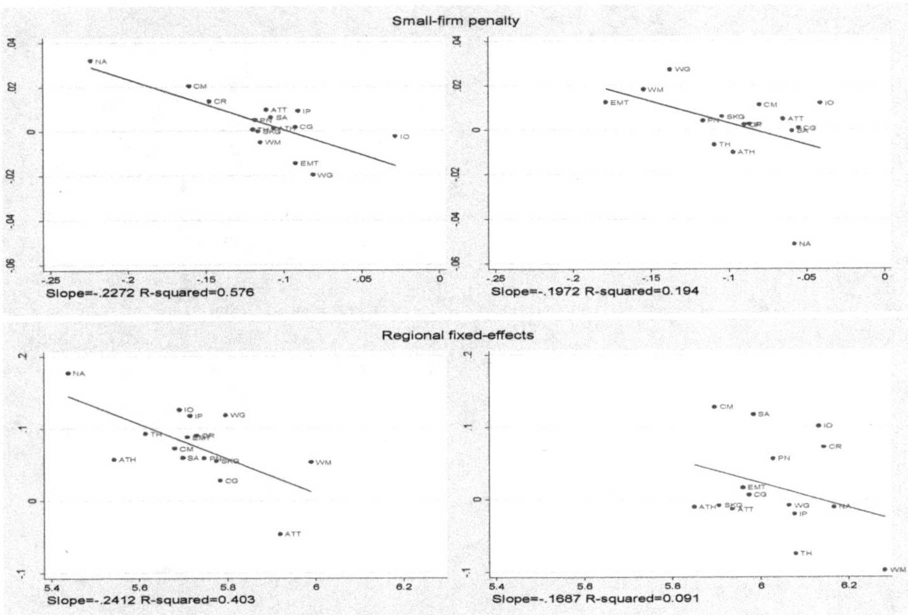

Early EMU period (2000-2004) **Pre-crisis (2005-2008)**

Appendix B: T-I analysis for characteristics (2000-2008 vs 2009-2012)

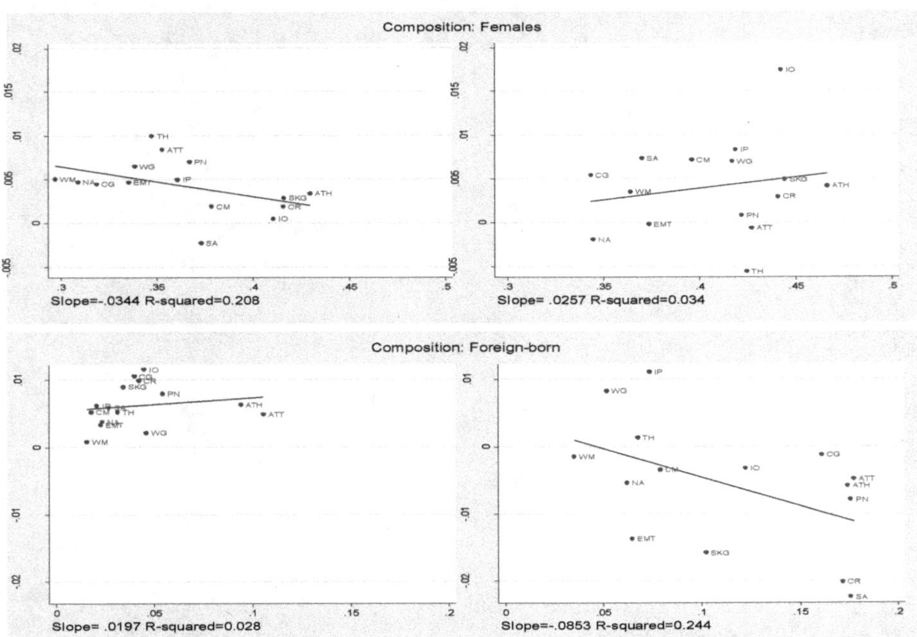

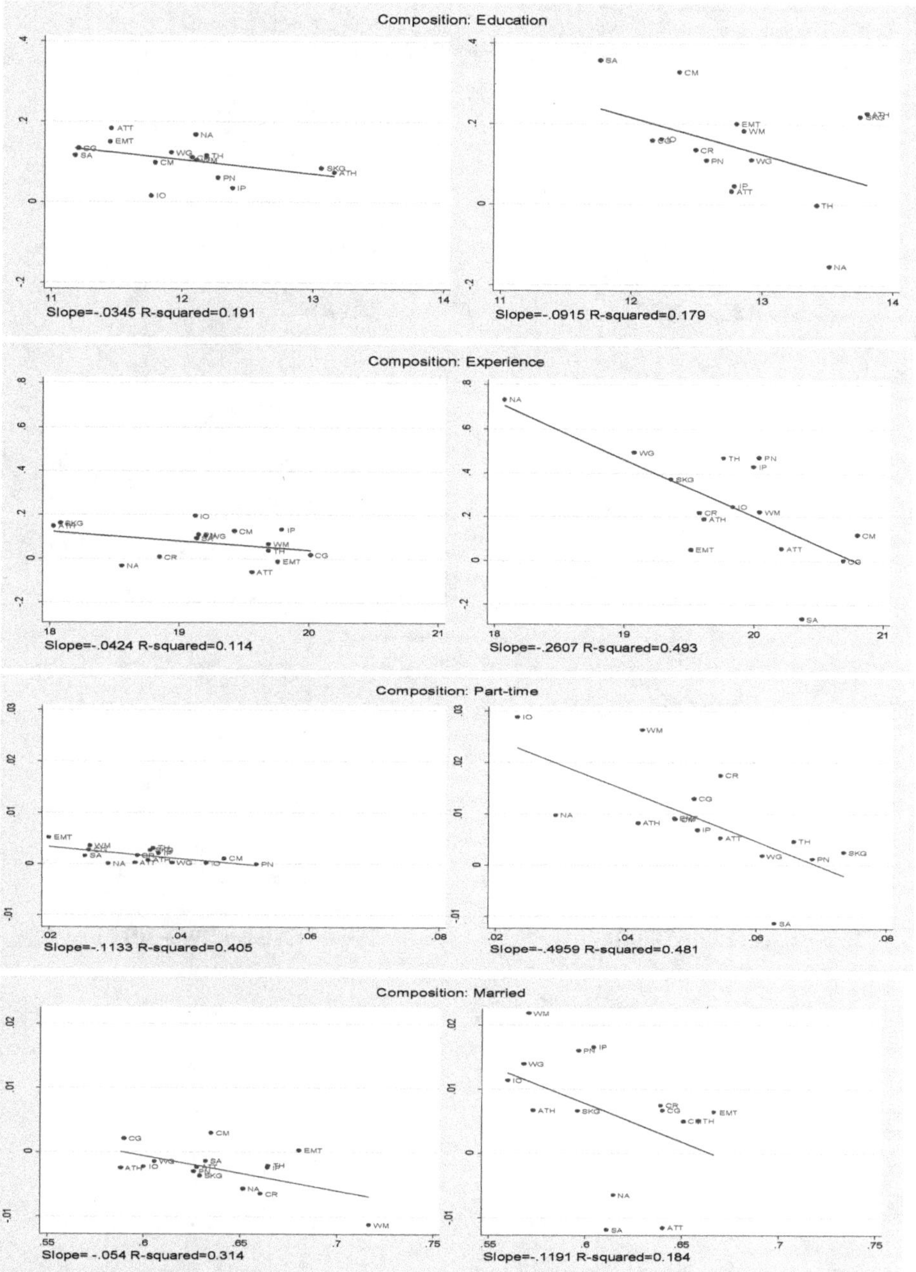

Pre-crisis (2000-2008) **Crisis (2009-2012)**

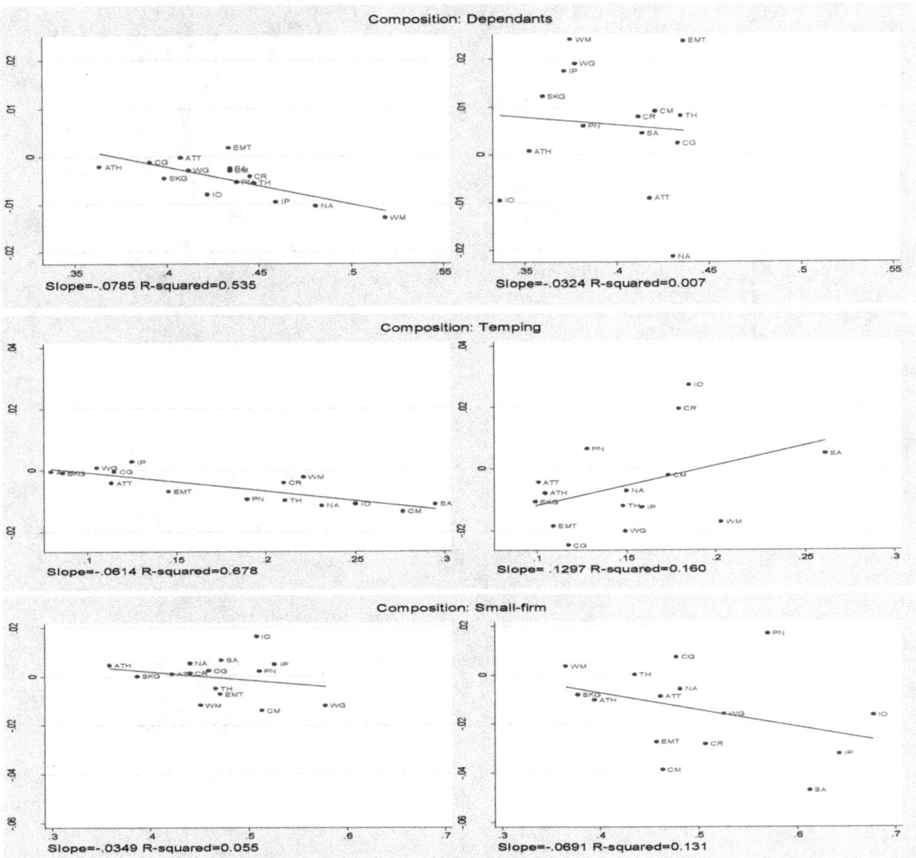

Pre-crisis (2000-2008) **Crisis (2009-2012)**

Appendix C: Sigma-convergence analysis for prices and wages

C.1: Sigma-convergence analysis for returns to characteristics

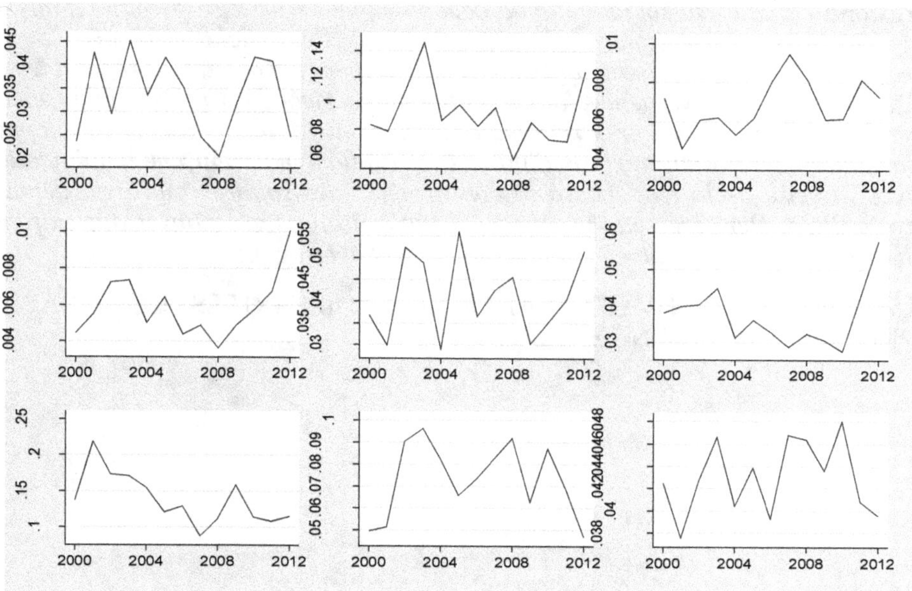

C.2: Sigma-convergence analysis for actual and baseline wages

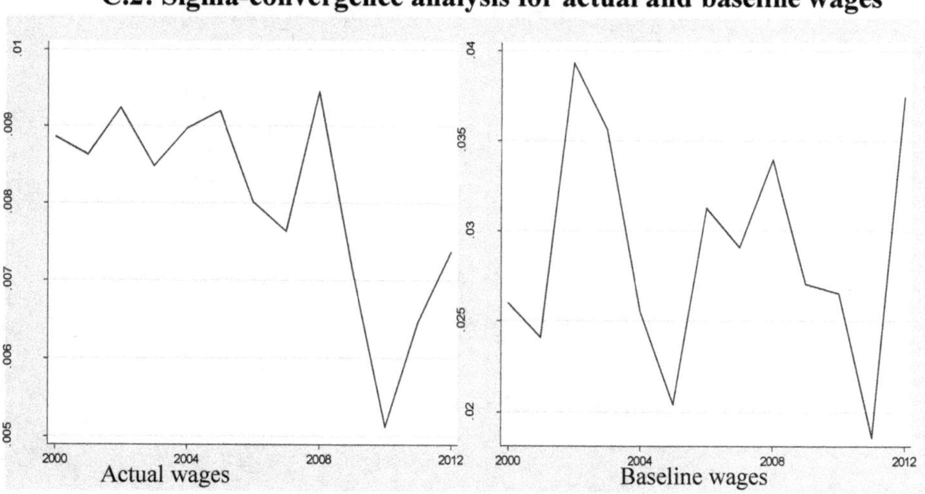

LA CONVERGENCE DES SALAIRES DURANT LA CRISE GRECQUE : UNE ANALYSE AU NIVEAU RÉGIONAL

Résumé - *L'analyse sociale et macroéconomique de la crise grecque a mis au second plan ses conséquences au plan régional. Cet article se focalise sur cet aspect de la crise en étudiant plus particulièrement les disparités régionales de salaires et leur convergence. Une équation mincérienne est utilisée pour analyser l'évolution des salaires régionaux en suivant la méthodologie développée par Duranton et Monastiriotis (2002). Les résultats montrent une amplification avec la crise de la tendance à la convergence des salaires qui avait débutée avant 2008. Derrière cette tendance, il apparaît que les réponses des marchés du travail régionaux face à la crise ont été fort hétérogènes.*

Mots-clés - AVANTAGES SALARIAUX, DISPARITÉS RÉGIONALES, GRÈCE, CONVERGENCE, CRISE

ECONOMIC CRISIS AND REGIONAL DEVELOPMENT IN GREECE

Yannis PSYCHARIS*, Antonis ROVOLIS**, Vassilis TSELIOS***, Panayotis PANTAZIS ****

Abstract *- This paper sets out to examine the determinants of regional development in Greece before and during the economic crisis. By proposing an econometric model with spatial effects for the years 2005-2008 and 2009-2011, which represent the sub-periods of growth and decline of the Greek economy respectively, we make it possible to capture the different factors that affect the regional economic development of the NUTS III regions in the country. Results highlight that the most urbanized and high income level regions are more affected by the economic crisis. However, these regions had been the ones that most benefited during the upturn of the economic activity. The same applies to the regions that are based on agriculture, which had benefited during the period of economic development but cannot sustain the gains of development during the recession. Specialization in manufacturing is an important determinant of regional development, either in times of growth or in times of crisis, while tourism generates benefits to the neighbouring regions in times of economic crisis. These results are also tested for geographical subsets of the country such as the North-South divide and regions belonging to the development axis of the country (PATHE) versus the rest regions of the country.*

Key words - ECONOMIC CRISIS, REGIONAL RESILIENCE, REGIONAL DEVELOPMENT, GREECE

JEL Classification - R11, R12, C21, C23, O21

Acknowledgments: This paper is based on research that has been co-financed by the European Union (European Social Fund) and Greek national funds through the Program "Education and Lifelong Learning" of the National Strategic Reference Framework - Research Funding Program: THALES.

* Panteion University of Social and Political Sciences, Department of Economic and Regional Development; psycharis@panteion.gr

** Panteion University of Social and Political Sciences, Department of Economic and Regional Development; rovolis@panteion.gr

*** University of Thessaly, Department of Planning and Regional Development; vtselios@prd.uth.gr

**** University of Thessaly, Department of Planning and Regional Development, Panteion University of Social and Political Sciences, Department of Economic and Regional Development; ppantaz@prd.uth.gr

1. INTRODUCTION

The reaction of regional economies during the economic cycle has been a longstanding issue in the literature of regional analysis and policy. While gains from growth or losses from recession are highly unevenly distributed across space, the underlying causes and circumstances that could offer plausible explanations to such differences are still open to debate. Theories of regional development offer contradictory views, while empirical research yields highly diversified findings based on different country experiences, methodological frameworks and availability of data.

In this paper we try to identify the determinants of regional economic development in Greece for the period 2005-2011. This period has some distinct characteristics that make Greece an interesting case study. During this period, the Greek economy experienced both economic growth and decline. For this reason, the entire period 2005-2011 has been divided into two sub-periods, 2005-2008 and 2009-2011, which represent periods of economic growth and recession respectively.

The year 2005, which is the starting year of our analysis, is the median year of the decade that started with the establishment of Eurozone which Greece joined in 2001. In addition, this year highlights the post-Olympic-Games period for the country. Throughout the decade and also during that period 2005-2008, the Greek economy showed well above the European average annual percentage growth rate in terms of its economic activity. The year 2009 highlights another turning point, with the start of the most severe, and still-evolving, economic crisis the country has experienced during its modern history. The impact of the crisis on the level of economic prosperity and living conditions for people and territories is still a little known and discussed issue and as such it constitutes a promising area for scientific investigation.

This paper tries to sets out to examine the interrelation between space and economy and investigates how the gains from development are distributed throughout different territories of the country, and also how losses from recession are spread and divided between different areas of the country. The principal goal of our paper is to identify and compare the drivers of regional development in Greece before and during the economic crisis.

We also attempt to see how these determinants are differentiated by the geographical subsets of national economy, such as for the regions that belong to the development axis of the country (known as PATHE) versus the rest of the country (Non-PATHE), as well as regions based on the North-South divide of the country.

This attempt is supported by a newly elaborated dataset with socio-economic, demographic and geographical variables, which capture different aspects of the morphology of NUTSIII regions of the country. Analysis which uses descriptive and spatial econometric analysis techniques offers some interesting insights for the determinants of the development in space.

This paper communicates with and contributes to the literature in many ways. Firstly, it makes an empirical attempt to study what determines the level of regional development in the country during periods of growth and recession. Secondly, it is related to regional resilience, which has been one of the core issues regarding the geography of crisis effects. Thirdly, analysis is conducted at the prefectural NUTS III level, which comprises a geographically disaggregated level, which in turn makes it possible to capture the crisis impact on relatively smaller areas. Fourthly, it applies spatial econometric analysis techniques accompanied with other descriptive methods of regional analysis, such as thematic mapping. Fifthly, analysis is based on a newly elaborated dataset with variables that capture socio-economic and demographic effects expected to explain the variation in the level of economic development across Greece. Finally, it provides evidence from a cohesion country for which regional development has been a policy priority for years. As a result, economic crisis puts at risk and also questions the viability-sustainability and resistance of regional economies to the crisis.

Summing up, the unique and timely dataset, the geographical level of analysis and the methodology applied give this study attempt a novelty that could communicate with the international audience and could offer insights from a country that was severely hit by the recent economic crisis and which was placed at the heart of economic discussion regarding interpretations of and responses to overcoming the current economic crisis.

2. LITERATURE REVIEW – ESTIMATING CRISIS IMPACT ON REGIONAL DEVELOPMENT

Fluctuations of the economic cycle, apart from the impact they have on national economy, have a distinct geographical dimension that has been a longstanding issue in regional analysis and policy literature. The upward 'tide' of economic activity generates benefits for the national economy that are spread geographically in a fairly unbalanced way (Richardson 1973: 138). Conversely, the downward trend of economic activity incurs costs that affect the economy of the regions across the country (Stillwell 1980). The rising and lowering tide spreads benefits and incurs costs in different geographical areas of a given economy that are subject to theoretical and empirical interpretations from different theoretical standpoints and scientific disciplines (Borts 1961; Myrdal 1957; Berry 1988; Krugman 1991).

In recent decades, the bulk of development literature has given relatively more attention to the growth performance of countries and regions rather than the determinants of the level of economic development (OECD 2009b: 13). This is probably due to fact that growth has been considered as the end-result of the economic activity and crises have been seen as the short-lived episodes of an unavoidable tendency to higher and converging levels of economic development. However, the intensity and duration of the current economic crisis, along with the unprecedented impacts it has had on people's lives and territories, has triggered a new surge of research regarding the impacts of the crisis on the level of economic and regional development (OECD 2009a: 13; Bachtler and Davies 2009). The question of what makes regions able to achieve and sustain a high level of economic development and which factors hinder the development potential and make regions more vulnerable to crises has (re)gained important salience these days.

One strand of the literature attempts to assess the heterogeneous impact of global recession on individual European countries and regions (De Groot *et al.* 2011). The overall conclusion of this analysis is that variation in the sectoral composition contributes to the variation of the current crisis impact at both country and regional level across the EU. However, as mentioned before, due to the lack of recent statistical data there are few examples of this type of research.

Other scientists have tried to investigate the impact of real estate and mortgage market crisis on cities and local economies, as the current crisis began as a crisis in the financial and real estate markets. Aalbers (2009) argues that the housing bubbles and changes in regulation in the financial sector dictated, to a large extent, the geography of the financial crisis at state and city level in the US (Aalberts 2009: 34). Martin (2011) depicts the geography of recession by analysing the locally varying impact of global credit crunch at macro and micro geographical levels in the USA. He concludes that geography stands as an essential element for analysing economic crisis. Holly *et al.* (2011) analyse the spatial and temporal diffusion of house prices in the UK, developing a model which captures the diffusion of the crisis across cities and regions in the real estate market. Marshall *et al.* (2012) offer another viewpoint of the credit crunch, with the collapse of Northern Rock in 2007, connecting this case with the peripheral financial region of Newcastle (where Northern Rock was based).

Another strand of research, which has been receiving growing attention, analyses the impact of the crisis on regional levels of unemployment. OECD (2011a) highlights the differentiated impact on the loss of jobs within OECD countries due to economic recession. Mussida and Pastore (2012) analyse regional unemployment in Italy and find that labour turnover is related to the regional unemployment rate and determined by structural change. Fingleton *et al.* (2012) investigate the effects of recessionary shocks in regional unemployment, with reference to UK regions during the period 1971-2010, and provide evidence that there are quite large differences in the way that regions react to recessionary employment shocks. Patuelli *et al.* (2012) use spatial filtering techniques to depict the geographical distribution and persistence of regional/local unemployment rates in Germany, and find widely heterogeneous but generally high persistence in regional unemployment rates.

Another notion that is central to the geography of economic crisis is that of "resilience". Martin (2012) develops the idea of resilience and examines its usefulness as an aid to understanding the reaction of regional economies to major recessionary shocks; he makes a preliminary empirical analysis of previous and recent crises in UK regions. In another relevant paper, Foster (2012) points out that resilience represents both the capacity to respond to a shock and the performance of a region once a shock has occurred. Then, she proceeds with a construction of a regional resilience index and applies it to USA cities. Bristow and Healy (2014), placing specific emphasis on the role of human agency, argue that that the inclusion of the human factor in resilience thinking ultimately means that the role of place and context must assume greater significance.

As regards Greece, the regional impact of economic crisis has been given limited attention by the literature. In a recent paper, Psycharis *et al.* (2014) investigate the impact of economic crisis on the Greek regions with the use of a composite indicator, and find that metropolitan regions are more vulnerable to economic crisis while islands more resilient. Monastiriotis (2011) analyses the impact of austerity measures on regional income and inequalities, arguing that the horizontal measures are widening existing disparities – something that may be difficult to redress in the future. Bakas and Papapetrou (2012) examine the nature of Greek unemployment allowing for cross-sectional dependence among Greek regions, and suggest that structural breaks should be taken into account when considering general models that relate unemployment to other macroeconomic variables, at national and regional level within Greece. From another more critical perspective, Hatzimichalis (2011) discusses certain issues of regional development theory in combination with the conditions of uneven geographical development, and the shift towards what we may call the neoliberal urban and regional development discourse, and he questions the lack of socio-spatial justice in the austerity policies applied in the cohesion countries. Regional inequalities during economic crisis were the focus of a research attempt by Caraveli and Tsionas (2012), who argue that the current debt crisis and the fiscal measures have put a strain on the regional economies most heavily dependent on public sector employment and investment.

However, there is a dearth of research on modelling the regional effects of economic crisis in the Greek regions. Today, the relatively higher availability of statistical data makes it possible to make a quantitative assessment of crisis impact on regional output and development. Our model examines the dynamics of regional development in Greece for the period before and after the economic crisis hit Greece. This approach will allow us to delve into the underpinnings of the development and decline of Greek regions and to highlight the determinants which may prove important for interpreting the regional impact of a crisis and detecting ways out of it.

Our attempt, supported by a newly elaborated dataset is aiming at filling, at least in part, the gap in existing literature on the regional impact of an economic crisis, and communicates with the international debate on these issues.

3. MAPPING REGIONAL DEVELOPMENT SOME STYLIZED FACTS

In this part of the paper we present some stylized facts regarding the evolution of the level of economic development of Greek regions during the period 2005-11 and the two sub-periods 2005-08 and 2009-11.

3.1. Trends in national economy

Figure 1 portrays the evolution of GDP per capital for Greece and the EU-27 over the period 2005-2011 and shows that post-2009 Greece has experienced a clear divergence trend compared with the average EU-27 level of economic development. This steady divergence contradicts the convergence process that was observed for Greece during the previous years of the decade. While the EU 27 shows signs of stabilization, Greece is converging steadily. This divergent trend, which reflects the polarization of the emerging new economic geography in Europe, is something that can be highlighted before we turn to the regional impact of economic crisis.

Figure 1. GDP per capita of Greece as percentage (%) of EU27 average

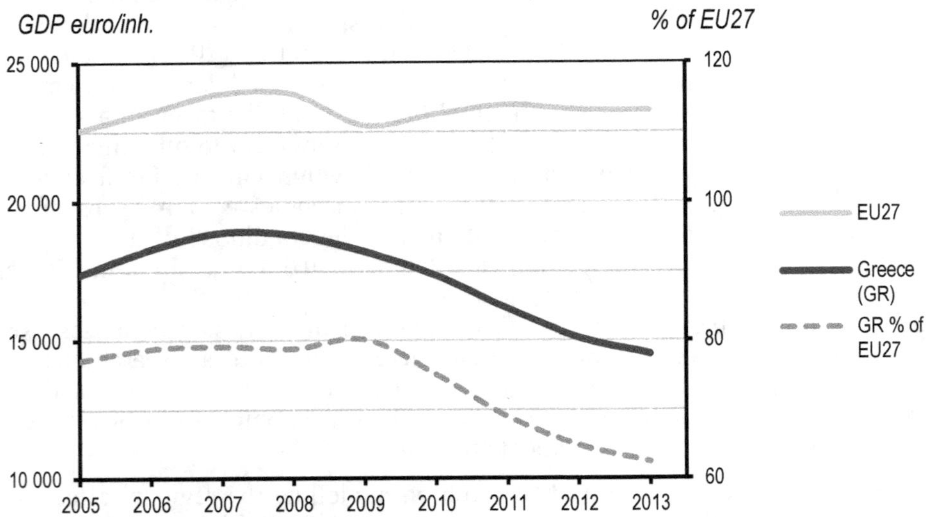

Source: AMECO online database - accessed at 26.08.2014, own calculations.

Table 1. Gross domestic product volume and per capita 2005-2013, EU27 and Greece

Variable	Unit	Change (%)			Compound Annual Growth Rate - CAGR (%)		
		2005-08	*2009-13*	*2005-13*	*2005-08*	*2009-13*	*2005-13*
Gross domestic product (constant prices 2005)	European Union (27 countries)	7.1%	3.41%	5.7%	2.3%	0.84%	0.7%
	Greece	9.0%	-21.02%	-16.6%	2.9%	-5.73%	-2.2%
Gross domestic product per capita (constant prices 2005)	European Union (27 countries)	5.8%	2.34%	3.1%	1.9%	0.58%	0.4%
	Greece	8.1%	-20.35%	-16.6%	2.6%	-5.53%	-2.2%

Source: AMECO online database - accessed at 26.08.2014, own calculations.

Table 1 provides some facts on the growth dynamics during this period. As the table shows, the annual growth of the Greek economy during the period 2005-2008 has been much higher than the European average. The reversed trend is observed for the period 2009-2013, which shows negative growth rates much higher than the EU average. As a result, high growth rates in the first period are accompanied with convergence of the Greek economy with the European average, while the reversed growth rates of the second period are accompanied by divergent trends from the European average.

Figure 2. GDP per capita, change (start year/end year), Greece NUTSIII spatial level

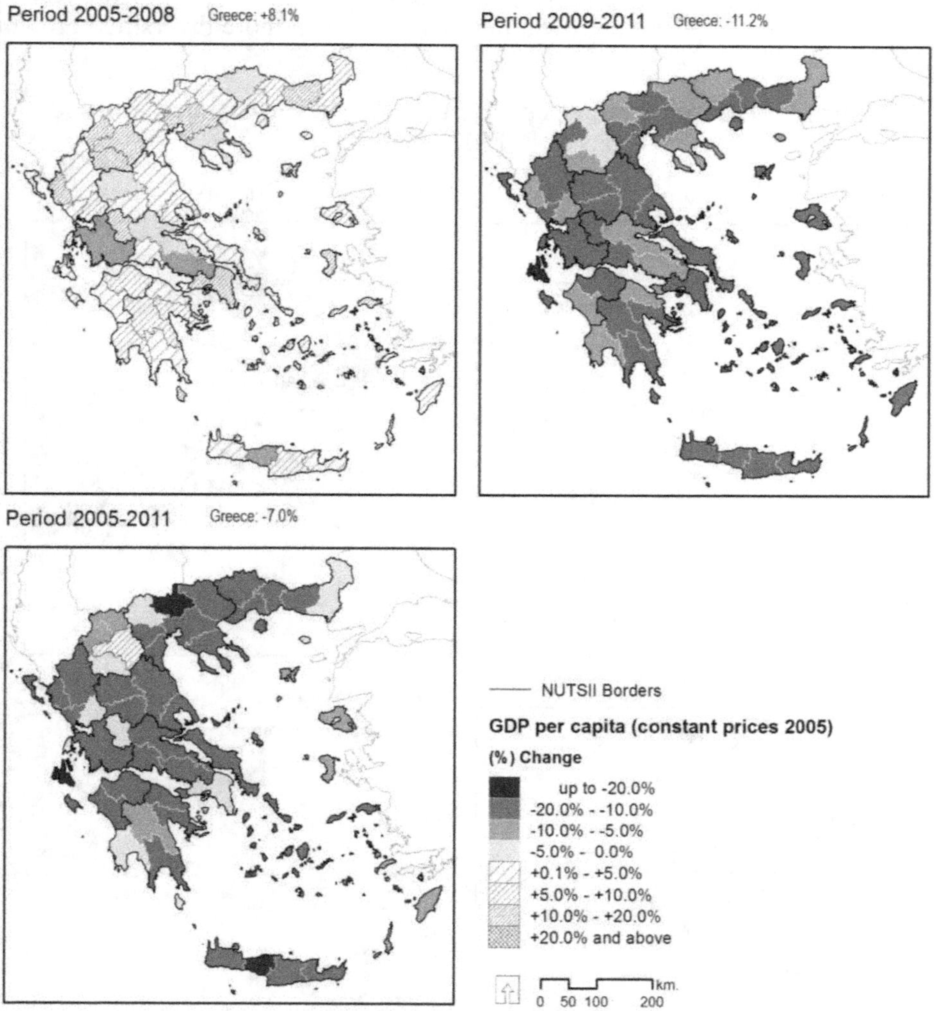

Source: Eurostat online database [nama_r_e3gdp] - accessed at 26.08.2014, own calculations.

3.2. Trends in regional growth

Now we can look at how these trends at national level are reflected at regional level. Figure 2 demonstrates that the growth performance of the economy during the period 2005-2008 is far from being equally distributed among the regions of the country. In addition, the economic decline during the period 2009-2011 shows a far from homogeneous spatial pattern.

The upward trend of economic activity during 2005-2008 includes almost all the NUTS III regions/prefectures of the country, with the exception of Voiotia, the neighboring region to Attiki and where the manufacturing activity of Attiki has been exported, the agricultural based prefecture of Aitoloakarnania in Western Greece and the prefecture of Rethymno in Creta. However, for the rest of the prefectures, the positive growth rates show a much more diversified growth pattern.

Figure 3. GDP per capita as percentage (%) of the national average, Greece NUTSIII spatial level

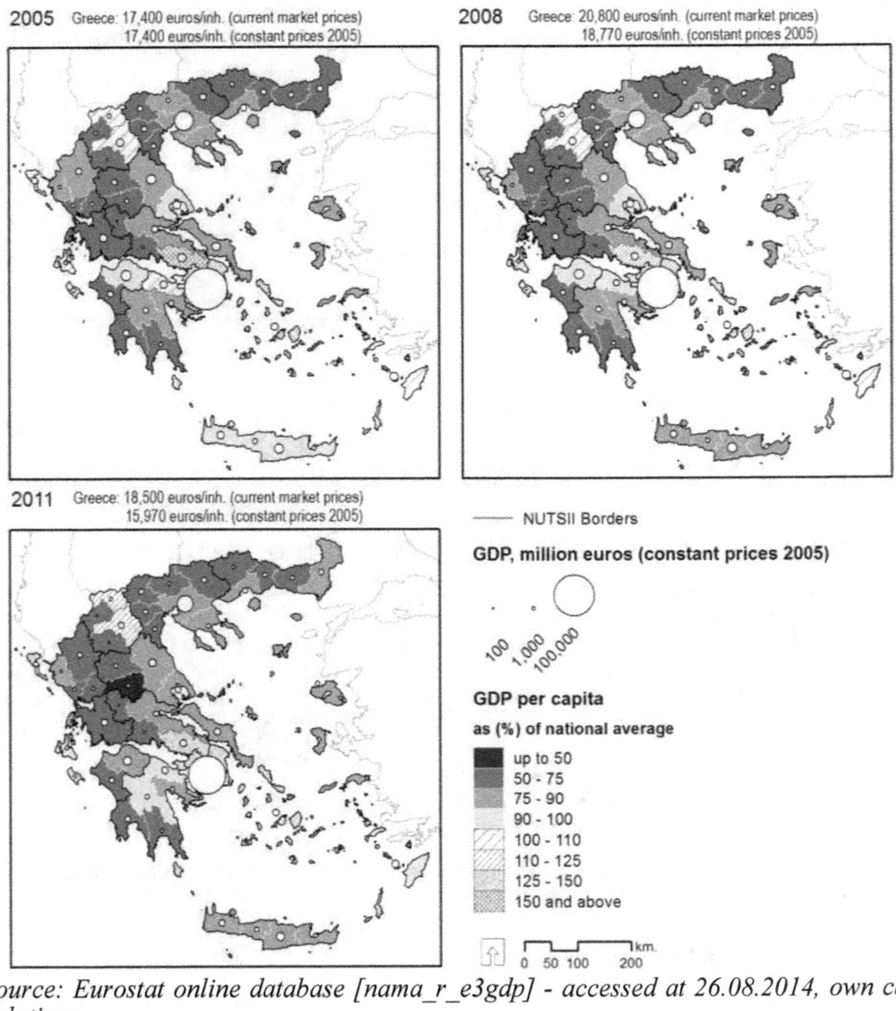

Source: Eurostat online database [nama_r_e3gdp] - accessed at 26.08.2014, own calculations.

The downwards trend of the period 2009-2011 affects all the NUTS III regions of the country. As a result, for the period 2005-2012 the majority of prefectures showed negative growth rates, with a few exceptions, including Kozani, which is the location of electrical production in Greece. Attiki stands out as one of the least affected and this is an important case because it includes Athens the capital city of Greece, and because the relative value of its economy accounts for almost 40% of the economic activity of the country. Other interesting cases include the prefectures of Grevena in Epirus, Evros in the north-east, Messinia in the south-west and Evritania and Arta in central-western Greece, and Pella in the north.

3.3. Trends in regional development and inequalities

Now we can study the map of regional development in Greece at NUTSIII level in comparison with the country average. Figure 3 shows the maps for regional GDP per capita as a percentage of the national average for the years 2005 (the starting year of the period under consideration), 2008 (the year before the start of the economic decline) and 2011 (the year with the latest available data on GDP at regional level). At constant prices, the GDP per capital for Greece in the year 2005 was 17,400 euro, in the year 2008 it was increased to 18,770, an increase of 7.8%. However, in 2011 it reduced to 15,970 indicating a fall of -14.9%. The lowering of the level of economic development of the country has impacted on the level of economic development of the regions.

Figure 4. Regional inequalities in Greece: coefficient of variation 2005-2011

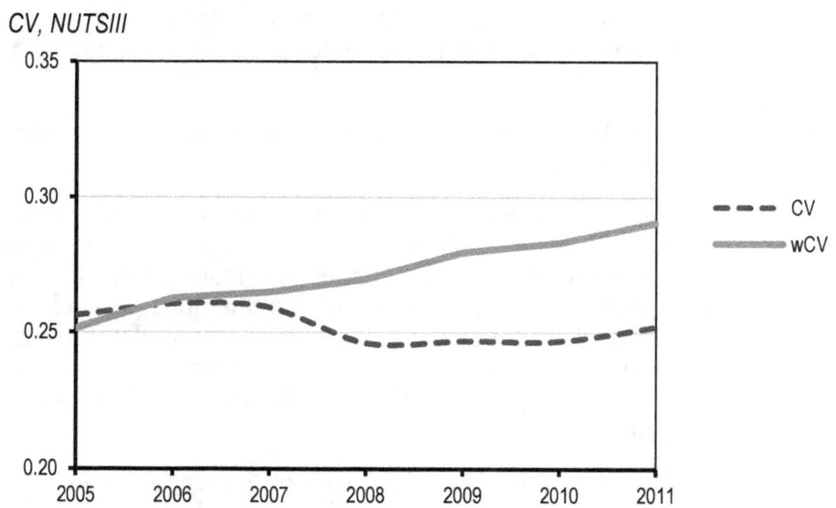

Source: Eurostat online database [nama_r_e3gdp] - accessed at 26.08.2014, own calculations.

As Figure 3 shows, the regional pattern of economic development has remained relatively stable throughout the study period and there are only a limited number of NUTS III regions that enjoy levels of economic development above the country average; these prefectures include Attiki, and its neighbouring prefectures, the Aegean Islands and Crete, as well as Kozani and Grevena, prefectures that are key energy suppliers for the country.

These trends have impacted on the level of regional inequalities across the country. As Figure 4 portrays, the coefficient of variation weighted with population shows that inequalities increase during the years of an economic crisis. However, using the simple coefficient of variance as a measure for regional inequalities, we can see that regional inequalities decrease after 2006 and remain stable during the economic crisis.

Summing up the finding of this section, we can observe the divergent trend of Greece from the European average, the relatively stable pattern of regional development, and the increase in regional inequalities.

4. MODELLING DETERMINANTS OF REGIONAL DEVELOPMENT

4.1. Description of variables

The variables that are included in the analysis stand for socio-economic, demographic and geographic features of the regional economies in Greece. Analysis is conducted at the NUTS III geographical level in the country. According to the recent administrative reform, these geographic units are sub-parts/subdivisions of the second tier of local government.

The dependent variable is *GDP per capita*, which stands for the level of economic development (Hellenic Statistical Authority, market prices). This indicator corresponds to one of the standard variables that have been found significant in growth and development models within neoclassical, endogenous or NEG theories (OECD 2009).

The explanatory variables include *urbanization*, *secondary sector, agriculture*, *tourism*, *and declared income*.

Urbanization has been measured by *Population density* of NUTS III regions. This variable has always been a standard variable in economic development models since it proxies agglomeration economies and market size. Literature suggests the differentiated impacts of crisis on cities and regions (Stilwell 1980, De Grout *et al.* 2012). Large agglomerations are more exposed to crisis and therefore sometimes experience higher impacts than the less-developed areas. However, these areas usually recover earlier than the rest of the country and become drivers of economic recovery.

Secondary sector (Manufacturing) and Agriculture are variables that proxy sectoral composition in regional economies, and question whether regional specialization in manufacturing or in agriculture account for the differentiation of the impact of a crisis across regions.

Tourism is another important factor for the level of economic development of the regions. In this model, we make use of total number of overnight stays of tourists in NUTSIII regions of the country.

Declared income reflects the level of prosperity among individuals across regions and is considered to be an important factor during a crisis.

4.2. Model specification

The empirical calibration of the economic development model includes a rather large set of independent variables, as described above. The calibrated equation has the form:

GDPperCapita = f(Urbanization, Agriculture, Secondary Sector, Tourism, Income)

The dataset has a relatively small time dimension, i.e. it covers the period 2005 to 2011, and a relatively larger cross-sectional dimension, i.e. the fifty one Greek prefectures (that is NUTS III regions in the European nomenclature). The estimated equation in compact form will be:

$$y_{it} = \alpha + \beta X_{it} + u_{it}$$

where subscript i denotes the cross-section dimension, t the time-series dimension, y_{it} is the dependent variable, X the $_{it}^{th}$ observation on K explanatory variables (not including the constant term), α is a scalar, and β is of M x 1 dimension. Finally, u_{it} is the disturbance term.

In the subsequent analysis, several different types of regression are employed; also different parts (subsets) of the basic dataset are used, differentiated either spatially or temporarily. Ordinary Least Squares (OLS), Panel Data Fixed Effects (FE), and Panel Data Random Effects (RE) were estimated, but only the FE results are reported here, as FE is the "preferable" estimation, based on the Hausman test (*see*, for instance, Baltagi 2008). Actually, we also used the robust version as suggested by Wooldridge (2002), which produced similar results rejecting RE estimators (these tests, as well as, OLS and RE estimations are available upon request). All sets of results are corrected for the presence of heteroskedasticity and serial correlation (for the methodology used to obtain these robust errors, see Arellano 1993 or Wooldridge 2002). In "compact" form, the panel estimators will be:

In the one-way Fixed Effects context, the disturbances will be:

$$u_{it} = \mu_i + \varepsilon_{it}$$

where μ_i denotes the unobservable individual specific effects and ε_{it} denotes the remainder disturbances. The FE estimators are computed on the assumption that the unobservable individual effects are fixed parameters and the remaining disturbances are independent and identically distributed (for the several alternative ways by which panel data estimators can be obtained, and give numerically identical results, see for instance, Baltagi 2008, or Greene 2011).

The Random Effects regression will be:

$$y_{it} = \alpha + \beta X_{it} + u_{it}$$

where, all symbols are as previously, but the error term now takes the form:

$$u_{it} = v_i + \varepsilon_{it}$$

where v_{it} are random variables (i.i.d. random-effects); the Cov(x_{it}, v_i) = 0 and the ε_{it} term denotes the remainder disturbances.

A potential problem is that the error terms are serially correlated and their standard errors are biased. A pooled GLS estimator provides here the Random Effects estimator (for the transformation procedure see, for instance, Baltagi 2008, or Greene 2011). As stated earlier, the results of RE estimators are available upon request.

The geographic nature of the data enabled the use of spatial regressions. There is now available an array of potential models to estimate spatial regression (Lesage and Pace, 2009, survey most of these models). Here, two of the most popular models, the Spatial Autoregressive Model (SAR) and the second the Spatial Error Model (SEM), have been used.

The SAR model has the compact form:

$$y_{it} = \rho * W * y_{it} + \beta X_{it} + \alpha_t + u_{it}$$

where W is the (spatial) weights matrix, ρ is the spatial autoregressive coefficient, and all other notation as before (for the u_{it} the classical assumptions are assumed). In the Spatial Autoregressive Model (which is also called Spatial Lag Model) setting it is assumed that the values of the dependent variable y in spatial unit j depend on the values of y in neighbouring spatial units; in this way SAR model captures “spatial spill-overs”. If coefficient $\rho = 0$, there is no spatial dependence, which means that the dependent variable y does not depend on the values of y in neighbouring spatial units.

The Spatial Error Model has the form:

$$y_{it} = \beta X_{it} + \alpha_t + v_{it}$$

where v_{it}:

$$v_{it} = \lambda * W * v_{it} + u_{it}$$

where λ is the spatial error coefficient, and all other notations are as before. It can be argued that SEM is the spatial analogous of the temporal correlation process. If there is no spatial correlation between the error terms, then the coefficient λ equals zero.

The SAR and SEM models in a panel data context can be estimated in fixed and random effects specifications (Lee and Yu 2012). LeSage and Pace (2009) have argued that the answer to the question 'which of these models is the "correct" one' is dictated by the specific empirical context.

In the estimation of spatial regression, one crucial factor is the selection of the "proper" spatial weights. Here the spatial weight matrix was calculated with the use of "3-nearest neighbours" method[1]. The reason for this is that Greece has a significant number of (real) islands which should be integrated into the spatial regression analysis; Ertur and Le Gallo (2003), who have argued that spatial weight matrices based on the *k*-nearest method, are preferable to the simple contiguity matrices for a number of reasons, such as in the aforementioned case of islands (that is to avoid rows and columns in the W matrix with only zeros). The use of *k*-nearest method also ensures that the number of neighbours is 'fixed' and thus avoids potential methodological problems (for a more extensive analysis, see for instance, Lopez-Bazo *et al.* 1999 or Ertur and Le Gallo 2003).

5. EMPIRICAL RESULTS

Table 2, with the variables' correlations matrix, shows that all pairwise correlations are relatively low. Table 3 presents some descriptive statistics.

Table 2. Correlation Matrix 2005-2011

	GDPpc	Urbanization	Agriculture	Secondary Sector	Tourism	Income
GDPpc	1.000					
Urbanization	**0.376** *0.000*	1.000				
Agriculture	**-0.531** *0.000*	**-0.317** *0.000*	1.000			
Secondary Sector	**0.349** *0.000*	-0.110 *0.038*	-0.028 *0.600*	1.000		
Tourism	**0.378** *0.000*	**0.423** *0.000*	**-0.382** *0.000*	-0.246 *0.000*	1.000	
Income	**0.466** *0.000*	**0.405** *0.000*	**-0.513** *0.000*	-0.010 *0.846*	0.247 *0.000*	1.000

The regression results are presented in Tables 4 to 5; all these tables show firstly three columns regarding the estimates for all regions (prefectures, i.e. NUTS III units), one column with results for PATHE prefectures, one column for Non-PATHE prefectures, one column for northern Greece prefectures, and one column for southern Greece. PATHE is the acronym for the main highway of Greece, linking the port (and city) of Patras in south-western Greece, with the northern borders of Greece, via the metropolitan area of Athens and Thessaloniki. The rational for the breakdown of the dataset in northern and southern Greece is to investigate the idea that the two main parts of the country have experienced different paths of development and different patterns of crisis. The

[1] It has to be noted that the use of other spatial weights schemes, such as the minimum threshold distance gave, more or less, similar results.

rationale behind the breakdown of the dataset to PATHE prefectures and Non-PATHE prefectures is to explore the idea that PATHE prefectures comprise the "growth" axis of the country (in the Greek bibliography these prefectures are called the "S of growth" as their spatial shape resembles the letter "S"; see Petrakos and Psycharis 2014 for this point).

Table 3. Descriptive statistics

Variable	Obs	Mean	Std. Dev.	Min	Max
Period 2005-2008					
GDPpc	204	15883.620	4140.581	9469.697	29423.530
Urbanization	204	78.289	146.939	10.700	1070.600
Agriculture	204	7.983	4.521	0.371	22.154
Secondary Sector	204	22.628	11.706	8.432	64.720
Tourism	204	1196595.000	2184492.000	22685.000	13000000.000
Income	204	6217.930	1026.732	3899.787	10597.550
Period 2009-2011					
GDPpc	153	15952.890	4002.575	9281.812	28054.610
Urbanization	153	79.210	150.168	10.600	1080.400
Agriculture	153	6.883	3.775	0.363	18.923
Secondary Sector	153	18.980	11.968	5.396	62.687
Tourism	153	1331180.000	2430922.000	22237.000	15300000.000
Income	153	7622.028	1135.681	5221.048	13510.600

Table 5 of the regression results replicates the first Table by using the same spatial breakdowns; however, the former Table refers to the pre-crisis period 2005-2008, and the latter, to the crisis period, 2009-2011. As growth trends show, the crisis in Greece was evident in 2009.

A first, general, conclusion which can be drawn from these tables is that results are "stable" across specifications, and spatial and temporal breakdowns. Moreover, the statistics for spatial regression (spatial rho and lambda) are positive and statistically significant, showing positive spatial autocorrelation.

Analysis regarding comparative assessment of regional development for the pre-crisis and crisis periods for Greece has yielded some interesting results.

The first important finding is that agglomeration economies, proxied by population density (*Urbanisation*), have always been a statistically significant determinant in explaining regional development in the country. However, while urbanization is positively related with the high rates of economic development, it turns to be a negative and statistically significant determinant for the level of economic development during economic decline. These results indicate that the most urbanized areas are the ones that are more vulnerable to economic crisis. However, these areas had been the ones that have benefited most during the upturn of the economic activity. Secondly, it seems that the same observation applies to the level of economic prosperity of the regions, which is proxied by the declared incomes of households (*Income*). Results show disproportionally higher gains for more prosperous regions during development and disproportionally higher losses during recession. This also applies to PATHE/NON-PATHE regions as well as SOUTH REGIONS of the country.

Table 4. Results, Time Period: 2005-2008 (Before the crisis)

Dependent variable: gdp/capita							
	ALL REGIONS			PATHE	NON-PATHE	NORTH GREECE	SOUTH GREECE
	FE	SAR FE	SEM FE	FE			
Variables							
Urbanization	111.3***	121.1***	121.9***	60.42***	155.9***	120.4***	107.5***
	(20.42)	*(16.79)*	*(15.80)*	*(18.61)*	*(23.85)*	*(22.03)*	*(25.14)*
Agriculture	172.4***	171.6***	179.7***	266.3***	168.4***	137.9**	179.8***
	(27.70)	*(20.93)*	*(20.54)*	*(46.84)*	*(32.59)*	*(55.05)*	*(30.48)*
Secondary Sector	187.9***	191.2***	200.9***	307.3***	166.2***	175.3***	181.6***
	(23.80)	*(15.28)*	*(14.90)*	*(45.36)*	*(26.53)*	*(42.96)*	*(29.98)*
Tourism	-0.0000578	-0.000306**	-0.0000808	0.000453**	-0.0000659	-0.000511***	0.000109
	(0.000162)	*(0.000140)*	*(0.000140)*	*(0.000176)*	*(0.000189)*	*(0.000156)*	*(0.000182)*
Income	2.145***	1.799***	2.089***	2.342***	2.157***	2.265***	2.085***
	(0.108)	*(0.0918)*	*(0.0874)*	*(0.166)*	*(0.126)*	*(0.161)*	*(0.132)*
Constant	-11728.6***			-19690.8***	-10372.6***	-12378.6***	-11072.9***
	(1758.4)			*(2432.2)*	*(1708.4)*	*(1999.3)*	*(2324.2)*
Spatial							
rho		0.0918***					
		(0.0153)					
lambda			0.188***				
			(0.0229)				
Variance							
sigma2_e		105132.8***	93697.8***				
		(10418.5)	*(9413.3)*				
adj. R^2	0.885	0.252	0.185	0.923	0.874	0.901	0.876
N	204	204	204	48	156	64	140

Standard errors in parentheses. * $p < 0.10$, ** $p < 0.05$, *** $p < 0.01$.

Thirdly, manufacturing (*Secondary Sector*) has always been a statistically significant driver of development during periods of growth and has shown significant resistance to crisis during recession. However, manufacturing areas proved to be more resilient to crisis. Contrary to that, the NON-PATHE and Southern agricultural areas (*Agriculture*) which had benefited from an upward turn in economic activity have turned to be more vulnerable to economic crisis while the PATHE and Northern regions are more resilient.

Tourism (*Tourism*) is positive for the level of economic development and in times of crisis generates benefits to the neighboring regions (second and third column). However, this result doesn't apply to NON-PATHE and Southern regions of the country.

Table 5. Results, Time Period: 2009-2011 (During the crisis)

Dependent variable: gdp/capita							
	ALL REGIONS			PATHE	NON-PATHE	NORTH GREECE	SOUTH GREECE
	FE	SAR FE	SEM FE	FE			
Variables							
Urbanization	-517.0***	-391.9***	-442.3***	-617.1***	-648.9**	-584.4***	-486.8***
	(115.9)	*(102.2)*	*(107.0)*	*(167.5)*	*(248.9)*	*(115.7)*	*(122.9)*
Agriculture	-194.9	-184.6**	-214.2**	192.2**	-496.1***	64.50	-432.6***
	(133.3)	*(81.23)*	*(88.98)*	*(85.64)*	*(152.1)*	*(60.23)*	*(146.8)*
Secondary Sector	186.1***	153.2***	127.8***	190.2***	156.2***	172.6***	188.6***
	(36.51)	*(25.28)*	*(27.70)*	*(39.14)*	*(44.82)*	*(25.16)*	*(50.61)*
Tourism	- 0.000543***	0.000654***	0.000623**	-0.00375	-0.000497***	0.00251*	-0.000571***
	(0.000133)	*(0.000237)*	*(0.000294)*	*(0.00297)*	*(0.000166)*	*(0.00127)*	*(0.000166)*
Income	-0.863***	-0.414***	-0.267**	-1.706***	-0.785**	-1.317***	-0.784**
	(0.318)	*(0.105)*	*(0.114)*	*(0.404)*	*(0.321)*	*(0.170)*	*(0.344)*
Constant	62014.2***			134183.6***	55855.6***	55540.5***	65124.9***
	(9844.8)			*(31383.3)*	*(13535.0)*	*(7943.7)*	*(11475.0)*
Spatial							
rho		0.176***					
		(0.0214)					
lambda			0.230***				
			(0.0230)				
Variance							
sigma2_e		158965.7***	184207.9***				
		(18312.1)	*(21666.8)*				
adj. R^2	0.648	0.248	0.150	0.851	0.614	0.744	0.625
N	153	153	153	36	117	48	105

Standard errors in parentheses. $* \; p < 0.10$, $** \; p < 0.05$, $*** \; p < 0.01$.

6. CONCLUSIONS AND POLICY IMPLICATIONS

The Great Recession that started in 2008 has offered new insights into the complexity of economic development and has brought up new ways of thinking and interpreting economic activity and its connection to the economy of the regions. The ways in which gains from growth and loses from recession are channeled to different regions of the country is a complex result of interrelations and connections between regional economies, the national economy and the international economy.

Analysis showed that crisis has impacted on different geographical levels. Firstly, crisis re-shapes the development map at the European level. Greece is seen to be diverging from the European average. Secondly, crisis has impacted on the level of economic inter-regional development and inequalities within country. Regional inequalities, weighted by population, have been increased. Finally, the intensity and duration of the crisis has impacted on the intra-regional development and spatial inequalities within regions and cities. The high dispersion of unemployment generates social polarization and segregation across the country and within cities.

The results highlight the importance of well targeted interventions such as with public investment in order to make regions more resilience to crisis (OECD 2011b; OECD 2011c). The very inegalitarian spread of crisis impact questions horizontal policy measures and call for a more counter-cyclical and carefully targeted fiscal policy.

Geography proves to be a significant determinant for the gains from development and the losses from recession. The most urbanized and high income regions either on PATHE/NON-PATHE or North-South are more favorable in times of development and more vulnerable in times of economic crisis. Furthermore, the agricultural NON-PATHE regions are more vulnerable to crisis impacts as well as the southern areas of the country. Finally, NON-PATHE and SOUTHERN regions based on tourism are more vulnerable to crisis than PATHE and NORTHERN regions. If this holds true, it poses certain questions for the "right" mix of regional policy.

Another interesting empirical finding is that there are some significant differences between the determinants of regional development in the pre-crisis and during-the-crisis period; for example, the role of the agriculture sector and the level of economic prosperity of the regions. That implies that not only are specific regional policies needed for economic recovery, but that these policies should be closely monitored and adjusted during the different phases of the economic (business) cycle.

Policy interventions are important for regions as well as cities and large agglomerations. Nevertheless, we need to delve deeper and look into social groups and sectors of economic activity that are more vulnerable to crisis and therefore require interventions for social protection and economic development. As a result, policy-targeted interventions to ameliorate crisis impact and to find ways out of it have to be framed very carefully, and need to cover the functioning of economic policy at European, national and local levels.

REFERENCES

Aalbers M. (2009, "Geographies of financial crisis", *Area,* 41: 34-42.

Arellano M. (1993), "On the testing of correlated effects with panel data", *Journal of Econometrics*, 59(1-2): 87-97.

Bachtler J.F. and Davies S.S. (2009), "The geography of the crisis in Western Europe: national and regional impacts and policy responses", in: *Financial Crisis in Central and Eastern Europe – from Similarity to Diversity*, Scholar, Warsaw.

Bakas D and Papapetrou E. (2012), "Unemployment in Greece: evidence from Greek regions", Bank of Greece Working Paper, 146. Available at: http://www.bankofgreece.gr/BogEkdoseis/Paper2012146.pdf.

Baltagi B. (2008), *Econometric analysis of panel data*, Chichester: Wiley.

Berry B. (1988), "Migration Reversals in Perspective: The Long-Wave Evidence", *International Regional Science Review*, 11(3): 245-251.

Bristow G. and Healy A. (2014), "Regional Resilience: An Agency Perspective", *Regional Studies*, 48(5): 923-935.

Borts G.H. (1961), "Regional Cycles of Manycacturing Employment in the United States 1914-53", Occasional Paper No. 75, National Bureau of Economic Research.

Caraveli H. and Tsionas E. (2012), 'Economic Restructuring, Crises and the Regions: The Political Economy of Regional Inequalities in Greece", GreeSe Paper No. 61, *Hellenic Observatory Papers on Greece and Southeast Europe*.

De Groot S.P.T., Mohlmann J.L., Garretsen J.H. and De Groot H.L.F. (2011), "The crisis sensitivity of European countries and regions: stylized facts and spatial heterogeneity", *Cambridge Journal of Regions, Economy and Society,* 4: 437-456.

Ertur C. and Le Gallo J. (2003), "An exploratory spatial data analysis of European regional disparities, 1980-1995", in: Fingleton B. (ed), *European Regional Growth*, Berlin: Springer-Verlag,.

Fingleton B., Garretsen H. and Martin R. (2012), "Recessionary shocks and regional employment: evidence on the resilience of U.K. regions", *Journal of Regional Science,* 52(1): 109-133.

Foster K. A. (2012), "In search of regional resilience", in: Pindus N., Weir M., Wial H. and Wolman H. (eds), *Building regional resilience: Urban and regional policy and its effects*, Washington D.C.: Brookings Institution Press, 24-59.

Greene W.H. (2011), *Econometric Analysis*, Essex: Pearson.

Holly S., Pesaran Hashem M. and Yamagata T. (2010), "Spatial and Temporal Diffusion of House Prices in the UK", *Journal of Urban Economics*, 69(1): 2-23.

Krugman P. (1991), "Increasing Returns and Economic Geography", *Journal of Political Economy*, 99:183-199.

Lee L.F. and Yu J. (2012), "Spatial panels: Random components versus fixed effects", *International Economic Review*, 53: 1369-1421.

LeSage J.P.and Pace R.K. (2009), *Introduction to Spatial Econometrics*, Taylor and Francis, Broken Sound Parkway NW.

Lopez-Bazo E., Vaya E., Mora A. and Surinach J. (1999), "Regional economic dynamic and convergence in the European union", *Annals of Regional Science* 33: 343-370.

Marshall J.N., Pike A., Pollard J.S., Tomaney J., Dawley S. and Gray J. (2012), "Placing the run on northern rock", *Journal of Economic Geography,* 12(1): 157-181.

Martin R. (2011), "The local geographies of the financial crisis: from the housing bubble to economic recession and beyond", *Journal of Economic Geography*, 11(4): 587-618.

Martin R., 2012, "Regional economic resilience, hysteresis and recessionary shocks", *Journal of Economic Geography*, 12(1): 1-32

Monastiriotis V. (2011), "Making geographical sense of the Greek austerity measures: compositional effects and long-run implications", *Cambridge Journal of Regions, Economy and Society,* 4(3): 323-337.

Mussida Ch. and Pastore F. (2012), "Is There a Southern-Sclerosis? Worker Reallocation and Regional Unemployment in Italy", IZA Discussion Papers 6954, Institute for the Study of Labor.

Myrdal G. (1957), *Economic Theory and Underdeveloped Regions*, London: University Paperbacks, Methuen.

OECD [Organization for Economic Cooperation and Development] (2009a), What regional-level action are you taking in response to the economic crisis?, Meeting of the Territorial Development Policy Committee at Ministerial Level

OECD [Organization for Economic Cooperation and Development] (2009b), How regions grow: trends and analysis, OECD Publishing.

OECD [Organization for Economic Cooperation and Development] (2011a), "Impact of the crisis on jobs in regions", in: *OECD Regions at a Glance 2011*, OECD Publishing.

OECD [Organization for Economic Cooperation and Development] (2011b), Public investment in regions, in: OECD *Regions at a Glance 2011*, OECD Publishing.

OECD [Organization for Economic Cooperation and Development] (2011c), Making the most of public investment in a tight fiscal environment: Multi-level governance Lessons from the Crisis, OECD Publishing.

Petrakos G. and Psycharis Y. (2014), *Regional Development in Greece*, second edition (in Greek) forthcoming.

Patuelli R., Schanne N., Griffith, D.A. and Nijkamp P. (2012), "Persistence of regional unemployment: application of a spatial filtering approach to local labor markets in Germany", *Journal of Regional Science,* 52(2): 300-323.

Richardson H.W. (1973), *Regional Growth Theory*, New York – Toronto: John Wiley and sons.

Stilwell J. (1980), *Economic Crisis, Cities and Regions*, Pergamon Press

Wooldridge, J.M. (2002), *Econometric Analysis of Cross Section and Panel Data*, Cambridge, MA:MIT Press.

CRISE ÉCONOMIQUE ET DÉVELOPPEMENT RÉGIONAL EN GRÈCE

Résumé - *Cet article propose d'examiner les déterminants du développement régional en Grèce avant et pendant la crise économique. En proposant un modèle économétrique avec effets spatiaux pour les années 2005-2008 et 2009-2011, qui représentent respectivement les périodes de croissance et de dépression de l'économie grecque, nous cherchons à saisir les différents facteurs qui influent sur le développement économique régional des régions de niveau NUTS III. Les résultats montrent que les régions à niveau de revenu élevé et les plus urbanisées sont les plus affectées par la crise économique. La spécialisation dans les activités industrielles est un déterminant important du développement régional quelle que soit la conjoncture.*

Mots-clés - CRISE ÉCONOMIQUE, RÉSILIENCE, DÉVELOPPEMENT RÉGIONAL, GRÈCE

THE EVOLUTION OF THE GREEK URBAN CENTERS: 1951-2011

Alexandra SCHAFFAR*, Sotiris PAVLEAS**

Abstract - *The aim of this paper is to study the evolution of urban hierarchies and the nature of urban growth processes in Greece from 1951 to 2011 using data provided by the Greek Statistical Authority. The paper delivers three series of results: firstly, when using an administrative definition of the city, the Greek cities converge towards a middle city-size population; secondly, when taking into account spatial dependence, the sizes of Greek cities still converge but this movement starts in the middle of the period, after 1981. In both cases, the preeminence of the Athens agglomeration slowly decreases; finally, the paper delivers evidence concerning the changes that affect urban demographical trends in Greece over the last decade. These changes can be related to the economic crisis and the profound socioeconomic upheaval that Greece has undergone since the beginning of the 21st century.*

Key words - URBAN GROWTH, URBAN HIERARCHIES, ECONOMIC CRISIS, GREECE

JEL Classification - J11, R10, R12, R23

* LEAD, University of Toulon. schaffar@univ-tln.fr
** Department of Planning and Regional Development, University of Thessaly. pavleas@mie.uth.gr

1. INTRODUCTION

Greece is among the countries that experienced limited and late industrialization (Petrakos and Economou, 2004). The growth rate and the socioeconomic evolution of its cities was associated less to the development of industry and more to historical circumstances, such as the massive arrival of refugees from Asia Minor in 1922 and the population displacements due to the Civil War (1946-1949). These events contributed drastically to the formation of the most dominant current economic and social structures in the country.

Over the past decades (Maloutas, 2000; Pavleas, 2014), the urbanization process developed rapidly in Greece, mainly because of the rural economy decline and the consequent transfers of rural population to urban areas to seek better living standards. The limited labor market of the smaller cities was becoming less attractive to the inhabitants of rural areas, compared to that of larger cities. The capital city of Athens, in particular, received the majority of the migration flows, due to the concentration of government agencies and the relatively higher share of employment opportunities. As a result, the already existing structure of the 'primate city' in the Greek urban system was enhanced, pooling in Athens the most dynamic part of human force and the largest share of the production activity in the country.

The post 2nd World War period included determining tendencies, such as a general upgrade of educational level, a reduction in manual occupations and a rise in tertiary sector's activities and high-skilled employment (Maloutas, 2000). The Greek urban system developed clear hierarchical patterns, which arise by the changes in labor market's structure, real estate and housing conditions. However, the growth of Greek cities took place without central State planning, relying basically on market forces and individual strategies. The Greek State influenced urban development through insufficient planning legislative framework and corruption phenomena, rather than applying integrated urban strategies (Giannakourou, 1999). In general, the urban areas lack of technical, environmental and social infrastructure. There are important omissions of open and green areas in the urban fringe, while uncontrolled and unauthorized residential expansion prevails. It has to be noted that urban space is mostly private, causing complex and costly obstacles to cities' administration, when policy intervention is aimed. In addition, high building and population densities are more than evident; the building stock is of low level of aesthetics, and in many cases, poor supervision of cultural and architectural heritage has degraded cities' historic centers. Finally, traffic congestion and the associated noise remain an important problem in Greek cities. (Pavleas, 2014)

Currently, the Greek urban system is affected by the adverse socioeconomic conditions, which emanate from the economic crisis, reflecting on the composition and level of employment, business initiatives and the quality of life. In spite of the fact that the crisis is an ongoing phenomenon and any attempt to estimate at this stage the urban socioeconomic footprint, gives an instantaneous picture and not conclusive medium or long-term aspects, it is quite safe to argue that the crisis and the subsequent fiscal squeeze accelerate changes in the structure of urban economy, multiplying threats and intensifying existing problems in cities.

The aim of this paper is to study the evolution of urban hierarchies and the nature of urban growth processes in Greece from 1951 to 2011 using data provided by the Greek Statistical Authority. The paper delivers three series of results: firstly, when using an administrative definition of the city, the Greek cities converge towards a middle city-size population; secondly, when taking into account spatial dependence, the sizes of Greek cities still converge but this movement starts in the middle of the period, after 1981. In both cases, the preeminence of the Athens agglomeration slowly decreases; finally, the paper delivers evidence concerning the changes that affect urban demographical trends in Greece over the last decade. These changes can be related to the economic crisis and the profound socioeconomic upheaval that Greece has undergone since the beginning of the 21st century.

The paper is built as follows: the second section of this paper deals with theoretical issues. The third section provides a descriptive analysis of the population dynamics in the Greek urban system. The fourth section delivers results on the evolution of urban hierarchies and urban growth in Greece. The fifth and concluding section discusses the findings of the previous section and focuses on the specific urban demographical trends over the last decade.

2. THEORETICAL ISSUES

An important amount of modern economic literature deals with urban hierarchies. Following Zipf's early work, several papers have studied the changes in a country's system of cities by using different specifications of a rank-size model (Rosen and Resnick, 1980; Parr, 1985; Soo, 2005). These studies deliver evidence that a lower-bound truncated city-size distribution is Pareto (Krugman's 1996, "urban mystery"). In this case the Pareto exponent is a very simple and elegant indicator of the urban concentration degree within a system of cities. Parr (1985) assumes that in many industrialized countries, the Pareto exponent follows an inverse-U curve: the exponent is high (low urban concentration) in the beginning of the industrialization process, then decreases with GDP/capita increase, because firms and industries tend to move to the largest urban areas in order to benefit from agglomeration economies. According to Parr, the inflexion point appears when economic growth diffuses and when the advantages of agglomeration decline because of growing congestion and higher real-estate prices. Firms and workers relocate to smaller cities which leads in demographical adjustment in urban areas (and the increase of the Pareto exponent).

Empirical studies have tested Parr's hypothesis (Eaton and Eckstein, 1997; Dobkins and Ioannides, 2001; Catin and Van Huffel, 2004; Duranton, 2006) with mitigated results. Although rank-size models remain the best option to study the evolution of urban hierarchies within a country, they only deliver a descriptive analysis that needs to be completed in order to understand the engine and the nature of urban growth.

Urban growth processes have been studied within two major analytical frameworks (Duranton, 2012; Dimou and Schaffar, 2011): the random growth and the endogenous growth theories. The first ones (Gabaix, 1999, Gabaix and Ioannides, 2004, Cordoba, 2008) admit that city-growth is a stochastic process depending upon randomly distributed exogenous shocks. In the stationary state, the urban growth processes lead to a city-size distribution that follows the Zipf law. The second ones (Eaton et Eckstein, 1997, Black et Henderson, 1999) consider that urban growth processes depend upon each city's characteristics and industrial specialization. City-growth is determined by city-size and the Zipf's law doesn't necessarily hold.

Random growth theories drive back to Simon's (1955) probabilistic model where city-growth appears as an additive process that confirms Gibrat's law. This means that the urban growth rate is independent from city-size. In the stationary state, the demographic growth of cities tend to the null and, when considering a truncated city-size distribution with a lower bound, the Pareto exponent is 1, which confirms the Zipf law for cities. Recent urban growth theories have been developed following Gabaix's (1999) original work, according to whom, under a series of restrictive hypotheses (no demographical change, constant return to scales and limited households' mobility – only for young workers), city-growth follows a random process. City-growth depends only upon exogenous shocks randomly distributed such as historical accidents, natural disasters and, more commonly, local policies improving a city's amenities or changing the local taxing system.

On the opposite, endogenous growth theories assume that a city's size depends upon the firms' localization choices. The firms compare each city's advantages (scale externalities) and disadvantages (congestion, real-estate market failures) in order to decide where to locate. These theories drive back to Lucas endogenous growth model and to Henderson's (1974, 1988) theoretical framework. Eaton and Eckstein (1997) and Black and Henderson (1999) have calibrated urban growth models where the demographical change of cities depends upon their stock of external economies and human capital spillovers. Urban growth is a determinist and smooth process (Duranton, 2012); the heterogeneity of cities is due to the differentiation of their human capital stock. Under some specific assumptions, urban growth may lead to conditional convergence in city size (Black and Henderson, 2003).

More recently, a series of papers have tried to combine the two theoretical backgrounds within some hybrid urban growth models that take into account both agglomeration economies and random shocks (Rossi-Hansberg and Wright, 2007; Duranton, 2007; Schaffar and Dimou, 2012). Urban growth studies aim to determine whether there is an optimal city-size or not and, if this is the case, under which conditions it occurs. Random growth models don't validate the optimal city-size hypothesis which implies that agglomeration economies are not an explanative factor for city growth. On the opposite, determinist growth theories produce city-size convergence which doesn't seem to correspond to empirical findings. By loosening some assumptions, hybrid growth theories deliver models that fit much better to empirical observation.

In this paper we study the evolution of urban hierarchies in Greece and we test the nature of the Greek cities' growth processes. We show that the Greek cities converge to a medium city-size while urban concentration decreases. This means that the Athens agglomeration importance declines, especially during the last thirty years. However, the recent economic crisis leads in reconsidering these long-time trends.

3. URBAN DEMOGRAPHICS IN GREECE

The density and the distribution of population is associated with the process of demographic urbanization (population masses shift from rural to urban areas), which is closely connected with the economic urbanization (shift of labor from primary to secondary and tertiary production sector) and the social urbanization (dissemination and copying of behavioral and consumption patterns). (Maloutas, 2004).

Table 1: Evolution of urban population in Greece, 1951-2011

Years	Total population	Urban Population	Share of urban population (%)
1951	7,632,801	2,948,903	38.6
1961	8,388,553	3,661,456	43.6
1971	8,768,372	4,680,770	53.4
1981	9,738,243	5,680,396	58.3
1991	10,258,364	6,057,823	59.1
2001	10,964,020	6,650,284	60.7
2011	10,815,197	6,931,633	64.1

Source: Hellenic Statistical Agency - Own elaboration.

The share of urban population in Greece showed a constant upward trend over time (Table 1), accompanied with a rather strongly uneven distribution. To be more specific, urban population added up to 38.6 % of the total population of the country in 1951 and it increased up to the level of 58.3% in 1981, while in 2011 it reached a peak of 64.1%. The geographical distribution of the urban population, at the beginning of the post 2nd World War period, showed a significant concentration in areas near the main highway axis of the country (Patra-Athens-Thessaloniki) and in several islands. Since the 1980s and mainly the 1990s, urban concentration diffused to other areas of the country, creating a second minor axis in western Greece (Patra - Ioannina), an area now crossed by the Ionian highway, which is under construction. Urban population growth showed, in the last three decades, a general trend of establishing in urban areas of local, regional or national importance. The dominant trend however regards the disproportionate growth of the two largest urban centers, Thessaloniki and especially Athens, compared with the rest of the urban areas (Map 1). At the same time, smaller urban centers (such as Patra, Larissa, Volos, Heraklio, Ioannina and Kavala) grew considerably gaining significant role at regional scale.

An analysis of the population census data for the period of 1951 to 2011 shows that the number of urban centers increased significantly over time. In 1951 the relative number was 55, in 1991 the number increased up to 71, while in 2001 and 2011, the number of urban centers seems to have relatively stabilized at 83 and 84 respectively (Table 1). It should be clarified that 'urban centers' are considered the settlements with a population over 10,000 inhabitants, according to the definition of the Hellenic Statistical Agency.

Map 1: Greek urban centres over 10.000 residents, 2011

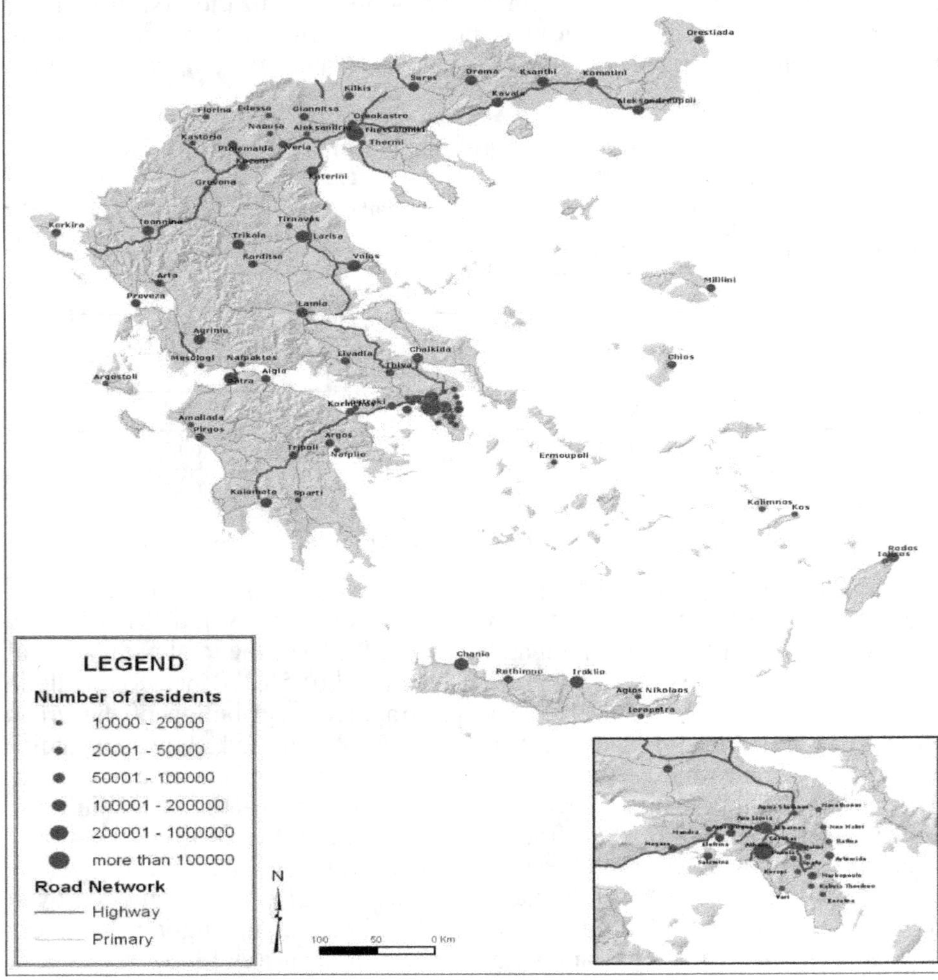

The growth of Greek cities has been quite diverse, since they grew at different rates. Map 2 verifies this argument and depicts population change for the cities, which are over 10.000 residents in 2011 and for the period 1951-2011. The range of changes begins from the minimum value of -53.9% (for the city of

Ermoupoli) to the maximum value of 2624.7% for the city of Oreokastro. It seems that the only two cases with negative change refer to the island cities of Ermoupoli and Chios, while, in general, the relatively smaller changes attribute to agglomerations in islands and to smaller cities of mainland. Moreover, Map 2 shows that there is a considerable number of cities that magnified over 5 and 10 times their size during this period and they are located dominantly in the area of Athens' metropolitan functional influence.

Map 2: Population change of Greek urban centres, 1951-2011

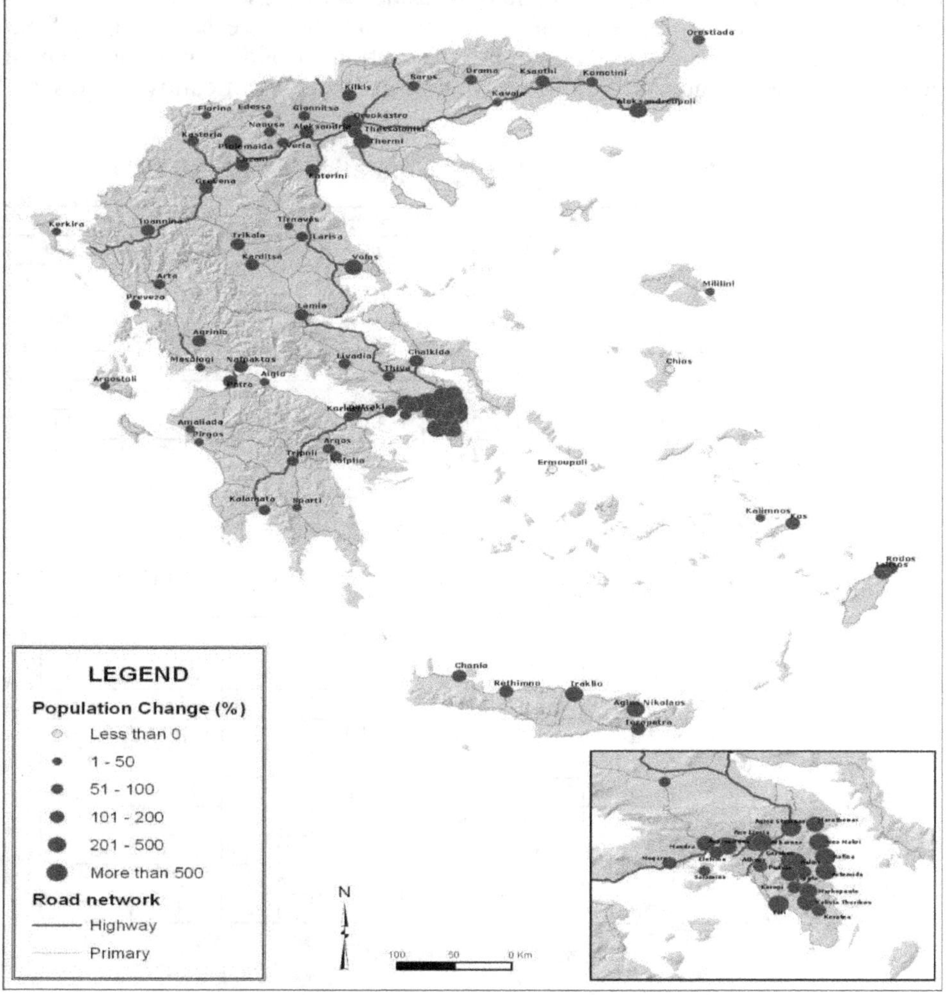

Table 2 shows the number of urban centers by population category, from 1951 to 2011. From a general point of view, the intense asymmetries of Greek urban space are corroborated. The urban complex of Athens is the only case, which exceeds 1,000,000 inhabitants, accounting for 46.75% (in 1951) and 44.57% (in 2011) of the total urban population (Table 3).

Likewise, the urban complex of Thessaloniki is the only settlement in the category of 500,000 to 1,000,000 inhabitants, participating in urban population with 11.90% (in 1971) and 11.38 % (in 2011). During the last decade, the population of the two largest urban centers showed for the first time signs of decline. It should be emphasized that the Greek urban system lacks urban agglomerations of size between 200,000 and 500,000 residents, which is the relative determinant framework for medium-sized cities in the European urban context (Pavleas and al, 2005). Interestingly, in the last thirty years (1981-2011) the number of cities from 100,000 to 200,000 residents increased from 4 in 1981 to 6 in 2011, while the cities between 50,000 and 100,000 increased abruptly from 2 to 14. The last trend was due to the penetration of additional cities, which belonged to the category of 20,000 to 50,000 and grew significantly at the same period.

Table 2: Number of cities by population size, 1951-2011

	Number of urban centers						
Population	1951	1961	1971	1981	1991	2001	2011
Over 1.000.000	1	1	1	1	1	1	1
500.000-1.000.000	0	0	1	1	1	1	1
200.000-500.000	1	1	0	0	0	0	0
100.000-200.000	0	1	1	4	4	4	6
50.000-100.000	3	3	4	2	7	5	14
20.000-50.000	22	25	27	32	29	35	30
10.000-20.000	28	25	23	23	29	37	32
Total	55	56	57	63	71	83	84

Source: Hellenic Statistical Agency – Own elaboration.

Table 3: Distribution of urban population by city-size, 1951-2011

Population	Share (%) of urban population						
	1951	1961	1971	1981	1991	2001	2011
1.000.000 <	46.75	50.6	54.7	53.29	50.73	47.66	44.57
500.000-1.000.000	0	0	11.9	12.43	12.37	11.93	11.38
200.000-500.000	10.25	10.4	0	0	0	0	0
100.000-200.000	0	2.84	2.58	8.37	8.69	8.82	12.19
50.000-100.000	7.28	5.65	6.39	2.09	6.56	10.24	12.53
20.000-50.000	22.47	20.5	17.59	18.09	15.03	13.56	12.43
10.000-20.000	13.25	10	7.27	5.73	6.62	7.79	6.90
Total	100	100	100	100	100	100	100

Source: Hellenic Statistical Agency - Own elaboration.

The tendencies presented above are also reflected in Table 3 and Graph 1, which show the evolution of urban population's distribution by population category for the same time period. The sum of shares of Athens and Thessaloniki in urban population reaches 63% in 1991, 59.59% in 2001 and 56 % in 2011, which may indicates that the relative importance of the two largest urban centers decreases in recent decades. At the same time, the participation of the cities from 50,000 to 200,000 residents seems to have been enhanced. Moreover, the share of smaller urban centers (20,000 to 50,000) presents diminishing trends in the last 30 years, while cities from 10,000 to 20,000 inhabitants show mixed trends over time, remaining however at relatively low levels of 6% to10%.

In total, the urbanization process in Greece, during the period 1951-2011, seems to have set off from a spatially polarized urban pattern (Athens - Thessaloniki), continued with growth of the relatively smaller urban centers, and resulted in a stabilization of a concentrated urban status, due to reduced demographic growth and migratory movements. In the last decades, the importance of cities from 50,000 to 200,000 has been enhanced, while the urban share of Athens and Thessaloniki seems to have tapered. The question (Pavleas and al, 2005) whether the trends analyzed above, can be really interpreted as evidence of deconcentration in the Greek urban system remains a crucial topic and only merely investigated in Greek literature.

Graph 1: Evolution of urban population's distribution, 1951-2011

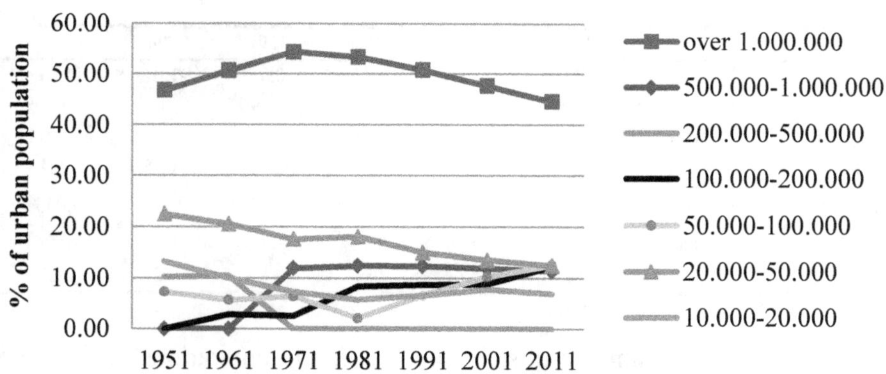

Source: Hellenic Statistical Agency - Own elaboration.

4. URBAN HIERARCHIES AND CITY-GROWTH

In order to study the evolution of urban hierarchies and the nature of urban growth in Greece between 1951 and 2011, we use two different samples: an administrative definition of the cities' sample and a geographical and economic definition of the cities' sample which takes into account agglomeration effects and spatial dependence, especially for the two major cities, Athens and Thessaloniki. Data is provided by the Hellenic Statistical Agency.

We use the Gabaix and Ibragimov (2011) correction for the rank size model (Schaffar, 2009:2).

$$\ln\left(R - \frac{1}{2}\right) = a + \beta \ln(S)$$

Then we study the convexity of the distribution, by using the Rosen and Resnick (1980) quadratic model.

$$\ln(R) = a + \beta \ln(S) + \theta \ln(S)^2$$

with R the rank of a city and S its demographical size. Table 4 delivers both the results for the rank-size model and the quadratic model, when we use the administrative cities sample.

The evolution of the Pareto exponent clearly shows that urban concentration decreases and that the medium-size cities become more important within the Greek urban landscape. After 2001, the Pareto exponent is stable and almost equal to 1. This means that when defined by an administrative point of view, medium-size Greek cities tend to grow and the distribution of urban population becomes less hierarchical over time. The quadratic model confirms that the number of medium size cities become more important within the distribution since the δ systematically increases during the whole period.

Table 4: Pareto exponent and quadratic model parameters for the Greek cities-size distribution (administrative definition)

Rank-size	*1951*	*1961*	*1971*	*1981*	*1991*	*2001*	*2011*
ln(Pop)	-0.72***	-0.79***	-0.83***	-0.87***	-0.95***	-1.01***	-1.01***
R^2 adjusted	0.81	0.86	0.89	0.92	0.96	0.97	0.96
Quadratic	1951	1961	1971	1981	1991	2001	2011
ln(Pop)	-0.26***	-0.22***	-0.29***	-0.76***	-0.93***	-1.15***	-1.18***
$\ln(Pop)^2$	-0.07***	-0.048***	-0.023**	-0.002	0.038***	0.059***	0.043***
R^2 adjusted	0.872	0.880	0.890	0.917	0.954	0.968	0.961
Number of obs.	87	87	87	87	87	87	87

*** *sig at 1%* ** *sig at 5%* * *sig at 10%.*

Table 5 gives the same results for the Greek agglomerations. This sample only contains 67 cities, since 20 cities from the previous sample belong to the Athens or to the Thessaloniki agglomerations.

Table 5: Pareto exponent and quadratic model parameters for the Greek cities-size distribution (agglomerations)

Rank-size	*1951*	*1961*	*1971*	*1981*	*1991*	*2001*	*2011*
ln(Pop)	-1.00***	-0.81***	-0.83***	-0.87***	-0.96***	-1.01***	-1.01***
R^2 adjusted	0.91	0.85	0.87	0.91	0.94	0.95	0.94
Quadratic	1951	1961	1971	1981	1991	2001	2011
n(Pop)	-1.26***	-0.26	-0.68**	-1.12***	-2.13***	-2.55***	-2.17***
$\ln(Pop)^2$	0.016**	-0.024**	-0.004	0.015**	0.057***	0.073**	0.056**
R^2 adjusted	0.893	0.856	0.867	0.896	0.945	0.958	0.896
Number of obs.	67	67	67	67	67	67	67

*** *sig at 1%* ** *sig at 5%* * *sig at 10%.*

Compared to the previous results, Table 5 shows a U curve trend for the Pareto exponent. Until the mid-70s there is a clear urban concentration dynamic, then the trend changes; this is also confirmed by the Rosen and Resnick's δ change over time. Although the definition of cities is different[1], both results show that after 1981 there is a tendency for urban diffusion and the importance of the largest cities slightly diminishes compared to the medium-size cities. This means that the prominence of the Athens' agglomeration has reached to a limit when compared to the other urban centers in Greece and slowly decreases after 1981 (which doesn't' mean that the Athens population diminishes! It just grows slower than other medium-size agglomerations).

We next study urban growth in Greece following a methodology developed by Schaffar (2009:1) and Schaffar and Dimou (2012). Firstly, we apply unit-root models on panel data to test whether city-sizes are stationary; secondly, we use a Markov chain procedure to study the relative growth of cities.

First generation panel data unit-root tests have been developed by Levin, Lin and Chu (2002), Maddala and Wu (1999), Im, Pesaran and Shin (2002) and Choi (2002). When using these tests, we assume that each city's growth process is independent from other cities' growth processes. Heterogeneity depends only upon each city's characteristics. The second generation panel data unit-root tests loosen this assumption and consider interaction between urban growth processes (Choi, 2002; Pesaran, 2003).

We test two different growth models both with fixed effects, with or without a drift.

Model with fixed effects without a drift:

$$\Delta \ln S_{it} = c_i + \gamma_i \ln S_{it-1} + \sum_{j=1}^{p_i} \beta_j \Delta \ln S_{t-j} + \mu_{it}$$

Model with fixed effects and a drift:

$$\Delta \ln S_{it} = c_i + \delta_i t + \gamma_i \ln S_{it-1} + \sum_{j=1}^{p_i} \beta_j \Delta \ln S_{t-j} + \mu_{it}$$

where c_i controls city heterogeneity, $\delta_i t$ the upward trending and p_i is the number of the lagged difference term for city i. $H_0 : \gamma_i = 0, \forall i$ is the instability hypothesis, where cities' sizes are not stationary, versus the alternative $H_1 : \gamma_i < 0, \forall i$ where the logarithms of cities' sizes converge to a constant value in the steady-state. The null hypothesis doesn't reject the Gibrat law for cities. Table 6 provides results for first generation tests.

[1] Chesire (1999) discuss the advantages for each definition, when studying urban hierarchies. Henderson (1988) considers only the agglomerations, since they are economically defined. However, other studies insist on the interest of using administrative cities since they allow taking into account urban policies differentiation.

The LL and the IPS tests reject the hypothesis H_0 for both samples. This means that whatever sample we use, the Gibrat law for cities doesn't' hold and cities' sizes converge.

Table 6: Results for the first generation panel unit-root tests

	Test	Stats	Model with drift	Model without drift
87 cities sample	Levin Lin and Chu (2002)	LL	18.541 (1.00)	11.928 (1.00)
	Im Pesaran and Shin (2003)	$\overline{Z}_t$	-12.225 (0.00)	-12.355 (0.00)
		$\overline{W}_t$	-12.452 (0.00)	-12.376 (0.00)
67 cities sample	Levin Lin and Chu (2002)	LL	18.662 (1.00)	12.296 (1.00)
	Im Pesaran and Shin (2003)	$\overline{Z}_t$	-13.662 (0,00)	-12,718 (0.00)
		$\overline{W}_t$	-13.058 (0.00)	-12.933 (0.00)

p-values in braquets.

Table 7: Results for the second generation panel unit-root tests

	Test	Stats	Model with drift	Model without a drift
87 cities sample	Choi (2002)	P_m	21.723 (0,00)	21.723 (0,00)
		Z	-9.840 (0,00)	-9.630 (0,00)
		L^*	-13.435 (0,00)	-13,105 (0,00)
	Pesaran (2003)	$CIPS$	-9.664 (0,01)	-9,411 (0,01)
		$CIPS*$	-6,501 (0,01)	-6,278 (0,01)
67 cities sample	Choi (2002)	P_m	21.567 (0.00)	21,011 (0,00)
		Z	-9.651 (0.00)	-9,110 (0,00)
		L^*	-12.121 (0.00)	-12.098 (0.00)
	Pesaran (2003)	$CIPS$	-7.214 (0.01)	-7.260 (0.01)
		$CIPS*$	-6.502 (0.01)	-6,.311 (0,01)

p-values in braquets.

The results from the most robust second generation panel unit-root tests (Table 7) confirm those from the first generation tests: the Greek cities' sizes converge. This is relevant with the results from the static analysis delivered by the rank-size model and the quadratic model. Cities' size convergence goes against the usual belief in Greece supporting the idea of a strong urban concentration movement in the Athens region. It is worthy reminding that these results are confirmed for both samples, although when using the agglomerations distribution, convergence and urban diffusion only appear after 1981.

Finally intra-distributional dynamics for the Greek cities are studied. Following Black and Henderson (2003) and Dimou and alii (2008), we use Markov chains techniques. This requires the discretization of the distribution by assigning each city to one predetermined number of groups, based on its relative size. In this paper, the discretization process is made with cut-off points exogenously defined at relative city sizes of 0.1m, 0.3m, 0.5m and 0.8m, where m is the average city size for a given year t. It is assumed that the distribution follows a homogenous stationary first-order Markov process and F_t denotes the vector of distributional shares for each group of the discretized distribution

$$F_{t+1} = M \times F_t$$

Each element P_{ij}^t of the transition matrix M_t represents the probability that a city moves from the group i to the group j in t. The transition probabilities are estimated with the maximum likelihood method. Tables 8 and 9 deliver the results for the transition matrices for both samples (87 and 67 cities).

Table 8: Transition matrix for the 87-cities sample

$\hat{p}_{ij}$	C_1	C_2	C_3	C_4	C_5
C_1	0.7142	0.2857	0	0	0
C_2	0.0147	0.9411	0.0441	0	0
C_3	0	0.1818	0.7727	0.0454	0
C_4	0	0	0.1	0.8555	0.0444
C_5	0	0	0.0161	0.1451	0.8387

Table 9: Transition matrix for the 67-cities sample

$\hat{p}_{ij}$	C_1	C_2	C_3	C_4	C_5
C_1	0.9658	0.0341	0	0	0
C_2	0.15	0.79	0.06	0	0
C_3	0	0.2461	0.6307	0.1230	0
C_4	0	0	0.1282	0.8461	0.0256
C_5	0	0	0	0.0952	0.9047

Tables 10 and 11 show the mean first passage time for a city from one group to another for each sample while Table 12 compare the initial and the ergodic distributions for the two samples.

The Markov chains procedure globally confirm our previous findings. The ergodic distributions for both samples show that there is a strong convergence to the lower city-sizes groups (the first for the 87-cities sample and the second for the 67-cities sample). Instability is extremely high in both distributions, which is rather rare for an industrialized country. One should note that even for the last group of cities (c_5) instability is rather high (the diagonal elements are equal to 0.83 and 0.90 for each group). Obviously, the discretization process plays an important role for these statistics, thus we have tested other discretization processes with various cut-off points for both distributions and they all confirm the high instability of the Greek cities' ranks.

The results in Tables 10 and 11 show the high rate of convergence process of the Greek cities' sizes. When using the administrative definition of cities' sample, it only needs 3.5 years for a city from group c_1 to reach the group c_2. In a similar way, when considering agglomerations, it takes 10.5 years for a city from the second group c_2 to pass to c_1. In general, downward mobility is higher when using the agglomeration sample and upward mobility is higher when using the administrative cities sample.

Table 10: Mean first-time passage for the 87-cities sample

M	C_1	C_2	C_3	C_4	C_5
C_1	0	3,5	27,3	144,6	431,1
C_2	93,6	0	23,8	141,1	427,6
C_3	102,2	8,5	0	117,3	403,8
C_4	114,4	20,7	12,2	0	286,5
C_5	119,4	25,7	17,1	17,9	0

Table 11: Mean first-passage time for the 67-cities sample

M	C_1	C_2	C_3	C_4	C_5
C_1	0	29,2	119,1	306,7	1284,3
C_2	10,3	0	89,8	277,5	1255,1
C_3	19,2	9,0	0	187,7	1165,2
C_4	29,1	18,9	9,9	0	977,5
C_5	39,7	29,4	20,4	10,5	0

Table 12: Initial and ergodic distributions

	C_1	C_2	C_3	C_4	C_5
87 cities sample					
Initial distribution	0.16	0.22	0.27	0.15	0.20
Ergodic distribution	0.04	0.70	0.17	0.07	0.02
67 cities sample					
Initial distribution	0.18	0.24	0.21	0.22	0.15
Ergodic distribution	0.74	0.17	0.04	0.04	0.01

5. THE CHANGING PATTERNS OF URBAN HIERARCHIES

Our findings in previous sections lead to three series of conclusions.

Firstly, urban concentration in Greece decreases after 1981 whatever definition of a city is used. This is confirmed from descriptive statistics but also from our findings when using the rank-size model and the quadratic model as well as from the tests concerning the nature of urban growth processes.

Secondly, cities' sizes converge towards a middle city-size. This confirms Parr's (1985) hypothesis that urban hierarchies follow a U-trend movement, according to the industrialization process. The Greek urban system has been characterized by demographic concentration during the early industrialization stages. After 1981, when the country's growth rate met a slight but steady decrease, urban concentration stopped and medium sizes cities emerged in a more dynamic way. Athens remains of course a huge agglomeration compared to the other Greek cities but grows slower than the rest of the country. It is important to note that in any case the Gibrat law for cities doesn't hold.

Thirdly, the cities' sizes convergence rate is extremely high, when considering distributional dynamics within the whole period, that is, from 1951 to 2011. Downward mobility for cities is almost as high as upward mobility.

Following these long-term results, one of the questions that occur is whether the recent economic crisis has changed the trends of the Greek urban system over the last decade. The results from the rank-size and the quadratic models show that in 2011 both the Pareto exponent and the Rosen and Resnick □□have slightly decreased (compared to 2001) which contrasts with the Greek urban demographics dynamics since 1981. This leads to the assumption that the convergence process has weakened and confirms previous findings for the Balkans cities delivered from Dimou and Schaffar (2009) according to whom, a country's city-size distribution is characterized by less mobility during a period of crisis.

We have applied the Markov chains method in the Greek cities' size distribution but this time we run the model only considering the intra-distributional movements that have taken place during the last decade. The results in Table 13 deliver some interesting complements on the previous information concerning urban hierarchies and urban growth in Greece during the crisis period.

Table 13: Transition matrix for the 67-cities sample (2001-2011 trend)

$\hat{p}_{ij}$	C_1	C_2	C_3	C_4	C_5
C_1	0.7857	0.2142	0	0	0
C_2	0.0714	0.7857	0.1428	0	0
C_3	0	0.0625	0.8125	0.125	0
C_4	0	0	0	0.9485	0.0514
C_5	0	0	0	0	1

The intra-distributional mobility is quite lower than the one observed in the previous matrices. For the two last groups of cities, this mobility almost falls down to 0. Moreover downward mobility is extremely law in all cases, on the opposite of what we have observed in the previous matrices. In the stationary state (ergodic distribution), there is convergence to the higher city-size so all cities reach the last group. However, the upward movements are extremely long and it needs more than 2 000 years for a city from the first group to reach the second one and an infinite time (40 000 years) to reach the last group c_5.

Obviously, these results must be considered with a lot of criticism and one should take into account the fact that they draw upon the intra-distributional movements of Greek cities within a single period (2001-2011). However, they clearly show the strong immobility in the Greek city-size distribution during the crisis decade. This also means that temporary shocks such as the economic and financial crisis that Greece is undergoing since 2009 don't produce instability in urban demographics but tend to "freeze" the existing urban hierarchies.

REFERENCES

Black D., Henderson J.V., 1999, A Theory of Urban Growth, *Journal of Political Economy*, 107, 252-284.

Black D., Henderson J.V., 2003, Urban evolution in the USA, *Journal of Economic Geography*, 3, 343-372.

Catin M., Van Huffel C., 2004, L'impact de l'ouverture économique sur la concentration spatiale dans les pays en développement, *Région et Développement*, 20, 123-157.

Cheshire P., 1999, Trends in sizes and structures of urban areas, in Cheshire P. and Mills J. (Eds), 1999, *Handbook of regional and urban economics*, vol.3, Elsevier Science B.B, Amsterdam, 1339-1773.

Choi I., 2002, *Combination Unit root tests for cross-sectionally correlated panels*, Mimeo, Hong Kong, University of Science and Technology.

Cordoba J.C., 2008a, On the Distribution of City Sizes, *Journal of Urban Economics*, 63 (1), 177-197.

Dimou M., Schaffar A., 2009, Urban hierarchies and city growth in the Balkans, *Urban Studies*, 46(13), 2891-2906.

Dimou M., Schaffar A., 2011, Les théories de la croissance urbaine, *Revue d'Economie Politique*, 121(2), 61-89.

Dimou M., Schaffar A., Chen Z., Fu S., 2008, La croissance urbaine chinoise reconsidérée, *Région et Développement*, 26, 109-131.

Dobkins, L., Ioannides, Y., 2001, Spatial interaction among U.S. cities 1900-1990, *Regional Sciences and Urban Economics,* 31(6), 701-731.

Duranton G., 2006, Some foundations for Zipf's law: product proliferation and local spillovers, *Regional Science and Urban Economics*, 36, 542-563.

Duranton G., 2007, Urban evolutions: the fast, the slow and the still, *The American Economic Review,* 97(1), 197-221.

Duranton G., 2012, La croissance urbaine : déterminisme vs bruits, Région et Développement, 36, 11-30.

Eaton J., Eckstein Z., 1997, Cities and Growth: Theory and Evidence from France and Japan, *Regional Science and Urban Economics*, XXVII, 443-74.

Gabaix X., 1999, Zipf's Law for Cities: an Explanation, *Quarterly Journal of Economics*, 114, 739-767.

Gabaix, X., Ibragimov, R., 2006, *Log(Rank – ½): a simple way to improve the OLS estimation of tail exponents*, Discussion paper 2106, Harvard Institute of Economic Research, Harvard University.

Gabaix, X., Ioannides, Y., 2004, The evolution of city sizes' distribution in Henderson J.V et Thisse J-F. (eds) *Handbook of regional and urban economics*, vol.4, Elsevier Science B.B, Amsterdam, 2341-2376.

Giannakourou G., 1999, The Legislative Framework of Urban Planning in Greece: Historic transformations and current debate in Economou D. and Petrakos G., *The Development of Greek Cities*, Gutenberg, Volos, 457-80.

Henderson V., 1988, *Urban Development: theory fact and illusion*, Oxford University Press.

Im, K., Pesaran, M., Shin, Y., 2003, Testing for Unit Roots in Heterogeneous Panels, *Journal of Econometrics*, 115, 53-74.

Jefferson M., 1939, The Law of the Primate City, *The Geographical Review*, 29, 226-232.

Levin, A., Lin C., Chu C., 2002, Unit root tests in panel data: asymptotic and finite-sample properties. *Journal of Econometrics*, 108, 1-24.

Maddala G., Wu S., 1999, A comparative study of unit root tests with panel data and a new simple test, *Oxford Bulletin of Economics and Statistics*, 12, 631-652.

Maloutas T., 2000, Cities: Economic and Social Atlas of Greece, National Centre of Social Research, University of Thessaly publications.

Maloutas T., 2004, Segregation and residential mobility, *European Urban and Regional Studies*, 11(3): 195–211.

Parr J., 1985, A note on the size distribution of cities over time, *Journal of Urban Economics*, vol.18, 199–212.

Pavleas S., 2014, The Structure and Development of the Greek Urban System, Doctoral Dissertation, Department of Planning and Regional Development, University of Thessaly (in Greek).

Pavleas S., Petrakos G., Anagnostou A., 2005, The Greek Urban System: Concentration or Deconcentration, and estimation of metropolitan concentration, in *'The City and the Region'*, eds Frank Eckardt and Dieter Hassenpflug, 117-142, Peter Lang, Germany.

Pesaran H., 2003, *The simple panel unit root test in the presence of cross-section dependence*, Mimeo, University of Southern California.

Petrakos G., Economou D., 2004, Spatial Asymmetries in Southeastern Europe, *Journal of Economic Asymmetries*, 2(1), 127-149.

Rosen, K., Resnick, M., 1980, The size distribution of cities: an examination of the Pareto low primacy, *Journal of Urban Economics,* 8, 165-186.

Rossi-Hansberg E., Wright M., 2007, Urban Structure and Growth, *Review of Economic Studies*, 74, 597-624.

Schaffar A., 2009:1, Croissance et Hiérarchies Urbaines dans les pays émergents, Thèse de Doctorat, Université de La Réunion, 350p.

Schaffar A., 2009 :2, La loi de Zipf dans la science régionale : entre anciennes controverses et nouvelles perspectives, *CyberGeo–Revue Européenne de Géographie*, n.450, Avril, 1-23.

Schaffar A., Dimou M., 2012, Rank size dynamics in India and in China, *Regional Studies,* 46 (6), 707-721.

Simon, H., 1955, On a class of skew distribution functions, *Biometrika*, 44, 425-440.

Soo K.T., 2005, Zipf's Law for cities: a cross-country investigation, *Regional Science and Urban Economics*, vol.35, 239-263.

CROISSANCE ET HIÉRARCHIE URBAINES EN GRÈCE (1951-2011)

Résumé *- Cet article propose d'étudier l'évolution des hiérarchies urbaines et la nature de la croissance urbaine en Grèce entre 1951 et 2011, en s'appuyant sur une base de données de la Greek Statistical Autority. Trois séries de conclusions apparaissent : (i) lorsqu'on utilise une définition administrative des villes, les villes grecques convergent vers une taille moyenne ; (ii) lorsqu'on tient compte des effets d'agglomération, on constate également une convergence, mais le processus démarre plus tardivement, après les années 1980. Dans les deux cas de figure, l'importance d'Athènes décroît ; (iii) la crise économique depuis 2008 a fortement modifié les trajectoires urbaines précédentes.*

Mots-clés - CROISSANCE URBAINE, HIÉRARCHIES URBAINES, CRISE ÉCONOMIQUE, GRÈCE.

THE IMPACT OF MONETARY SHOCKS ON REGIONAL OUTPUT: EVIDENCE FROM FOUR SOUTH EUROZONE COUNTRIES

Angeliki ANAGNOSTOU*, **Stephanos PAPADAMOU****

Abstract - *This paper quantifies the importance of Optimal Currency Area (OCA) criteria for the monetary policy transmission mechanism at the regional level. The study employs a Bayesian PVAR model to measure the impact of monetary policy shocks on regional output of 58 regions of four South Euro-Zone countries: Greece, Spain, Italy and Portugal over the period 1980-2009. The results provide evidence of different regional responses of regional GDP on monetary policy shocks. The policy's asymmetric effects are explained by employing the OCA framework.*

Key words - MONETARY POLICY, INTEREST RATE CHANNEL, PANEL VAR, OCA CRITERIA

JEL Classification - E52, R11

* Department of Economics, University of Thessaly. aganag@uth.gr
** Department of Economics, University of Thessaly. stpapada@uth.gr

1. INTRODUCTION

Studying the Euro-Zone area, the monetary policy is structurally designed at the aggregate level as a stabilisation policy, aiming mainly at controlling the inflation of the area. Given the financial crisis, however, questions concerning the practical conduct of monetary policy in the European Monetary Union (EMU) are moving to the front of the policy debate. Problems are engendered from the weak regional capacity to cope with adjustment requirements of a common currency. In other words, there are doubts on whether Euro-zone regions can be characterized as members of an optimum currency area (OCA)? Conducting monetary policy in a common currency union assumes a homogeneous and an undifferentiated effect at all regions at the sub-national level, ignoring the fact that any regional economy may present different economic characteristics and activities, or it may be in a different phase of economic cycle compared to the others. Whether or not regions at the sub-national level of a currency union can meet the OCA criteria can affect significantly the final magnitude and accurate time of the monetary policy effect on these economies.

Mundell (1961) identifies a common set of OCA criteria the regions must fulfil when conducting countercyclical monetary policy for multiple regions: a) the regions must share similar business cycles, or b) have in place shock absorbers such as factor mobility, flexible prices and wages, national fiscal transfers and a diversified portfolio of sectors in their real economy. If the regions share the same business cycle then the targeted national monetary policy should be stabilising for all regions. If however, the regions experience dissimilar cycles, then the monetary policy will be destabilising for some regions, unless they have in place the above mentioned economic shock absorbers (Guiso et al, 1999; Beckworth, 2010).

Assessing the regional impact of national economic policies such as monetary policy has now become more operational and reliable, and research has been directed to the study of possible asymmetric effects at a spatially disaggregated scale. A pioneered work by Carlino and DeFina (1998) by making use of structural VAR indicates that real income in each of the eight U.S. major regions is affected quite differently to a common monetary policy shock. Regional variations are due to different responses of regional output coming from interest-rate sensitive sectors. One year latter Carlino and DeFina (1999) extended their analysis of the effects of monetary policy to the state level. Their results for the U.S. states are in line with their previous work in regions.

Other studies also raise questions about the OCA status of the United States are those by Antzoulatos and Yang (1996), Owyang and Wall (2009), Partridge and Rickman (2005), and Crone (2005) who argue that asymmetric effect of monetary policy across regions may be attributed to a not-similar business cycle across US regions. In case of Canada Georgopoulos (2009) found that a monetary policy shock negatively affects employment in primary based regions and, to a lesser degree in manufacturing-based regions. Further, Potts and Yerger (2010) report that U.S. monetary policy shocks have a discernible impact on Canadian regional economic activity, but the impact varies across regions.

Additionally and among studies focusing on the regional effect of monetary policy in China, Cortes and Kong (2007) by using VEC-generated impulse response functions, found that coastal provinces responded more to shocks in monetary policy than inland provinces. Moreover, according to Jiang and Chen (2009) the regions with high productivity level responded more to the monetary policy shock.

Evidence against an optimum currency area has been also provided for Indonesia by Ridhwan et al. (2011). Cross-regional differential responses to monetary policy actions can be primarily explained by the region's industrial composition (economic structure). They argue that manufacturing and construction are the most interest sensitive sectors (see also Ridhwan, 2010). Other significant sources of heterogeneity are the share of small firms and small banks in the regions. Evidence has been provided for the US case by Kashyap and Stein (2000).

Relevant studies have been conducted in Europe, also, but mainly investigating OCA criteria within a country. For instance, Hayo and Uhlenbrock (2000), Arnold and Vrugt (2004) studied the effects of monetary policy in the German regional output. Rodriguez-Fuentes (2005) and de Lucio and Izquierdo (2002) conducted a similar exercise for the Spanish regions; While Dow and Montagnoli (2007) investigated the impact of monetary policy on the regional economic disparities in the UK and Scottish economies. Arnold and Vrugt, (2002) in case of Netherland argue that sectorial rather than regional effects account for the variation in interest rate sensitivity. Therefore particular attention should be given on the sectoral composition of each region. Svensson (2012) by investigating the effect of a monetary policy shock on employment in 21 Swedish regions found that regions with larger shares of employment in the goods sector and higher export intensity are adversely affected.

This paper contributes to the existing literature twofold. Firstly, treats regions of South Eurozone countries as members of Eurozone area and not within their national borders, in our effort to provide evidence whether these regions can be part of an OCA. According to Mundell (1961), a currency area should be a region, whose borders needed not necessarily coincide with the state borders. It may be beyond the state borders or within the borders. Secondly, by adopting a panel VAR approach, allows some degree of heterogeneity between impulse responses to a common monetary policy shock. The use of a panel VAR which is becoming increasingly widespread in macroeconomic analysis (Beetsma et al. 2006, Almunia et al. 2010), allows us to take advantage of the resulting large sample dimension, given the non-parsimonious nature of our model and the data frequency. Therefore our findings add to previous related U.S. and European regional literature. We should note here, that there are alternative frameworks, such as large scale Bayesian VARs (e.g. Banbura et al, 2010), spatial econometric models (see Anselin, 2010), factor models (see e.g. Stock and Watson, 1989, 2003), and global VARs (see Dees et al., 2007 and Pesaran, et al., 2004), which can be used in such analysis[1]. We will limit however our analysis to just using a Baysian PVAR model and we will consider the application and comparison of the results for some of the above mentioned models to a future research.

This paper proceeds as follows: Section 2 employs a Bayesian Panel VAR model to estimate the effects of monetary policy shocks on regional output of 58 South European regions and presents the empirical results by analysing the impulse response functions obtained from the estimated model. The results show that the national monetary policy shocks do generate asymmetric effects across the 58 regions' economic activity. Section 3 attempts to explain these asymmetries using the OCA criteria. Section 4 concludes.

2. ESTIMATING THE REGIONAL EFFECTS OF MONETARY POLICY SHOCKS

2.1. The Empirical Model: A Bayesian Panel VAR model

In order to carry out the first part of our analysis, we estimate a Panel VAR model developed by Canova and Ciccarelli (2004), which is based on the Bayesian shrinkage estimators and predictors proposed by Garcia Ferrer et al. (1987), Zellner and Hong (1989), Zellner et al. (1991).

In general the model specification in the above studies is as follows:

$$y_{it} = A(L)y_{it-1} + \varepsilon_{it} \tag{1}$$

where y_{it} is $Gx1$ vector, $i = 1, \dots, N$; $A(L)$ is a matrix in the lag operator; $\varepsilon_{it} = \alpha_i + \delta_i + u_{it}$, where δ_t is a time effect; α_i is a unit specific effect; u_{it} a disturbance term. According to Canova and Ciccarelli (2004), two main restrictions characterize this specification. First, it assumes common slope coefficients. Second, it does not allow for interdependencies across units. With these restrictions, the interest is typically in estimating the average dynamics in response to shocks (the matrix $A(L)$). Canova and Marcet (1995), Pesaran and Smith (1997), instead, use a univariate dynamic model of the form:

$$y_{it} = \alpha_i + \rho_i y_{it-1} + x'_{it}\beta_i + v'_{it}\delta_i + \varepsilon_{it} \tag{2}$$

where y_{it} is a scalar, x_{it} is a set of k exogenous unit specific regressors, v_{it} is a set of h exogenous regressors common to all units, while, ρ_i, β_i, and δ_i are unit specific vectors of coefficients. Canova and Ciccarelli (2004) relax the above two restrictions and study the issues of specification, estimation and forecasting in a macro-panel VAR model, taking into consideration the Bayesian view of VAR analysis. Such an approach has been widely used in the VAR literature since the works of Doan et al. (1984), Litterman (1986), and Sims and Zha (1998) and provides a convenient framework where one can allow for both interdependencies and meaningful time variations in the coefficients. We should note here that the above mentioned VAR approach allows us to address the

[1] See Canova and Ciccarelli (2013) for the main features of the mentioned models and how they compare to the PVAR models.

endogeneity problem by allowing the endogenous interaction between the variables in the system. The model is specified as follow:

$$y_{it} = A_{it}(L)y_{it-1} + \varepsilon_{it} \quad (3)$$

Following Canova and Ciccarelli (2004), we adapt the so-called Minnesota prior to a panel VAR framework. The Minnesota prior, described in Litterman (1986), Doan et al. (1984), Ingram and Whiteman (1994), Ballabriga et al. (1998) among others, is a way to account for the near nonstationarity of many macroeconomic time series and, at the same time, to weakly reduce the dimensionality of a VAR model. Given that the intertemporal dependence of the variables is believed to be strong, the prior mean of the VAR coefficients on the first own lag is set equal to one and the mean of remaining coefficients is equal to zero. The covariance matrix of the coefficients is diagonal (so we have prior and posterior independence between equations) and the elements are specified in a way that coefficients of higher order lags are likely to be close to zero (the prior variance decreases when the lag length increases). Moreover, since most of the variations in the VAR variables are accounted for by their own lags, coefficients of variables other than the dependent one are assigned a smaller relative variance. The prior on the constant term, other deterministic and exogenous variables, is diffuse. Finally, the variance–covariance matrix of the error term is assumed to be fixed and known.

2.2. Data, Regional Characteristics and Model Estimation

2.2.1. The Data

The model is estimated for 58 regions of the 4 South European countries: Greece (GR–13 regions), Italy (IT–21 regions), Portugal (PT-5 regions), and Spain (ES-19 regions), using core macroeconomic variables. Table 1 in the appendix provides all the 58 regions per country and their notation. The sample spans the time period 1980-2009. This span of data includes two main structural changes such as joining the EURO as well as the financial crisis of 2007; therefore, dummy variables are employed to capture these events.

We retain the following variables in our empirical analysis: national GDP proxying national economic activity; regional GDP proxying regional economic activity calculated by deflating annual data on nominal GDP for each region during the period 1980-2009 with the national CPI. The use of national CPI is forced due to the unavailability of the regional price indices. We employ interest rates as an indicator of monetary policy; specifically, we utilize the money market interest rates. Finally, we employ the national inflation rate to account for aggregate supply shocks. All variables are extracted from the EUROSTAT database. National and regional GDP are expressed in logarithms.

2.2.2. Stylised Facts of the 58 Regions

Before we proceed with our econometric analysis, it is important to summarize some important stylized facts about the 58 regions. Tables 2.A to 2.D provide some basic economic indicators regarding the regions and the four countries respectively. More specifically, the above mentioned tables present the total gross value added and the value added of the five broad sectors [Agriculture (AGR), Energy & Manufacturing (ENM), Construction (CONS), Market Services (MS) and Non-Market Services (NMS)], as a percentage of GVA averaging over the period 1980-2009 in each country and in each region. Further, the tables report unemployment rates and relative manufacturing wages. From the first glance in the Tables, the figures reveal that the highest contributors sectors to GVA are the Markets Services in all four countries (Greece: 49.77%, Spain: 46.22%, Italy: 47.32% and Portugal: 44.86%) followed by Non-Market Services in all countries except Italy, in which the second largest sector is Energy and Manufacturing. Agriculture is the lowest sectoral contributor to GVA in all countries except in Greece, where Construction appears to be the lowest sectoral contributor to GVA. The more disaggregated view reveals striking differences among the sectors and among regions. In Greece, Attiki (ATT - 41.87%) is the region with the highest contribution to GVA followed by Kentriki Makedonia (KM - 15.25%). The regions with the lowest contribution to GVA are the Voreio Aigaio (VAIG - 1.49%), Ionia Nisia (IN – 1.69%) and Dytiki Makedonia (DM - 2.51%). In the case of Spain, Catalunia (CAT – 18.58%), Comunidad de Madrid (CDM – 16.91%), and Andalusia (AND – 13.56%) are the regions with the highest contribution to GVA, while Ciudad Autónoma de Ceuta (CADC – 0.16%), Ciudad Autónoma de Melilla (CADM - 0.15%) and La Rioja (LR) are the regions with the lowest contribution. In Italy, Lombardia (LOMB - 20.88%) and Lazio (LAZ – 10.35%) are the regions with the highest share to the national GVA, while Basilicata (BAS – 0.73%), Provincia Autonoma Bolzano-Bozen (PABB – 1.07%), and Provincia Autonoma Trento (PAT – 0.99%) have the lowest shares to national GVA. Finally, in the case of Portugal, Lisboa (LISB – 39.13%) and Norte (NORT - 30.01%) are the regions with the highest shares in GVA, while Algavre (ALGA – 3.87%) is the region with the lowest.

In terms of sectoral value added, across the 58 regions, Attiki (ATT-GR – 36.18%), Cataluna (CAT-ES – 24.72%), Lombardia (LOMB-IT- 28.37%) and Norte (NORT-PT – 40.43%) are the regions with the highest shares to national Energy and Manufacturing sectoral GVA. Regions such as Kentriki Makedonia (KM-GR – 17.88%), Andalucia (AND-ES – 23.90%), Lombardia (LOMB-IT – 11.03%) and Centro (CENTRO-PT – 34.48%) are the regions with the highest contribution to the national agricultural value added.

Observing the unemployment rates, out of the four countries, at the national level, Spain has the highest rate, while Portugal the lowest. At the regional level, regions which are observed to have the highest rates are Dytiki Makedonia (DM-GR-15.8%), Andalusia (AND-ES-23.7%), Calabria (CAL-IT-21.5%) and Alentejo (ALEN-PT-7.3%); while the lowest unemployment rates are observed in the regions of Kriti (KRI-GR-8.1%), Comunidad Foral de Navarra (CFDN-ES-7.7%), Provincia Autonoma Bolzano-Bozen (PABB-IT-2.9%), Centro (CENTR-PT-3.2%).

Finally, observing the Relative Manufacturing Wages across the 58 regions, we conclude that the Regions of Sterea Ellada (SE-GR-27.41%), Cataluna

(CAT-ES-67.59%), Piemonte (PIEM-IT-7.57%), and Norte (NORT-PT-8.85%) have the highest percentages, while regions such as Attiki (ATT-GR-7.90%), Ciudad Autónoma de Ceuta (CADC –ES-5.73%), Ciudad Autónoma de Melilla (CADM-ES-5.73%), Povincia Autonoma Bolzano-Bozen (PABB-IT-6.24%), Provincia Autonoma Trento (PAT-IT-6.24%), Veneto (VEN –IT), Alentejo (ALEN-PT-4.79%).

2.2.3. Model Estimation

In order to examine empirically how economic activity in each of the 58 regions responds to monetary policy actions, we obtain estimates of the monetary policy transmission mechanism in specific regions using the Bayesian PVAR model (discussed in section 2.1) expressed as follows:

$$z_{it} = (y_t^n, infl_t, r_t, y_{it}^r) \tag{4}$$

where $i = 1,2,3,\dots,N$ indexes regions and $t = 1,2,3,\dots,T$ indexes time. y_t^n is the national real output; $infl_t$ is the national level of inflation rate; r_t is the short-term "policy" interest rate proxied by the money market interest rate, and y_{it}^r is the real regional GDP. In our multivariate VAR model, the speed and degree of adjustment of the regional economic activity variables due to an interest rate shock is investigated. The estimated model captures the dynamic feedback effects in a relatively unconstrained fashion, and is therefore a good approximation of the true data-generating process. Before getting into the analysis of impulse response functions, we have to mention that unit root tests on all variables of our models provide evidence for I(1) processes.[2] Following the fact that all of our VAR models estimated involve variables admitting stationary linear combinations[3], we estimate the Bayesian PVAR in levels rather than cointegrated VARs (arguments on this can be found in Sims and Zha 1998)[4]. Additionally, VAR in first differences provides no information on the relationship between the levels of the variables in the VAR, and it is this aspect on which economic theory is most informative. The model is estimated in RATS software.

2.3. Impulse Response Functions

Once the model is estimated, we examine how a positive shock to the interest rate is transmitted to the regional economic activity, by examining the impulse responses of the 58 regions' GDP. Impulse responses (IRFs) give the dynamic responses of each variable to an innovation of this variable as well as of the other variables included in the VAR system. In our case, IRFs are used to

[2] The augmented Dickey–Fuller and Phillips–Perron tests have been applied. Moreover, the Elliott et al. (1996) test and the modified Z tests of Perron and Ng (1996) have been applied because they have superior power and size properties.
[3] Cointegration tests based on the Johansen procedure are not presented for economy of space. However, they are available upon request from the authors.
[4] Diagnostic tests (F-statistic versions of the Breusch–Godfrey test for autocorrelation and the ARCH test) on residuals from estimation of Eq. 1 do not indicate any problem concerning autocorrelation and heteroskedasticity issues.

show the dynamic response of regional GDP to a standard deviation monetary policy shock. If there are statistically significant differences among IRFs, monetary policy is generating asymmetric regional effects.

Figure 1. Impulse Response Functions - PVAR

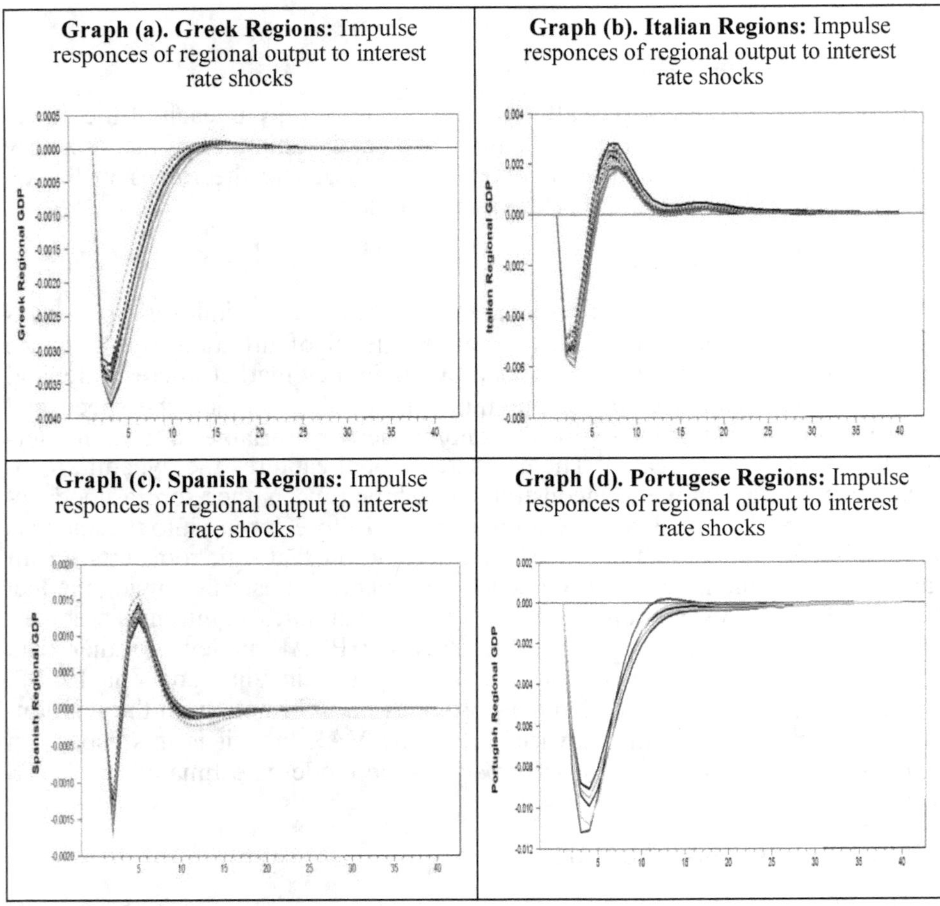

Graph (a). Greek Regions: Impulse responces of regional output to interest rate shocks

Graph (b). Italian Regions: Impulse responces of regional output to interest rate shocks

Graph (c). Spanish Regions: Impulse responces of regional output to interest rate shocks

Graph (d). Portugese Regions: Impulse responces of regional output to interest rate shocks

In Figure 1 (Graphs (a)–(d)), we present the impulse responses of regional output to a positive interest rates shock under standard Choleski decompositions (responses to one S.D. innovations) for each of the 58 regions. The IRFs of the 58 regions are grouped per country in each graph. In general, these figures show that positive monetary policy shocks have a negative impact on regional economic activity in all 58 regions, nonetheless the magnitude of the responses defers across regions. The impulse responses indicate that monetary policy shocks have their maximum impact on Greek regional output at the 3rd year in four out of thirteen regions, while the maximum impact occurs in the 2nd year for eight out of thirteen regions. In the case of Italy, the maximum impact occurs in the 2nd year in 19 out of 21 regions, while the maximum impact occurs in two out of 21 regions in the 3rd year. In the case of Spain, the maximum impact occurs in the 2nd year in all regions; whereas, in Portugal the maximum impact of the monetary shock occurs in the 4th year in all five regions. Furthermore, the magnitude of the responses is very different across regions of the four countries. Generally speaking, a restrictive monetary policy shock seems to affect significantly in magnitude and time Greece and Portugal, while recovery is much quicker for Spain and Italy.

To help summarize the information on the magnitude of the impulse responses across the four grouped regions, we construct tables 3 and 4.

Table 3. Statistics for the 12, 24 and 36 month response functions for 58 regions grouped by country

	IRFs_GR12	IRFs_GR24	IRFs_GR36	IRFs_ES12	IRFs_ES24	IRFs_ES36
Mean	-0.00328	-0.00341	-0.00297	-0.001437	5.16E-07	0.001117
Max	-0.002935 (DM)	-0.002776 (KM)	-0.002242 (KM)	-0.001226 (EXTR)	0.00017 (PVAS)	0.001399 (GAL)
Min	-0.003416 (KRI)	-0.003815 (KRI)	-0.003488 (KRI)	-0.001635 (RDM)	-0.000235 (EXTR)	0.000922 (CANT)
Std Dev.	0.00014	0.000271	0.000327	9.91E-05	0.000108	0.000114
Obs	13	13	13	19	19	19
National IRFs	-0.003272362	-0.004078	-0.004058	-0.001083	-6.733E-05	0.000845
	IRFs_IT12	IRFs_IT24	IRFs_IT36	IRFs_PT12	IRFs_PT24	IRFs_PT36
Mean	-0.005273	-0.005084	-0.002827	-0.001437	5.16E-07	0.001117
Max	-0.004774 (VEN)	-0.003988 (FVG)	-0.001353 (FVG)	-0.001226 (NORT)	0.00017 (NORT)	0.001399 (NORT)
Min	-0.005601 (SIS)	-0.00601 (BAS)	-0.004096 (BAS)	0.011223 (ALEN)	-0.015778 (ALEN)	0.015793 (ALEN)
Std Dev.	0.000259	0.000458	0.000594	0.000829	0.000993	0.000767
Obs	21	21	21	5	5	5
National IRFs	-0.004037	-0.004498	-0.003444	-0.002299	-0.003066	0.002926

Note: The abbreviations in the parentheses indicate the regions that experience the minimum and the maximum values of IRFs.

Table 3 reports summary statistics of the 12-month, 24-month and 36-month impulse responses for all regions grouped by country; while, Table 4 reports the IRFs at 12 months, 24 months and 36 months for each region. The regions are ranked in descending order according to the size of their decline, indicating each region's position relative to the national one.

Using the national value of the impulse response as a benchmark, we observe that for the Greek regions, the regional average decline in output is smaller than that of the national in all three periods; while in the case of Portugal, the average is much greater than that of the national in all three periods. In the cases of Italian regions, in the 1st and 2nd year, the national decline is smaller than that of the regional average, while in the 3rd year, the national becomes greater than that of the regional. In Spain and in all three periods, the national IRFs values are smaller than that of the regional average. Finally, the abbreviations in the parentheses of Table 3 present the regions that experience the minimum or the maximum IRFs values. More or less, there is a consistent pattern across the regions, which experience the minimum or maximum values of IRFs over the three periods.

Table 4. IRFs at 12, 24 and 36 months per region relative to the national ones

Greek Regions					
	IRFs 12 mon		IRFs 24 mon		IRFs36 mon
DM	-0.0034157	Greece	-0.0040785	Greece	-0.0040583
KM	-0.0034145	KM	-0.0038148	KM	-0.0034875
IP	-0.0034055	IP	-0.0037616	IP	-0.0034399
VAIG	-0.0033850	DM	-0.0036662	DM	-0.0032591
TH	-0.0033719	PEL	-0.0035753	PEL	-0.0031649
PEL	-0.0033345	TH	-0.0034457	TH	-0.0029620
SE	-0.0033247	VAIG	-0.0034300	DE	-0.0029546
Greece	-0.0032724	SE	-0.0033859	AMT	-0.0029362
AMT	-0.0032711	AMT	-0.0033835	VAIG	-0.0029295
NAIG	-0.0032391	DE	-0.0033697	SE	-0.0028970
IN	-0.0032341	IN	-0.0033167	IN	-0.0028670
DE	-0.0031961	ATT	-0.0032097	ATT	-0.0028112
ATT	-0.0031148	NAIG	-0.0031910	NAIG	-0.0026566
KRI	-0.0029345	KRI	-0.0027763	KRI	-0.0022418

Spanish Regions					
	IRFs 12 mon		IRFs 24 mon		IRFs36 mon
RDM	-0.0016348	PVAS	-0.0002352	Spain	0.0008459
PVAS	-0.0016168	RDM	-0.0001798	GAL	0.0009215
CANT	-0.0015685	GAL	-0.0001373	PVAS	0.0009226
CFDN	-0.0015318	CYL	-0.0000751	CYL	0.0009791
CDM	-0.0014861	AND	-0.0000695	RDM	0.0009826
AND	-0.0014624	Spain	-0.0000673	AND	0.0010638
CAT	-0.0014577	PDA	-0.0000459	PDA	0.0010759
CLM	-0.0014237	CFDN	-0.0000316	IB	0.0010879
CADC	-0.0014195	CDM	-0.0000177	CFDN	0.0011168
CANT	-0.0014123	IB	0.0000267	LR	0.0011266
CADM	-0.0014056	CV	0.0000289	CDM	0.0011302
IB	-0.0014034	CAT	0.0000326	CV	0.0011410
CV	-0.0014027	CLM	0.0000342	ARAG	0.0011423
PDA	-0.0014005	LR	0.0000351	CAT	0.0011691
GAL	-0.0013965	CANT	0.0000460	CANT	0.0011709
LR	-0.0013912	ARAG	0.0000569	CLM	0.0011781
CYL	-0.0013587	CADC	0.0000920	CADC	0.0011884
ARAG	-0.0013122	CADM	0.0001096	CADM	0.0012027
EXTR	-0.0012263	EXTR	0.0001696	EXTR	0.0012297
Spain	-0.0010835	CANT	0.0001703	CANT	0.0013992

Italian Regions					
	IRFs 12 mon		IRFs 24 mon		IRFs36 mon
VEN	-0.0056013	FVG	-0.0060097	FVG	-0.0040958
FVG	-0.0055989	ER	-0.0057039	ER	-0.0037505
PIEM	-0.0055905	LOMB	-0.0054224	Italy	-0.0034448
LOMB	-0.0055149	PIEM	-0.0053983	TOSC	-0.0033561
BAS	-0.0055045	BAS	-0.0053867	BAS	-0.0032262
ABRU	-0.0054948	VEN	-0.0053823	PAT	-0.0031769
ER	-0.0054612	UMBR	-0.0053367	UMBR	-0.0031189
VAMOL	-0.0054323	TOSC	-0.0053280	LOMB	-0.0030527
CAMP	-0.0053666	PAT	-0.0051821	PABB	-0.0030058
UMBR	-0.0053355	VAMOL	-0.0050918	VEN	-0.0029449
LAZ	-0.0052995	PABB	-0.0050886	PIEM	-0.0029043
PABB	-0.0051767	LAZ	-0.0050130	LIG	-0.0028507
TOSC	-0.0051702	LIG	-0.0050040	MOL	-0.0026657
PAT	-0.0051609	MOL	-0.0049059	SIS	-0.0026503
LIG	-0.0051586	ABRU	-0.0048917	LAZ	-0.0026375
MOL	-0.0050846	CAMP	-0.0048900	VAMOL	-0.0026105
PUG	-0.0049600	SIS	-0.0047252	MARC	-0.0023164
SIS	-0.0049177	MARC	-0.0045327	CAMP	-0.0022990
MARC	-0.0048656	Italy	-0.0044981	CAL	-0.0022974
CAL	-0.0047741	CAL	-0.0043992	ABRU	-0.0022226
Italy	-0.0040374	PUG	-0.0039881	PUG	-0.0013529
Portugish Regions					
	IRFs 12 mon		**IRFs 24 mon**		**IRFs36 mon**
ALEN	-0.0112231	ALEN	-0.0157778	ALEN	-0.0157926
ALGA	-0.0104898	ALGA	-0.0151281	ALGA	-0.0156184
CENTR	-0.0095630	CENTR	-0.0140369	CENTR	-0.0148846
LISB	-0.0093950	LISB	-0.0136734	LISB	-0.0143635
NORT	-0.0093230	NORT	-0.0134738	NORT	-0.0140301
Portugal	-0.0022997	Portugal	-0.0030668	Portugal	-0.0029264

For instance, in Portugal, the region which experiences the lowest IRF value is Norte (NORT) in all three periods, while the region that experience the highest IRF value over all three periods is Alentejo (ALEN). In the case of the Italian regions, Veneto (VEN) is observed to have the lowest value of IRFs in the 12-month period, while Sicilia (SIS) has the highest IRF value in the same period. Friuli-Venezia Giulia (FVG) and Basilicata (BAS) are the two regions that are observed to have the lowest and the highest values of IRFs respectively over the 24 and 36-month periods. In the case of the Greek Regions, the region of

Kriti (KRI) is observed to have the highest IRF value in all three periods, while Dytiki Makedonia (DK) has the lowest IRF value in the 12-month period and Kentriki Makedonia (KM) in the 24 and 36- month periods. Finally, the Spanish regions have a different pattern compared to the regions of the preceding countries. Different regions experience different values of IRFs in each of the three periods. More specifically, in the 12-month period, Extremadura (EXTR) has the minimum IRF value, while Region de Murcia (RDM) has the highest in the same period. In the 24-month period, Pais Vasco (PVAS) has the lowest IRF value and Extremadura (EXTR) has the highest. Finally, in the last period, the 36-month, Galicia (GAL) is observed to have the minimum IRF value and Canarias region (CANT) to have the greatest.

Summing up Table 4, we can report that among the Greek Regions, 6 regions perform better than Greece in the 1st year, while in the second and third year all regions perform better than Greece, having lower decline in their output. In Italy in the first year, output decline is greater than that of the national in all regions; while in the third year, the results are reverse for 19 regions. We observe a similar pattern in the Spanish regions. Finally, in Portugal, the decline in real economic activity is greater at the regional level than that of the national in all three periods.

We conclude this section by making two distinct points of the above empirical analysis: a) the monetary policy shocks do generate asymmetric effects across regional economic activity, and b) there is a pattern on the magnitude of the decline in regional economic activity: in the 1st year the regional decline is greater than that of the national, exception is Greece; while, in the third year the regional decline is smaller than that of the national, exception is Portugal.

3. EXPLAINING ASYMMETRIC MONETARY POLICY SHOCKS WITHIN AN OCA FRAMEWORK

Our general findings from the preceding Bayesian PVAR analysis have shown compelling evidence of differences in regional responses following monetary policy actions. Our results are consistent with many studies which also have documented disparities in the regional responses to monetary policy shocks. Carlino and DeFina (1998) show that certain Bureau of Economic Analysis (BEA) regions respond differently from the U.S. aggregate response to a monetary policy shock. Furthermore, while repeating the exercise for state-level data, Carlino and DeFina (1999) indicate substantial within- and cross-region variability. Additionally, Ridhawan *et al.* (2011) documented regional disparities in Indonesia; Arnold and Vurugt (2002) reported differential effects of monetary policy in Netherlands; Ahlefeldt et al. (2009) reported regional and sectoral asymmetries in Denmark and Sweden; Beskworth (2010) documents regional disparities of monetary policy transmission in the 48 USA states. Other papers [Mihov (2001), Hanson et al. (2006)] have shown that these regional asymmetries exist at varying levels of disaggregation, for different datasets, and various identifying restrictions governing the propagation of policy shocks.

Given the fact that monetary policy affects some regions of the country more than others, a review of the large stance of empirical studies examining how monetary policy may affect regions differently and why, reveal that certain regions of the country are consistently more affected by monetary policy than others due to the fact that those regions have a relatively high share of their economy in interest sensitive industries, i.e. manufacturing, which is more susceptible to negative monetary policy shocks. An interesting conclusion from the review of all these studies is that different mix of industries in the regions is the only convincing explanation of regional asymmetric responses to monetary policy shocks. Any traditional effect through a credit channel that may be operating at the national level is not reflected in the regional asymmetries (Crone, 2007). As pointed by Crone (2007), we should search for other reasons for these types of asymmetries.

In our study and following Beckworth (2010), we give a different direction to explaining regional asymmetries in the response to the monetary policy shock by using the OCA framework; since, very few studies have explained regional asymmetries of monetary policy shock through the perspective of the Optimal Currency Area (OCA) framework. The OCA is useful here because it provides criteria to determine whether multiple regions are best served by a single monetary union.

3.1. Shock Absorbers based on Optimal Currency Area (OCA) Theory

According to OCA theory (Mundel's (1961)), when authorities conduct a monetary policy in multiple regions, the regions must share similar business cycles or have in place economic shock absorbers in order to minimize the costs of a positive monetary shock. These absorbers are well defined within the OCA theory and they are the following:

a) High degree of labor mobility

The idea is that the cost of sharing the same currency would be eliminated if the factors of production, capital and labor, were fully mobile across borders. Since it is conventionally assumed that the real hurdle then comes from the lack of labor mobility. High factor market integration within a group of regions can reduce the need to alter real factor prices and the nominal exchange rate between countries in response to disturbances (Mundell (1961)). Trade theory has long established that the mobility of factors of production enhances both efficiency and welfare. Such mobility is likely to be modest in the very short run and could display its effect over time. The mobility of factors of production is limited by the pace at which direct investment can be generated by one region and absorbed by another. Similarly, labour mobility is likely to be low in the short run, due to significant costs for migration and retraining. Mobility, however, may increase in the medium and long run, easing the adjustment to permanent shocks.

b) Flexible wages and prices

When nominal prices and wages are flexible between and within regions contemplating a single currency, the transition towards adjustment following a shock is less likely to be associated with sustained unemployment in one region and/or inflation in another. This will in turn diminish the need for nominal exchange rate adjustments (Friedman, 1953). Alternatively, if nominal prices and wages are downward rigid some measure of real flexibility could be achieved by means of exchange rate adjustments. The loss of direct control over the nominal exchange rate instrument represents a cost (Kawai, 1987).

c) Budgetary transfers
Countries sharing a supranational fiscal transfer system to redistribute funds to a member country affected by an adverse asymmetric shock would also be facilitated in the adjustment to such shocks and might require less nominal exchange rate adjustments (Kenen, 1969). However, this would require an advanced degree of political integration and willingness to undertake such risk-sharing.

d) Economic Diversification
It is widely held that a diversified economy is less sensitive to the ups and downs associated with any particular industry because risk is spread more evenly across a number of industries. With diversification, even if some industries are suffering, other stronger industries will help the economy maintain healthy growth. The presence of many industries would be expected to offer opportunities for employment in growing sectors to compensate for employment losses in declining sectors (Kenen, 1969).

e) Similar Business Cycles
Finally, if the regions share the same business cycle then monetary policy, which typically targets the aggregate business cycle or an anchor region's business cycle, should be stabilizing for all regions. If, on the other hand, there are regional economic shocks generating dissimilar business cycles among the regions, then one monetary policy will be destabilizing for some of the regions unless the above mentioned economic shock absorbers are in place (Beckworth 2010).

In general, the greater the dissimilarity of a region's business cycle with the rest of the currency union the more important these economic shock absorbers become for the region to be a successful part of an OCA. Basically, how a region responds to countercyclical monetary policy relative to the other regions provides a summary measure of whether that region shares a similar business cycle with the rest of the monetary union or it has in place the appropriate economic shock absorbers to accommodate the shock. If some regions cannot comply with the above OCA criteria, an important question arises: Should have these regions been a part of a common currency area?

The objective of the second part of our empirical analysis is to answer the above raised question by investigating whether the absolute value of the asymmetric regional impulse responses to monetary policy shocks obtained from the Bayesian PVAR estimates, regardless of the sign, can be explained by the OCA criteria; this leads to the following empirical analysis.

3.2. Empirical Analysis

In order to explain the regional asymmetric effects of monetary policy evidenced in section 2 of our paper and using the OCA framework explained in Section 3.1, we employed the following data sets for all 58 regions: national and regional GDP; national and regional manufacturing wages; national and regional unemployment rates; national and regional sectoral output (sectors included: Manufacturing (MAN) and Non-Market services (NMS). The choice of the particular sectors is attributed to the fact that manufacturing is more susceptible to negative monetary policy shocks, since it is considered to be a high interest sensitive industry, while an industry such as the non-market services is a low interest sensitive industry, hence it is less susceptible to negative monetary policy shocks. The above data came from two different sources: OECD and EUROSTAT. The period analyzed is 1980-2009 and all the variables are in constant prices. From the above data, we computed the following main variables that were used in our OCA analysis.

Firstly, we computed the absolute values of the 12, 24 and 36-month impulse responses obtained from the estimated Bayesian PVAR model.

Secondly, we computed wage flexibility (Relative Manufacturing Wage-RMW) by taking the average percent deviation of a region's manufacturing wage from the national manufacturing wage for the period 1980-2009. The wage flexibility measures are rates of change relative to the national average, hence, they should have a mean of zero if they are perfectly flexible; while they will be downwardly sticky and less flexible compared to the nation, if wages are persistently higher than the national average.

Thirdly, we constructed the labor mobility variable (Unemployment Persistence-UP) by estimating the relative persistence in a region to an unemployment shock (Eichengreen, 1990; Beckworth, 2010). More specifically, we took the difference between the IRF 5 years out from 1 unit shock to a region's unemployment rate and a similar shock to the national unemployment rate over the period 1980-2009. In order to obtain the IRFs, we estimated a simple 1-lag autoregressive model for each region and each country. The larger the IRF 3 years out the greater the unemployment persistence is, hence the greater the labor immobility.

Fourthly, and in order to quantify the diversification of each region's economy, we constructed the shares of a region's economy (Relative Sectoral Share of a sector) in a particular sector minus the share of the national economy in that economic sector. The closer to zero this measure is for a regional economy, the closer it is to being diversified along the lines of the national economy. Even if all the sectors are investigated for economy of space reasons we present only the statistically significant ones (NMS, MAN).

Finally, we estimate a business cycle coincident indicator (CCI) measure in order to obtain the differences between the regions' and nations' business cycles. The variable is constructed as follows for each region and nation: we use annual observations of the GDP in constant prices covering the period 1980-2009. For the identification of the business cycle, we use the deviation cycle proposed by Lucas (1977), defined as a cyclical fluctuation in the cyclical component of a variable around its trend. The deviation cycle is identified by isolating the cyclical component from the trend component, and for this purpose, it is necessary to apply a specific de-trending technique, which transforms the non-stationary variable of regional output into a stationary one. There are a variety of filtering techniques to extract the cyclical components of the macroeconomic series. In our analysis, we use the Hodrick-Prescott filter (1997), which estimates the trend component by minimizing deviations from trend, subject to a predetermined smoothness of the resulting trend (de Haan et al. 2008).

Our model is empirically specified as follows:

$$AIRF(no.mon)_i = \alpha + \beta_1 RMW_i + \beta_2 UP_i + \beta_3 RS(MAN)_i + \beta_4 RS(NMS)_i + CCI_i + \varepsilon_i \quad (5)$$

where $i = 1,2,3,\ldots,N$ indexes the number of regions; $AIRF(no.mon)_i$ are the absolute values of the impulse responses at 12-month, 24-month and 36 month period obtained from the estimated Bayesian PVARs; RMW_i is the relative manufacturing wage; UP_i is the unemployment persistence; $RSMAN_i$ is the relative manufacturing share; $RSNMS_i$ is the relative Non-Market Services share; CCI_i is the Coincident Correlation Indicator; ε_i refers to the disturbance term (which follows normal probability distribution with zero mean and constant variance).

The above model is estimated for the 58 observation, using the standard OLS method. All regressions were checked for heteroskedasticity using the Breusch-Pagan Test, and where evidence of heteroskedasticity found, the models were re-estimated using robust standard errors. The results are presented in Table 5.

We report two different versions of the estimated model to explain the 12-month, 24-month and 36-month AIRFs. The main four economic shock absorbers used in both versions are the wage flexibility, labor mobility, manufacturing diversification and non-market services diversification.

In the first model, the estimated equations with dependent variables AIRF-12mon, and AIRF-24mon, report statistically significant coefficients of the four economic shock absorbers and the signs are as expected. The higher the relative manufacturing wage (i.e. the lower the wage flexibility), the greater the unemployment persistence (i.e. the less is labor mobility) the greater are the absolute responses of the state economies to a negative monetary policy shock. However, what is really interesting and contributes to existing relevant literature is that the larger the share of non-market services and manufacturing relative to the national one, the smaller are the absolute responses of the regional economies to a negative monetary policy shock. For European countries the role of manufacturing is crucial in contrast to other countries such as USA or Canada.

Table 5. Using the OCA criteria a to explain the asymmetric effects of monetary policy shocks in the 58 regions

	Variables	(1) AIRF (12 month)		(2) AIRF (24 month)		(3) AIRF (36 month)	
		Coeff.	t-Stat	Coeff.	t-Stat	Coeff.	t-Stat
Model 1.	C	0.005693***	7.64	0.006323***	4.87	0.00491***	3.28
	RMW	0.007114***	4.52	0.010247***	3.95	0.006346***	2.21
	RSMAN	-0.007603***	-2.03	-0.01231**	-1.96	-0.008463	-1.36
	RSNMS	-0.011906***	-3.62	-0.020143***	-3.65	-0.015361***	-2.14
	UP	0.003001***	2.35	0.003894*	1.81	0.002755	1.32
	R^2	42.43%		35.38%		16.78%	
	Adj. R^2	38.09%		30.50%		10.50%	
Model 2.	C	0.005871***	7.67	0.006979***	5.43	0.00528***	3.72
	RMW	0.00703***	4.11	0.009936***	3.50	0.006171***	2.02
	RSMAN	-0.007088**	-1.95	-0.010401	-1.68	-0.007389	-1.10
	RSNMS	-0.011752***	-3.40	-0.019572***	-3.30	-0.01504***	-2.00
	UP	0.003149***	2.13	0.004441**	1.89	0.003063	1.49
	CIC	-0.00031	-0.31	-0.001148	-0.77	-0.000646	-0.53
	R^2	42.54%		35.98%		16.99%	
	Adj. R^2	37.02%		29.83%		9.01%	

*Note: ***, **, and * significant at 1%, 5% and 10% significance level respectively.*

Interestingly, the estimated coefficients on these variables and the overall explained variation get larger in the second period, while they become smaller in the 3rd period. In the 3rd period, manufacturing diversification and unemployment persistence becomes less statistically significant. An also interesting observation is that the R^2 decrease with the time horizon. These models explain between 42.43% at the 12-month horizon, 35.38% at the 24-month horizon and 16.78% at the 36-month horizon the corresponding AIRFs.

Further, we re-estimate the above models including the CCI variable (Model 2). Nevertheless, the correlation measure is negative as expected but statistically insignificant in all cases. Concerning the main four economic absorbers, still remain statistically significant and with the expected sign in the case where the dependent variable is the AIRF-12mon; however, the variables of manufacturing diversification and unemployment persistence become less statistically significant in the cases of AIRF-24mon and AIRF-36mon.

To summarize the above analysis, there are economically meaningful contributions made by all the OCA variables. Their importance, however, changes over the time period. Wage flexibility and labor mobility are more important during the first two horizons while the industry diversification variable and the correlation measure become more important during the latter two horizons. Overall, then, the OCA criteria appears to provide a good framework for understanding the asymmetric regional effects of the monetary policy shocks on South European countries. These findings suggest that some regions may have gained from having their own currency.

4. CONCLUSIONS

The recent Eurozone crisis reveals significant difference between North and South of Eurozone. It is implied by a number of economists that countries of South Europe could be possible to have their own common currency. Therefore an interesting question arises: Are South Euro-Zone regions best served by a single currency? This study tries to shed light on this direction by using annual data from 1980 to 2009 for the 58 regions of the four South EU-zone countries: Greece, Italy, Spain and Portugal.

A Bayesian Panel VAR model that includes real and monetary variables is employed in order to identify the responses of regional output to monetary policy. The results show that the monetary policy shocks do generate asymmetric effects across regional economic activity. Generally speaking, a restrictive monetary policy shock seems to affect significantly in magnitude and time Greece and Portugal, while recovery is much quicker for Spain and Italy. This can be characterized as a first sign that the birth of a new currency union covering all South European countries is not an easy task. Spain and Italy could be members of a new currency union but not with Portugal and Greece as can be implied by our analysis.

By analyzing further impulse response functions an interesting finding is that in the 1st year following the restrictive shock the regional decline is greater than that of the national (exception is Greece); while, in the third year the regional decline is smaller than that of the national (exception is Portugal). This result discloses a short lived regional asymmetry with possible implications for policy makers and economic agents.

In attempting to explain the evidenced asymmetries in monetary policy responses, we used the OCA criteria. The results showed that there are economically meaningful contributions made by all the OCA variables used. More specifically, our results indicate that the higher the relative manufacturing wage (i.e. the lower the wage flexibility), and/or the greater the unemployment persistence (i.e. the less is labor mobility) the greater are the absolute responses of the state economies to a negative monetary policy shock. Furthermore, what is really interesting and contributes to existing relevant literature is that the larger the share of non-market services and manufacturing relative to the national one, the smaller are the absolute responses of the regional economies to a negative monetary policy shock. Their importance, however, changes over the time period. Wage flexibility and labor mobility are more important during the first two horizons while the industry diversification variable and the correlation measure become more important during the latter two horizons.

Our results support the findings of Beckworth, 2010, who used the same framework analysis to examine the regional effects of US monetary policy shocks through the perspective of the optimal currency framework. He concluded that some regions may have been benefited from having their own currency.

In this paper, we argue that the South European Country regions constitute a puzzle from the standpoint of OCA criteria. Overall, in our analysis, the OCA criteria appear to provide a good framework for understanding the asymmetric effects of the monetary policy shocks in the South European Regions. The regions have successfully maintained a currency union despite their failure to meet a number of important OCA criteria.

The theory of optimum currency areas postulates that when authorities conduct a monetary policy in multiple regions, the regions must share similar business cycles or have in place the following economic shock absorbers in order to minimize the costs of a positive monetary shock: a) High degree of labor mobility; b) Flexible wages and prices; c) Budgetary transfers; and finally d) Economic diversification.

Our analysis suggests that:

a) Labor is relatively immobile in South European regions; labor mobility – that is geographically mobility – is unlikely to form a major mechanism of adjustment to asymmetric shocks within the South European Regions.

b) Real wages and prices have been inflexible between the South European Regions, which leads to the conclusion that wage-price flexibility may prove even less significant as a mechanism of adjustment to asymmetric shocks of a common monetary policy.

Given that fact these labour market rigidities remain, then fiscal redistribution adjustments will be the only instrument available to offset the consequences of asymmetries in shocks at the regional level resulting from a common monetary policy. Hence, fiscal policy instruments should play an active role in smoothing regional inequalities in the South European countries. Therefore, fiscal policies forcing wage flexibility and labor mobility by governments can serve as the economic absorbers needed in the occurrence of a negative economic shock. Moreover, in this path can help the increase of sectors like manufacturing and non-market services.

REFERENCES

Almunia, M., Benetrix, A., Eichengreen, B., O'Rourk, K.H., Rua, G., 2010. From great depression to great credit crisis: similarities, differences and lessons. *Economic Policy*, 25. 62, 219-265.

Antzoulatos, A.A. and Yang, J., 1994, Exchange Rate Pass-Through in U.S. Manufacturing Industries: A Demand Side Story, Working Papers, New York University.

Anselin, L., 2010. Thirty Years of Spatial Econometrics. *Papers in Regional Science*, 89, 3-25.

Arnold, J, Vrugt, E., 2002. Regional Effects of Monetary Policy in the Netherlands, *International Journal of Business & Economics,* 1(2), 123-134.

Arnold, I. J., Vrugt, E. B., 2004. Firm Size, Industry Mix and the Regional Transmission of Monetary Policy in Germany, *German Economic Review*, 5(1), 35-39.

Ballabriga, F.C., Sebastian, M., Valles, J., 1998. European asymmetries. *Journal of International Economics* 48, 233-253.

Banbura, M., Giannone, D., and Reichlin, L., 2010. Large scale Bayesian VARs, *Journal of Applied Econometrics*, 25, 71-92.

Beetsma, R., Giuliodori, M., Klaassen, F., 2006. Trade spill-overs of fiscal policy in the European Union: a panel analysis. *Economic Policy,* 121. 48, 639-687.

Beckworth, D., 2010, One nation under the fed? The asymmetric effects of US monetary policy and its implications for the United States as an optimal currency area. *Journal of Macroeconomics*, 32, 732-746.

Ben S. Bernanke & Mark Gertler, 1995. Inside the Black Box: The Credit Channel of Monetary Policy Transmission, *Journal of Economic Perspectives*, 9(4), 27-48.

Binder, M., Hsiao, C., Pesaran, M.H., 2000. Estimation and inference in short panel vector autoregressions with unit roots and cointegration. DAE Working Paper 0003, University of Cambridge.

Canova, F., 1995. VAR: specification, estimation, testing, forecasting. In: Pesaran, H., Wickens, M.R., (Eds.), *Handbook of Applied Econometrics*, Vol. 1. Macroeconomics. Blackwell, 73-138.

Canova, F., Marcet, A., 1997. The poor stay poor: non-convergence across countries and regions. UPF Working Paper 137.

Canova, F., Ciccarelli, M, A., 2004. T Forecasting and turning point predictions in a Bayesian panel VAR model. *Journal of Econometrics*, 120, 327-359.

Canova, F., Ciccarelli M (2013) Panel Vector Autoregressive Models: A Survey, European Central Bank, working Paper Series, 1507.

Carlino, G, DeFina R., 1998. The differential regional effects of monetary policy. *Review of Economics and Statistics*, 80, 572-587.

Carlino, G., DeFina R, 1999. The differential regional effects of monetary policy: Evidence from the U.S. *Journal of Regional Science* 9(2), 339-358.

Chamberlain, G., 1982. Multivariate regression model for panel data. *Journal of Econometrics* 18, 5-46

Chamberlain, G., 1984. Panel data. In: Griliches, Z., Intriligator, M.D. (Eds.), *Handbook of Econometrics*, Vol. 2. North-Holland, 1247-1318.

Cohen J., Maeshiro A. 1977. The significance of money on the State level, *Journel of Money, Credit & Banking* 9, 672-78.

Cortes, B. S., Kong, D. 2007. Regional effects of Chinese monetary policy. *The International Journal of Economic Policy Studies*, 2, 15-28.

Costa-i-Font, J., Tremosa-i-Balcells, R., 2002, Spanish Regions and the Macroeconomic Benefits of the European Monetary Union, Working Paper, Universitat de Barcelona.

Crone, T. 2005. An Alternative Definition of Economic Regions in the United States Based on Similarities in State Business Cycles, *The Review of Economics and Statistics*, 87(4), 617-626.

Crone, T. 2007, Pattern of regional differences in the effects of monetary policy.*Federal Reserve Bank of Philadelphia Business Review*, Q3, 9-19.

Dees, S, Di Mauro, F., Pesaran, H., Smith, V. 2007. Exploring the International Linkages of the Euro area: A Global VAR analysis. *Journal of Applied Econometrics*, 22, 1-38.

De Grauwe, P., 2000, *Economics of Monetary Union*, Oxford: Oxford University Press.

De Haan J, Inklaar R, Jong-A-Pin R, 2008. Will business cycles in the Euro area converge? A critical survey of empirical research. *Journal of Economic Surveys*, 22, 234-273.

De Lucio, J., Izquierdo, M. 2002. Local responses to a global monetary policy: The regional structure of financial systems. *Journal of Economic Studies*, 29 (3), 205-221.

Doan, T., Litterman, R., Sims, C., 1984. Forecasting and conditional projections using realist prior distributions. *Econometric Review* 3, 1-100.

Dow S., Montagnoli A., 2007, The regional transmission of UK monetary policy, *Regional Studies,* 41, 797-808.

Eichengreen, B., 1990, One Money for Euroep? Lessons from the US Currency Union, Working Paper 90-132, University of California at Berkeley.

Friedman, M., 1953. The case for flexible exchange rates. In: Friedman, Milton (Ed.), *Essays in Positive Economics*. University of Chicago Press, 157-203.

Garretsen H, Swank J. 2003. The bank lending channel in the Netherlands: the impact of monetary policy on households and firms. *De Economist* 151(1):35-51.

Garrison B. and Chang H., 1979, The effects of monetary forces in regional economic activity, *Journal of Regional Science*, 19, 15-29.

Garrison B. and Chang H., 1979, The effect of monetary and fiscal policies on regional business cycles, *International Regional Science Review*, 4, 167-80

Garcia Ferrer, A., Highceld, F., Palm, F., Zellner, A., 1987. Macroeconomic forecasting using pooled international data. *Journal of Business and Economic Statistics* 5, 53-67.

Georgopoulos, G. 2009 Measuring regional effects of monetary policy in Canada, *Applied Economics*, 41: 16, 2093-2113.

Guiso I., Kashyap A., Panetta F. Terlizzese D. 1999. Will a Common European Monetary Policy Have Asymmetric Effects? *Economic Perspectives*, 23(4). 56-75.

Hanson, M. S. Hurst, E. and Park. K. Y., 2006, Does monetary policy help least those who need it most? *Wesleyan Economics Working Papers*, 06,

Hodrick, R.J. and E.C. Prescott 1997, Postwar US Business Cycles: An Empirical Investigation, *Journal of Money, Credit, and Banking*. 29, 1-16.

Holtz-Eakin, D., Newey, W., Rosen, H., 1988. Estimating vector autoregressions with panel data. *Econometrica* 56, 1371–1395.

Hsiao, C., Pesaran, M.H., Tahmiscioglu, A.K., 1999. Bayes estimation of short run coeGcients in dynamic panel data models. In: Hsiao et al. (Eds.), *Analysis of Panels and Limited Dependent Variable Models*. In Honor of G.S. Maddala. Cambridge University Press, Cambridge, 268-296.

Ingram, B., Whiteman, C., 1994. Supplanting the Minnesota prior: forecasting macroeconomics series using real business cycles model prior. *Journal of Monetary Economics* 34, 497-510.

Jiang Y., Chen Z., 2009, Empirical analysis of regional effects of monetary policy in China by SVAR model, *Journal of Financial Research*, 346(4): 180-195.

Jiao J, Sun T., Liu X., 2006, Analysis of regional difference in the effect of monetary policy, *Journal of Financial Research*, 309(3): 1-14.

Kawai, M., 1992. Optimum currency areas. In : Newman, P., Milgate, M., Eatwell, J. (Eds.), *The New Palgrave Dictionary of Money and Finance*, 3, 78-81.

Kenen, P.B., 1969. The theory of optimum currency areas: an eclectic view. In: Mundell, R.A., Swoboda, A.K. (Eds.), *Monetary Problems of the International Economy*. University of Chicago Press, Chicago, 41-60.

Lindley, D.V., Smith, A.F.M., 1972. Bayes estimates for the linear model (with discussion). *Journal of the Royal Statistical Society B* 34, 1-41.

Litterman, R.B., 1986. Forecasting with Bayesian Vector Autoregressions - years of experience. *Journal of Business and Economic Statistics* 4, 25-38.

Lucas, R., 1977. Understanding business cycles, Stabilization of the domestic and international economy, Carnegie-Rochester Conference Series.

Marelli, E. 1985. Economic policies and their effects upon regional economies, *Papers in Regional Science*, 58(1), 127-139.

Mathur, K., Stein S., 1980, Regional Impact of Monetary and Fiscal Policy: An Investigation into the Reduced Form Approach, *Journal of Regional Science*, 20(3), 343-51.

Mathur, K., Stein S., 1983, Regional Impact of Monetary and Fiscal Policy: A Reply, *Journal of Regional Science*, 23(2), 263-65.

Mihov, I. 2001, Monetary policy implementation and transmission in the European Monetary Union, *Economic Policy*, 16(33):369-406.

Mundell, R. 1961. A Theory of Optimal Currency Areas, *American Economic Review* 51: 657-665.

Owyang, M. T., & Wall, H. J. 2009. Regional VARs and the channels of monetary policy. *Applied Economics Letters*, *16*(12), 1191-1194.

Papadamou, S., Siriopoulos, C., 2012. Banks' lending behavior and monetary policy: evidence from Sweden. *Review of Quantitative Finance and Accounting*, 38 (2) 131-148.

Partridge M., Rickman, S. 2005. Regional cyclical asymmetries in an optimal currency area: an analysis using US state data, *Oxford Economic Papers*, 57(3), 373-397.

Pesaran, M.H., Smith, R., 1996. Estimating long run relationships from dynamic heterogeneous panels, *Journal of Econometrics*, 68, 79-113.

Pesaran, H., Schuerman, T., Wiener, S., 2004. Modelling regional interdependencies using a global error-correcting macroeconomic model. *Journal of Business and Economic Statistics*, 22, 129-162

Potts, T. Yerger, D. 2010. Variations across Canadian regions in the sensitivity to U.S. Monetary Policy, *Atlantic Economic Journal*, 38, 443-454.

Ridhwan, M. M., de Groot, H. L.F., Rietveld, P., Nijkamp, P., 2011, The Regional Impact of Monetary Policy in Indonesia, *Tinbergen Institute Discussion Paper*, TI 2011-081/3, Amsterdam.

Ridhwan, M.M., De Groot, H.L.F., Nijkamp, P. and Rietveld, P. 2010. The impact of monetary policy on economic activity: Evidence from a Meta-Analysis. *Tinbergen Institute Discussion Paper*, 043/3.

Rodríguez-Fuentes, C. J. (2005), Credit Availability and Regional Development, *Papers in Regional Science*, 77(1), 63-75.

Sims, C., Zha, T., 1998. Bayesian methods for dynamic multivariate models. *International Economic Review* 39, 949-979.

Stock, J., H. Watson, M. W., 1989. New Indices of Coincident and Leading Indicators, in Blanchard, O. and Fisher, S. (eds.), NBER Macroeconomic Annual, 4.

Stock, J. Watson, M., 2003. Understanding Changes in International Business Cycle Dynamics. *Journal of European Economic Association*, 3, 968-1006

Svensson, E. 2012, Regional Effects of Monetary Policy in Sweden, Department of Economics, Lund University, *Working Paper 2012:9*, Lund.

Zellner, A., Hong, C., 1989. Forecasting international growth rates using Bayesian shrinkage and procedures. *Journal of Econometrics* 40, 183-202.

Zellner, A., Hong, C., Min, C., 1991. Forecasting turning point in international output growth rates using Bayesian exponentially weighted autoregression, time varying parameter. *Journal of Econometrics* 49, 275-304.

ANNEX

Table 1. The 58 regions under study grouped by country

Greek Regions		Spanish Regions		Italian Regions		Portugish Regions	
AMT	AMakedThraki	GAL	Galicia	PIEM	Piemonte	NORT	Norte
KKM	K Makedonia	PDA	Asturias	VAMOL	Valle d'Aosta	CENTR	Centro
DDM	DMakedonia	CANT	Cantabria	LIG	Liguria	LISB	Lisboa
TH	Thessalia	VAS	Pais Vasco	LOMB	Lombardia	ALEN	Alentejo
IP	Ipeiros	FDN	Navarra	PABB	Bolzan	ALGA	Algarve
IN	Ionia Nisia	LR	La Rioja	PAT	Trento		
DE	Dytiki Ellada	RAG	Aragón	VEN	Veneto		
SE	Sterea Ellada	CDM	Madrid	FVG	Friuli-Venezia		
PEL	Peloponnisos	CYL	CastillaLeón	ER	Emilia-Roma		
ATT	Attiki	CLM	CastillaManc	TOSC	Toscana		
VAIG	Voreio Aigaio	EXTR	Extremadura	UMBR	Umbria		
NAIG	Notio Aigaio	CAT	Cataluña	MARC	Marche		
KRI	Kriti	CV	Valenciana	LAZ	Lazio		
		IB	Illes Balears	ABRU	Abruzzo		
		AND	Andalucia	MOL	Molise		
		RDM	Murcia	CAMP	Campania		
		CADC	Ceuta	PUG	Puglia		
		CADM	Melilla	BAS	Basilicata		
		CANT	Canarias	CAL	Calabria		
				SIS	Sicilia		
				SARD	Sardegna		

Table 2.A. Economic Variables for NUTS II Regions in Greece, 2009 (% of total)

Region	GVA	AGR	EMAN	CONS	MS	NMS	UN	RMW
GR	**103076**	**8725**	**14375**	**7760**	**51304**	**20911**	**1.4**	
AMT	4.26%	9.53%	4.45%	6.24%	3.18%	3.84%	11.6	26.38%
KM	15.25%	17.88%	16.07%	17.18%	14.68%	14.29%	11.4	26.50%
DM	2.51%	3.87%	5.46%	1.00%	1.92%	1.91%	15.8	25.39%
TH	5.76%	13.56%	5.45%	7.62%	4.87%	4.21%	11.5	25.96%
IP	2.40%	3.80%	1.51%	2.17%	2.12%	3.20%	12.8	25.93%
IN	1.69%	2.17%	0.51%	1.88%	1.86%	1.80%	9.2	25.96%
DE	4.94%	9.85%	3.88%	5.18%	4.62%	4.28%	11.1	26.02%
SE	6.93%	9.33%	15.76%	11.11%	4.93%	3.20%	12.8	27.41%
PEL	4.87%	11.43%	5.99%	4.63%	4.06%	3.46%	8.4	25.77%
ATT	41.87%	4.26%	36.18%	34.00%	47.22%	51.24%	11.8	7.90%
VAIG	1.49%	2.30%	0.66%	3.80%	1.38%	1.15%	10.3	25.97%
NAIG	3.01%	2.64%	1.68%	1.19%	3.83%	2.74%	11.2	25.99%
KRI	5.03%	9.40%	2.39%	4.00%	5.32%	4.69%	8.1	25.60%

Table 2.B. Economic Variables for NUTS II Regions in Spain, 2009 (% of total)

Region	GVA	AGR	EMAN	CONS	MS	NMS	UN	RMW
ES	**507303**	**20503**	**102951**	**43414**	**234451**	**105984**	**14.5**	
GAL	5.51%	9.73%	5.61%	6.31%	4.87%	5.69%	15.0	14.03%
PDA	2.41%	1.75%	3.24%	2.83%	2.06%	2.32%	15.7	14.17%
CANT	1.28%	1.45%	1.43%	1.33%	1.21%	1.21%	13.9	14.23%
PVAS	6.45%	2.74%	9.79%	5.07%	5.65%	6.25%	12.5	14.07%
CFDN	1.71%	1.88%	2.57%	1.52%	1.37%	1.66%	7.7	14.13%
LR	0.77%	1.75%	1.08%	0.67%	0.62%	0.64%	8.6	14.27%
ARAG	3.20%	4.57%	3.91%	3.00%	2.85%	3.10%	8.8	14.10%
CDM	16.91%	1.01%	13.09%	15.04%	19.98%	17.64%	11.8	5.79%
CYL	5.85%	11.61%	6.11%	6.03%	5.07%	6.14%	13.5	67.39%
CLM	3.48%	9.94%	3.33%	4.40%	2.75%	3.60%	13.1	67.32%
EXTR	1.70%	4.76%	0.92%	2.48%	1.37%	2.27%	23.0	67.36%
CAT	18.58%	8.58%	24.72%	16.19%	18.64%	15.40%	10.9	67.59%

CV	9.69%	8.24%	10.45%	9.68%	9.89%	8.78%	12.9	67.35%
IB	2.38%	0.99%	1.00%	2.31%	3.31%	1.96%	8.8	67.37%
AND	13.56%	23.90%	9.01%	16.15%	13.17%	15.79%	23.7	67.33%
RDM	2.40%	4.61%	2.14%	2.59%	2.22%	2.53%	13.2	67.33%
CADC	0.16%	0.02%	0.06%	0.12%	0.11%	0.41%	23.0	5.73%
CADM	0.15%	0.04%	0.04%	0.14%	0.10%	0.38%	19.6	5.73%
CANT	3.83%	2.44%	1.50%	4.15%	4.75%	4.21%	14.4	21.88%

Table 2.C. Economic Variables for NUTS II Regions in Portugal, 2009 (% of total)

Region	GVA	AGR	EMAN	CONS	MS	NMS	UN	RMW
PT	**83856**	**3856**	**17241**	**5684**	**37616**	**19460**	**5.4**	
NORT	30.01%	27.55%	40.43%	34.37%	25.86%	28.00%	5.5	8.85%
CENTR	19.70%	34.48%	24.66%	17.50%	15.87%	20.44%	3.2	7.62%
LISB	39.13%	6.19%	26.39%	38.28%	47.89%	40.25%	6.8	5.18%
ALEN	7.30%	25.90%	7.46%	5.70%	5.44%	7.52%	7.3	4.79%
ALGA	3.87%	5.87%	1.06%	4.14%	4.94%	3.79%	5.1	4.92%

Table 2.D. Economic Variables for NUTS II Regions in Italy, 2009 (% of total)

Region	GVA	AGR	EMAN	CONS	MS	NMS	UN	RMW
IT	**957744**	**26234**	**224000**	**55794**	**453167**	**198549**	**9.6**	
PIEM	8.60%	6.79%	11.15%	7.41%	8.42%	6.72%	6.6	7.57%
VAMOL	0.27%	0.11%	0.17%	0.47%	0.26%	0.34%	4.5	6.81%
LIG	2.94%	2.15%	1.74%	2.40%	3.55%	3.17%	8.6	6.81%
LOMB	20.88%	11.03%	28.37%	17.23%	21.10%	14.25%	4.6	7.29%
PABB	1.07%	1.69%	0.68%	1.20%	1.21%	1.07%	2.9	6.24%
PAT	0.99%	1.13%	0.86%	1.15%	0.99%	1.08%	4.5	6.25%
VEN	9.06%	9.06%	11.77%	10.13%	8.57%	6.83%	5.2	6.24%
FVG	2.35%	2.49%	2.40%	2.43%	2.30%	2.39%	5.9	6.79%
ER	8.87%	10.77%	11.21%	8.20%	8.55%	6.87%	4.9	6.37%
TOSC	6.68%	5.23%	7.14%	5.48%	6.84%	6.30%	7.0	7.00%
UMBR	1.40%	1.76%	1.38%	1.53%	1.32%	1.52%	7.8	6.79%
MARC	2.54%	2.96%	2.99%	2.45%	2.37%	2.38%	6.4	6.82%
LAZ	10.35%	5.53%	5.18%	8.94%	11.84%	13.85%	9.8	7.07%
ABRU	1.86%	2.61%	1.87%	2.08%	1.70%	2.05%	9.2	6.80%
MOL	0.43%	0.75%	0.33%	0.69%	0.35%	0.59%	13.5	6.81%
CAMP	6.36%	7.12%	3.96%	7.63%	6.27%	8.83%	18.4	6.93%
PUG	4.61%	9.88%	3.19%	5.91%	4.28%	5.92%	12.2	6.91%
BAS	0.73%	1.58%	0.51%	1.26%	0.59%	1.01%	14.9	6.80%
CAL	2.18%	4.49%	0.89%	3.04%	2.10%	3.29%	21.5	6.77%
SIS	5.64%	9.65%	2.84%	7.17%	5.36%	8.47%	20.0	6.78%
SARD	2.18%	3.23%	1.36%	3.20%	2.02%	3.06%	16.8	6.80%

Notes and Abbreviations: GVA – Gross Value added, AGR –Agriculture, Forestry and Fishing; EMAN-Energy and Manufacturing; CONS- Construction; Market Services; Non-Market Services; UN-Unemployment Rate; RMW-Relative Manufacturing Wages. The Sectoral GVA are expressed as shares of the national totals. The sectoral GVA values are expressed in 2000 real terms; and the shares have been calculated after taking the averages over the period 1980-2009. National GVA is expressed in Levels - 2000m euros.

L'IMPACT DES CHOCS MONÉTAIRES SUR L'ACTIVITÉ PRODUCTIVE DES RÉGIONS : UNE COMPARAISON DE QUATRE PAYS DE LA ZONE EURO

Résumé - *Cet article utilise un modèle bayésien VAR afin de mesurer et comparer l'impact des chocs monétaires sur le PIB de 58 régions des pays du sud de la zone euro (Grèce, Espagne, Italie, Portugal) sur la période 1998-2009. Les résultats montrent la différence des réponses régionales aux chocs monétaires globaux.*

Mots-clés - POLITIQUE MONÉTAIRE, TAUX D'INTÉRÊT, PANEL VAR, ZONE EURO, PIB RÉGIONAUX

MAPPING POVERTY AT REGIONAL LEVEL IN GREECE

Panagiotis ARTELARIS[*], **George KANDYLIS**[**]

Abstract - Poverty *has been a matter of great academic and political concern for decades. In the recent years, the interest has increased considerably at the European Union level because poverty seems to be a relatively persistent phenomenon and a* threat to *economic prosperity and social cohesion of the Union. The aim of this paper is to* assess *and map, for the first time, the distribution of poverty at the NUTS III level in Greece, as well as to evaluate and map the regional impact of the ongoing economic crisis on poverty, by comparing the poverty rates before and during the crisis. For this purpose a Small Area Estimation technique is employed in order to estimate poverty rates at low levels of geographical aggregation. Spatial variation is a relatively neglected dimension of poverty analysis and poverty maps that provide a description of the spatial distribution of welfare and poverty within a country at different spatial levels may be a useful tool for policy-making.*

Key words - INCOME, REGION, GREECE, POVERTY MAPPING, SMALL AREA ESTIMATION

JEL Classification - C53, D63, I32, R13

This research was conducted as part of the project TIPSE - Territorial Dimensions of Poverty and Social Exclusion in Europe, - as part of the ESPON 2013 programme, (European Observation Network for Territorial Development and Cohesion), funded by the European Union. Texts and maps stemming from research projects under the ESPON programme presented in this report do not necessarily reflect the opinion of the ESPON Monitoring Committee.

[*] Harokopio University of Athens, partelar@hua.gr
[**] National Centre for Social Research, gkandyli@ekke.gr

1. INTRODUCTION

In the recent years, the interest for poverty has increased considerably both at the global and at the European Union (EU) level. At the global level, several scholars have concluded that poverty has declined significantly in the last decades in both absolute and relative terms (Sala-i-Martin, 2004; Chen and Ravallion, 2004; Nielsen, 2009)[1], although the rate of decrease has not been uniform in different countries (Fosu, 2010) and many studies have shown that poverty and inequality are likely to rise in the future (Hillebrand, 2008).

At the EU level, poverty seems to be a relatively persistent phenomenon and *a* threat to economic prosperity and social cohesion of the Union. In their introduction for *Breadline Europe*, Gordon and Townsend (2000) expressed their concern that poverty might become intractable and that the wounded confidence on the ability to combat it had to be restored. Ten years later, similar concerns were evidently present in the adoption of the Europe 2020 strategy, while many European countries were starting to face the impacts of the global economic crisis. Meanwhile, in an environment marked by continuous growth at least until 2007, the EU-15 at-risk-of-poverty (AROP) rate showed no signs of decrease. On the contrary, it had increased from an estimated 15% in 2000 to 16.3% in 2010, when the AROP rate of the enlarged EU-27 was almost identical, at 16.4%. In addition to this, according to the last available Eurostat data (SILC data) that reflect the impact of economic crisis, the EU-27 AROP rate rose to 16.9% in 2011 and 2012. Since the Eurostat AROP rate refers to a relative income threshold (60% of the median income) which is not fixed and decreases in times of recession, the increase of poverty would be quite higher if seen in absolute terms. Indeed, using the corresponding threshold of 2005 the EU-28 AROP rate increased by 2.1 percentage units between 2010 and 2012 (from 13.5 to 15.6%), while the condition is more alarming the eighteen Eurozone countries, where the AROP rate rose from 14.6 in 2010 to 17.8 in 2012.

In light of all these facts, it is not surprising that the reduction of poverty (as well as social exclusion) is now one of the central objectives of the EU and its member States[2]. At the Lisbon meeting in 2000, the European Council set the strategic goal of "greater social cohesion" and committed to take steps "to make a decisive impact on the eradication of poverty". This strategy put poverty and social exclusion at the heart of EU social policy and led to the adoption in 2001 of the Laeken social indicators including, among others, poverty indicators. Tackling poverty is also one of the objectives of the Europe 2020 Strategy. This objective is defined on the basis of three indicators: the number of people considered "at-risk-of-poverty", the number of materially deprived persons and the number of people aged 0–59 living in "jobless" households (European Commission, 2010b).

[1] The decrease in poverty concerns the reduction of people considered as poor using either absolute or relative thresholds. There are indices that the ratio of the income of the poor to the income of the non-poor tends to decrease (Nielsen, 2009).
[2] For a discussion about poverty issues in the EU see Marlier and Atkinson, 2010; Whelan and Maıtre, 2010 and Betti et al., 2012.

In the context of broader European developments, Greece is in any sense a remarkable case. The country faces one of the most serious economic crises in its modern history caused by exogenous (i.e., the global financial crisis) as well as endogenous (i.e. clientelism, bureaucracy and structural weaknesses) factors (Psycharis et al., 2014). The national GDP showed a rapid decrease since 2008, even in nominal terms. With an AROP rate of 20.9% (representing about 2.15 million people), Greece scored poorly among the EU-15 countries as early as in 2003. After some fluctuations, the corresponding figure was almost the same in 2010, but three points higher in 2012. More tellingly, if one uses the fixed 2005 threshold, the AROP rate increases from 22.9% to 32.3% in the same two years. At the same time, Greece is in the bottom-five EU countries regarding income inequalities, as depicted by the Gini coefficient (Mitrakos, 2014). In this situation, the response of the Greek welfare state seems to be inadequate (Lyberaki and Tinios, 2014).

Spatial variation is a relatively neglected dimension of poverty analysis both at the national and at the EU level. Typically, poverty analysis is based on national level indicators that are compared over time. This kind of analysis ignores the fact that large variations may exist among different spatial entities, i.e. that poverty is a spatially heterogeneous phenomenon. The comparison of the regional dispersion of poverty in different national contexts might reveal the relationship between national performance and regional disparities in the sense that higher national poverty rates may be accompanied by concentration of poverty in specific regions or, on the contrary, by widespread poverty across regions (Jesuit et al., 2002; Lelkes and Zólyomi, 2008). Positive or negative changes in the national value may equally mask contradictory trends between regions, which means that there might exist regions in which poverty increases despite aggregate decrease or the opposite. The risk of poverty might be more prevalent in this or that kind of regions (for example in urban as opposed to rural ones), thus revealing constant spatial patterns.

Furthermore, differences between regions may relate to regional growth rates as well as to dynamic structural transformations of the regional economies (Förster et al., 2003). For example, the current crisis is not a monolithic and homogenizing process. On the contrary, it has broadly transformed the socio-economic status of various areas, affecting their income levels as well as poverty in a very unequal way. This has been confirmed both for Greece (Monastiriotis, 2011; Psycharis et al., 2011; Bakas and Papapetrou, 2012; Psycharis et al., 2014) and for the EU (Committee of the Regions, 2010: 3).

All in all, regional differentiations of poverty risk should be taken into serious consideration in policy making and policy implementation. Poverty might have strong local characteristics and this is something that should be carefully examined by policy makers because, sometimes, targeted policies might be more effective than general interventions. National level indicators are useful to monitor the global trends but disaggregated information for lower geographical (administrative) areas is probably more useful for policy-makers. On the other hand, regional explanations of poverty should not be overestimated and the same applies to regionally differentiated (i.e. area based) policies. It is possible that inequalities between regions come as the result of restructuring at higher geographic levels and/or policy decisions taken at the national or supranational level and from that perspective interventions focused especially on 'problematic' areas may have poor results in reducing poverty. If, for example, poverty in specific ageing regions has to do with reforms in the national pension system, then it is questionable whether policies to increase employment in those regions would be more effective than a reconsideration of the redistribution effect achieved through pensions.

From all these perspectives, poverty maps that provide a description of the spatial distribution of welfare and poverty within a country at different spatial levels and can be used to investigate the relationship between poverty and other economic, social and geographic factors, might be a useful tool for analysis and policy-making.

The aim of this paper is to *assess* and map, for the first time, the distribution of poverty at the NUTS III level, as well as to evaluate and map the impact of the ongoing economic crisis on poverty, by comparing the regional AROP rates before and during the crisis (in 2005 and 2011). The data used were obtained from two sources: survey data obtained from EU-SILC micro datasets and population census data obtained from the Hellenic Statistical Authority (EL.STAT.) In order to estimate poverty rates and to elaborate poverty maps, a sophisticated statistical technique, known as Small Area Estimation (SAE) is used. The goal of this technique is to generate estimates of households' living standards at low geographical levels, combining both the detailed information about living standards usually included in survey databases and the more extensive geographical coverage of census databases (Baschieri et al., 2005).

The remainder of the paper is organized as follows: The next section presents an overview of the main and most recent empirical studies concerning poverty in Greece. Section 3 gives a description of the methods used in empirical analysis, section 4 gives a description of the data and variables used in the study and discusses poverty measurement issues, while section 5 maps the estimated AROP rates before and during the economic crisis. A brief summary and discussion of the results and suggestions for future research follow in the final section.

2. (REGIONAL) POVERTY IN GREECE

Greece is divided into 13 NUTS II Regions (*Perifereies*) and 51 NUTS III Regions (*Nomoi*). The latter have an average resident population size of 212,084 (2011 census) but with a high coefficient of variation (2.6). In fact, with its 3.8 million inhabitants, the capital region of Attiki (mainly consisting of the metropolitan region of Athens) accommodates about 35% of the total population, while the second biggest region of Thessaloniki is responsible for another 10%. There are large differences among the NUTS III regions in terms of development level and regional economic structures, reflected in varying employment structures and inequalities in regional GDP per capita. In 2011 the richest NUTS III Region had an average income 2.9 times higher than that of the poorest. Relatively recent investments in transportation and communication infrastructure have started to alter the historical fragmentation of the national space. However, the NUTS III regions continue to be internally homogeneous spatial economic units, as it is indicated by the importance of their boundaries in the delineation of local labor markets (Kallioras et al., 2012).

The literature on regional poverty in Greece is scanty mainly due to data availability reasons (regional micro-data available only at NUTS I level)[3]. As a result, the few previous studies that have examined regional poverty in the EU have not included Greece in their analysis (e.g. Jesuit et al., 2003).

According to a series of studies based on data from the national Household Budget Surveys (HBS) and European data sources (ECHP, EU-SILC), poverty and inequalities in Greece declined almost continuously during the last four decades, but remain at levels higher than the European average (Tsakloglou, 1990; Tsakloglou and Panopoulou, 1998; Mitrakos and Tsakloglou, 2012; Mitrakos, 2014). The decrease of relative poverty was remarkable especially in the first decade after the collapse of the dictatorship in 1974 and showed signs of stabilization afterwards, while the decrease of absolute poverty continued during the whole period. Kikilias et al. (2005) and Georgiadis (2007) depict the variance of AROP rates across demographic groups and socioeconomic categories. At the individual level, AROP rate is higher than the average for people aged less than 25, i.e. for children and those still in education or at the early steps of their working life. The lowest rate is that for those between 25 and 44, while then the AROP rate tends to increase with age, showing the highest scores for people older than 75. Relatively higher AROP rates appear among the economically inactive persons, the unemployed and the less educated, although there seems to be an increase of the AROP rate among those with medium and higher education (Mitrakos, 2014).

Some recent studies, analyzing the impact of economic crisis on national economy, highlight the increase of poverty in Greece. Matsaganis and Leventi (2013), focusing mainly on their distributional effects of economic crisis, suggest that the relative income poverty has risen slightly in the last years (until 2011). Matsaganis and Leventi, (2014), show that poverty in Greece increased moderately from 20 per cent in 2009 to 21.3 per cent in 2012, but when fixing the poverty line at pre-crisis levels, poverty have risen sharply to 37 per cent in 2012. Dagoumas and Kitsios (2014), examining the impact of the economic crisis on energy poverty (using the electricity consumption per capita), suggest that economic crisis has a considerable effect on the electricity consumption, as well as on the capability (or willingness) of people to pay their bills. The effect of the crisis seems to be more obvious in bigger cities (e.g. Athens, Piraeus and Thessaloniki) while more remote areas, such as Peloponnese and Epirus have been affected less. This is an indication that the shift of poverty from rural to

[3] Most regional income studies have focused on inequality issues rather poverty (Petrakos and Artelaris, 2008). However, the findings about disparity might be different from the results about poverty because of distributional effects.

urban areas that started four decades ago (Mitrakos, 2014) continues in the period of crisis.

Poverty analysis at the regional level has been conducted only by Kikilias et. al. (2005). The authors identified three groups of NUTS II regions with different performances. Trying a more detailed categorization of five groups (using the natural breaks classification technique) the picture that emerges shows the distinctive disadvantaged position of the Region of Ipeiros in North Greece. The best performing Region of Attiki is followed by a group shaped by the islands Region of Kriti and V. Aigaio. The rest of the country is divided in two parts, one with low-medium rates comprising the northern Regions of K. Makedonia, D. Makedonia, Thessalia, the Ionian island and the N. Aigaio islands; and one with medium-high rates, comprising the central and southern Regions of D. Ellada, S. Ellada and Peoloponnisos and the Northern Region of A. Makedonia – Thraki. However, the values provided by Kikilias et al. are based on relatively small samples at the NUTS II level and consequently exhibit high standard errors. As a result, though these values are the first attempt to measure regional poverty in Greece at the NUTS II level, they should be interpreted with caution.

The decrease of the national GDP is not experienced in a similar way by all sub-national regions, even those located relatively close to each other. Indicatively, using 2005 as the base year, the regional GDP in 2011 had remained stable in Kozani but had been reduced by almost one third in Kilkis, both NUTS III regions in North Greece. An emerging question is whether regional disparities in AROP rates are connected with disparities in regional level of prosperity as represented by the GDP per capita[4].

3. METHOD OF ANALYSIS

Poverty mapping involves employing relatively new methods to estimate poverty rates at lower aggregation levels (e.g. regions, provinces, municipalities), using data that are usually available at the national level. These methods are based heavily on the literature on Small Area Estimation techniques. The aim of these sophisticated techniques is to estimate quantities of interest within a partition of a country (Haslett and Jones, 2010) combining, in the case of poverty, sample survey and population census information. Typically, household surveys, such as the EU-SILC, collect very detailed information on household characteristics, including measures of income and/or consumption on which the estimation of poverty rates can be based. However, these samples are rarely reliable at low levels of aggregation mainly because of small sample sizes. On the other hand, census data enable (spatial) disaggregation but do not usually

[4] There is a vast literature on the relationship between poverty and growth in various countries and regions of the world (Ravallion, 2001; Kalwij and Verschoor, 2007; Fosu, 2010), although only a part of it concerns the sub-national regional dimension of this relationship directly (Ferreira et al., 2010). Findings are commonly suggestive of a negative relationship, as higher growth tends to be coupled with poverty reduction, but this relationship is mediated by income distribution (and in turn by those factors that influence income distribution, such as regional economic structure or regional disparities in social protection systems).

provide information on income or consumption, or measure these variables poorly (Elbers et. al., 2003). This has led to the need of developing alternative and sophisticated methods aimed at combining data from the aforementioned databases (Baschieri et al. 2005). As a result, the main aim of the poverty mapping statistical procedure (small area estimation) is to combine data from both sources to estimate poverty rates at low levels of geographical aggregation (Elbers et. al. 2002).

This field is rapidly expanding since small area statistics have become an increasingly important analytical means of estimating and detecting poverty trends as well as guiding policies in several countries. Currently, there is a project of the World Bank supported by the European Commission, aiming at producing small-area estimation (SAE) poverty maps for new Member States of the European Union (Bulgaria, Czech Republic, Estonia, Hungary, Latvia, Lithuania, Poland, Romania, and Slovenia).

Elbers et al. (2003) developed a small area estimation approach for income-based (or expenditure-based) poverty measures to estimate poverty rates based on regression models of income (or expenditure) at the level of survey clusters[5]. To estimate poverty rates, survey data are used to elaborate a model of income (income prediction model), employing a series of explanatory variables that are common in both databases. The parameter estimates from this model are then applied to census data to produce estimates of household income as well as poverty rates at smaller geographical units.

This method includes three stages of poverty mapping. First, in the stage of comparability, common variables from both sources are identified, selected and compared. Evidently, these variables have to be strongly related with households' living conditions and welfare (as for example the variables of age, gender, education, marital status, status in employment, nationality etc). Only variables that have the same definition and similar distribution in both databases can be used in the second stage, described as the stage of modeling. In this stage, a number of regressions are run in order to model the household income (or expenditure) and decompose the random unexplained components[6]. In this stage, only the variables that contribute significantly to the explanation of household income are selected for inclusion in the final model. In other words, the rest of the variables are dropped from the model. In this stage, a statistical test for heteroscedascity is necessary determining the method employed. Finally, in the last stage, known as simulation stage, the model parameters are applied to the census database, the income is predicted and the poverty statistics are derived at a variety of levels of spatial disaggregation.

[5] This technique has been used by the World Bank to estimate poverty rates in several countries; it has been incorporated into the World Bank software "PovMap".

[6] It is worth noting that endogeneity that typically hampers the interpretation of the parameter estimates can be ignored in this model, because the objective of the model is not the interpretation of the parameters but the prediction of income.

Following Elbers et al. (2003), the empirical model of household income (consumption) is defined as:

$$\ln y_{ch} = E(y_{ch} \mid x_{ch}) + u_{ch}$$

where *c* is the subscript for the cluster or location (a spatial aggregation level common in the two databases which is typically defined by survey data), *h* is the subscript for the household within cluster *c*, $\ln y_{ch}$ is the logarithm of per capita income (or expenditure) of household *h* in cluster *c* , X_{ch} is a vector of observed household characteristics for household *h* in cluster *c* (available in both the survey and the census datasets) and u_{ch} is the error term ($\varepsilon \sim N(0,\sigma^2)$). The model is simplified by using a linear approximation to the conditional expectation $E(y_{ch} \mid x_{ch})$ and decomposing u_{ch} into uncorrelated terms:

$$u_{ch} = n_c + \varepsilon_{ch}$$

where n_c a location error term common to all households within the location (cluster component) and ε_{ch} is a household specific error term (household component). It is further assumed that n_c is uncorrelated across locations and ε_{ch} is uncorrelated across households. Under these assumptions, the fully specified simulation model is defined as follows:

$$\ln y_{ch} = x_{ch}\beta + n_c + \varepsilon_{ch}$$

4. POVERTY MEASUREMENT, DATA AND VARIABLES

4.1. Poverty measurement

Poverty is sometimes seen as an unproblematic unidimensional concept that reflects the conditions in which peoples' basic needs are not met. This one-dimensional view is questionable because it ignores other crucial aspects of poverty such as health and education (Sen, 1985). The definition of poverty and the identification of the poor is a controversial and multi-faceted issue. Until now, there is no commonly accepted way of identifying who is poor. Despite the wide problematization, not only about causes and effects but also about the indices of poverty, unidimensionality seems to be the result of official definitions that focus on income distribution (Azpitarte, 2012). Thus, while there has been extensive discussion on whether poverty has to be considered in absolute or relative terms (or both), i.e. defined according to a fixed poverty line or a poverty line somehow related to the median income of a society[7], available income has emerged as the most common poverty indicator, adopted as a legitimate measure in national and international contexts.

[7] The concept of absolute poverty appears to be more relevant to low income countries, while relative poverty is of more relevance to high income countries (cf. Garroway and de Laiglesia, 2012).

In this study, poverty is estimated following the Eurostat definition (European Commission, 2010a). According to this, the common threshold applied to at-risk of- poverty indicators is that of 60 % of (national) median equivalised disposable income (after social transfers). In other words, the poverty rate is defined in relative terms, as the percentage of people or households who have a net income of less than 60% of the national median equivalised disposable income. In order to take into account the size of the household, Eurostat uses the OECD modified equivalence scale[8]. Poverty thresholds can be defined in each region separately, according to the regional median income or, alternatively, global thresholds may be applied, following the median income at the national level (Jesuit et al., 2003; Kangas and Ritakallio, 2007). Here we selected the latter method that is representative of the comparative position of each region against the national poverty rate.

4.2. Data

The two sources of data are used to extract poverty rates for Greece are (i) the EU-SILC 2005 and 2011 databases[9] and (ii) the population census databases of 2001 and 2011. The European Union Statistics on Income and Living Conditions (EU-SILC) survey is conducted every year, contains information on a wide range of variables including, among others, demographics, education, health status, as well as income measures This database is the main reference source for the three indicators of the target of poverty and social exclusion adopted in the Europe 2020 strategy (European Commission, 2010b). EU-SILC for Greece[10] produces poverty estimates at national level as well as for large geographical divisions, allowing reliable spatial analysis of poverty only at the NUTS I level. Both census databases offer a complete coverage of all households in each point in time.

4.3. Variables

Twelve common variables were identified in the two databases. From them, eleven explanatory variables were selected and used in the elaboration of the income model as they present similar distributions in both databases, while ten of them contribute significantly to the explanation of the (log) household income. Table 1 presents the dependent and the explanatory variables that are selected by the stepwise method for the final two models.

---

[8] This assigns a weight of 1.0 to the first adult, 0.5 to the second and each subsequent person aged 14 and over and 0.3 to each child aged under 14.

[9] It would be desirable that the two databases had the same reference year, as one main requirement of this technique is that the census and the survey databases represent the same population and implicitly the same point in time (Baschieri et. al., 2005). However, the selection of the 2005 EU-SILC database corresponds better to our objective to compare poverty rates before andduring the crisis.

[10] EU-SILC for Greece collects data on the characteristics of over 6,000 households and 13,000 individuals.

Table 1. Dependent and explanatory variables

Variables used for 2005	Variables used for 2011
Equivalised disposable income (Dependent Variables)	
Before housing costs	Before housing costs
After housing costs	After housing costs
Demographic characteristics	
Household size: (HX040)	Household size: (HX040)
Age: (RX020)	Age: (RX020)
Sex: (RB090)	Sex: (RB090)
Citizenship: (PB220A)	Citizenship: (PB220A)
Socio- economic characteristics	
Basic Economic Activities: (RB210)	Basic Economic Activities: (RB210)
Highest ISCED attained: (PE040)	Highest ISCED attained: (PE040)
Tenure: (HH020)	Tenure: (HH021)
NACE (REV 1.1): (PL110)	Marital Status: (PB190)
Housing characteristics	
Bathroom/toilet: (HH080)	Bath or shower in dwelling: (HH081)
Indoor flushing toilet : (HH090)	Indoor flushing toilet (HH091)

5. EMPIRICAL RESULTS

The estimated AROP rates[11] at the NUTS III level for 2005 (Model 1) range between 17.3% in Attiki and 28.2% in Zakynthos (an island in Ionia Nisia). With a coefficient of variation of a mere 0.09 and only 13 out of the 51 regions falling more than one standard deviation below or above the national average, the distribution of the regional values gives a picture of relative evenness regarding regional performances.

On the other hand, the related spatial pattern (Map 1) reveals at least one cluster of regions with similar high and medium-high AROP rates in western Greece, consisting of eight both continental and island NUTS III regions, shared by four different NUTS II regions. A second smaller cluster appears at the north-western borders of the country, while the northern border can be described altogether as an area of medium to high AROP rates, at least with the exception of the eastern end (bordering on Turkey). Medium to medium high values emerge also in the NUTS III regions of Peloponnese in the South. Two other clusters of medium rates appear in the central and in the northern part of continental Greece, while a cluster of low-medium rates is located in the eastern part of the mainland, shared between the NUTS II regions Thessalia and D.

[11] All calculations of this section refer to the estimated AROP rates *after housing cost*. The differences in regional AROP rates before and after housing cost range between 2.4 and 6.2% and they show a moderate level of variation across Greece (coefficient of variation: 0.30).

Makedonia. All island regions in the Aegean are characterized by either low-medium or medium values. Last but not least, the two metropolitan NUTS III regions of Attiki and Thessaloniki are on the top of the list, presenting the lowest values. Interestingly enough, they are both surrounded by regions with either medium or medium-high rates.

Map 1. Estimated 2005 AROP rates at NUTS III level, 2001 census data and 2005 SILC data

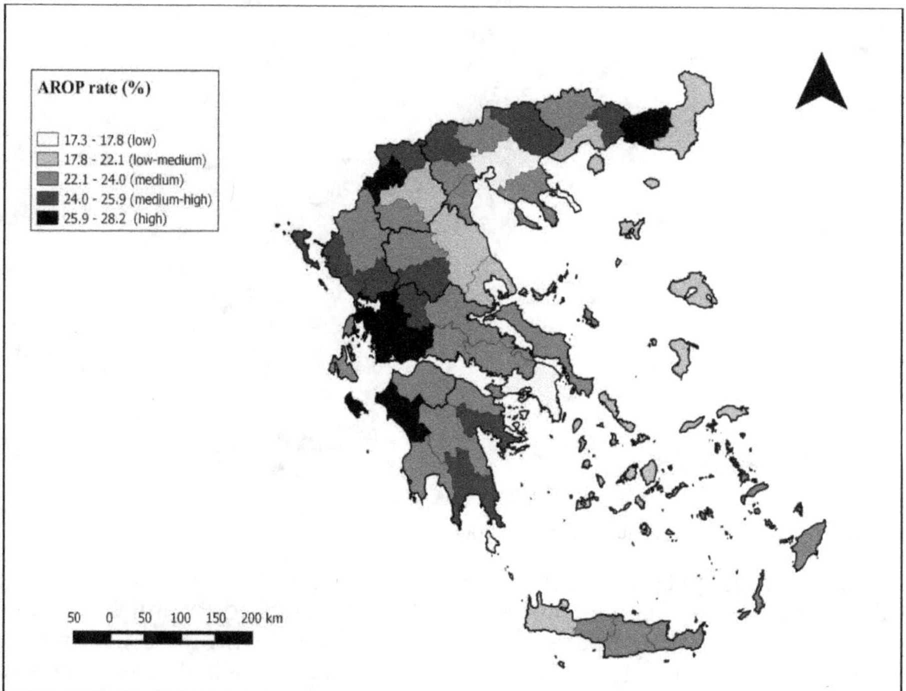

© EuroGeographics for the administrative boundaries.

A comparison of the above picture with the regional AROP rates in 2011 (Model 2) shows that the risk of poverty decreased in 48 out of 51 NUTS III regions. In 26 regions the level of decrease exceeds 10% of the 2005 AROP rate. On the other hand, the evenness of the spatial distribution of the values is confirmed, with an even lower coefficient of variation (of 0.06). There is now only one NUTS III region that can be classified as of high AROP rate (the Region of Xanthi in A. Makedonia-Traki). In most parts of the country the NUTS III regions are clustered together in the way they did in Model 1, with minor differences that mainly have to do with relative improvement or relative decline in specific parts of the previous clusters. Not surprisingly, *no significant differences* are noted in the ranking of the NUTS III regions. The Region of Attiki shows again the lowest rate, while the Region of Thessaloniki falls in the low-medium category, but both metropolitan regions are among the three NUTS III regions that present a slight increase in their AROP rates.

Map 2. Estimated 2011 AROP rates at NUTS III level, anchored at the 2005 median income, 2011 census data and 2011 SILC data

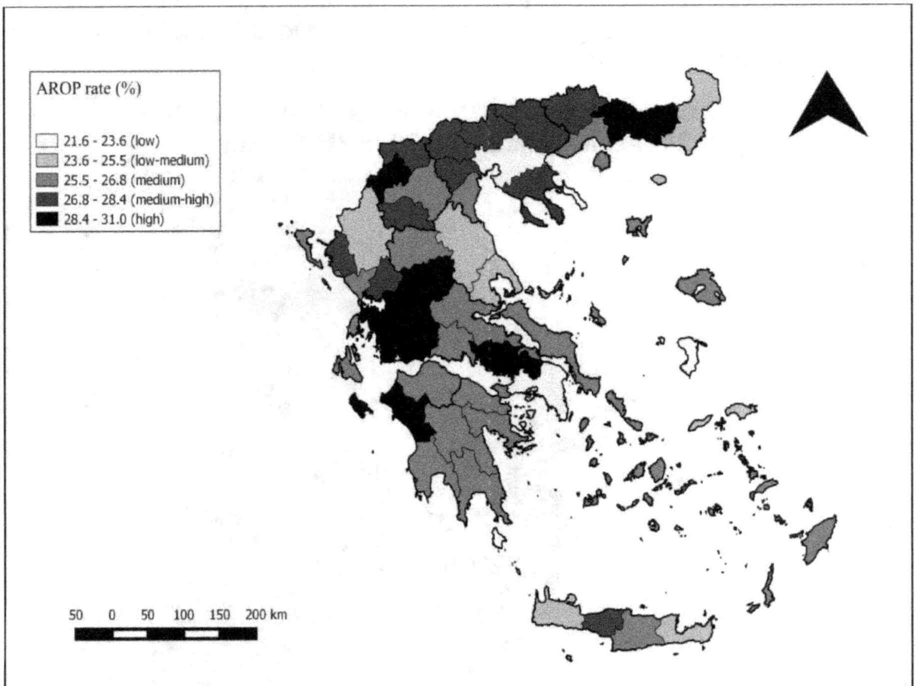

© EuroGeographics for the administrative boundaries.

The picture is quite different if one takes a look at the regional AROP rates of 2011 anchored at the median income of 2005 (adjusted for inflation), as an increase of the rate in comparison to the 2005 values is then recorded in every single NUTS III region. The level of increase exceeds 10% in 41 cases and even 20% in 9 cases, while the AROP rates range between 21.5 and 31%. However, despite sharp increases, the spatial pattern of the AROP rates remains again quite stable, exhibiting almost the same clusters of similar performance (Map 2), especially those in the central-western part of the country and at the north border. The two metropolitan regions are again at the top two positions of the hierarchy. Additionally, the coefficient of variation of the regional AROP rates (0.06) is again lower than in Model 1.

On the other hand, the similarity of the spatial distributions in the two models should not mask the varying trends in different NUTS III regions. In fact, the two metropolitan regions show a dramatic increase of their AROP rates (by 25% in Attiki and 33% in Thessaloniki), ranked in the top two positions in the list of AROP rate change. From a broader perspective, the spatial distribution of increase rates seems to produce an inversion of the previous pictures (Map 3). This is an indication that, between the two points in time, the AROP rates increased more in those NUTS III regions that had lower initial values. Indeed, the 2005 AROP rates and the 2005-2011 increase rates have a negative correlation coefficient (Pearson correlation) of -0.77 (significant at the 0.01 level). Accordingly, there is evidence that after the outbreak of the economic crisis the Greek NUTS III regions tended to become even more uniform in terms of the risk of poverty faced by their inhabitants, but this equality is 'achieved' at a higher aggregate level of risk.

Map 3. Percentage change of AROP rates at NUTS III level, 2005-2011

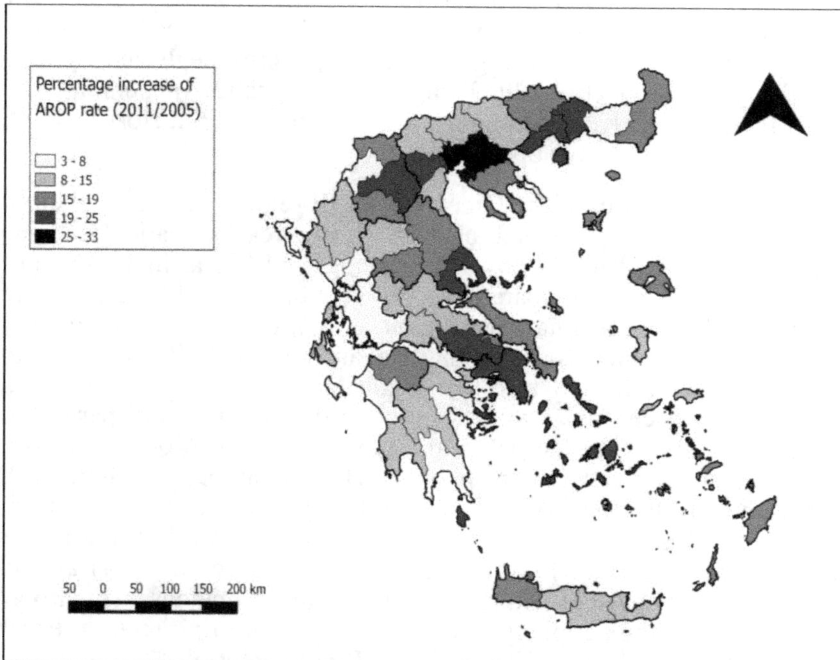

© EuroGeographics for the administrative boundaries.

The next question is whether this trend is connected with changes in regional GDP occurring in a period of recession in Greece. Both in 2005 and 2011 a weak negative correlation between the AROP rates and GDP per capita is observed at the NUTS III level, as indicated by Pearson correlation coefficients of -0.29 and -0.28 respectively (both significant at the 0.05 level). This is a limited indication that the AROP rate is lower in regions with higher GDP per capita before as well as during the economic crisis. Nonetheless, there is an equivalent positive correlation between the increase of the AROP rates and the GDP per capita in 2011 (correlation coefficient: 0.31; sig. level: 0.05). This means that the NUTS III regions that experienced higher increase in AROP rates were those that ended up with higher GDP in 2011. From this point of view, it seems that maintaining higher regional GDP in a period of recession is not a safeguard for regions against increasing poverty. This might happen because the maintenance of comparatively higher GDP is accompanied by intra-regional redistribution in the benefit of the non-poor of the region. The extent to which this or other alternative explanations (based for example on regional sectoral structures) are valid is a matter of future research.

6. SUMMARY, CONCLUSIOS AND FUTURE RESARCH

Poverty is a spatially heterogeneous phenomenon in the sense that poverty rates can vary widely across space. Regional differentiations of poverty risk should be taken into serious consideration in policy making and policy implementation, since poverty might have strong local characteristics. Sometimes, targeted policies might be more effective than general interventions. As a result, there is a strong need for sound spatial poverty statistics mainly for policy decision and policy making. In this context, poverty maps might be a useful tool since they can uncover possible geographical patterns neglected by national level analysis. As Crow et al. (2009) suggest, visualization matters in the study of inequality and poverty, since maps might present powerful stories about progress, social change and development.

In this paper a portrait of the Greek NUTS III regions regarding their levels of relative poverty was presented, using a Small Area Estimation technique in order to disaggregate data on poverty that are available at higher geographic levels. In a country with comparatively high national AROP rate (seen from a European perspective), sub-national regional disparities seem to be quite moderate. The significant increase in the national anchored AROP rate in a period of severe recession is reflected in every single NUTS III region. However, this occurs at varying paces, in a way that further reduces regional disparities, obviously at a level inferior to that before the economic crisis. Moreover, it is especially in the vast and relatively prosperous metropolitan regions where the highest increase in AROP rates takes place. The findings of the study are consistent with other previous studies showing increased poverty rates during the recent years (at the national level) (e.g. Matsaganis and Leventi, 2014) as well as showing that the impact of economic crisis is more obvious in metropolitan areas rather than in the periphery (e.g. Peloponnese and Epirus) (e.g. Psycharis et al., 2011; Dagoumas and Kitsios, 2014; Psycharis et al., 2014). This is of great importance in a country characterized by high population concentration.

The presented analysis provides a starting point and further research should be conducted using additional explanatory variables from other data sources, focusing at smaller spatial levels, including alternative poverty indicators, as well as examining a wide variety of related issues (e.g. drivers of regional poverty) that can shed light on regional poverty.

REFERENCES

Azpitarte F. (2012), Measuring poverty using both income and wealth: a cross-country comparison between the U.S. and Spain, *Review of Income and Wealth,* 58(1):24-50.

Bakas D. and Papapetrou E. (2012), Unemployment in Greece: Evidence from Greek regions, Bank of Greece, *Working Paper 146,* June 17th, 2014.

Baschieri A., Falkingham J., Hornby D. and Hutton C. (2005), Creating a poverty map for Azerbaijan, *World Bank Policy Research Working Paper 3793,* http://elibrary.worldbank.org/doi/book/10.1596/1813-9450-3793.

Betti G., Gagliardi F., Lemmi A. and Verma V.(2012), Subnational indicators of poverty and deprivation in Europe: methodology and applications, *Cambridge Journal of Regions, Economy and Society*, 5: 129–147.

Chen S. and Ravallion M. (2004), How have the world's poorest fared since the early 1980s? *The World Bank Research Observer*, 19(2):141–169.

Committee of the Regions (2010), *European Economic Recovery Plan in Regions and Cities,* Publications of the European Communities.

Crow B., Zlatunich N. and Fulfrost B. (2009), Mapping global inequalities: Beyond income inequality to multi-dimensional inequalities, *Journal of International Development,* 21(8):1051-1065.

Dagoumas A. and Kitsios F. (2014), Assessing the impact of the economic crisis on energy poverty in Greece. *Sustainable Cities and Society,* http://dx.doi.org/10.1016/j.scs.2014.02.004

Elbers C., Lanjouw J. and Lanjouw P. (2002), Micro-level Estimation of Welfare, *Research Working Paper 2911*, World Bank, Washington, D.C.

Elbers C., Lanjouw J. and Lanjouw P. (2003). Micro-level estimation of poverty and inequality. *Econometrica*, 71: 355-364.

European Commission, (2010a), *Combating poverty and social exclusion, A statistical portrait of the European Union*, Eurostat Statistical Books.

European Commission (2010b), *Income and living conditions in Europe*, Eurostat Statistical Books, *European* Union, Luxembourg.

Ferreira F., Leite P.G. and Ravallion M. (2010), Poverty reduction without economic growth?: Explaining Brazil's poverty dynamics, 1985–2004", *Journal of Development Economics*, 93(1):20-36.

Förster M., Jesuit D. and Smeeding T. (2003), Regional poverty and income inequality in Central and Eastern Europe, *WIDER Discussion papers, No 2003/65*, World Institute for Development Economics.

Fosu A. (2010), Growth, inequality and poverty reduction n developing countries: Recent global evidence, *Background paper for the Global Development Outlook 2010.*

Garroway C. and de Laiglesia J.(2012), On the relevance of relative poverty for developing countries, *OECD Working Paper, No 318.*

Georgiadis T. (2007), Poverty and material deprivation in Greece: Growing together and getting old?, 3rd Hellenic Observatory PhD Symposium, Contemporary Greece: Structures, Context and Challenges.

Gordon D. and Townsend P. (2000), Introduction: the measurement of poverty in Europe. In: Gordon D. and Townsend P. (eds), *Breadline Europe: The Measurement of Poverty*, The Policy Press, 1-22.

Haslett J. and Jones G., (2010), Small-area estimation of poverty: the aid industry standard and its alternatives, Australian & New Zealand Journal of Statistics, 52(4):341-362.

Hillebrand E., (2008), The Global Distribution of Income in 2050, *World Development* 36(5): 727–740.

Jesuit D., Rainwater L. and Smeeding T. (2003) *Regional Poverty within the Rich Countries*, in Amiel Y. and Bishop J.A. (eds.), *Inequality, Welfare, and Poverty: Theory and Measurement*, 9, 345–377.

Kallioras D., Kandylis G., Kromydakis N., Pantazis P. (2012), Commuting-based delineation of local labor markets in Greece, *Geography*, 20: 99-116.

Kalwij A. and Verschoor A. (2007), Not by growth alone: The role of the distribution of income in regional diversity in poverty reduction, *European Economic Review*, 51: 805-829.

Kangas O. and Ritakallio V. (2007), Relative to what? Cross-national picture of European poverty measured by regional, national and European standards, *European Societies*, 9(2):119-145.

Kikilias E., Gazon E. and Ntontis D. (2005), Regional Aspects of Poverty in Greece, *Social Cohesion Bulletin,* 1/2005.

Lelkes O. and Zólyomi E. (2008), Poverty across Europe: The latest evidence using the EU-SILC Survey, *European Centre, Policy Brief.*

Lyberaki A and Tinios P. (2014), The Informal Welfare State and the Family: Invisible Actors in the Greek Drama, *Political Studies Review*, 122:193–208.

Marlier E. and Atkinson A. (2010), Indicators of Poverty and Social Exclusion in a Global Context, *Journal of Policy Analysis and Management*, 29(2):285–304.

Matsaganis M. and Leventi C. (2014), Poverty and Inequality during the Great Recession in Greece, *Political Studies Review*, 12: 209–223.

Matsaganis M. and Leventi, C. (2013), The distributional impact of the Greek crisis in 2010. *Fiscal Studies*, 34: 83–108.

Mitrakos T. (2014), Inequality, poverty and social welfare in Greece: Distributional effects of austerity, *Bank of Greece, Working paper 174.*

Mitrakos T. and Tsakloglou P. (2012), Inequality, poverty and material welfare: from the restoration of democracy at the crisis, In: Bank of Greece, *Social policy and cohesion in Greece under conditions of economic crisis*, 23-64.

Monastiriotis V. (2011), Making geographical sense of the Greek austerity measures: Compositional effects and long-run implications. *Cambridge Journal of Regions, Economy and Society,* 4: 323–337.

Nielsen L. (2009), Global relative poverty, *IMF Working paper, 09/93*.

Petrakos G. and Artelaris P. (2008), Regional Inequalities in Greece, in H. Coccossis and Y. Psycharis (eds.), *Regional Analysis and Policy. The Greek Experience*, Heidelberg: Physica-Verlag, 121-139.

Psycharis Y., Kallioras D., Artelaris P., Tsiapa M. and Pantazis P. (2011), *A study for the impact of economic crisis on the economy of the Greek regions*, Report Commissioned by the Greek Ministry of Development.

Psycharis Y., Kallioras D. and Pantazis P. (2014), Economic crisis and regional resilience: detecting the 'geographical footprint' of economic crisis in Greece, *Regional Science Policy & Practice,* doi:10.1111/rsp3.12032

Ravallion M. (2001), Growth, inequality and poverty: Looking beyond averages, *World Development*, 29(11):1803-1815.

Sala-i-Martin X. (2004), The disturbing 'Rise' of global income inequality, *NBER Working Paper 8904*, Cambridge, MA, April.

Sen A. *(1985), Commodities and Capabilities*, Amsterdam: North-Holland.

Tsakloglou P., (1990), Aspects of poverty in Greece, *Review of Income and Wealth*, 36(4):381-402.

Tsakloglou P. and Panopoulou G. (1998), Who are the poor in Greece? Analysing poverty under alternative concepts of resources and equivalence scales, *Journal of European Social Policy*, 8(3): 229-252.

Whelan C. and Maıtre B., (2010), Comparing Poverty Indicators in an Enlarged European Union, *European Sociological Review*, 26(6):713–730.

UNE ANALYSE DE LA PAUVRETÉ RÉGIONALE EN GRÈCE

Résumé - *L'objectif de cet article est de dresser une carte de la pauvreté au niveau des régions NUTS III en Grèce et d'évaluer les effets de la crise actuelle. Le travail s'appuie sur une technique (Small Area Estimation) permettant d'estimer les taux de pauvreté à différents niveaux géographiques.*

Mots-clés - PAUVRETÉ, ANALYSE SPATIALE, REVENU, RÉGION, GRÈCE

SOCIAL AND SPATIAL IMPACT OF THE CRISIS IN ATHENS

FROM CLIENTELIST REGULATION TO SOVEREIGN DEBT CRISIS

Thomas MALOUTAS*

Abstract *- Following a brief introduction to the impact of globalization and economic restructuring on urban social structures, the paper depicts the formation of the socio-spatial structure of Athens in recent decades, the problems accumulated by the traditional regulation of urban sociospatial issues, and concludes with a discussion of the impact of the Greek sovereign debt crisis on these issues. The discussion focuses on the rather weak social polarization and segregation resulting from global forces until the mid 2000s, and on the subsequent change of socioeconomic and demographic conditions forming a new social and political environment in which the socially dividing impact of the current crisis is potentially becoming deep.*

Keys words - HOUSING, SOCIAL DISPARITIES, ATHENS

JEL Classification - R21, R28, I24

* Harokopio University. maloutas@hua.gr

1. GLOBALIZATION AND URBAN SOCIOSPATIAL REARRANGEMENT

Capitalist globalization increased pressure for convergence in economic and social regulation modes starting from the industrially developed countries. Economic restructuring in these countries –evidenced by extensive deindustrialization and the gradual shrinking of welfare states– became the dominant paradigm in facing the crisis of the previous accumulation regime that depended on large and vertically integrated productive units as well as on the stimulation of substantial and socially diffused demand. The new paradigm opted for the liberalization-deregulation of markets (Harvey 1989; Amin 1994; Knox, Agnew and McCarthy 2003; Perrons 2003). In real terms, however, deregulation policies were implemented in very selective ways by preserving protectionist walls for countries and international coalitions that had the power to enforce them, while deregulation within countries was mainly performed at the expense of redis-tributive policies and the state's welfare role.

The redistribution of resources in favour of capital brought up by globalization had important social and spatial repercussions. On the regional level, changes were mainly related to the re-localization of different activities –the decentralization, for instance, of simple manufacturing to countries of lower labour cost– as the model of the large and vertically integrated corporation was progressively abandoned in favour of more complex schemes in terms of both business organization and geographic location. Investors were increasingly liberated from local/national ties and dependencies to choose locations for each of the processes involved in the production of their commodities. The spatial and temporal fluidity of investment/disinvestment –enhanced by the financialization of capital– became important leverage for capital in its claim for more incentives in order to invest. This leverage became especially persuasive through the bleak fate of areas of disinvestment, where it materialized as deindustrialization and high unemployment.

On the metropolitan level, changes were also important. Large metropolises, and especially world cities became privileged spaces for particular types of investment. According to different authors (Sassen 1991; Mollenkopf and Castells 1991; Feinstein et al. 1992) globalization increased the role of these areas in the management of international economic processes, especially regarding the crucial sectors of financial markets, insurance and banking, accounting and legal services, IT systems, real estate management etc. According to these authors, this led to an increase in both income inequality and social polarization– i.e. there was growing concentration of people at the extremes of the socioeconomic hierarchy while the breadth of its middle positions was diminished– but also in residential segregation– i.e. there was growing social distance among the areas where different social groups reside. These claims convey the idea of transition to a socially divided or dual city, and can be related to arguments about social exclusion. Certain authors consider, however, that the social and spatial division of these large cities is more complex, involving important subdivisions and stratifications (Marcuse 2002).

The mechanism that produces social polarization in major world cities is related to the attraction of highly skilled and highly remunerated work force used by high-end service providers to multinational corporations and, at the same time, to the attraction of large numbers of workers without particular skills for menial/routine jobs, including those related to the provision of personal services to the corporate elite (Sassen 1991). Social polarization according to Sassen (1991) leads also to spatial polarization by increasing segregation of lower socioeconomic groups; this is produced by gentrification processes triggered or facilitated by the housing demand of the corporate elite as well as by the appropriation of privileged urban areas for corporate use.

More recent approaches are less unequivocal regarding the catalytic impact of economic restructuring by leaving some space to the State, to policies in deter-mining actual trends. These approaches are mainly related to the role of the welfare state (Hamnett 1994 and 1996; Marcuse and van Kempen 2002; Musterd and Ostendorf 1998) and usually dissociate the economic and social regulation in the US from regulation models in large parts of Western and Northern Europe where developed welfare systems are still important. Other approaches stress the contextual character of theoretical constructs like social polarization that generalize features and trends that derive from, and largely remain attached to the US economic and political situation. These approaches reveal the contextual diversity of several determinant factors –apart that is from the European welfare state– like the East Asian developmental state (Hill and Kim 2000; Hill and Fujita 2003) or the clientelist and familist social regulation in South European countries. In this sense, they ultimately stress the contextual character of what is often implicitly considered as general and global (Maloutas and Fujita, forthcoming).

These alternative approaches claim that the impact of globalization on cities is much more diverse and complex from the diagnoses of an ever increasing social dichotomy. In most of these approaches there is emphasis on local processes which lead to creating increasingly diverse micro areas with particular social and spatial features. Some authors focus on special types of micro-areas –like gated communities, gentrified spaces, ghettos, regenerated waterfronts and 'citadels' for higher social groups. The spaces developed to such types of areas are in fact the soft underbelly of cities facing the attack of globalization, in the sense that they are easier to reshape according to the new economic environment (Marcuse and van Kempen 2000).

No one denies, however, that the pressure from global economic trends leads towards a widening gap of social inequality; however, the impact on social structures and on spatial constructs is not predetermined. Most of the approaches that criticize the social polarization thesis, stress that sociospatial outcomes are not resulting from immutable economic processes, but from their political regulation. The gradual shrinking of welfare structures in Western and Northern Europe and the difficulties to sustain the East Asian developmental state, witness the increasing difficulties to resist the rise of social inequality and urban division. At the same time, the claim for social equality is de-legitimated as a counter incentive for the undeserving poor, as economically unproductive and, ultimately, as socially unjust.

The strength of neoliberal domination is witnessed by the fact that although the most dynamic and geographically mobile part of international capital with its unbridled speculative practice brought the international economy to its knees –through the US subprime loan crisis– it suffered no significant consequences. On the contrary, the sovereign debt crisis that immediately followed was treated in a very different way by the assault on labour rights and public policies that did not abide by neoliberal orthodoxy.

2. GLOBALIZATION SOVEREIGN DEBT CRISIS AND SOCIAL IMPACT ON ATHENS

2.1. The origins of reduced segregation in the pre-crisis era

The Greek city –with Athens as the main example– had not experienced a clear growth of sociospatial division as a consequence of globalization processes, at least until the recent crisis. This claim is founded on the fact that residential segregation did not increase since the early 1990s. On the contrary, indices of segregation for most occupational categories have been decreasing (Maloutas et al. 2012; Maloutas forthcoming), except for the declining number of industrial workers whose spatial concentration increased during the 1990s.

A closer look shows that segregation processes are not distributed across the city in a uniform way. Areas at the social extremes –like the bourgeois suburbs of *Psychico* and *Ekali* on the one hand or the working-class areas of *Ano Liosia* and *Aspropyrgos* on the other– have increased their socially homogenous profile and have thus contributed to the increase of social segregation. These area types comprise, however, a rather small part of the city's population, while the much larger and much more populated areas of intermediate social strata have exhibited an increase in social mix (Maloutas 2007). Moreover, the massive inflow of immigrants since the 1990s has counter intuitively contributed to the decrease of social segregation. In fact, it was this immigrant inflow that induced the residential de-segregation of lower occupational categories following the residential location of the new settlers in different areas from those of the native Greek working-class. The latter are mainly located as homeowners in the city's working-class suburbs (western part of the urban periphery) while immigrants were attracted by affordable housing supply for rent in the densely built areas around the centre (Arapoglou 2006 and 2007; Arapoglou and Sayas 2006; Maloutas 2007; Arapoglou and Sayas 2009). But, de-segregation and spatial proximity in Athens, like in many other South European cities (Arbaci 2007 and 2008) and beyond, do not necessarily lead to social proximity. Thus, despite the spatial proximity with native Greek middle-class groups, immigrants live under clearly inferior housing conditions (Arapoglou et al. 2009) and usually have no access to the same important services –like schools– that are crucial for the social mobility prospects of their children.

The relatively reduced level of segregation in Athens is accompanied by a rather weak presence of other important processes of sociospatial division. Gentrification of inner city areas –i.e. the invasion of such areas by upper-middle social groups and the displacement of older residents of lower social status within a process of urban regeneration that also induces the substitution of former land uses by new uses of higher rank (Atkinson & Bridge 2005; Lees et al. 2008; Porter and Shaw 2009)– appears to be rather weak and segmented in Athens (Maloutas and Alexandri 2009; Alexandri 2013 and 2014). The construction of gated communities (i.e. housing projects, enclosed by material or symbolic walls, providing protection services) is almost non existent. The functionally autonomous middle-class areas at the periphery that provide locally an important number of jobs enabling their residents and those of surrounding areas to work and live in relative isolation from the city centre (edge cities), is also embryonic if not completely absent (Sayas 2004 and 2006). Finally, upper-class 'citadels' (Marcuse and van Kempen 2000) in Athens refers to a very limited number of self-promoted properties in high status suburban areas, like *Kavouri* or *Ekali*, rather than to some sizeable form of organized housing provision for very high income groups.

The question is therefore what were the causes that induced the relatively reduced degree of social division in the distribution of different social groups among the residential areas of Athens. First of all, housing provision in Greece has never been the object of large projects, either private or public. As a South European metropolis where industrial activity has never been dominant –and thus has not left an important imprint on the city's organizational structure[1]– Athens has never seen the development of social services in the ways and the magnitude they acquired in the industrial European countries, i.e. in the form of a developed classic welfare state. The local model of welfare arrangements – bearing important similarities with the rest of Southern Europe (Mingione 1996; Ferrara 1996), especially concerning housing (Allen et al. 2004)– left much broader margins to the family to organize and invest in its members social reproduction using resources often transmitted by the state through clientelist processes in ways that reinforced and consolidated the dominant political system. The profile of the house-building sector was shaped within this type of welfare arrangements. The average size of building companies remained extremely small and their operations rarely involved the construction of more than one building unit, while specific arrangements prevented the involvement of large constructors in house-building activity and of private banks in housing credit (Economou 1988). The processes of housing production that prevailed almost up to the 1990s –i.e. the low cost self-promotion at the city's periphery and the *antiparochi* system that produced condominiums through the joint venture of small landowners and small building entrepreneurs[2]– supplied very

[1] For a comprehensive discussion of differences between the urbanization of the industrial metropolis and urbanization in the European South, where industry has not been the major component of urban attraction, see Allen et al. (2004: chapter 3).

[2] The house building system of *antiparohi* provided massively low cost housing in the 1960s and the 1970s (Antonopoulou, 1991). Operations were small scale, as they entailed the joint venture of a small landowner and a small builder who got a share of the

large numbers of affordable housing units that covered, to a large extent, the housing needs developed in a rapidly expanding metropolis. At the same time, however, they created a rather poor urban environment, since an important factor that reduced housing cost was the lack of urban infrastructures and public space. The affordable cost and the socially diffused access to housing resulted in sustaining and increasing the high rates of homeownership. On the other hand, the rationale of the two dominant housing systems (self-promotion and *antiparochi*) was compatible with the constitution of stable self-help networks in residential areas based on kinship and common origin. The importance of these proximity-based networks for social reproduction, combined with the extreme segmentation and social diffusion of landed property and the heavy taxation of property transfers, created conditions of low residential mobility – therefore of a rather stable residential location for households during most of their lifetime– which prevented the sociospatially dividing pressure of a constant sifting and sorting.

The second important parameter related to the rather weak sociospatial division in Athens is the profile of housing demand and especially the demand from higher social strata that did not exercise substantial segregation pressure. Native Greek middle and upper-middle strata followed, to a large extent, similar housing practices to those of lower social categories and contributed to segregation only through their gradual relocation to the new middle-class suburbs since the 1970s. At the same time, these categories unintendedly contributed to increasing the social mix in the inner city by being the main actors in the *antiparochi* system, which provided abundant affordable housing in and around the city centre.

City residents of foreign origin belonging to upper-middle strata –and especially those who belong to the highly mobile corporate elite– usually exercise an important pressure on the local housing market by increasing demand for high quality housing in central locations often fuelling processes of gentrification. In Athens, this group is relatively small due to the scarcity of high level corporate activities and of high-end producer services. If globalization did not have an important impact on the Athenian housing market through this type of demand, the presence of large numbers of immigrants, relegated to the lower parts of the occupational hierarchy, had a significant impact on local housing. However, the growing presence of immigrants did not induce the increase of residential segregation since they were not attracted by the same areas where native Greeks in similar occupational categories usually reside: the concentration of immigrants in the traditional working-class –but also owner-occupied– municipalities of Western Athens is lower than their average in the whole city region. Immigrants were much more concentrated in areas where small and affordable apartments for rent were available, i.e. in the

---

building at the end of the works according to an initial agreement. The popularity of this system was due to generous tax relief that made any other form of condominium production not competitive. Almost 35.000 units of five floors or higher were produced between 1950 and 1980 in a city that, before that period, had less than 1.000 (Maloutas and Karadimitriou, 2001).

degraded neighbourhoods around the centre following their dense building using the *antiparochi* system in the 1960s and 1970s (Maloutas 2007).

The third, and probably most important, cause of reduced segregation is the increased importance of intermediate social categories, which remain remarkably dominant in Athens. The quick integration of post war rural migrants to the urban society and their rapid access to intermediate social positions relied on the sustainability of the small family business in the city and on the important social mobility produced by the wide access to educational credentials and skills. Social mobility through education mitigated the anti-meritocratic ways that access to the labour market (especially the public sector) was regulated, following strict political discrimination during the first post war decades and subsequently using more relaxed clientelist procedures. As a result, Greece presented –and still does– the highest rate of self-employment amongst OECD countries, and, until a few years ago, a relatively high rate of public employment; both self-employment and employment in the public sector were essential in consolidating the importance and relative stability of intermediate occupational positions.

2.2. Issues of social regulation in Athens since the 1990s

The impact of the two dominant housing systems of the post-war period (self-promotion and antiparochi) on the city's built and social environment was especially clear until the end of the 1970s; it started fading after the 1980s when population growth came almost to a full stop. Since the 1990s the housing question in Athens became much more related to the social redistribution of the existing stock than the massive production of new housing. The main source for new housing demand was limited to the gradual relocation of large numbers of households to the suburbs and the broader periphery through processes that left a substantially different social imprint from those of the first post war period. The second important source of housing demand were immigrant groups and was targeted to rented accommodation in central areas. Segregation was reinforced in the new and socially homogeneous middle-class suburbs. Moreover, during the last two decades, social access to homeownership was considerably limited following the decline of the two dominant housing systems that promoted working-class homeownership. This outcome was further reinforced by the rapid growth of housing credit that boosted –but also socially differentiated– housing demand as, at the same time, it led to strong increases of housing prices from the mid 1990s to the beginning of the sovereign debt crisis (Emmanuel 2004).

During the same period, changes in the labour market have also been important. The small family business was in constant retreat, in spite of the unexpected resource it found in the abundant and cheap immigrant labour force. Access to employment in the public sector was radically reduced affecting disproportionately lower social groups whose social mobility depended on it much more than the rest. Important problems have, however, also affected categories at the higher end of the occupational hierarchy, –like doctors, legal professionals and engineers– whose increasing numbers decreased individual opportunities leading them to substantial difficulties[3]: underemployment for the self-employed, employment in lower grade jobs than those expected following their training, pressure on their remuneration.

Demographic changes in the city have also had significant social effects. The population of Athens –as in most cities in economically developed countries– is ageing. In 1951 those over 64 years old represented approximately 5% of the total population, while in 2001 they had reached 15% (16,2% in the native Greek population) and 17,4% in 2011 (ESYE 1951; EKKE-ESYE 2005). Ageing –resulting both from the increase in life expectancy and the decrease in fertility rates– in the Greek familist welfare system does not only affect the solvency and the prospects of pension funds, but also the ability to provide care through the family: increasingly less children have to provide care for their parents, while the increasing number of childless people is by definition deprived of this type of resource. During the last twenty years, the (female) immigrant work force has covered a substantial part of this need, since it was difficult for native Greek women to combine traditional roles of domestic work with their increasing participation in the official labour market. In 1961 the percentage of Greek women aged 19-64 that were economically active was approximately 29%, while in 2001 it had reached 55% and was especially high (70%) for those between 25 and 34 (EKKE-ESYE 2005). It is obvious that these changes and the problems they lead to in the familist welfare context are a much greater burden for those who have no access to alternative solutions, i.e. for lower social groups and migrants.

Immigration has been the other very important facet of demographic change in Athens during the last twenty years. A large number of immigrants has settled in Greece and many of them –especially those that settled during the first fifteen years (1990-2005)– were able to get integrated rather smoothly in the local economy and society in spite of the lack of active policies to facilitate their integration (Cavounides 2002). The rather smooth integration of immigrants can be attributed to the positive economic climate that culminated in the preparation for the 2004 Olympic Games and, on the other hand, to available and accessible niches in both the labour and housing markets. In the former, it was mainly jobs that were abandoned by native Greeks as they moved upwards in the occupational hierarchy following the strong social mobility of the previous decades; and in the latter, it was the housing stock around the inner-city but also in peripheral locations that was devalued and often abandoned before the immigrant inflow (Maloutas 2014). In the second half of the 2000s, however, the rather smooth integration of immigrants started to change following the deterioration of the economic climate, but also following the change in the profile of new immigrants who no longer originated from the neighbouring Balkan countries but from war zones of the broader Middle-East, and were disproportionately male with very low educational skills. These changes led to the end of the serendipitous coincidence between qualities of

[3] Similar problems for these occupational categories seem to exist in Spain: from the mid 1990s to 2007 the increase in their remuneration was the smallest compared to all other occupational groups (Dominguez et al. 2012).

migrants and needs of the local economy and society (Arapoglou et al. 2009). Under current conditions it becomes increasingly harder to face immigration issues. New difficulties related to the scarcity of resources invested for immigrant integration have to be taken into account on top of the long absence of positive immigration policies. In this sense, immigrant groups –and especially those situated at the lower social positions (Arapoglou et al. 2009)– are in danger of being entrapped in conditions with no mobility prospects and in permanent threat of effective marginalization.

Therefore, changes in the labour and housing markets, as well as demographic changes during the last 20 years increased inequalities in terms of living conditions and mobility and paved the way for a deeper crisis impact.

3. THE IMPACT OF THE CRISIS

3.1. Increasing inequalities in education and employment

The negative social trends depicted earlier resulted from policies followed by Greek governments during previous decades and from features of the Greek economy that became increasingly problematic in a context of growing globalization. The policies adopted to face the crisis made the preservation of social rights a defensive battle and limited acceptable solutions to what neoliberal orthodoxy would prescribe. The dominant political discourse led to de-legitimating the policies of the past, putting forward their outdated clientelist character and avoided to address their socially redistributive effect that kept social inequality on a lower level than what could be reasonably expected from the absence of a properly organized welfare state. As a result, de-legitimation affected not only clientelist political management –an easy target on grounds of both morality and efficiency– but also social rights. Clientelist populism appeared as a relation of mutual guilt between political parties and the electorate, supposedly leading to excessive and unsustainable income redistribution, while other facets of former policies (like tolerance to tax evasion from elite groups) were much less visible in public debate and did not seriously affect anti-crisis policies.

The ongoing deregulation in the labour market (substantial shrinking of the public sector, free access –for investors– to formerly protected professions, precarization of working conditions in both the private and public sectors, compression of labour cost) has led to a social restructuring bearing significant similarities with the restoration of capitalism in former socialist countries: multifaceted increase of social inequality that theoretically should increase economic performance. An important difference, however, is that in Greece, and in the rest of South European countries, these changes could not be dissimulated behind claims for the restitution or expansion of political liberties.

Changes in education are also following a course that enhances social division in the name of boosting educational and eventually economic performance. From primary to higher education the option to increase diversity among educational units –justified by stressing the increasingly diverse demand– is leading to the increase of already substantial educational inequalities. Education is increasingly commodified as it is considered a service that has to satisfy the expectations of consumers (students/families) diversified in terms of both preference and solvency; it is also commodified following its new management ethics and the way its humanistic mission is increasingly downplayed. The changes in education along these lines –especially in higher education– started to be implemented in 2005 by introducing elements of foreign educational systems (especially from the US and the UK) that have pioneered such changes. The discourse was about modernizing the Greek educational system and about increasing its social accountability and efficiency, but the policy change can be summed up as a naive and superficial attempt to produce positive results through the adoption of isolated elements belonging to educational systems whose overall rationale was neglected or ignored. Some changes (e.g. the appointment of governing bodies on criteria of 'excellence' rather than on democratic vote from institutions' congregations or the evaluation of university departments following ill-prepared evaluation procedures) have been adopted, while others (e.g. the establishment of private universities) remain pending. As these changes begun to be implemented before the crisis, the most important impact of the latter was the substantial reduction of funding for education and research and the shrinkage of human resources through the complete stop of new hiring, the non-replacement of retiring personnel and the recent attempt to lay off a large number of university administrative employees that seriously disturbed the two older universities in Greece and led to long strikes during 2013.

The decision to increase choice and to diversify curricula and services to address a socially unequal demand in secondary education follows an international trend and leads to a growing social diversity in education, which is then translated to a more unequal access to higher education and to an enlarged reproduction of social inequality. Social and spatial differentiation of school quality was already an important factor of chances for social mobility in Athens before these policy changes (Maloutas et al. 2013). On the contrary, policies following a different direction –like the Zones of Educational Priority that would address educational and social problems in areas of multiple deprivation (Koutouzis et al. 2012)– were given insufficient resources and were quickly abandoned. The prospect of increasing inequality through education in a country under acute crisis is even gloomier when countries with a much more equitable social distribution of educational opportunities, like Denmark, face increasing difficulties in bridging social differences through education (Andersen 2012).

3.2. Housing and sociospatial inequalities

Changes in housing conditions and policies have affected the city in more direct ways. Homelessness has attained unprecedented levels (over 22.000 homeless in the whole country and 15.000 in Athens reported by Balampanidis et al. 2013) in a country where it used to be insignificant. If homelessness is the extreme form of housing deprivation, a host of other problems appeared in the housing market following the rapidly growing unemployment that reached 27%

in 2013. This is especially important in conditions of absence of social housing provision; social rented housing was never developed in Greece (Allen et al. 2004). This means that the neediest social groups were always unprotected by social housing policies, the latter being almost exclusively turned towards lower middle and working-class groups (namely workers and employees) with an income that made them eligible for access to homeownership (Economou 1987). The shock from the crisis had, therefore, to be absorbed within the private rented market; and it was partly absorbed due to the social profile of private landlords who are almost entirely small property owners whose total income largely depends on the rent of each of their very few tenants since they rarely own more than one or two units. These landlords are often retirees having invested their life's savings in small property holdings. Rent for them is often a complement to a small pension or their only income. Thus, the decreasing ability of tenants to face former rent levels resulted much more in substantial rent reductions than in evictions.

The situation became more complex when the impact of new property taxation policies reached the housing market. Following a long tradition, current property taxation was once more not decided considering its consequences on housing. Such policy measures were usually triggered, throughout the post-war period, by the expectation to mobilize the broader economy through house-building activity or to produce positive political effects by enabling access to homeownership rather than to improve housing conditions for the neediest part of society. Following the same approach, the new property taxes were decided to face sovereign debt, without considering their impact on housing. At first sight, taxing property seems a measure of social justice, drawing resources from those who have more instead from those who have less. However, in Southern Europe the social consequences of taxing real property are quite complex since homeownership and urban landed property are socially diffused.

Until recently, real property in Greece was taxed at a low rate through local tax (a centrally imposed tax in favour of municipalities collected together with the residence tax through electricity bills) and heavily taxed when transferred. Exemptions or lower tax rates applied for the acquisition of a first principal residence and for intra family transfers up to a certain amount of real property value. Large properties (over 300.000 euros) were taxed additionally following a progressive rate, but the owners of very large properties often avoided taxation through offshoring. The first new measure was to impose a substantial emergency/temporary property tax on all properties using electricity (therefore under some form of effective or potential use) with the explicit objective to meet the conditions of Greece's bailout memorandum by maximizing tax collection. The next step was to change the way income from property was taxed. This tax is henceforth calculated independently from other income. The most recent change was the introduction of a new property tax affecting all forms of real property independently of their actual use that unifies previous property taxes. At the same time, transfer taxes are considerably lowered (from over 10% to 3%) since 2014.

Lowering the transfer tax is supposed to facilitate transactions in a stagnating market. It may also be considered a response to a change of context. A high transfer tax was effective during the rapid urbanization years when transactions were abundant and inevitable, even though residential mobility within urban areas was very low both for new settlers and old urban residents.

The rationale of the new property tax policy is unrelated to housing concerns as it is absolutely turned to macroeconomic objectives. There are two main objectives in the recent changes concerning this policy:

- The increase of tax revenue from extending the taxation base and, consequently, the social diffusion of the tax burden.

- The mobilization of the economy through real property recommodification.

Recent changes introduced substantial taxation for all properties independently of their use, their value and the income they generate. A large number of small property owners are henceforth subject to taxation as income from property is taxed with a fixed rate independently and, therefore, is not exempt from tax if it is part of an annual income below the taxation threshold. At the same time, tax is substantially reduced for large income from property (the high tax rate on real property income (33%) is considerably lower than the high tax rate on other income (42%)) while the issue of tax evasion for large property holders is still not addressed, and special incentives are provided to foreign investors in properties over 250.000 euros (five year residence permit).

The stimulation of the property market through taxation seems to be a strongly defended position by the troika (EU, ECB, IMF) but somehow reluctantly adopted by the Greek government fearing its social and political impact. The idea is that idle properties make no sense and owners should be coerced to make their properties provide rent or sell them to others that would do so. Moving from transfer to withholding property taxes is a way of coercing owners to put their properties on the market for a lower price in order to face the cost of their properties' idleness. The impact of this policy may be very different depending on the social profile of landowners. When idle properties belong to large owners whose retreat from the market is a form of self-serving regulation of property values, policies of coercion through taxation may be justified. On the contrary, when most properties belong to small landowners who keep them vacant due to absent demand or rent them at any price offered by the market since they depend on that income or –in most cases– use them as their own residence, things are quite different. This type of petty landownership cannot refuse lower rent levels, especially in times of crisis, and thus has to accommodate lower levels of tenant solvency. Such flexibility of the private rented sector is especially important in a country without a social rented sector. Moreover, a large number of elderly outright homeowners use their decommodified properties as their main shield against poverty. The demise of small property owners in the effort to increase public revenue may be pregnant with unexpected social consequences.

The recommodification of small properties through taxation pressure means in fact dispossession of petty owners in favour of some other type of investors under the ideological conviction that a more mobile housing market is always a solution rather than a problem. Taxing the idle outright owned properties coerces their holders to sell in order to face their tax and other obligations produced under crisis conditions. This happens regularly since owners' other income is seriously reduced and the market value of properties has spectacularly decreased, while taxes are still calculated on the fictitious pre-crisis level of property values in the official tables used for that matter. Thus, owners are compelled to sell at extremely low prices and are in fact dispossessed. This is why there is complete reluctance to sell when it is possible to avoid it, and the number of transactions in recent years is very small.[4] Prospective buyers are not many within national borders, but could be found amongst middle-class pensioners or leisure home seekers from other European or more distant countries. This type of demand, however, is mainly related to properties in tourist areas and affects much less urban neigbourhoods in distress, where the percentage of small property owners is very high.

Under these new conditions it should increasingly start to make sense being a tenant in a low rent market, where homeownership is heavily taxed, compared to the previous long period when affordable cost led eventually to homeownership that was free of substantial tax charges after its acquisition. However, cataclysmic changes and a paradigm shift in tenure should not be expected unless the crisis and austerity policies remain long enough to really exhaust petty homeowners' reserve resources (see also Emmanuel, in this volume).

Homeownership in Southern Europe is the highest on the continent (it exceeds 80% in Greece and Spain and is quite close in Italy and Portugal (Allen et al. 2004)). For very long years the growth of homeownership has been a dynamic and lucrative process, often with important differences among these countries regarding the actors involved (e.g. large construction companies, banks and big landowners in Spain versus small constructors and petty landowners in Greece) and the patterns of sociospatial outcomes. In spite of differences, massive access to homeownership solidified conservative –and sometimes authoritarian– political regimes in the region during the first post-war decades: homeownership was one of the major socially integrating assets provided in these rapidly urbanizing poor countries since it constituted the foundation, as well as a clear symbol, of social mobility. Through the years, most of the housing stock in these countries have eventually become outright owned properties. At the same time, the demand for new stock for homeownership decreased due to demographic changes (less geographic mobility within the countries and reduced fertility rates that make family assets sufficient to cover current and future needs even if those are increased by the internal division of family households). We have reached a point where housing

[4] The number of transactions fell precipitously: -10% in 2010, -28% in 2011 and -38% in 2012 (Bank of Greece 2014).

properties are relatively decommodified and transactions –outside intra-family readjustments– are not decreasing only due to insolvent demand.

This makes previous policies that facilitated access to homeownership much less important, while rented housing begins to be reappraised both as a household strategy and a business prospect. The idle fixed capital embodied in the outright owned housing stock is seen as a problem by those who consider that commodifying everything leads to an ever increasing growth, and that this is the only way to insure economic and social sustainability. The destruction of social relations embedded in this idle form of fixed capital seems a probable unintended consequence of the current taxation policies of real property.

The dominant discourse about the crisis unearthed the clientelist policy frame of social regulation in post war Greece and easily de-legitimated it, implying that clientelism and whatever it was related to were the main culprits for current problems. This critique of clientelism on grounds of morality and efficiency has been absolutely eclectic in targeting redistributive policies and made no reference to other aspects of clientelist management, especially to relations of state power with elite groups. This critique of clientelism aimed eventually at de-legitimating social rights as resulting from clientelist arrangements and to make any claim to social equity seem out of place.

The deep crisis of public debt in Greece continues to bring important social consequences for the capital city due to the direct impact of the recession and to the impact of policies imposed by the bailout agreement (restructuring of social expenses and decrease of labour cost) that reduce considerably chances for future growth. These consequences contribute to strengthening social inequality, since crises usually create opportunities to violently redistribute income and wealth. Athens is therefore experiencing through the crisis the socially dividing impact of globalization that other cities experienced in less abrupt ways, while adjustment policies are exacerbating rather than attenuating the socially dividing effects.

After six years of crisis and recession the impact continues to be strong and the prospect for positive change continues to seem distant. The lower social strata in Athens are further losing their chances for social mobility, and part of them is in danger of persistent marginalization following long term unemployment. Marginalization in the labour market is coupled by increasing marginalization in education, where these strata are relegated, more than in the past, to options that are increasingly dissociated from future employment. Competition with the middle-classes, when the latter become also very anxious and intensify their family strategies to insure the prospect for their children's social mobility, makes things even harder. The situation is even worse for immigrants who have to face the enduring lack of integration policies, their curtailed social rights and their much smaller social capital. For the broader middle-class groups there is a tangible growing fear of declining social mobility. The loss of many family businesses and the limited prospects for self-employment in many prestigious professions, along with the drastic limitation of hiring by the public sector, make the reproduction of these strata an increasingly difficult process. The intergenerational fall to lower occupational positions, the high unemployment rate, the employment by necessity in jobs unrelated to training, the long wait for a satisfactory job, the long financial dependence from the parental household, the prolonged stay in the parental home, and the new wave of emigration are processes affecting middle and lower social categories that started before the crisis and were clearly reinforced since. We are probably facing the end of what Tsoukalas (1984) called the miracle of a lower middle-class society. The end of a social and political com-promise in the post-war period in which the ruling classes enjoyed an unequal share and privileged access to all kinds of important resources, while intermediate and working-class groups were not marginalized, but could reasonably hope for social mobility through education, self-employment and homeownership. This end of an era may be carrying further consequences due to its previous social and political organization, i.e. to the lack of an adequately organized system of social protection, to the familist limitation of the traditional solidarity culture and to the complete unawareness by current policies of the fact that they operate (within) a major change of the welfare paradigm. However, nothing is lost until it is really lost; the considerable opposition to current policies may always bring unexpected outcomes.

REFERENCES

Alexandri, G. (2013) *Social and spatial change at the centre of Athens: The case of Metaxourgheio*, PhD thesis, Harokopio University.

Alexandri, G. (2014) Reading between the lines: Gentrification tendencies and issues of urban fear in the midst of Athens', *Urban Studies.*

Allen, J., Barlow, J., Leal, J., Maloutas, T., Padovani L. (2004) *Housing and welfare in Southern Europe,* Oxford, Blackwell.

Amin, A. (ed.) (1994) *Post-Fordism: A Reader*, Oxford, Blackwell.

Andersen, H.T. (2012) The Solidity of Urban Socio-spatial Structures in Copenhagen, in Maloutas, T., Fujita, K. (eds) *Residential Segregation in Comparative Perspective. Making Sense of Contextual Diversity*, Farnham, Ashgate, 177-96.

Antonopoulou, S. (1991) *Postwar Transformation of the Greek Economy and the Residential Phenomenon,* Athens: Papazisis.

Arapoglou, V.P., Sayas, J. (2006) Urban sprawl and immigrant segregation in peripheral areas of the Athens metropolis, paper presented at the conference *Immigration in Greece: Experiences – Policies – Expectations*, Athens].

Arapoglou, V.P., Kavoulakos, K.J., Kandylis, G., Maloutas, T. (2009) The new social geography of Athens: Immigration, diversity and conflict, in Ventoutra, L. & Papataxiarchis, E. (eds) *The challenge of immigration, Synchrona Themata,* special issue, 31/107, 57-66.

Arapoglou, V.P. (2006) Immigration, Segregation and Urban Development in Athens: The Relevance of the LA Debate for Southern European Metropolises, *The Greek Review of Social Research*, 121(C), 11-38.

Arapoglou, V.P., Sayas, J. (2009) New Facets of Urban Segregation in Southern Europe: Gender, Migration and Social Class Change in Athens, *European Urban and Regional Studies*, 16(4), 345-362.

Arapogou, V.P. (2007) Immigrant segregation and housing inequalities in Athens: Exposed to affluence or deprivation? *Proceedings of the 8th National Geography Conference*, Athens, Greek Geographical Society.

Arbaci, S. (2007) Ethnic Segregation, Housing Systems and Welfare Regimes in Europe, *European Journal of Housing Policy*, 7(4), 401-33.

Arbaci, S. (2008) (Re)Viewing Ethnic Residential Segregation in Southern European Cities: Housing and Urban Regimes as Mechanisms of Margina-lisation, *Housing Studies*, 23(4), 589-613.

Atkinson, R., Bridge, G. (eds) (2005) *Gentrification in a Global Context: The New Urban Colonialism,* London, Routledge.

Balampanides, D., Patatouka, E., Siatitsa, D. (2013) The right to housing within the crisis in Greece, *Geographies*, 22: 31-44 [in Greek].

Bank of Greece, Direction of Economic Analysis, Department of Real Estate Analysis (2014) *Analysis results of the national real estate registry*, 1st trimester 2014.

Cavounides, J. (2002) Migration in Southern Europe and the case of Greece, *International Migration* 40(1), 45–69.

Domínguez, M., Leal, J.,, Martinez Goytre, E. (2012) The Limits of Segregation as an Expression of Socioeconomic Inequality: The Madrid Case, in Maloutas, T., Fujita, K. (eds) *Residential Segregation in Comparative Perspective. Making Sense of Contextual Diversity*, Farnham, Ashgate, 217-36.

Economou, D. (1987) Housing policy in post war Greece, *The Greek Review of Social Research*, 64, 56–129.

Economou, D. (1988). Land and Housing System in Post-war Greece: Functional Equivalents to the Keynesian Welfare State. In D. Economou, T. Maloutas (Eds) *Problems in the development of welfare state in Greece*, Athens, Exandas, 57-113.

EKKE and ESYE (2005) *Panorama of Census Data 1991–2001, Database and mapping application,* Athens.

Emmanuel, D. (2004) Socio-economic Inequalities and Housing in Athens: Impacts of the Monetary Revolution of the 1990s, *The Greek Review of Social Research*, 113A, 121-144.

ESYE (National Statistical Service of Greece) (1951) Census results of April 7 1951, vol. II.

Feinstein, S.S., Gordon, I., Harloe, M. (eds) (1992) *Divided Cities. New York and London in the Contemporary World,* Oxford, Blackwell.

Ferrara, M. (1996) The 'Southern' Model of Welfare in Social Europe, *Journal of European Social Policy* (6), 17-37.

Hamnett, C. (1994) Social polarisation in global cities. Theory and evidence. *Urban Studies*, 31, 401–24.

Hamnett, C. (1996) Social polarisation, economic restructuring and welfare state regimes, *Urban Studies* 33, 1407–30.

Harvey, D. (1989) *The Condition of Post-Modernity*, Oxford, Blackwell.

Hill, R.C., Fujita, K. (2003) The nested city: introduction, *Urban Studies*, 40(2), 207-17.

Hill, R.C., Kim, J.W. (2000) Global cities and developmental states, *Urban Studies*, 37(12), 2167-98.

Knox, P., Agnew, J., McCarthy, L. (2003) *Geography of the World Economy*, London, Arnold (4th edition).

Koutouzis, M., Kyrides, A., Maloutas, T., Papadakis, N., Syrigos, S. (2012) *Educational Priority Zones. Executive summary of the work of the Social Research Group*, Ministry of Education.

Lees, L., Slater, T., Wyly, E. (2008) *Gentrification,* London, Routledge.

Maloutas, T. (2007) Segregation, Social Polarisation and Inequality in Athens during the 1990s: Theoretical Expectations and Contextual Difference, *International Journal of Urban and Regional Research,* 31(4), 733-58.

Maloutas, T. (2014) The archeology of the decline of the city center: Residential location choices of affluent groups, in Tsilimpounidi M., Walsh A. (eds) *Remapping 'Crisis'. A guide to Athens*, Winchester, Zero Books, 26-42.

Maloutas, T., Alexandri, G. (2014). La gentrification dans des villes non gentrifiables ? Rénovation urbaine et changement des structures sociales dans le centre d'Athènes. In C. Rhein, E. Preteceille (eds.) *Gentrification, transformations des quartiers populaires et couches moyennes : notion unique, processus pluriels*, Paris, La Découverte.

Maloutas, T., Fujita, K. (eds), forthcoming, *Residential Segregation Around the World. Why Context Matters*, Faringham, Ashgate.

Maloutas, T., Karadimitriou, N. (2001). Vertical social differentiation in Athens: Alternative or complement to community segregation?, *International Journal of Urban and Regional Research*, *25*(4), 699–716.

Maloutas, T., Arapoglou, V., Kandylis, G., Sayas, J. (2012) Social Polarization and De-segregation in Athens, in Maloutas, T., Fujita, K. (eds), *Residential Segregation in Comparative Perspective. Making Sense of Contextual Diversity*, Farnham, Ashgate, 257-84.

Maloutas, T., Hadjiyianni, A., Kapela, A., Spyrelis, S., Valassi, D. (2013) Education and social reproduction: The impact of social position, school segregation and residential segregation on educational performance in Athens, RC21 Conference 'Resourceful Cities', Berlin.

Marcuse, P. (1989) Dual city: A Muddy Metaphor for a Quartered City, *International Journal of Urban and Regional Research*, 13(4), 697-708.

Marcuse, P. (2002) The Partitioned City in History, in P. Marcuse and R. van Kempen (eds) *Of States and Cities. The Partitioning of Urban Space*, Oxford, Oxford University Press, 11-34.

Marcuse, P., Van Kempen, R. (2000) Introduction, in P. Marcuse, R. van Kempen (eds) *Globalizing Cities. A New Spatial order?*, Blackwell, 1-21.

Marcuse, P., Van Kempen, R. (eds) (2002) *Of States and Cities. The Partitioning of Urban Space,* Oxford, Oxford University Press.

Mingione, E. (1996) Urban Poverty in the Advanced Industrial World: Concepts, Analysis and Debates, in E. Mingione (ed.) *Urban Poverty and the Underclass. A Reader*, Oxford, Blackwell, 3-40.

Mollenkopf, J.H., Castells M. (eds) (1991) *Dual city: Restructuring New York,* New York, Russel Sage Foundation.

Musterd, S., Ostendorf, W. (eds) (1998) *Urban Segregation and the Welfare State. Inequality and Exclusion in Western Cities,* London, Routledge.

Perrons, D. (2003) *Globalization and Social Change*, London, Routledge.

Porter, L., Shaw, K. (eds) (2009) *Whose Urban Renaissance? An International Comparison of Urban Regeneration Strategies,* London, Routledge.

Sassen, S. (1991) *The Global City: New York, London, Tokyo,* Princeton, Princeton University Press.

Sayas, J.P. (2004) An exploration of the social and spatial division of labour in the Athenian urban space', *The Greek Review of Social Research*, Social Change and Segregation Trends in European Cities, 113 (A), 167–200.

Sayas, J.P. (2006) Urban sprawl in peri-urban coastal zones', *The Greek Review of Social Research,* Social transformation and Governance issues in Eastern and Southern European Cities, 120 (B), 71–104.

Tsoukalas, K. (1984) Employment structure and the miracle of small and medium size firms, *Anti*, 213, 36.

Wacquant, L. (2008) *Urban Outcasts. A Comparative Sociology of Advanced Marginality,* Cambridge, Polity.

L'IMPACT SOCIAL ET SPATIAL DE LA CRISE À ATHÈNES

Résumé - *Cet article analyse l'impact de la crise financière sur les structures urbaines et sociales de la ville d'Athènes. Il montre le passage progressif d'une régulation traditionnelle du marché immobilier et du logement, aux accents fortement clientélistes, à une forte dérégulation durant la crise qui conduit à un net renforcement de la ségrégation sociale et spatiale.*

Mots-clés - HABITAT, INÉGALITÉS SOCIALES, ÉDUCATION

Région et Développement n° 39-2014

THE GREEK SYSTEM OF HOME OWNERSHIP AND THE POST-2008 CRISIS IN ATHENS

Dimitris EMMANUEL*

Abstract - *In order to examine the impact of the economic crisis on the home ownership pattern, we first review the basic structural features of the Greek housing system. This necessarily involves a discussion of the distinctive home ownership regimes found in Southern European countries as well as the place of the Greek case in this comparative framework. The main relevant distinctive characteristics of southern countries are high outright ownership rates, limited bank financing and strong "familism". After reviewing these aspects of the Greek "established" housing regime with data for Athens, the paper examines the major changes that took place during both the monetary revolution in housing finance from the late 1990s to 2007 and then during the current crisis, troika control and memorandum policies for strict austerity and "modernization" of the labor market. We conclude that these changes foreshadow a shift to a sharply modified "southern" housing regime rather than simply a prolonged economic shock.*

Key words - HOUSING, HOME OWNERSHIP, GREECE, SOUTH EUROPE

JEL Classification - R21, R28, I24

The original statistical material in this paper is based on preliminary survey results of the still ongoing research project SECSTACON ("Socioeconomic Class, Social Status and Consumption") awarded by action "Research Excellence" of the General Secretariat of Research and Technology and financed by the European Union and the Greek State.

---

* National Centre for Social Research, demmanuel@ekke.gr

1. GREECE AND THE SOUTHERN EUROPEAN HOME OWNERSHIP REGIME

It is widely recognized that Southern European countries have housing systems with distinctive characteristics. Allen et al. (2004, p.190) summarize their comprehensive review by pointing out a number[1] of major aspects in which Greece, Italy, Portugal and Spain are distinctive:

- High rates of home ownership coupled with sparse social rented housing.
- Relationship between access to housing and family structures (the extended family plays a strong role in supporting access to housing).
- Role of self-promotion and self-provision in supplying housing.

These three – or, rather, four aspects, since the absence or limited extent of social rented housing should be distinguished from the dominance of home ownership – make, at first glance at least, for a good description of a distinctive Southern housing regime. Given the preponderance of home ownership in the mixture, they also describe a distinctive home ownership regime. In this sense, are the family, the lack of social housing and self-promotion/self-provision integral aspects of a Southern home ownership regime and, furthermore, are they the only important ones? For instance, Mulder and Billari (2010) have argued that European home ownership regimes should be distinguished according to their place along two dimensions: the extent of home ownership and the extent of mortgage financing. The second dimension is a very important one for Southern housing where mortgage financing of owner-occupiers has historically been very limited and is still relatively limited, especially in Italy and Greece, even after the post-2000 credit expansion. However, the emphasis on mortgage financing availability essentially implies that getting a loan is the obvious "normal" road to home ownership: hence lack of financing should result in great difficulties for accessing ownership and limited ownership shares among middle and low incomes. It also implies an essentially economic decision of weighting the costs and benefits of alternative tenures.

This misses important aspects of the southern case where home ownership expanded despite limited financing and despite conditions in the rental sector (which, in Greece at least were very favorable). Its rationale was mainly about security, independence and accumulation of wealth that will also contribute to the support of the extended family. Thus, undue emphasis on the determinant role of limited credit availability without equal emphasis on the major role of high savings towards the accumulation of housing wealth will not suffice for the southern countries[2]. It is the accumulation of wealth and the achievement of independent ownership i.e. outright ownership that is the preferred goal rather

[1] In fact, their list includes a fourth aspect – " high level and significance of secondary housing" – which is not directly relevant to the system of housing provision for main residences that concerns us here.

[2] Mulder (2006) and Mulder, Dewilde & Smits (2014) essentially make this apparent in their examination of the role of credit availability as major determinant of home ownership patterns.

than the rational utilization of one's access to credit. Hence the importance of savings and the high extent of outright ownership in Southern countries even in recent times when easy financing has been more available. Thus, it is the extent of outright ownership that is the crucial aspect rather than its reverse, the limited extent of mortgage financing (which could very well imply increased renting). In this context, the crucial role of the familist system as a source of support in the form of real assets and funds for the reproduction of the home ownership regime (and therefore its significance as an integral part of the regime) becomes apparent (Cabre Pla and Modenes Cabrerizo, 2004; Kurz & Blossfeld, 2004a).

Things are more ambiguous for the role of self-promotion in the supply of housing or the role of the owner-building sector. This sector of housing production has been quite extensive in Greece in the past, especially for the working class, and it has arguably played a pivotal role in the formation of the pattern of widespread home ownership, however systematic data on its extent through time for the rest of the South are not easily available[3]. Moreover, we know that in relation to the predominant economic forms of housing production, land ownership and urban development, there are substantial differences between the four Southern countries. At the one extreme we have Spain where relatively large-scale organized land development and business-based large apartment building is the norm and at the other, Greece where land ownership is extremely diffuse and fragmented and building is dominated by a combination of owner building and small scale speculative developers most of which do not depend on bank financing.. In between, lie Portugal, more similar to Spain, and Italy, regionally divided in this matter and in many respects more similar to Greece.

However, there is an additional important distinctive aspect of the southern regime that has not been recognized as such in the European literature and clearly deserves to popular access to home ownership. In Southern European countries the extent of home ownership among the urban working class differs little from that of the middle class despite the lack of extensive policies favoring low-income households and despite the fact that tax relief policies favor more affluent strata. This egalitarian pattern, moreover, is in sharp contrast with inequalities in all other regions of economically advanced Europe though it often compares unfavorably with the extent of class equality in home ownership in Eastern Europe – the countries of the former Eastern Block. Eastern European countries, however, should be considered a special case in the context of this discussion since there has clearly been a massive transfer of house ownership after the fall of communist regimes and the emerging housing market has most probably not yet crystallized.

Until recently, there was very little in the comparative literature on North-South differences in the class pattern of home ownership. The major review by Allen et al. (2004) offers little on this matter while economic studies that confront this issue (e.g. Andrews et al., 2011) relate the extent of home ownership

[3] Allen et al. (2004) provide only sparse material but it seems that owner building was not developed as much and declined early in Spain and Italy.

to income categories – a notoriously inappropriate variable since household income is strongly related to the size of the household and the age of the head, both of which correlate positively with the extent of home ownership. Moreover, it is well known that social classes include households with very wide differences in current income as well as in wealth that differ in their success in achieving ownership. As a result, grouping by income category cuts across classes and, predictably, shows a more positive effect of income on the incidence of home ownership compared to class-based "structural" measures of economic resources. Based on such problematic material and on received ideas about "normal" housing economics, a common expectation is that there will be pronounced social inequalities in access to ownership in Southern countries (Kurz & Blossfeld, 2004b)[4]. These issues are reviewed in the massive collection of studies edited by Kurz and Blosffeld (2004a) on social inequality and home ownership in comparative perspective which explicitly examines the role of occupational class controlling for other significant determinants – especially the birth cohort, the stage in the life cycle and the urban-rural continuum.

The results show that in Spain simple distributions by age cohort show no significant correlation between class and the rate of home ownership save for differences in the *age* of achieving ownership. In Italy, similar conditions prevailed during the first three post-war decades while class inequalities have become more pronounced after the 1980s. Comparisons between the South and other European countries (and the U.S.) show that in most other countries – including some Northern "social democratic" regimes – inequalities are higher though direct comparisons are often quite difficult due to the complexity of statistical methods used and differences in data definitions and modeling.[5] There is also explicit consideration of the role of intergenerational transfers and the "self-building" sector in making for greater access to ownership – especially for the working class. The summary of results is somewhat inconclusive: though the importance of these factors is significant in Spain and Italy, their role is not as clear in other European cases (Kurz & Blossfeld, 2004c).

The review of the case studies on Spain and Italy in conjunction with the Greek evidence[6] shows that southern countries went through a first phase during the three post-war decades of massive urbanization and fast economic growth which established the main components of their particular home owning regime: extensive popular access to ownership based, on the one hand, on high

[4] An important exception is the Norris & Winston (2012) study that uses broad quartile income groupings and recognises both the major importance of the north-south division and the lack of significant inequalities in access to ownership in the south.

[5] I have used EU-SILC 2008 microdata comparing the differences in home ownership and *outright* (debt-free) ownership between major occupational groups. The findings show, that, excepting Eastern Europe, Southern countries consistently show minor inequalities compared to substantial ones in Scandinavian, Central and Western European countries. In any case, this argument is secondary to the purposes of this paper to burden it with a long series of tables. The statistical results are available on demand from the author.

[6] For the period up to 1991 cf. Emmanuel et al. (1996), Maloutas (1990).

rates of saving and family support rather than institutional financing and, on the other, on suitably "elastic" forms of housing production and supply that to an important extent, though in varying degrees, included popular access to land and owner-building. While the 1980s were, more or less, a period of stasis and gradual change, by the start of the 1990s a new phase was entered with accelerating deindustrialization, liberal pro-market reforms, increasing economic and monetary integration to the EU and fast expansion of mortgage and consumer credit. To these we may add the increasingly perceived impacts of the broader trends of increasing consumerism and demographic changes towards smaller households and later marriage – what, in combination, have been described as the "second demographic revolution" (Lesthaege, 2010).

2. THE CLASS PATTERN OF ACCESS TO HOME OWNERSHIP AND ITS CORRELATES: SOME DATA FOR ATHENS

Having established the outlines of the distinctive southern home ownership regime and its relationship with the Greek case, we may turn to a more detailed examination of the Greek urban housing pattern as it developed up to the time of the post-2008 crisis.

By the late 1950s, 60% of the urban middle class (professional, technical, administrative and managerial heads of households) owned their home. Households of industrial, construction and transport workers owned their homes by a significantly larger percentage - 69% - based on extensive owner-building (in part illegal on owned land) fuelled by the wave of rural-urban migration in the 1950s and early 1960s. By 1974, after the imposition of the junta, the speculative apartment boom and the slowdown in internal migration, the respective shares were 58% and 56%.[7] This reversal towards a more equal footing, was sustained up to the end of the 1980s. By 1988, the ownership shares in Greater Athens were 52.0% and 52.5%.[8]. During the 1990s there seems to have been a gradual increase in disparities in access to ownership. However, by the end of the 1990s ownership rates have started to be affected by the massive influx of immigrants. Using micro data from the 2001 census and excluding foreign nationals originating outside EU15, the respective ownership shares in Athens were 65.4% and 60.5% – an inequality ratio of 1,08 – thus there was indeed increasing inequality but at a much modest pace.

The explosive expansion of housing credit after 2000 apparently has shifted things towards a more equal class pattern though it had not, surprisingly, led to any significant increase in the rate of home ownership. Table 1 shows the tenure pattern in the whole Athens region for 2011 and 2013[9].

[7] Data from the 1957/58 and 1974 Urban Household Expenditure Surveys.

[8] Our estimates from micro data from the 1987/88 HES.

[9] Estimates for 2011 based on the rates for urban areas in 2011 adjusted by the difference between urban areas and the Athens Region calculated from the 2004/2005 HES. Data for 2013 for this and the following tables are from the SECSTACON 2013 NCSR survey. It should be noted that the Athens region for the NCSR survey is smaller, by a small percentage, than the Attika region reported in the HES surveys.

The class distribution of tenure types in 2013 Athens is shown in Table 2. In this case we are able to use a more theoretically concise model of the class structure, namely, the well-known European Socioeconomic Classification (ESeC) presented in summary form in the following matrix for the 9-class and 5-class versions (Harrison & Rose, 2006).

Table 1: Tenure forms, Athens Region 2011 & 2013[10]

Tenure forms	HES 2011 estimate	% Owners w Loan	2013 Survey	% Owners w Loan
Owned without loan etc.	55,0%		45,9%	
Owned with loan etc.	11,9%	17,8%	17,7%	27,8%
Offered free by the employer	0,1%			
Offered free by the family or others	6,8%		6,6%	
Rented at market rent	25,9%		29,8%	
Reduced rent by the employer	0,1%			
Reduced rent by the family or others	0,2%			
	100,0%		100,0%	

ESeC9		ESeC5	ESeC9
1	Large employers, higher mgrs/professionals	1	1 & 2
2	Lower mgrs/professionals, higher supervisory & technicians		
3	Intermediate occupations	2	3 & 6
4	Small employers and self-employed (non-agriculture)	3	4 & 5
5	Small employers and self-employed (agriculture)		
6	Lower supervisors and technicians		
7	Lower sales and service workers	4	7
8	Lower technical workers	5	8
9	Routine workers	5	9

Table 2 shows the rates for each tenure type for the broad working class (7,8 & 9) with and without migrant households. In the second case the rates of rental housing fall drastically – especially in the case of older skilled workers (8). Thus, the ownership inequality ratio, the ratio of the ownership rate of class 1 to that of working class categories, reaches values very close to unity. Regarding the other "southern" aspects of the home ownership regime, they are clearly present in 2013 Athens: a low percentage of owners with active mortgage loans (below 30% with the exception of small employers and own account workers), a high extent of ownership for a large city and a significant share of units offered free by the extended family – an attribute that is common across classes. The only attribute that shows a clear positive correlation with class position is

[10] It should be noted that while the ownership rate difference between the two estimates (66,9% - 63,6%) is most probably due to sampling errors – though a limited shift away from owner occupation towards renting due to the effects of the crisis after 2011 should not be ruled out, the difference in the rates of mortgaged properties is surprising given the fact that housing financing between 2011 and 2013 has been minimal to zero.

the rate of mortgage financing. This is more evident if we examine how owners acquired their home in the simpler 5-class ESeC schema in Table 3. The table also shows the insignificant role of state housing provision.

Table 2: Tenure type shares by socioeconomic class (ESeC9) Athens Region 2013

ESeC9h	Owners w/o Loan	Owners w Loan	Free	Renters	Total Households	%Owners w Loan	Inequality ratio
1	51,0%	21,7%	7,9%	19,4%	100,0%	29,8%	1,00
2	49,4%	21,3%	5,9%	23,5%	100,0%	30,1%	
3	46,3%	16,3%	7,5%	29,9%	100,0%	26,1%	
4	47,8%	16,9%	5,1%	30,2%	100,0%	26,1%	
5*							
6	41,2%	22,0%	6,2%	30,5%	100,0%	34,8%	
7	41,3%	13,3%	6,4%	39,0%	100,0%	24,4%	1,24
8	42,4%	17,1%	7,4%	33,2%	100,0%	28,7%	1,20
9	39,5%	13,6%	5,2%	41,6%	100,0%	25,7%	1,29
	46,0%	**18,1%**	**6,3%**	**29,6%**	**100,0%**	**28,3%**	
	w/o migrants						
7	44,3%	14,3%	6,9%	34,5%	100,0%	24,4%	1,15
8	54,9%	20,4%	8,6%	16,0%	100,0%	27,0%	0,93
9	50,2%	16,1%	6,3%	27,4%	100,0%	24,3%	1,02

Source: SECSTACON survey micro data, our calculations. (*) Farmers not included.

The main importance of Table 3 lies in the measurement of family transfers of property. If we add the cases of acquisition through inheritance or family transfer and "antiparochi" i.e. the exchange arrangements between owners (mainly by inheritance) of plots or older low-rise buildings and developers[11], we have nearly 40% of owners that had the benefit of some family property (last column). We must add to that substantial shares of "buying" or "building" without loans that were essentially based on the sale of inherited or transferred family properties[12].

Family contribution is not limited to the utilization of real wealth: cash transfers and assistance in the repayment of a loan are also important. Table 4 shows the extent of family contribution recognized by its recipients without reference to its specific form. It is notable that "medium" and "small" support, presumably more in the nature of cash transfers, is positively correlated with higher class positions.

Table 3 also shows the extent of owner building. This, for the 2013 Athens owners, reaches a rather modest share of 12,6% - much lower than rates in the past. However, a substantial share of owning through family transfers or inheritance is based on past owner building within the extended family, a fact we must also take into account. As is evident in the data shown in Table 5, small-scale building, which largely implies owner-building, was much more extensive

[11] "Antiparochi" was much more important during the 1960s and 1970s where massive house building and redevelopment of low-rise housing stock took place.

[12] I have estimated that the direct or indirect contribution of family property in the late 1980s clearly surpassed 50% (Emmanuel, 1994).

in the past given the structure of current building stock. Since in the Greek context, buildings with one to three dwellings are near-exclusively owner build, the contribution of this mode of housing production for home ownership, especially for the lower working class is clearly significant.

Table 3: How owners acquired their home, Athens Region 2013

ESeC5h	Bought w/o loan	Bought w loan	Inher transf.	Anti*	Built w/o loan	Built w loan	State progr	Total hous/ld	Bought w loan	Family propert
1	15,7%	35,8%	33,0%	2,3%	6,2%	6,7%	0,3%	100%	42,5%	35,3%
2	14,4%	29,2%	40,1%	2,0%	6,9%	5,4%	2,0%	100%	34,7%	42,1%
3	17,7%	25,1%	36,0%	3,9%	10,6%	5,5%	1,3%	100%	30,5%	39,9%
4	21,5%	28,9%	34,7%	2,5%	5,8%	4,1%	2,5%	100%	33,1%	37,2%
5	21,7%	25,2%	36,2%	2,1%	6,9%	2,1%	5,9%	100%	27,2%	38,3%
	17,5%	30,3%	35,2%	2,5%	7,3%	5,2%	1,9%	100%	35,6%	37,8%

*Antiparochi: Exchange arrangement with the developer of the plot owned by the household.

Table 4: Family contribution

	Family contribution				
ESeC5h	Large	Medium	Small	No contrib.	All
1	29,3%	18,8%	11,3%	40,6%	100%
2	31,6%	18,4%	8,1%	41,9%	100%
3	29,1%	16,4%	9,9%	44,6%	100%
4	42,7%	10,1%	9,0%	38,2%	100%
5	27,2%	12,2%	8,0%	52,6%	100%
	30,2%	16,3%	9,8%	43,6%	100%

The Greek urban home ownership regime has been formed and sustained through the four decades after the end of the Civil War (1949) by growing incomes and high savings rates mainly due to economic growth. In addition, it has been supported by an inflow of funds from the Greek diaspora. It also benefited greatly by the land value gains brought by rapid urbanization and the growth of tourism and by the increasing prosperity of farmers who sent their offspring to the cities. These flows of capital were spread throughout each social class, and most especially the working class, both "horizontally" through relationships of kinship and marriage and across generations through inheritance and transfers. Thus, accumulation of wealth should not be viewed from the perspective of an atomistic household model but rather as a collective process spanning – through social networking – over a whole class.

Table 5: Home owners, size of building

ESeC5h	One-two dwellings	Three to five dwellings
1	31,4%	53,2%
2	33,8%	50,0%
3	37,5%	63,1%
4	27,7%	51,3%
5	37,0%	55,5%
All	33,8%	55,1%

To these factors we may add the relative favorable trends in housing costs. The introduction of mechanization in construction that lasted well into the 1980s and the overproduction of dwellings that was fuelled by high savings, the inflow of resources and liberal planning controls kept construction costs, rents and prices in step with inflation. Even by the second half of the 1990s when prices have started to increase much faster than inflation, the affordability index (the ratio of average dwelling price to annual income) for all social classes in Athens was within very reasonable limits (Table 6). Estimates for the end of the 1980s for Athens, a time of high prices and stagnant incomes, show index values higher by about 20%. [13] The relative uniformity of the affordability index across classes is based on extensive differences on the size and quality of the average dwelling between classes. Popular access to property depends on flexible housing standards: the acquisition or building of often sub-standard dwellings and the gradual move through improvements or additions to socially acceptable conditions.

Table 6: Affordability index by class, Athens 1998/99

Social Class	Avg. Annual consumption	Avg.Dwelling current price	Affordability Index
Middle Class	11.404	28.699	2,52
Lower m.class	8.369	23.250	2,78
Working class	7.179	18.354	2,56
Lower w.class	5.228	16.085	3,08

The lack of strict planning or quality controls, moreover, allows the operation of marginal production forms such as owner building and petty commercial developments that make possible the adequate supply of lower income housing. In the long run, partly through income growth and partly through the major demographic shift, common to all Southern European countries, that started in the early 1980s toward much lower fertility and smaller households, even the acquisition of housing of modest size allowed for significant improvement in housing conditions.

3. IMPACTS OF THE CREDIT BUBBLE AND THE 2008 CRISIS

The Greek crisis started as a banking crisis in 2008, became a fiscal crisis in 2009 and then, with the imposition in 2010 of international control by the "troika" of IMF, EU and the ECB and the strict austerity measures turned into a deep recession of unprecedented proportions (Diagram 1). From the point of the housing sector, problems were accentuated by the fact that the general economic crisis was preceded by a severe building slump that started in 2006 due to overbuilding caused by the explosion of building starts fuelled by credit expansion and the excessive peak in 2005 caused by the untimely announcement of planned changes in housing taxation. The combination of recession with the

[13] Our estimates of the affordability index across classes for the end of the 1980s in Athens show larger values ranging between 3,0 and 3,6.

building slump resulted in a drop of house building to near-zero levels (Diagram 2).

The bubble of housing credit expansion that have started in the second half of the 1990s when low interest rates and more relaxed loan-to-value ratios became available for the first time in Greek post-war history, lasted until 2007. Since then, the drop in the flow of funds for housing was rapid and steep : by 2011 the flow was negative i.e. the household sector advanced more for loan repayment than it received for financing of housing (Diagram 3). The Greek household sector showed during the first post-war decades exceptionally high savings ratios. After the stagnation of the 1980s, the economic slump of the early 1990s and, then, the expansion of consumer credit after the mid-1990s, the saving ratio fell to fluctuating slightly above zero. The credit-led growth after 2004 increased this ratio somewhat but it soon fell to near-zero levels again. When the crisis struck, the savings ratio dropped rapidly to *negative* levels approaching -10% (Diagram 4).

Fuelled by too much liquidity chasing a slowly growing housing supply, relative i.e. real housing prices more than doubled from the mid-1990s to 2007 during the credit bubble. Following the combined effects of the building slump and the crisis, dwelling prices, according to the Bank of Greece index, fell rapidly reaching 1999 levels by 2013 – a fall by more than 40% (Diagram 6).[14] Surprisingly, real rents (adjusted for inflation) also rose at a steep pace steadily after the early 1990s up to 2010 when they started to fall. The index of housing expenses (rents plus heating, water and electricity), however, continued to rise despite the fall of consumption demand (Diagram 5).

Unemployment in the country as a whole was about 11% by the end of the 1990s. After the period of growth (2001-2008) it fell to 7,2% (2008 second quarter, Athens Region: 6,0%). By the second quarter of 2013 it had risen to a disastrous 27,1% and, in Athens, to 28,1%. Moreover, unemployment was sharply skewed by class: as Table 7 shows, it was as much as three times higher among the working class than among the "Salariat" (class 1 in ESeC5). The rates for the intermediate class and the self-employed were much lower but still more than double that of the salariat. Obviously, such high unemployment rates and such wide class disparities will have a major impact on household incomes, security and savings. However, of greater importance for the class pattern of income distribution in the long-run are the wide-ranging changes effected during 2011-2013, in implementation of memorandum policies, in minimum wages, protection from layoffs, work contracts, collective wage agreements–and, more generally, deregulation towards more "flexible" employment relations (INE-GSEE, 2013).

In the field of housing policy three major changes took place as part of memorandum policies.

[14] The index was based on realtors data up to a point and then on bank data on mortgage loans. While I have no quarrel with the index up to 2009, the number of sales backed by loans decreased drastically after that point. There is a very strong possibility that the index reflects expediency conditions and has a strong downward bias.

1. National Net Disposable Income 1994-2013 (2009 prices, peak 2007)

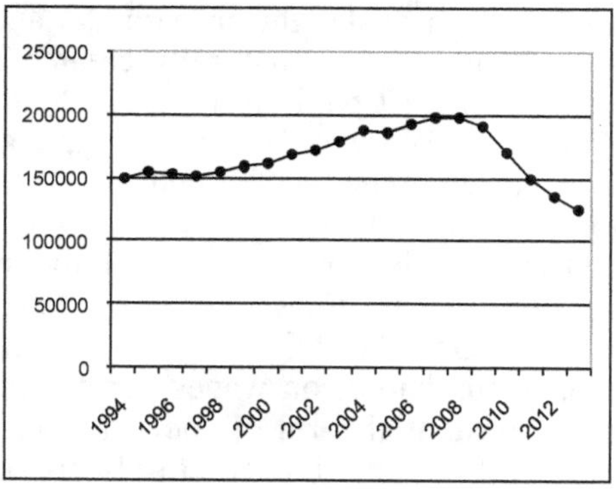

2. New dwelling permits 1980-2013, (peak 2005)

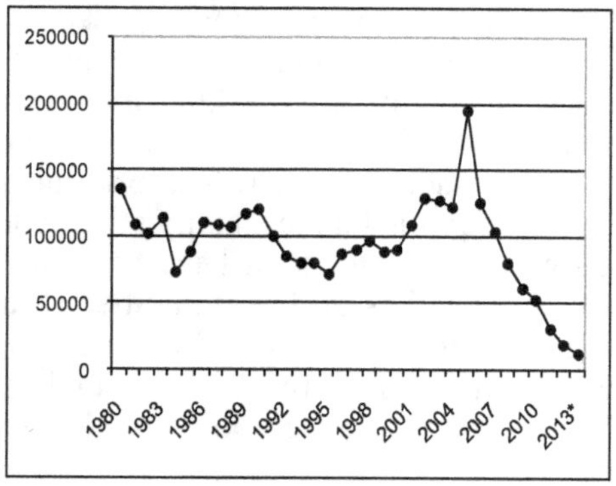

3. Housing finance 1994-2013 (change in balances) (2009 prices, peak 2007)

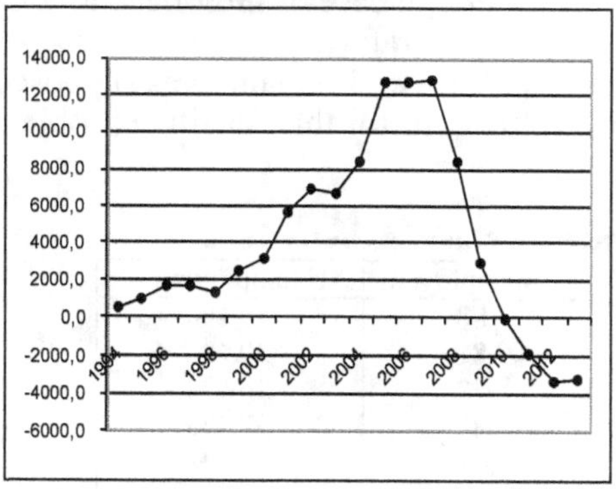

4. Household gross savings ratio 2000-2013 (peak 2007)

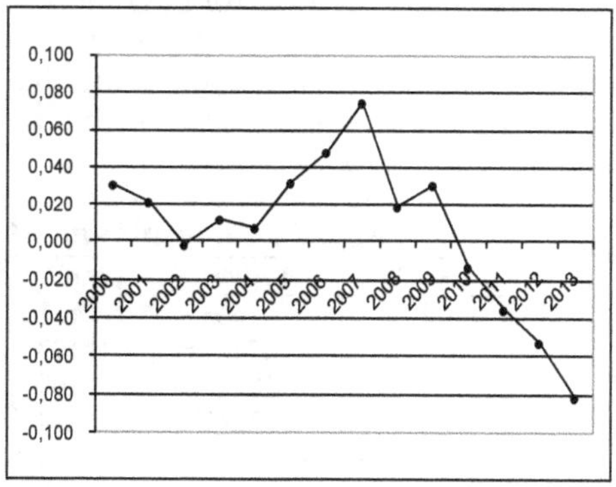

5. Relative Price Index for Rents & Housing Expenses (1994 – 2013, rents peak 2011)

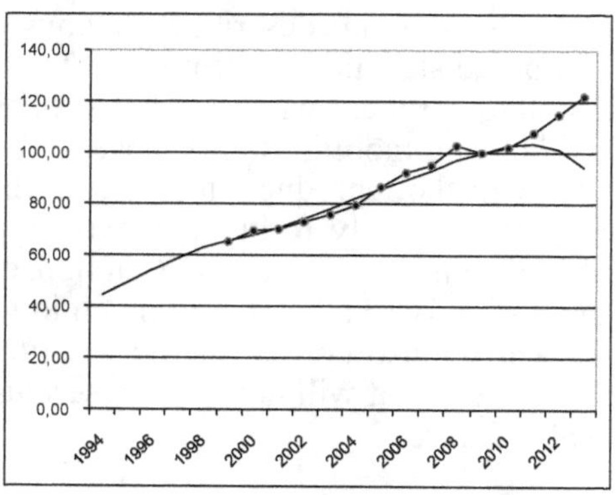

6. Relative Price Index for Dwellings, Athens Urban Area (1993-13 peak 2007)

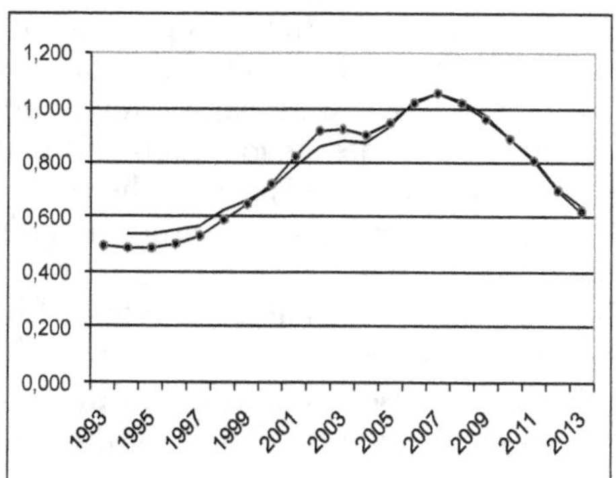

Notes: Series based on data drawn from the sites of ELSTAT (Greek Statistical Authority) and the Bank of Greece. Constant 2009 magnitudes and "relative" price indices are adjusted by the consumer price index with 2009 as the base year. The time series data are available on demand from the author.

First, starting in 2011, a new property tax was imposed, for purely fiscal purposes, on all built property. The tax as a rule did not amount to more than 1% of housing values but imposed at a time of an onslaught on earnings and pensions, general tax increases and rising unemployment, naturally created a furor. Secondly, all subsidies and tax relief on interest paid on mortgage loans were repealed. Thirdly, and most importantly, the Workers Housing Organization was sacked in 2012 (its programs were discontinued at the end of 2011). W.H.O supplied a marginally small number of built housing (for ownership) but a significant number of heavily subsidized loans to buyers and owner-builders and an equally significant number of lump-sum rent subsidies to renters belonging to a broad category of wage and salary earners.[15] W.H.O. programs, which were self-financed by special social insurance surcharges on wages partly paid by the employer, were, effectively the only substantial form of social housing policy in the Greek context. Its dissolution had obvious immediate effects on the class patterning of access to housing. To these policy changes we may add, somewhat on the positive side, legislation passed with the aim of protecting mortgage loan debtors from eviction and auctioning in case of prolonged arrears when their dwelling was the main residence. This moratorium on evictions from main residences, that helped avoid the dramas observed in Spain, was supposed to end by the beginning of 2014 but a final settlement for this sensitive problem will have to wait.

Table 7: Unemployment rate by class, Athens 2013

ESEC5	Active	Employed	Unemployed	Unemployment
1	646	558	88	13,6%
2	274	193	81	29,6%
3	286	209	77	26,9%
4	221	134	87	39,4%
5	294	171	123	41,8%
N.A.	33	1	32	97,0%
All active	1754	1266	488	27,8%

Source: SECSTACON Survey data.

The impacts of the sweeping negative economic trends described previously will obviously take some time to register in broad statistical indicators of housing conditions and housing tenure patterns although there was already by 2013 evidence of widespread actual and planned housing mobility in response to the problems of the crisis. From the point of view of the reproduction of the established home ownership regime conditions are extremely forbidding: we have the drastic fall in access to stable jobs and in incomes and, as a result, in household savings – the latter accentuated by the difficulty of adjusting to much lower levels of consumption, coupled with the near standstill of housing production and the precarious condition of the banking system that will not allow a serious restart of housing financing for the foreseeable future.

[15] We estimate, based on 1999 survey data for Athens (MRC-DEPOS Survey) that WHO loans and rent subsidies reached much less than 10% of owners and renters, respectively, within a broad working class category. During 2007-2011 WHO faced severe economic problems due to excessive commitments in the past few years and programs were curtailed substantially.

On top of all that, there is the legacy of the pre-2008 credit bubble that appears to have shifted housing prices, despite the drastic price reductions during the crisis, to disproportionately higher levels relative to incomes. While the affordability index fluctuated around 2,5-3,0 before the bubble across all classes, even conservative estimates for 2013 show values significantly above 5,0 and possibly even approaching 6,0 – again in similar levels among classes (Table 8).[16] Given that transactions in the housing market add up to minimal numbers, it all depends on the extent to which owners will resist further price reductions below these levels (much reduced as they are compared to the peak of the price boom) when market activity resumes.[17]

Table 8: Estimated housing affordability index by class, Athens 2013

ESeC3h	Monthly Income (EUSILC) (2008)	Reported Monthly Income	Adjusted by +25%	Estimated Price of dwellings	Affordability Index	A.I. with price adj by -15%
1	3.118	1.837	2.296	172.280	6,25	5,31
2	2.108	1.234	1.542	115.256	6,23	5,29
3	1.624	978	1.223	91.573	6,24	5,30

Estimates based on EU-SILC08 and the 2013 SECSTACON survey.

4. ECONOMIC SHOCK OR HOUSING REGIME SHIFT?

That the Greek housing system is undergoing a major economic shock that will shape housing outcomes for more than a decade from now is undisputable. Will these changes shift the system substantially towards a new housing regime? This question clearly invites answers close to pure speculation but, nevertheless, we may consider some responses. An obvious candidate for the new home ownership regime is, of course, the model of liberal housing systems based on the dominance of bank financing for housing acquisition and class inequality in access to housing wealth given inequalities in incomes and job security and the imposition of market-based norms for housing supply. In such a system the role of household savings towards housing wealth and family transfers will atrophy since both economic policies and market conditions will favor alternative assets and savings among lower incomes will be minimized.

I think that the available evidence makes any across the board realization of such a scenario improbable. First, mortgage financing, given the problems of the Greek banking system and the legacy of mortgage finance excesses both in Greece and abroad, will at best – for the foreseeable future – recover up to a

---

[16] The 2013 SECSTACON survey recorded respondents' estimates on their monthly income range and the market value of their dwelling. We adjusted income figures upwards according to EU-SILC data for 2008 and the currently estimated average fall in household incomes. We also adjusted dwelling values downwards by a reasonable 15% since households tend to make somewhat inflated estimates.

[17] The fall in the Bank of Greece price index for dwellings implies much lower values and therefore, an affordability index in the order of 3,5. However, as noted already, it is based after 2010 on a minute number of transactions and cannot be considered representative of conditions at much higher levels of market activity.

point that will resemble its limited and class-biased role in pre-2000 days. Second, the familism system and the associated propensity for saving towards housing ownership c strengthened by the small property system – are aspects of social organization that will persist, albeit much weakened. Third, there is the legacy of accumulated real wealth that, assisted by lower fertility and lower rates of household formation, can sustain, to a diminishing but substantial extent, property transfers across next generations.

To risk a prediction, the general home ownership rate will most probably decrease by a substantial margin given the squeeze on savings and the shift in affordability conditions while the extend of class inequalities in access to ownership, given the removal of existing working class housing assistance and the new sharp inequalities in unemployment and labor market conditions, will certainly increase. But, unless an onslaught on small property of proportions akin to historical cases of "primitive accumulation" takes place, the over-all pattern will continue to be a case of the traditional southern regime, albeit a sharply modified one – an impoverished and more unequal pattern.

REFERENCES

Allen J., Barlow J., Leal J., Maloutas T., Padovani L. (2004) *Housing and Welfare in Southern Europe,* London: Blackwell.

Andrews, Dan and Aida Caldera Sánchez (2011), “The Evolution of Homeownership Rates in Selected OECD Countries: Demographic and Public Policy Influences”, *OECD Journal: Economic Studies*, 2011/1.

Bank of Greece (2013) *Report of the Governor,* Athens: Bank of Greece.

Bernardi, F., Poggio, T. (2004) "Home ownership and social inequality in Italy" 187-232 in Kurz K., Blossfeld H., (2004), op.cit.

Cabré Pla, A., Módenes Cabrerizo, J. A. (2004) "Home ownership and inequality in Spain", pp. 233-254 in Kurz, K., Blossfeld, H.P. (2004), op.cit.

Dewilde, C., Lancee, B. (2013) "Income inequality and access to housing in Europe", *European Sociological Review,* 29:6:1189-1200.

Doling, J., Ronald, R. (2010) "Home ownership and asset-based welfare", *Journal of Housing and the Built Environment,* DOI 10.1007/s10901-009-9177-6.

Emmanuel D. (1994) "On the Structure of Housing Accumulation and the Role of Family Wealth Transfers in the Greek Housing System" 168-201 in R. Forrest & A. Murie (eds) *Housing and Family Wealth,* London: Routledge.

Emmanuel D., Velidis S., Stroussopoulou E. (1996) *Low income Housing in Greece*, Athens: DEPOS.

Emmanuel, D. (2013) "Balancing autonomy, status and family in the transition to adulthood: class and housing aspects of the Southern European model in Athens, 1987-2004", 19-41 in Forrest, R. & Yip, N. (eds) *Young People and Housing: Transitions, Trajectories and Generational Fractures, Routledge.*

Hajnal J. (1983) "Two Kinds of Pre-Industrial Household Formation System" in Wall R., Robin J., Laslett P. (eds) *Family Forms in Historic Europe,* Cambridge: Cambridge University Press.

Harrison, E., Rose, D. (2006) *The European Socio-economic Classification (ESeC) User Guide,* Institute for Social and Economic Research, University of Essex, Colchester.

INE-GSEE (2013) *The Greek Economy and Employment*, Athens:INE-GSEE.

Kaila, E. (2014) "The Experience of Social Housing as Self-financed Benefit: Prospects and Potential", Paper delivered in the Workshop on Housing, National Technical University, April 4.

Kertzer D. I. (2002) "Living with Kin", 40-72 in Kertzer, D. I., Barbagli, M. (eds) *Family Life in the Long Nineteenth Century 1789-1913,* New Haven and London: Yale U.P.

Kurz, K., Blossfeld, H.P. (eds), (2004) *Home Ownership and Social Inequality in Comparative Perspective,* Stanford: Stanford University Press.

Kurz, K., Blossfeld, H.P. (2004) "Introduction: social stratification, welfare regimes and access to home ownership", pp. 1-20 in Kurz and Blossfeld (2004), op.cit.

Kurz, K., Blossfeld, H.P. (2004) "Summary and conclusions" pp. 365-378 in Kurz & Blossfeld (2004), op.cit.

Lesthaeghe R. (2010) "The Unfolding Story of the Second Demographic Transition", *Population and Development Review*, 36 (2): 211–251.

Maloutas, T. (1990) *Athens, Housing, Family: Analysis of the Post-war Housing Practices,* Athens: EKKE & Exantas.

Mulder, C.H. (2006) "Home-ownership and family formation", *Journal of Housing and the Built Environment,* DOI 10.1007/s10901-006-9050-9.

Mulder, C.H. and Billari, F.C. (2010) "Home-ownership regimes and low fertility", *Housing Studies*, 25(4), 527-541.

Mulder, C.H., Dewilde, C., Smits, A. (2014) "The Intergenerational transmission of homeownership across Europe", paper for the European Population Conference, Budapest, June.

Norris, M., Winston, N. (2012) "Home –ownership, housing regimes and income inequalities in Western Europe", *International Journal of Social Welfare,* 21, 2: 127-138.

Poggio, T. (2013) "The first steps into the Italian housing system: inequality between generational gaps and family intergenerational transfers", 42-63 in Forrest, R. & Yip, N. (eds) *Young People and Housing: Transitions, Trajectories and Generational Fractures,* London:Routledge.

Reher, D. S. (1998) 'Family Ties in Western Europe: Persistent Contrasts', *Population and Development Review,* 24(2): 203-234.

PROPRIÉTÉ IMMOBILIÈRE ET LOGEMENT EN GRÈCE APRÈS LA CRISE DE 2008

***Résumé* -** *Cet article étudie l'impact de la crise économique de 2008 sur le logement en Grèce. Il montre comment les caractéristiques du système de propriété immobilière se rapprochent des autres pays du sud de l'Europe, à savoir la forte propension des ménages à être propriétaire, le poids de l'héritage et des donations familiales et le faible recours au crédit immobilier. Cet article examine l'évolution du logement et du marché immobilier à Athènes entre 1990 et 2007 puis après la crise de 2008, grâce à une base de données originale permettant de considérer les différentes catégories de résidents.*

***Mots-clés* -** HABITAT, ÉCONOMIE IMMOBILIÈRE, GRÈCE

NOTE ET DOCUMENT

TOURISM AND THE ECONOMIC CRISIS IN GREECE - REGIONAL PERSPECTIVES

Andreas PAPATHEODOROU[*] and Pavlos ARVANITIS[**]

Abstract - *The ongoing deep recession has largely affected the great majority of economic activities in Greece in the primary, secondary and service sector. Not surprisingly, therefore, tourism is not an exception to this pattern although any generalization should be treated with caution due to the complex character of the particular activity and the inherent asymmetries between domestic and inbound tourism. For this reason, the present paper aims at investigating the impact of the Greek economic crisis on inbound and domestic tourism flows (measured by nights spent in hotel accommodation establishments) in Greece at NUTS2 (i.e. periphery) and NUTS3 (i.e. prefecture) levels using also supportive evidence from a hotel supply point of view. Based on different spatial indexes, the paper assesses the tourism profile of each spatial unit under consideration and studies patterns of regional tourism concentration (convergence and divergence) for the period 2005-2012. Building on the results, a new geography of tourism seems to emerge in Greece where the clear losers are those regions, which had specialized predominantly in domestic tourism. From a policy perspective, this stresses the need to expedite the internationalization of the tourism profile of the regions in question to overcome the adverse effects of the economic crisis.*

Key words - TOURISM, GREECE, ECONOMIC CRISIS, NUTS2, NUTS3

JEL Classification - R12, R58, L83

The authors would like to cordially thank Dr George Tataris, Laboratory of Cartography and Geoinformatics, Department of Geography, University of the Aegean for kindly designing and providing Map 1.

[*] University of the Aegean; a.papatheodorou@aegean.gr
[**] University of the Aegean; p.arvanitis@aegean.gr

1. INTRODUCTION

Tourism is a major sector of the service economy at a world level. According to the United Nations World Tourism Organization (UNWTO) 1,087 million international tourist arrivals were recorded in 2013, accounting for 873 billion euros in tourism receipts, i.e. close to 803 euros per arrival (UNWTO, 2014). These figures refer solely to international tourism and hence do not include the significant economic impact of domestic tourism, which is admittedly, however, difficult to measure from a statistical point of view. Interestingly and in spite of all contestable methodological issues regarding the concept of the tourism multiplier (i.e. the equivalent of the Keynesian multiplier – for a related discussion *see* Stabler, Papatheodorou and Sinclair, 2010), tourism seems to account for 9% of world GDP and is responsible for one every eleven jobs when all direct, indirect, induced effects are considered (UNWTO, 2013). At a national level, Greece had 17.9 million international tourism arrivals (excluding cruise passengers), which accounted for 12.2 billion euros in 2013 (UNWTO 2014). This corresponded to 681 euros per arrival, i.e. 15.2% less than the world average. In any case, Greece has about a 1.5% share of the world tourism market and a 2.9% of the European one (SETE 2014); moreover, and when all different impacts are considered, tourism contributes by 16.4% to the Greek GDP generating 18.3% of total employment in the country (SETE 2014).

Ironically, perhaps, the importance of tourism for the Greek economy became widely acknowledged and understood by policymakers in the aftermath of the recent economic recession, which has been the severest suffered by Greece in the last fifty years. In particular, Greece has experienced six consecutive years of recession between 2008 and 2013 as a result of the austerity measures introduced to face the public debt crisis with devastating effects on the welfare of its citizens. In 2008, GDP per capita amounted to 20,795 euros while in 2013 this was reduced to 16,302 euros, i.e. a 21.6% decrease in just five years. Moreover, the unemployment rate rose from 7.6% in 2008 to 26.9% in 2013 and general government gross debt as a percentage of GDP from 112.9% in 2008 to 175.7% in 2013 (IMF 2014). All the above have naturally resulted in major discontent among Greek citizens setting the fundamentals for civil unrest unless the problem is successfully addressed the soonest possible. Inbound tourism (i.e. foreigners visiting Greece) is now treated as the potential *Deus ex Machina*, which can generate new wealth helping the country to overcome the crisis: after all, domestic tourism (i.e. Greeks visiting areas in Greece outside their usual residence) has primarily wealth redistribution effects within the country and is expected to have strongly suffered as a result of the economic crisis; while outbound tourism (i.e. Greeks visiting places abroad) has a negative impact on the current account balance and limited effects on total employment in Greece.

Yet, the majority of policymakers do not seem to realize that a sole focus on the aggregate scale of international tourism arrivals is likely to cause more problems than benefits. According to the World Economic Forum (2013) the ranking of Greece in the world tourism competitiveness index list has significantly deteriorated since the beginning of the crisis, as the country ranked 24th

in 2009 but only 32nd in 2013 out of 140 countries. Greece seems to offer a typical, non-sophisticated 4S (i.e. sea, sun, sand and sex) tourism product of low value-for-money in terms of price competitiveness (127th position) while the impact of bureaucracy on foreign direct investment is extremely negative (133rd position) as a result of lack of transparency in policymaking (118th position) and political rivalries at national and local level. Therefore, and given the overall concern about the environmental sustainability of the Greek tourism industry development (106th position), a simple reduction of labour costs and related tourism prices may have a short-term positive impact on tourism arrivals but a doubtful long-term effect on per capita tourism receipts, which is a good proxy for successful delivery of augmented service quality.

In addition, and before introducing any grandiose tourism plans, it is very important to properly assess the impact of the recent economic crisis on tourism in Greece at both national and regional levels. In fact, from a supply point of view, tourism in Greece is highly concentrated as 40% of hotel beds in 2013 (out of a total of 773,445) were located in just two areas namely the island (and NUTS2 administrative region) of Crete (166,370 beds) and the Dodecanese islands (143,864 – part of the South Aegean NUTS2 administrative region (Hellenic Chamber of Hotels 2014). This concentration is unlikely to have changed at least significantly over the last few years due to the significant time involved in building new hotels and the reluctance to close down existing ones. Nonetheless, concentration of demand in terms of inbound and domestic tourism may have been affected by the recent economic crisis for many reasons with subsequent repercussions for regional policy and future hotel supply initiatives. This paper aims at studying this important issue in further detail. In particular, section two reviews the available literature on the impact of economic crisis on tourism setting theoretical hypotheses regarding the possible evolution of inbound and domestic but also (albeit to a much lesser extent) of outbound tourism at national and regional levels. Section three reports the empirical results of the study, which puts the emphasis on the evolution of bed-nights spent by foreigners and Greek tourists in hotel accommodation establishments at national, NUTS2 and NUTS3 level between 2005 (i.e. shortly before the crisis) and 2012 (i.e. the last year of available data to date). Finally, section four summarises and concludes, acknowledging limitations and making suggestions for future research.

2. LITERATURE REVIEW AND HYPOTHESES AT ISSUE

The literature review is structured into two parts. The first discusses the impact of an economic crisis on tourism (with a very clear emphasis on leisure activities) while the second focuses on potential implications for Greek tourism, making a number of research hypotheses which are subsequently explored empirically.

2.1. Tourism and Economic Crisis – A Generic Approach

An economic crisis may affect tourism as a result of both economic and non-economic factors (Goh 2012). Using a traditional microeconomics approach, an economic crisis is expected to affect tourism as a result of changes in income and prices. More specifically, an economic crisis has a recessionary effect on the economy leading to the reduction of GDP as well as of disposable income at a household level. Interestingly perhaps, in a world of rational, forward-looking individuals with perfect information, such a crisis should not affect tourism consumption: this is because the latter is not a function of current income but of permanent one as outlined by Modigliani and Brumberg (1954) and Friedman (1957) in their related theory. In essence, any adverse impacts caused by economic crises have already been discounted and incorporated into the consumption pattern of tourism and any other goods, as this depends on the income made by an individual throughout their entire life cycle. In reality, however, nobody has perfect information as the future is unknown and characterised by stochastic disturbances: moreover, the very idea of rationality of economic agents has been challenged long time ago; at best individual behaviour may be characterised by bounded rationality, where behaviour is intentionally rational but up to a certain extent only (Simon 1961). Consequently, tourism demand is expected to be largely affected not by permanent but by current income as argued by Keynes (1936) in his *ad hoc* yet powerful macroeconomic consumption function.

Having the above in mind, it may be consistently assumed that an economic crisis may have two major effects on tourism consumption as a result of a reduction in current income. The first is related to a cutback decision, i.e. individuals keep travelling to the same tourism destination and/or enjoying the same holiday characteristics in terms of accommodation, catering, etc. albeit to a lesser degree compared to the period before the crisis (Eugenio-Martin and Campos-Soria 2014, Page et al 2012, Smeral 2009). For example, instead of holidaying over a period of two weeks, people may now decide to travel away only for ten days. The second effect emerges as a result of substitution due to the income elasticity mechanism. Although tourism is generally regarded as an income elastic service, when different destinations and services are considered then the concept of inferiority (which is related to goods and services whose consumption increases when income falls) may become valid (Stabler et al 2010). In particular, an income reduction is expected to negatively affect relatively luxurious tourism destinations and/or services (e.g. a five star hotel) due their high income elasticity and positively destinations of low sophistication and/or tourism services of basic standards. Worryingly perhaps, and in case the Environmental Kuznets Curve hypothesis is valid, then consumers are also likely to move away from the consumption of more expensive, "green" tourism services favouring cheaper alternative activities and service providers who do not internalise the negative production externalities of tourism (Papatheodorou et al. 2010), thus leading to an environmental "race to the bottom" (Stabler et al 2010). Admittedly, the reality is even more complex as income elasticities are not constant over time but are usually asymmetrically affected by the business cycle because "the relative fall in tourism demand during a severe economic downturn –reflecting, as it does, the greater threat to a person's financial situation and job security– will be steeper than the relative increase in demand during an economic upturn of a similar magnitude" (Smeral 2010: 37).

In any case, however, the impact of income elasticity is likely to have important spatial connotations affecting among others the relation between outbound and domestic tourism. In particular, under the blanket assumption that outbound tourism is usually more income elastic than domestic tourism, an economic crisis is likely to make individuals switch away from international travel to the benefit of domestic destinations. As discussed by Sheldon and Dwyer (2010), this may have positive implications for the domestic tourism industry in terms of both employment and income. Domestic tourism is not an important generator of new income but predominantly contributes to the redistribution of income at a country level possibly to the benefit of remote regions with tourism interest as is the case of the Aegean islands in Greece. In periods of serious recession, however, domestic tourism is largely associated with a rise in VFR (Visiting Friends and Relatives) flows: therefore, people who previously travelled abroad on holidays now decide not only to stay at their home country but even to go to a relative's or friend's second/holiday house to avoid spending money on tourism accommodation and restaurants. In such a case, an economic crisis may negatively affect outbound tourism without benefiting (at least to a major extent) tourism providers at a domestic level. Moreover, the above is also a matter of spatial scale: travelling domestically in Luxembourg is a very different thing from travelling domestically in France due to a sheer difference in the size of the two countries. Similarly travelling abroad but within the European Union may be more expensive for the inhabitants of the Eastern Aegean Sea Islands who can visit Turkey (i.e. travelling outside European Union) simply by crossing the sea with a ferry, i.e. the role of border regions should be also somehow considered; whereas the very remoteness of the Canary Islands may explain to a large extent (in addition to the good climate) why people there may prefer to stay at home during their holidays.

In addition to the impact of an economic crisis on tourism as a result of changes in income, it is also important to consider the possible effect of changes in prices. In a neo-classical economic context, prices of goods and services as well as the remuneration rates of all factors of production is characterised by upward and downward flexibility. Hence, a decrease in tourism demand as a result of a reduction in income may also lead to a reduction in prices as tourism service providers try to stay competitive in the marketplace incentivising consumers accordingly (Ritchie et al 2010). Such a reduction in prices may prove financially sustainable provided that input production costs (especially wages) also decrease as a result of the recession. As a result of the above, real income (i.e. in terms of purchasing power) increases and the negative effects of the initial fall in nominal income on tourism demand are somewhat mitigated. Ironically perhaps, domestic tourism may now become more expensive as the substitution away from outbound tourism may put an upward pressure on local tourism prices; nonetheless, to the extent that the economic crisis is serious enough and the VFR tourism flow proves substantial such an effect is not likely to materialize.

In any case, the very assumption behind the flexibility characterising the price mechanism is the existence of competitive markets. Nonetheless, in the case of imperfect competition the outcome may be different (Stabler et al 2010). More specifically, in good economic times powerful oligopolies may acquire supernormal profits by potentially abusing their position in the market due to a relaxed consumer mentality. Subsequently, these profits may be used to sustain the operations of these companies in a recessionary period without reverting to a price reduction. In fact, if the oligopolists expect that the economic crisis will be only of transitory nature, they may prefer to keep their prices constant instead of reducing them as it may prove too difficult to raise them again when the crisis is over as a result of potential customer discontent. This neo-Keynesian argument (Campell and Mankiw 1991) may explain price stability in the tourism sector even in a period of crisis. As argued by Papatheodorou (2004), tourism is characterised by a notable dualism in its market structure as large transnational conglomerates in transport, accommodation and tour operations co-exist with small traditional firms. While the latter belong to the competitive fringe and may decide to cut significantly their prices in a period of economic crisis, this may not be the case with transnational companies, which may decide to keep their prices constant, at least for a while, supported by their strong brand name in the market. Of course, if an economic crisis is no longer regarded as transitory but as permanent, then it is expected that all tourism service providers, including the large oligopolists, will respond accordingly.

The last argument highlights the very important role of expectations in shaping the behaviour of both tourism consumers and producers in a period of economic crisis. If people become pessimist about the future fearing that they may lose their job as a result of the recession then the end effect on tourism consumption may be far greater than what would be predicted by the current reduction in income [as discussed previously in Smeral (2010) but also in Alegre et al. (2013)]: in that case, price reductions are expected to have only a limited effect and people may switch towards the consumption of other goods and services altogether (Sheldon and Dwyer 2010). Of course not all consumers react in the same way as tourism behaviour is characterised by substantial heterogeneity (Nicolau and Masiero 2013). Moreover, the very fact that people have experienced rising incomes over an extended period of time, makes it difficult to predict the exact impact of an economic crisis on their consumer behaviour (Bronner and Hoog 2012) as both under-reaction (due to emotional denial of the new situation) and over-reaction (due to exaggerated fear) may emerge.

This consumer pessimism may also be reflected in reduced business confidence among tourism service providers who then decide to avoid any new investments in the sector with potentially detrimental effects on service quality as a result of the gradual degradation in the existing tourism infrastructure. Still, an economic crisis may also have a positive impact. Using a Schumpeterian argument, Papatheodorou et al (2010) argue that an economic crisis makes inefficient firms exit the market while at the same time it may provide the remaining tourism companies with the necessary time to undertake deep organizational restructuring due to low opportunity costs. Such a restructuring may set the fundamentals for increased efficiency in the future and hence assist tourism enterprises in exiting the crisis. The very assumption behind this argument, however, is that the crisis will not last too long to deny any financial opportunity for restructuring altogether.

In conclusion, the implications of an economic crisis for tourism may be largely explained via the effects triggered by changes in income and prices. Still, these are by no means easy to predict while it is important in any case to consider the specificities of the market suffering from an economic crisis, as now discussed in the next sub-section of the paper.

2.2. Tourism and Economic Crisis – The Case of Greece

The economic crisis has largely affected Greek tourism as also discussed in the introduction of this paper. In the following, the possible implications are studied at two different levels, namely inbound and domestic tourism with reference also to outbound tourism.

Based on the analysis of the previous sub-section, and by making the very realistic assumption that the global economic crisis has affected Greece to a much larger extent than the tourism origin countries in Northern Europe but also elsewhere in the world, it is expected that Greek inbound tourism may be positively affected. This is because Greek tourism service providers may reduce their prices to gain competitiveness, while North Europeans may also switch away from long-haul sunlust destinations to the benefit of those in the vicinity, i.e. in the Mediterranean Region.

On the other hand, however, and while the international literature suggests that a crisis in a tourism destination may not have a negative effect in inbound tourism arrivals (Prideaux 1999) the very crisis in Greece has created very bad publicity for the country essentially destroying any good brand name achieved in the aftermath of the 2004 Olympic Games. As a result, increased perceived country uncertainty may discourage visitation leading to reduction of inbound tourism due to its inherent risk-aversion (Araña and León 2008). A fortiori, the economic crisis results in a decrease of demand for business tourism as the level of economic activity lowers. The latter may also result in a loss of scale economies, market exit and eventual monopolization of certain tourism and other services. Illustratively, back in 2008 (i.e. before the recession), the Athens – Chios (i.e. a Greek island off the Turkish Aegean coast in the area of Izmir) air route was serviced by three competing carriers, namely Olympic Airlines, Aegean Airlines and Athens Airways. This active competition had resulted in low prices and a relatively high level of service quality. Nonetheless, shortly after the recession started Athens Airways went bankrupt while later on Aegean Airlines pulled out of the market; moreover, in October 2013 Aegean was given the green light by the European Commission to acquire Olympic (which was facing very severe financial problems as a result of the crisis) leading to the creation of a monopoly in the majority of domestic routes in Greece with possibly negative repercussions on prices and quality.

All the above may then be taken advantage by international tour operators who may put great pressure on Greek tourism service providers to accept substantially reduced prices if they are to remain on the tourism map. If Greek tourism service providers succumb to this pressure, then inbound tourism is likely to rise from an arrivals perspective although the end result on tourism receipts may be difficult to predict. On these grounds, the following research hypothesis may be stated:

Hypothesis 1: As a result of the economic crisis, inbound tourism arrivals are expected to increase but related tourism receipts may decrease at least when considered at a per capita level.

Moreover, no clear classification into luxury and income-inferior tourism destinations can be made in Greece, at least when considering NUTS 2 and NUTS 3 levels of analysis. Consequently, the economic crisis is not expected to have resulted in a substantial change of the existing spatial pattern of inbound tourism. Hence, it is reasonable to make the following hypothesis:

Hypothesis 2: The economic crisis is not expected to have affected the existing pattern of inbound tourism spatial concentration at NUTS 2 and NUTS 3 levels.

As for domestic tourism in Greece, this may be positively affected by the economic crisis as a result of people switching away from the consumption of more expensive outbound tourism activities. Still, it is important to note that the nature of domestic tourism in Greece is very different from the one of outbound: the former is mainly related to sunlust, while the latter to wanderlust activities (i.e. primarily related to city-breaks for cultural and shopping tourism purposes). Hence, any expected substitution will be rather limited.

Moreover, the extent of economic crisis in Greece has led to the emergence of the 'staycation' phenomenon (as elsewhere in Europe too), where people prefer to spend their annual leave from work at home, i.e. not going away on holidays, in order to save money. In addition to the above, the impact of VFR tourism flows should be considered as Greeks who previously spent money staying in local tourism accommodation establishments (usually at much higher prices compared to those paid by foreign tourists as part of an inclusive package), now prefer to holiday as guests of their friends and relatives. Finally, domestic tourism is likely to have suffered as a result of the reduction in economic activity and business tourism. In fact, Greeks who usually stay in tourism accommodation establishments outside the high season are usually those engaged in business tourism activities such as industrial visits. Therefore, and given also that no clear classification into luxury and income-inferior tourism destinations can be made in Greece at least when considering NUTS 2 and NUTS 3 levels of analysis, the following hypotheses can be made:

Hypothesis 3: The economic crisis is expected to have negatively affected domestic tourism

Hypothesis 4: The economic crisis is not expected to have affected the existing pattern of domestic tourism spatial concentration at NUTS 2 and NUTS 3 levels.

As a final remark, it is important to note that inbound and domestic tourism in Greece show different patterns of spatial distribution. Leisure tourism in Greece is dispersed throughout the country with some emphasis on the islands while business tourism is expectedly located in the two main urban centres of Athens (part of the Region of Attiki at NUTS 2 and the Prefecture of Attiki at NUTS 3 levels) and Thessaloniki (part of the Region of Central Macedonia at NUTS 2 and the Prefecture of Thessaloniki at NUTS 3 level). On the other hand, inbound tourism (which is clearly of leisure nature) is predominantly concentrated on the Region of Crete (which has four prefectures at NUTS 3 level) and the Region of South Aegean (which has two prefectures at NUTS 3 level). As a result, the concentration of internal tourism (i.e. inbound + domestic) is less acute compared to inbound tourism. Nonetheless, as a result of the economic crisis, domestic tourism in both Athens and Thessaloniki is expected to have suffered considerably. Hence the final hypothesis to be made is as follows:

Hypothesis 5: The economic crisis is expected to have positively affected the existing pattern of internal tourism spatial concentration at NUTS 2 and NUTS 3 levels.

3. METHODOLOGY AND EMPIRICAL RESULTS

In the following, the validity of the above discussed research hypotheses is assessed diagrammatically based on secondary data analysis. First, the evolution of inbound tourism at a national scale between 2005 and 2013 is assessed using data collected from the UNWTO, the IMF and the Bank of Greece. This is complemented by an analysis of key features in hotel supply. Subsequently, the evolution of nights spent by inbound, domestic and all internal tourists in hotel accommodation establishments between 2005 and 2012 at NUTS2 level (13 regions) is analysed using data collected from the Hellenic Statistical Authority. Nights spent by domestic tourists in hotel accommodation establishments cannot capture the substantial effect of VFR flows but is the best possible proxy to somehow measure domestic tourism. Finally, the evolution of the concentration pattern exhibited by inbound, domestic and total internal nights spent in hotel accommodation establishments between 2005 and 2012 at both NUTS 2 and NUTS 3 levels (51 prefectures) is discussed based on calculations of the Gini coefficient: this ranges between zero and one, taking the former value in case of an equal distribution and the latter in case of total polarization. A similar analysis is also undertaken at NUTS2 level for the available hotel supply to provide an integrated approach and hence enhance the understanding of developments in tourism demand.

3.1. Analysis at National Level

Graph 1 shows the evolution of five different time series with respect to inbound tourism in Greece over the period 2005-2013 namely arrivals, nominal receipts, per capita receipts (i.e. nominal receipts divided by arrivals), real receipts (i.e. deflated nominal receipts) and real per capita receipts (i.e. real receipts divided by arrivals). It is evident from the graph that while arrivals (14.7 million in 2005 as compared to 17.9 million in 2013) and nominal receipts (13.7

billion USD in 2005 as compared to 15.9 billion USD in 2013) have risen over time, this is not the case of the other three series, which are of crucial importance when strategic sustainability issues are also considered. Illustratively, real per capita receipts fell from 929.9 USD in 2005 to 745.6 USD in 2013 in constant 2005 prices, i.e. a reduction of 19.8%! Thus, it seems that Hypothesis 1 is empirically validated, at least diagrammatically.

Graph 1. Inbound Tourism in Greece, 2005-2013

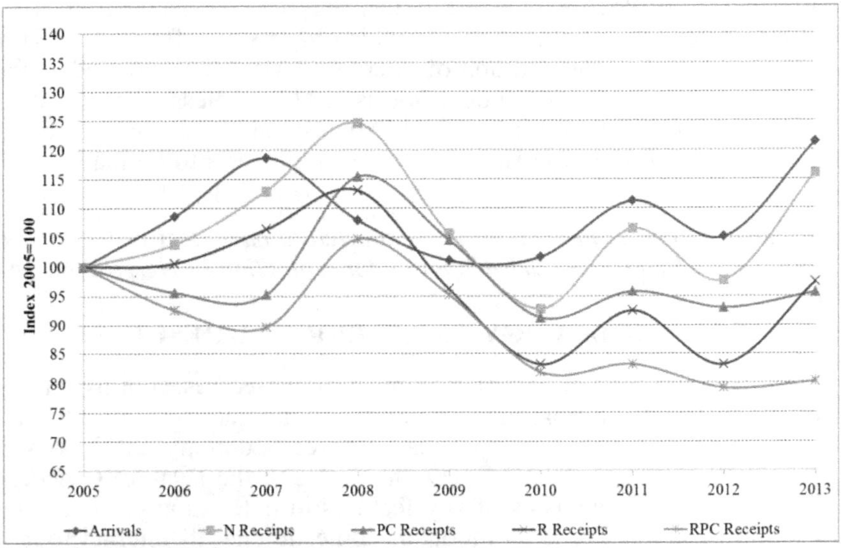

Source: UNWTO, IMF, Bank of Greece - compiled by the authors.

Graph 2. Operating Hotel Beds in Greece, 2006-2012

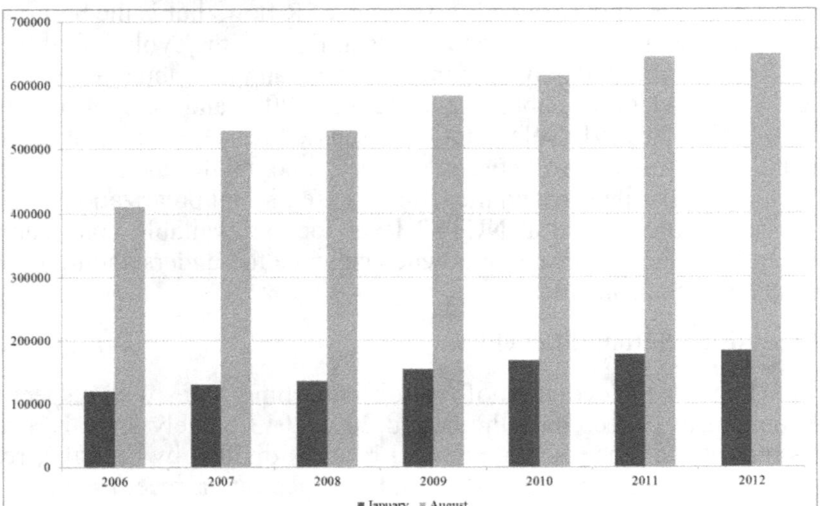

Source: Hellenic Statistical Authority - compiled by the authors.

Graph 2 shows the evolution of hotel beds available for sale (i.e. in operation) over the period 2006 – 2012 in January and August. Because of the seasonality characterizing the Greek tourism product, studying bed availability in both the off-peak and the peak period is justified. As expected, bed availability in August is much higher than in January with the related ratio ranging between 3.41 and 4.05 over the period examined. In both months, there is a clear increasing trend which levels off in 2012. One could possibly argue that there is still an increase in capacity well after the economic crisis has started. This is because a building process has been probably under development well before the financial crisis emerged; therefore the completion of the investment might have taken place in either 2011 or 2012. In any case, SETE has often argued against the pathology of overcapacity characterizing the Greek hotel accommodation market. This is also consistent with the negative trend exhibited by real per capita tourism receipts as discussed earlier.

Table 1. Hotel Supply in Greece, 2013

	5*	4*	3*	2*	1*	Total
Units 2013	361	1277	2358	4203	1478	9677
% Units 2013	3,73	13,20	24,37	43,43	15,27	100,00
Rooms 2013	57878	100289	95674	119157	28334	401332
% Rooms 2013	14,42	24,99	23,84	29,69	7,06	100,00
% Rooms 2009	11,60	25,30	23,60	31,80	7,70	100,00
Beds 2013	117555	194010	183722	223932	54226	773445
% Beds 2013	15,20	25,08	23,75	28,95	7,01	100,00
Beds/Unit 2013	325,64	151,93	77,91	53,28	36,69	79,93
% 1-20 Rooms 2013	12,20	34,80	37,60	42,80	65,40	42,80
% 21-50 Rooms 2013	13,00	24,10	35,50	45,90	32,70	37,30
% 51-100 Rooms 2013	15,50	15,30	19,90	10,30	1,70	12,20
% Over 101 Rooms 2013	59,30	25,80	7,00	1,00	0,10	7,80
% Seasonal 2013	48,50	48,70	44,90	59,40	56,60	53,60
% All-Year Round 2013	51,50	51,30	55,10	40,60	43,40	46,40
RevPAR Aug 2013	176,06	114,33	68,11	55,99	46,57	102,16
RevPAR Aug 2011	156,90	107,42	69,99	62,67	48,51	100,16
Employees / Room Aug 2013	0,62	0,38	0,25	0,18	0,12	0,36

Source: Hellenic Chamber of Hotels (2014).

Table 1 presents some key statistics regarding hotel supply in Greece in 2013; comparison with previous years is also made in several cases. In particular, the total number of hotel units in Greece amounted to 9,677 in 2013 – almost half of them (i.e. 43.43%) belonged to the 2* category confirming the widespread perception that the majority of Greek hotels aim primarily at the price-conscious budget traveller who is likely to have been adversely affected by the financial crisis. This is consistent with the reduction of Revenue Per Available Room (RevPAR) in the case of 1*, 2* and 3* hotels between 2011 and 2013; illustratively, for 2* hotels this reduction was close to 10.6%, i.e. from 62.67 down to 55.99 euros. Quite different is the case of upmarket hotels. Although 5* hotels represent a tiny part of the overall number of hotel units (3.73%), their share in the number of rooms and beds is much higher, i.e. in the area of 15%, as 59.30% of them have over 101 rooms. In fact, a typical 5* hotel has 8.8 times the beds of a 1* hotel, i.e. 325.64 vis-à-vis 36.69. Interestingly, the share of 5* hotels in the total number of available rooms increased between 2013 and 2009, i.e. to 14.42% from 11.60%: moreover, and given that the RevPAR for 5* and 4* hotels increased between 2011 and 2013 by 12.21% and 6.4% respectively raises hope that the decline of real per capita international tourist receipts shown in Graph 1 will be eventually reversed. To support the above it should be also noted that the majority of 5* hotels operate all-year round sustaining employment 5.1 times more than 1* hotels, which are usually very small, family-owned businesses facing substantial financial problems as a result of the recent crisis.

3.2. Analysis at Regional Level

Map 1 presents the thirteen (13) administrative regions of Greece at NUTS2 level. The Region of Attica and the Region of Central Macedonia are characterized by the existence of large urban centres, namely Athens and Thessaloniki respectively. Both cities have a large number of hotels to cater primarily for domestic business tourism. Likewise, the Region of Crete and the Region of South Aegean are very popular among inbound tourists and many hotels in these regions operate solely on a seasonal basis.

Map 1. Administrative Regions of Greece

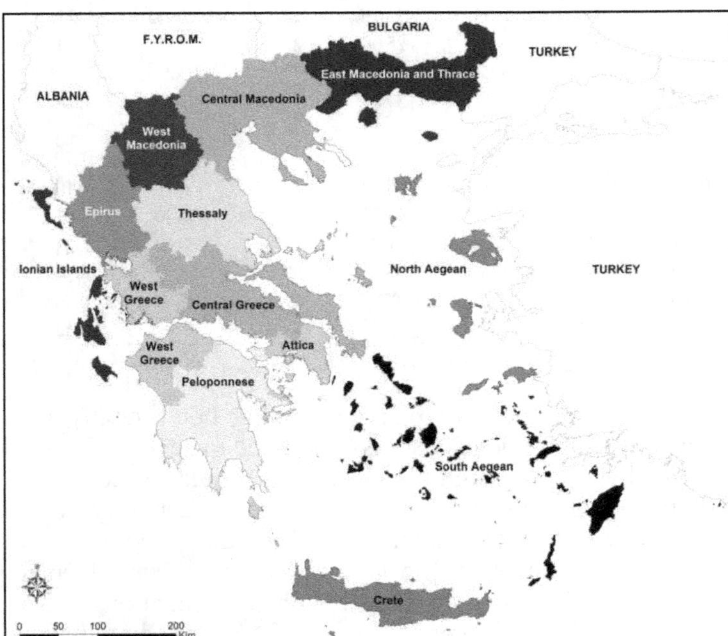

Graph 3 shows the evolution of domestic hotel nights at NUTS2 level over the period 2005-2012. This clearly reflects the impact of the economic crisis. There is a peak in 2009 followed by a sudden and substantial decrease since then which continues up to 2012. The decrease in the number of nights is on average 30% when comparing 2012 to 2009. As expected Attica and Central Macedonia dominate the picture, but the Ionian Islands seem to be the region most severely affected by the crisis in relative terms experiencing an almost 40% decrease in the nights spent by domestic tourists. Having the above in mind, Hypothesis 3 is largely validated.

Building on Graph 2, Graph 4 shows the evolution of hotel supply (i.e. available beds for sale) in January over the period 2005-2012. Given that January is very representative of the off-peak season, studying the evolution of hotel supply during that month provides a good proxy of the hotel supply available primarily for domestic tourists. As expected and similarly to Graph 3, Attica and Central Macedonia dominate the picture. Nonetheless, and in contrast with Graph 3, supply shows an upward trend in all regions throughout the period (which somewhat stabilizes between 2011 and 2012) possibly due to construction inertia and lag effects discussed earlier in Graph 2. As a result, hotel occupancy rates have decreased to the detriment of profitability in an era of severe financial crisis. Illustratively, occupancy rate in Attica (Central Macedonia) was 27.9% (24.4%) in January 2009 and 23.4% (21.7%) in January 2012.

Graph 5 shows the evolution in the number of inbound hotel nights at NUTS 2 level between 2005 and 2012. This exhibits an upward trend up to 2011 especially in the regions of Crete and South Aegean, which are very popular with inbound tourists due to their exceptional sunlust product – on the other hand, 2012 was associated with a reduction in the majority of the regions with the exception of Central Macedonia. Stability characterizes the pattern of the Ionian Islands; the region of Attica, on the other hand, had been severely affected by the negative publicity as a result of the civil unrest and violence in the streets which is reflected into the number of hotel nights that decreases constantly since 2008. Graph 6 shows the evolution of internal (i.e. domestic + inbound) hotel nights at NUTS 2 level over the period 2005 - 2012. The regions of Crete and South Aegean account for over 40% of total nights spent in Greece. The region of South Aegean and Attica are the ones recording the most severe decrease in the nights spent over the period under consideration.

Graph 7 shows the evolution of hotel supply (i.e. available beds for sale) in August over the period 2005 – 2012. Given that August represents the peak season par excellence, studying the evolution of hotel supply during that month provides a good proxy of the hotel supply available to both domestic and inbound tourists. Because of the seasonal nature of the tourism product and the great weight of inbound tourism in the internal market, Crete and South Aegean dominate the picture followed by the Ionian Islands, Central Macedonia (where in addition to Thessaloniki, tourists visit the very popular area of Halkidiki) and Attica. In the majority of regions, hotel supply exhibits an upward trend, although in the case of Attica, a plateau seems to have been reached since 2009. Yet, the substantial reduction of total nights in 2012 has caused a dramatic reduction in occupancy rates at least in the main metropolitan region. Illustratively, occupancy in Attica was 48.5% in August 2009 but only 40.8% in August 2012! Similarly, occupancy in Crete (South Aegean) was 83.2% (84.7%) in August 2009 and 82.7% (78.8%) in August 2012.

Graph 3. Domestic Hotel Nights in Greek Regions, 2005-2012

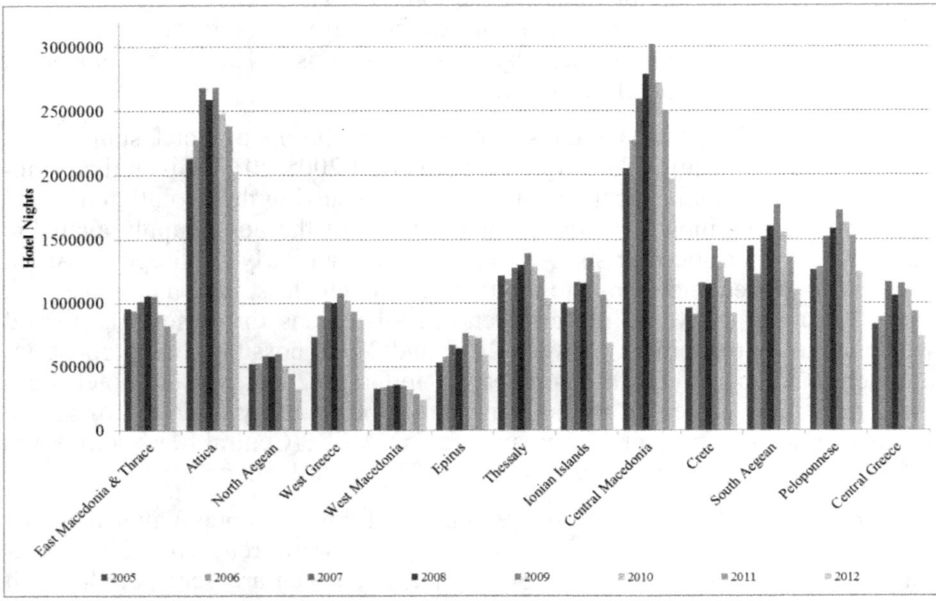

Source: Hellenic Statistical Authority - compiled by the authors.

Graph 4. Hotel Supply in Greek Regions, 2005-2012 (January)

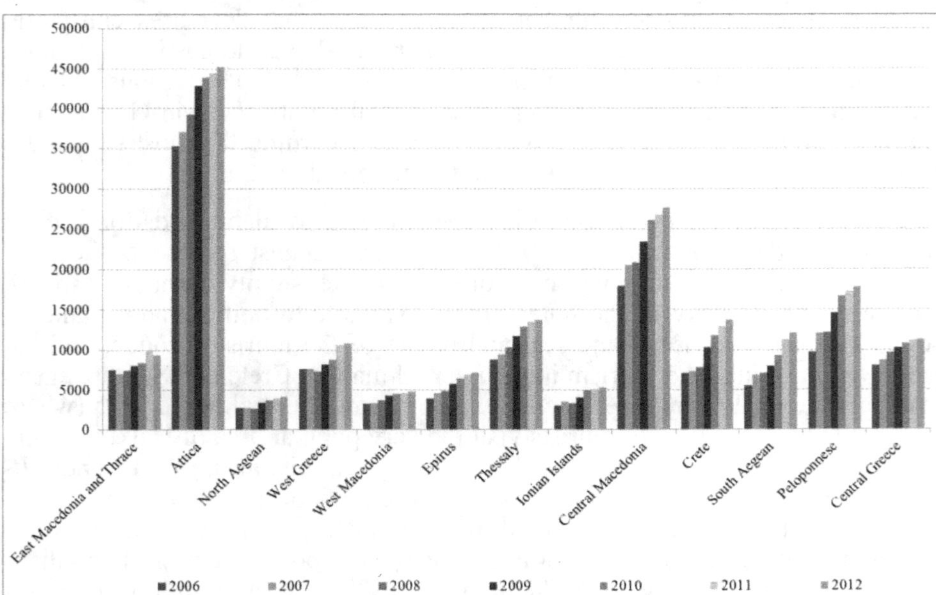

Source: Hellenic Statistical Authority - compiled by the authors.

Graph 5. Inbound Hotel Nights in Greek Regions, 2005-2012

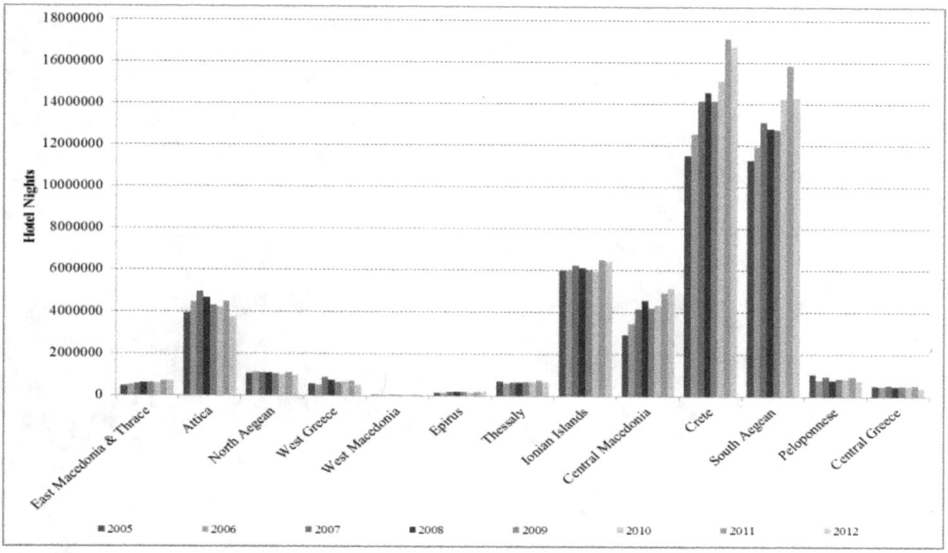

Source: Hellenic Statistical Authority - compiled by the authors.

Graph 6. Internal Hotel Nights in Greek Regions, 2005-2012

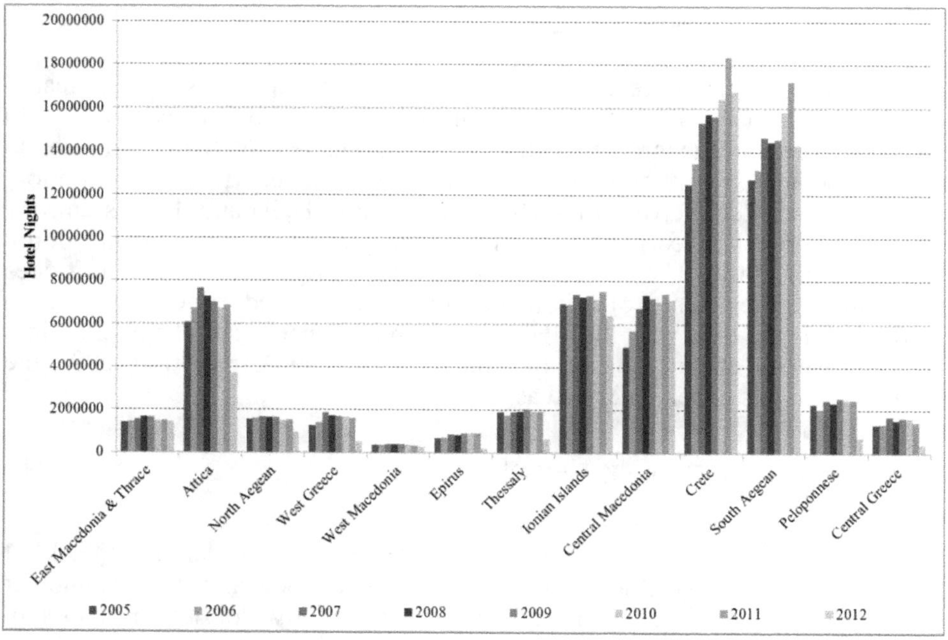

Source: Hellenic Statistical Authority - compiled by the authors.

Graph 7. Hotel Supply in Greek Regions, 2005-2012 (August)

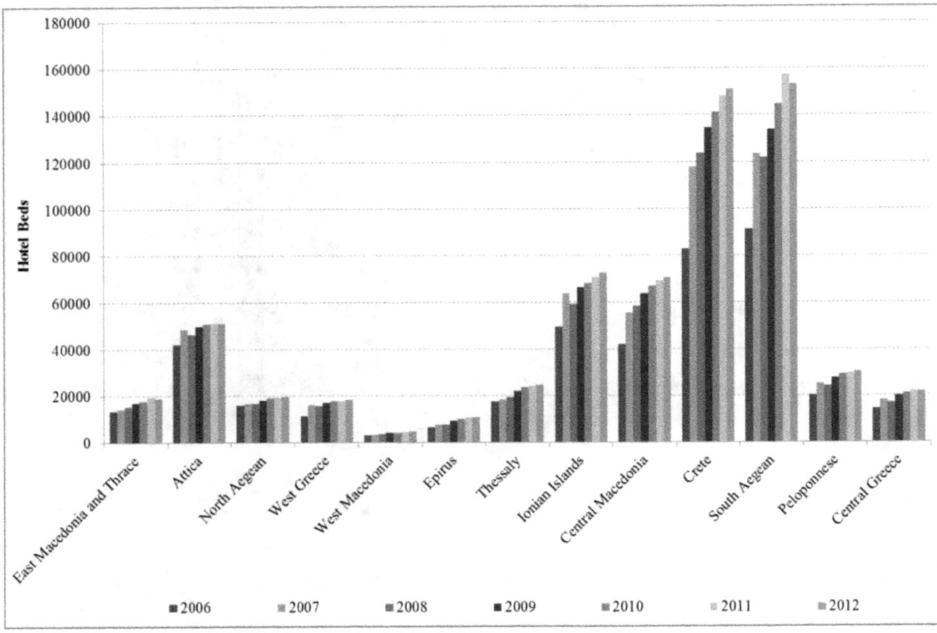

Source: Hellenic Statistical Authority - compiled by the authors.

3.3. Spatial Concentration Analysis

To further highlight the evolution of tourist flows and hotel supply, a spatial concentration analysis has been undertaken based on the Gini coefficient. In fact, the economic geography literature has considered alternative indexes to measure spatial concentration traffic flows, such as the coefficient of variation, the Gini index, the Herfindahl – Hirschman Index (HHI) and Theil's entropy measure (Curry and George 1983, Frenken 2007, Novotný 2007, Papatheodorou and Arvanitis 2009). The main advantage of the Gini coefficient is that it does not require the existence of a homogeneous (product and/or geography-wise) market (as is the case with the HHI for example), hence it may be applied in a rather universal context. Based on Papatheodorou and Arvanitis (2009), the Gini index in this paper is defined as:

$$G = \left| 1 - \sum_{i=1}^{N} (\sigma X_i - \sigma X_{i-1})(\sigma Y_i + \sigma Y_{i-1}) \right| \qquad (1)$$

where N is the number of administrative regions under consideration (i.e. 13 at NUTS2 and 51 at NUTS3 level), σX is the cumulative percentage of the number of regions considered each time and σY is the cumulative tourist (or hotel supply) market share of regions appearing in descending order. The coefficient takes values between zero (when absolute equality occurs) and one (in the context of the most unequal distribution). Moreover, in the present case is constant and equal to 1/N, taking values 1/13=7.69% for NUTS2 and 1/51=1.96% for NUTS3 regions. Consequently, equation (1) reduces to:

$$G = \left| 1 - \frac{1}{N} \sum_{i=1}^{N} (\sigma Y_i + \sigma Y_{i-1}) \right| \tag{2}$$

Having the above in mind, Graph 8 shows the evolution of the Gini coefficient for hotel nights at NUTS2 level over the period 2005-2012. Domestic nights (domhot) concentration is far less than inbound (inthot); both, however, exhibit limited fluctuation over time. On the other hand, internal (tothot) lies in between of the two but exhibits a clearly upward trend over the last few years. Graph 9 shows similar results at NUTS3 level, although the upward trend for internal concentration is in this case less pronounced. As a result, it seems that both graphs validate Hypotheses 2, 4 and 5.

Moreover, Graph 10 shows the evolution of the Gini coefficient for hotel supply in January and August at NUTS2 level over the period 2005-2012. Changes in both cases are minimal albeit of different direction. In particular, concentration in January is modest and somewhat downward sloping possibly because of the reduction in occupancy rates experienced by Attica, the dominant region in January. This very reduction may also explain the upward trend in August as the balancing effect of Attica over the dominance of Crete and South Aegean has decreased as a result of the crisis.

Graph 8. Gini Coefficient for Hotel Nights at NUTS2 Level, 2005-2012

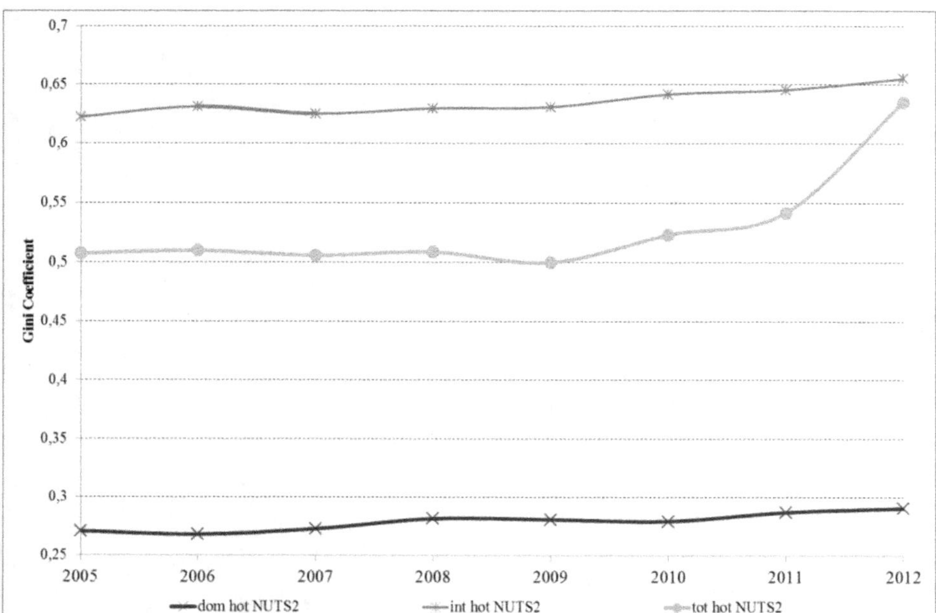

Graph 9. Gini Coefficient for Hotel Nights at NUTS3 Level, 2005-2012

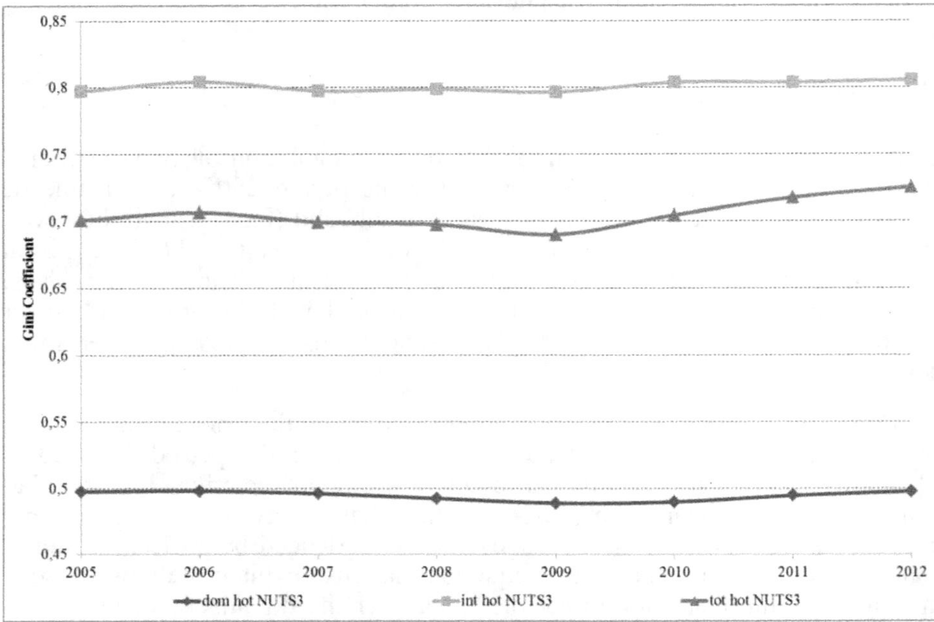

Graph 10. Gini Coefficient for Hotel Supply at NUTS2 Level, 2005-2012

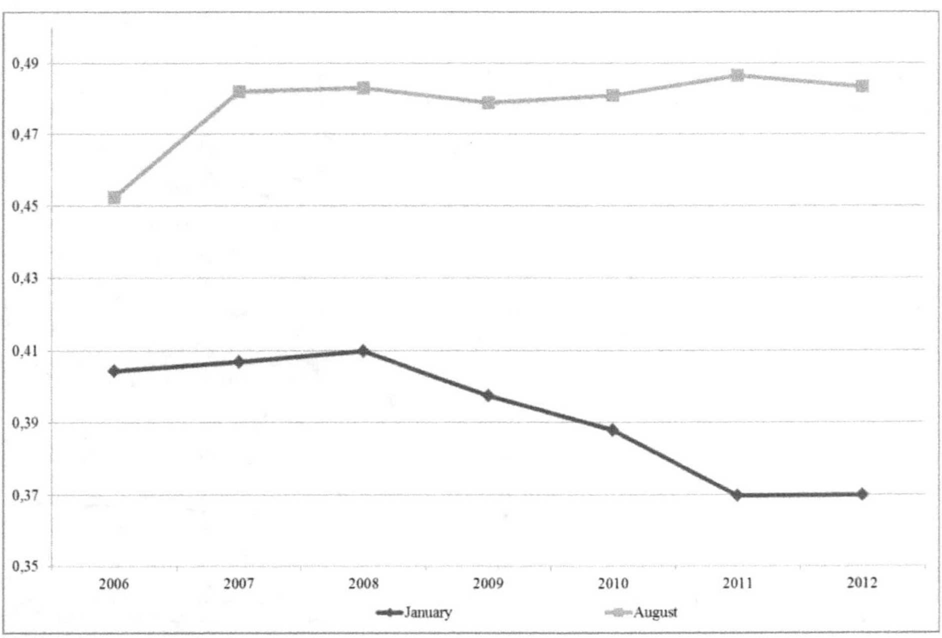

4. CONCLUSIONS

This paper aimed at analyzing the impact of the current economic crisis on Greek tourism. Emphasis was put on inbound and domestic tourism over the period 2005-2012. The related diagrammatical analysis based on nights spent in hotel accommodation establishments as well as of the available hotel supply reveals that the large majority of the research hypotheses made in the theoretical part of the paper have been validated. Although a diagrammatic analysis has certain limitations as it does not allow for a full evaluation of the economic crisis on tourism, still it seems legitimate to argue that the areas that have traditionally specialized in domestic tourism have been severely hit compared to tourism destinations focusing predominantly on inbound tourism. This has undoubtedly important implications for regional policy. In particular, while domestic tourism is eventually expected to recover as the economy rebounds, this process is likely to be slow and painful especially due to the high rate of unemployment at national and regional levels. Thus, the government and local authorities should assist these regions in their effort to overcome the negative effects of the crisis. Working together with tour operators and other bodies focusing on inbound tourism to promote these areas to the international tourism market may possibly be a way forward in order to increase the aggregate tourism flows in these regions. Nonetheless, diversification of spatial functionality may also prove beneficial, especially by encouraging these areas to also focus on primary sector products of high added value for export reasons. If successful, such a policy will help these areas overcome their current disadvantage but also set the fundamentals to better face future crises which are sector-specific and/or geographically dependent. Future research is worth focusing on this important issue of strategic spatial risk management.

REFERENCES

Alegre J., Mateo S., Pou L. (2013) Tourism participation and expenditure by Spanish households: The effects of the economic crisis and unemployment, *Tourism Management*, 39: 37-49.

Araña J., and León C. (2008) The impact of terrorism on tourism demand, *Annals of Tourism Research*, 35(2): 299–315.

Bank of Greece (2014) Developments in the Greek Travel Balance of Payments, Athens: Bank of Greece.

Bronner, F. and de Hoog, R. (2012) Economizing strategies during an economic crisis, *Annals of Tourism Research*, 39(2): 1048-1069.

Campbell J. Y. and Mankiw N. G. (1991) The response of consumption to income: a cross-country investigation, *European Economic Review*, 35: 715-721.

Curry B. and George K. D. (1983) Industrial Concentration: A Survey, *Journal of Industrial Economics*, 31(3): 203-255.

Eugenio-Martin, J. L. and Campos-Soria, J. A. (2014) Economic crisis and tourism expenditure cutback decision, *Annals of Tourism Research*, 44(1): 53-73.

Frenken K. (2007) Entropy statistics and information theory, in Hanusch H. and Pyka A. (eds.) *The Elgar Companion to Neo-Schumpeterian Economics*, Cheltenham: Edward Elgar, 544-555.

Friedman M. (1957) *A theory of the consumption function*, Princeton: Princeton University Press.

Goh C. (2012) Exploring impact of climate on tourism demand, *Annals of Tourism Research*, 39(4): 1859-1883.

Hellenic Chamber of Hotels (2014) Developments in Tourism and the Greek Hotel Sector in 2013 Athens: Hellenic Chamber of Hotels (in Greek).

International Monetary Fund [IMF] (2014) World Economic Outlook Database: Greece".

Keynes J. M. (1936) The general theory of employment, interest, and money, San Diego/New York/London: Harvest/HBJ.

Modigliani F. and Brumberg R. (1954) Utility analysis and the consumption function: An interpretation of cross-section data, in K. K. Kurihara (Eds.) *Post-Keynesian economics,* New Brunswick, NJ: Rutgers University Press, 388-436.

Nicolau J. L. and Masiero L. (2013) Relationship between price sensitivity and expenditures in the choice of tourism activities at the destination, *Tourism Economics*, 19(1): 101-114.

Novotný J. (2007) *On the measurement of regional inequality: does spatial dimension of income inequality matter?*, *Annals of Regional Science*, 41: 563-580.

Papatheodorou A. (2004) Exploring the evolution of tourist resorts, *Annals of Tourism Research*, 31: 219-237.

Papatheodorou A. and Arvanitis P. (2009) Spatial Evolution of Airport Traffic and Air Transport Liberalization: The Case of Greece, *Journal of Transport Geography*, 17: 402-412

Papatheodorou A., Rossello J., Xiao H. (2010) Global economic crisis and tourism: consequences and perspectives, *Journal of Travel Research*, 49(1): 39-45.

Prideaux B. (1999) Tourism Perspectives of the Asian Financial Crisis: Lessons for the Future, *Current Issues in Tourism*, 2(4): 279-293.

Ritchie J. R. B., Molinar C. M. A., Frechtling D. C. (2010) Impacts of the world recession and economic crisis on tourism: North America, *Journal of Travel Research*, 49(1): 5-15.

SETE (2014) The Importance of Tourism for Greece.

Sheldon P. and Dwyer L. (2010) The global financial crisis and tourism: Perspectives of the academy, *Journal of Travel Research*, 49(1): 3-4.

Simon H.A. (1961) *Administrative behavior*, (2nd edition), New York: Macmillan.

Smeral E. (2009) The impact of the financial and economic crisis on European tourism, *Journal of Travel Research*, 48(1): 3-13.

Smeral E. (2010) Impacts of the World recession and economic crisis on tourism: Forecasts and potential risks, *Journal of Travel Research*, 49(1): 31-38.

Stabler M. J., Papatheodorou A. and Sinclair M. T. (2010) *The Economics of Tourism*, (2nd edition), London: Routledge.

United Nations World Tourism Organization [UNWTO] (2013) Tourism Highlights, Madrid: UNWTO.

United Nations World Tourism Organization [UNWTO] (2014) World Tourism Barometer, Madrid: UNWTO.

World Economic Forum [WEF] (2013) The 2013 Travel and Tourism Competitiveness Report, Geneva: WEF.

CRISE ÉCONOMIQUE ET TOURISME EN GRÈCE

Résumé - *Cet article cherche à étudier les impacts de la récession qui frappe la Grèce depuis 2008 sur le tourisme étranger et domestique (mesuré par les nuitées) au niveau NUTS2 (région) et NUTS3 (préfecture). En s'appuyant sur différents indicateurs de concentration spatiale, l'article montre les processus d'évolution des régions grecques en matière de tourisme entre 2005 et 2012. Les résultats obtenus montrent que les régions qui enregistrent les plus grandes pertes à l'issue de la crise sont les régions qui avaient particulièrement investi dans le tourisme domestique.*

Mots clés - TOURISME, RÉGIONS, GRÈCE, CRISE ÉCONOMIQUE

NOTE ET DOCUMENT

LE RETOUR À LA CAMPAGNE DANS LA GRÈCE EN CRISE

Marie-Noëlle DUQUENNE*

Résumé - *Les conditions de vie dans les grandes villes de Grèce, plus spécialement dans l'agglomération d'Athènes et de Thessalonique, se sont très fortement dégradées au cours des cinq dernières années de crise. Le pays connaît des niveaux de chômage jamais atteints, alors que la population à risque de pauvreté et d'exclusion représente près de 35% de la population totale. La crise, en frappant avant tout les grands centres urbains, a généré une forte migration interne au profit des zones rurales. Ce travail examine, à l'aide des premiers résultats du recensement de 2011, les changements intervenus dans la distribution spatiale de la population entre 2001 et 2011 au niveau des municipalités.*

Mots-clés - MIGRATIONS RÉGIONALES, RETOUR À LA CAMPAGNE, GRÈCE

Classification JEL - J11, J64

*Department of Planning and Regional Development, University of Thessaly. mdyken@prd.uth.gr

1. INTRODUCTION

Depuis le début de la crise et avec la mise en place des plans successifs d'austérité, les conditions de vie dans les grandes villes de Grèce, plus spécialement dans l'agglomération d'Athènes et de Thessalonique, se sont très fortement dégradées. Le pays connaît notamment des niveaux de chômage jamais atteints, touchant désormais des familles entières, aussi bien les jeunes ménages que ceux approchant l'âge de la retraite. En décembre 2013, la Grèce présente le plus fort taux de chômage (27,5% contre 8,1% pour le même mois en 2008) parmi l'ensemble des 28 pays de l'UE, dépassant l'Espagne qui, depuis le début de la crise, détenait systématiquement les plus forts taux de chômage[1]. La population menacée de pauvreté ou d'exclusion sociale représente près de 35% de la population totale, soit environ 3,8 millions d'habitants (EL.STAT, 2013a). Le nombre de ménages au sein desquels tous les membres en âge de travailler sont au chômage s'accroît, atteignant plus d'un million d'individus (16,1% des personnes entre 18 et 59 ans). De récentes études estiment que près d'un ménage sur deux vit en partie grâce à l'aide de la famille et en particulier grâce aux retraites des proches (CGPACG, 2014). Face à cette situation et en l'absence de renversement notable des tendances, le pays est évidemment soumis à un risque réel d'émigration, spécialement des jeunes dont le taux de chômage, conformément aux données d'Eurostat, dépasse les 58% (décembre 2013).

Parallèlement, la crise pourrait générer une autre forme de migration, cette fois interne et au profit de certaines zones rurales. Le phénomène d'exode urbain vers la province, et non plus uniquement vers les zones périurbaines, dans un contexte de crise économique, est désormais au cœur du discours politique et scientifique (Goussios, 2011; Ghartzios, 2013; Verdier, 2013). Dans ce contexte de très grande précarité du travail et de détérioration des conditions de vie, spécialement dans les grandes villes, un mouvement de repli vers le rural ne serait-il pas en train d'émerger? En d'autres termes, le rural et plus spécialement les territoires d'origine des citadins ne deviendraient-ils pas un « espace de refuge », selon les termes mêmes de Lepicier et Sencébé (2001). Certaines études récentes semblent confirmer cette hypothèse, reflétant un désir d'abandonner la ville pour s'installer en province.

Dès lors, la question que nous nous proposons d'examiner est la suivante : au travers d'une analyse systématique, à l'échelle locale, des données de recensement (2001-2011) et des soldes migratoires, peut-on détecter une tendance réelle de migration vers la province et l'espace rural? Si une telle tendance pouvait être mise en évidence, cela suggèrerait que la crise économique à laquelle est confronté le pays depuis 2008 contribuerait à alimenter un certain retour au rural. Certains territoires ruraux ne seraient-ils pas une « porte de sortie » pour les ménages en grande difficulté, issue qui serait facilitée par le maintien de liens traditionnels et bien vivants au territoire d'origine (Goussios, 2006 ; Duquenne, 2010).

[1]Données Eurostat, dernière mise à jour : 13-03-2014.

2. L'APPROCHE DES MIGRATIONS VILLE-CAMPAGNE EN PÉRIODE DE CRISE

Après une longue période de dévitalisation, voire même de désertification, la campagne grecque voit sa population se stabiliser à la fin des années 1980. Si l'intensité et la rapidité du phénomène expliquent en partie l'arrêt de l'exode rural, le « réservoir humain » s'étant largement tari (Burgel, 2001:3), d'autres facteurs vont également être déterminants. Le pays se transforme non sans difficulté, au cours de la décennie 1990, en territoire d'accueil pour de nombreux migrants économiques, venant en majeure partie d'Albanie. Si ceux-ci s'installent essentiellement dans les principaux centres urbains du pays, les zones rurales vont néanmoins bénéficier de l'installation de cette population active, permettant à des secteurs clés – spécialement l'agriculture, le bâtiment et le tourisme – de trouver la main-d'œuvre nécessaire à leur bon fonctionnement (Kasimis et Papadopoulos, 2005; Papadopoulos, 2011) alors qu'en même temps, on observe un retour de migrants grecs, spécialement ceux qui étaient partis travailler en Europe lors de la grande période d'exode.

Au-delà de ces mobilités qui ont fait l'objet de nombreuses études, le quasi retournement démographique dans les zones rurales grecques à partir des années 90 s'explique également par la transformation et la modernisation des modes de vie ainsi que d'importantes mutations socio-économiques au sein de cet espace, favorisant non seulement son hybridation (Burgel, 2001) mais également l'émergence de nouvelles logiques socio-spatiales et stratégies des ménages. Deux des caractéristiques essentielles de ces nouvelles logiques méritent d'être mentionnées :

(i) le développement de la pluriactivité, favorisée par le fait que l'espace rural ne se limite plus à sa fonction traditionnelle de production agricole. Il est désormais un espace multifonctionnel (Wilson, 2009 ; Woods, 2009), « consommé » par les citadins du fait de ses nombreuses aménités mais également un espace résidentiel, les motivations d'installation étant aussi bien objectives que subjectives car liées aux perceptions du rural (Mitchell, 2004),

(ii) l'émergence de nouvelles territorialités autour désormais des petites et moyennes villes rurales (Goussios, Duquenne, 2005). De nouvelles formes de mobilité se mettent en place au sein de l'espace rural, avec l'installation de jeunes ménages non plus dans les grands centres urbains mais beaucoup plus dans les petites villes de plus en plus polarisantes (Goussios, 1999 ; Koutsou, Anthopoulou, 2008). Ce choix, favorisé par le maintien de la solidarité familiale, permet un fonctionnement de l'exploitation agricole familiale en se libérant des contraintes spatiales et temporelles (exploitation à distance), tout en bénéficiant de la proximité aux services, spécialement l'éducation et la santé au sein du système spatial de la petite ville (Goussios, Duquenne, 2003).

Le regain d'intérêt pour la vie à la campagne n'échappe pas au constat largement admis de nos jours (Halfacree, 2008, Gkartzios, 2013), qu'il s'agisse de phénomènes faisant référence à une diversité de situations, de motivations plus ou moins désirées ainsi qu'à des perceptions plus ou moins idylliques du monde rural dans l'imaginaire des citadins (Torre et Filippi, 2005).

S'il est sans doute peu approprié, avant la crise économique, de parler de retour à la campagne, on peut néanmoins admettre que le processus de dévitalisation a été stoppé grâce non seulement à l'arrivée durable de migrants étrangers relativement jeunes et à l'installation de jeunes retraités (Alvanides, 2006; Kaklamani, Duquenne, 2013) mais également au développement de réseaux sociaux, bien souvent liés aux originaires des villages, installés dans les grands centres urbains du pays voire même à l'étranger. Ces originaires ont en général conservé leur patrimoine (terres et habitat), contribuant ainsi au maintien de liens culturels avec le territoire d'origine. S'ils n'y sont plus des résidents permanents, ils ont un rôle essentiel dans la vie de leurs villages par leur présence par intermittence, l'entretien de leur patrimoine foncier, la consommation des produits locaux (Duquenne, Kaklamani, 2008) voire même leur implication active dans la vie économique de leur village (Goussios, 2011), renforçant ainsi les liens entre le rural et l'urbain.

Avec la crise économique que traverse la Grèce depuis 2008, le regain d'intérêt pour le rural prend une nouvelle dimension. L'espace rural semble mieux résister à la crise et s'il n'échappe pas au chômage, les pertes d'emploi, spécialement dans l'agriculture, y sont relativement moins fortes (Kasimis, Papadopoulos, 2013; Kasimis, Zografakis, 2013, p. 156) De récents travaux (spécialement à Athènes et Thessalonique) mettent en évidence que certains citadins envisagent clairement, dans ce nouveau contexte, l'éventualité d'une installation en province (Gkartzios, 2013). Une enquête réalisée en 2012 (KAPA Research) montre que plus de 68% des personnes interrogées envisagent leur départ vers la province, un peu plus de la moitié d'entre elles n'y ayant jamais vécu. Ce sont en majorité des populations relativement jeunes (30-44 ans) qui songent à quitter la ville. Il s'agit donc aussi bien d'un retour – plus ou moins durable – au territoire d'origine (Goussios, 2011; Verdier, 2013) que d'un désir de quitter la ville. Si les motivations reposent sur des considérations économiques (diminution des revenus, emploi précaire, chômage, moindre coût de la vie en province), elles sont également liées à un souci de qualité de vie et à une recherche d'une plus grande sécurité (la crise étant effectivement perçue comme un facteur d'accentuation de l'insécurité en ville).

Pour autant et spécialement dans le cas de la Grèce, un élément important doit être retenu pour mieux saisir les perspectives d'installation en province dans ce contexte de crise. En effet, une des caractéristiques fondamentales du fonctionnement du monde rural grec concerne, comme déjà mentionné, le maintien des liens culturels avec le territoire d'origine. Cette attache explique que nombre de citadins maintiennent leurs droits civiques dans leur village d'origine, permettant ainsi un certain continuum entre le rural et l'urbain. Si les liens n'ont pas été rompus, cela s'explique aussi par le fait que « les familles ont conservé leur capital, les terres et les biens familiaux ayant été confiés aux membres de la parenté restés au village » (Goussios, 2011, p. 7). Il n'est alors pas surprenant que les études récentes mettent en exergue le rôle non seulement de ce patrimoine mais également de la solidarité familiale dans la motivation à quitter la ville.

3. MÉTHODE D'APPROCHE ET DONNÉES

Pour répondre en toute certitude à notre questionnement concernant l'amplitude de la migration vers la province, il serait nécessaire de disposer de données permettant de mesurer directement les flux de migration interne entre les régions voire même entre les municipalités - dèmes[2]. Les données relatives au lieu de résidence lors du recensement et 5 ans avant ne sont pas encore disponibles or celles-ci seraient nettement plus adéquates puisqu'elles permettraient réellement de détecter l'origine et la destination des mobilités et ce, au cours d'une période débutant tout juste avant la crise. Il est néanmoins possible d'aborder le sujet au travers non seulement de l'étude comparative des résultats des deux derniers recensements de population de 2001 et 2011 mais également grâce aux données annuelles relatives au mouvement naturel (naissances et décès). Nous disposons donc de la structure par âge de la population pour 2001 (année initiale) et 2011 (année finale) ainsi que des naissances et décès par âge pour l'ensemble de la période étudiée.

Si les données relatives au mouvement naturel sont fiables, il faut néanmoins souligner que les résultats du recensement de 2011 ne sont pas totalement comparables à ceux de 2001, la méthodologie du recensement ayant été quelque peu modifiée (EL.STAT, 2013b). Par conséquent l'analyse comparative doit être menée avec grande prudence ainsi, éviterons-nous de commenter toute inflexion de faible amplitude entre les deux dates. On peut néanmoins admettre que les régions et municipalités présentant d'importantes variations de population et modification de structures par âge sont marquées par un changement de dynamique et/ou comportement démographique au cours de la décennie. Dès lors que de telles variations (positives tout comme négatives) peuvent être détectées, il est intéressant de les situer dans l'espace grec afin de vérifier si elles ne seraient pas révélatrices de l'émergence d'une nouvelle forme de migration interne au profit de certaines zones rurales.

A l'échelle nationale, la variation intercensitaire de population est la résultante de trois composantes : le solde naturel (SN), le solde migratoire (SM) et enfin un ajustement s'expliquant par une différence de qualité au niveau des résultats des deux recensements successifs alors que le solde migratoire est généralement entaché d'une certaine marge d'imprécision. Du fait qu'à tout échelon géographique plus fin, il est impossible de procéder à une répartition de l'ajustement, la variation de population pour un territoire donné, ne peut être décomposée que selon deux composantes : le solde naturel (SN) et le solde migratoire apparent (SMA) appelé encore « solde apparent des entrées-sorties ». Ce dernier mesure la variation de population non expliquée par le mouvement naturel (INSEE, 2009). Le SMA étant différent du solde migratoire réel, il ne fournit qu'une tendance quant au poids et au rôle des migrations au niveau local.

[2] Les dèmes correspondent aux unités administratives locales LAU1 selon la nomenclature d'Eurostat. Il s'agit en fait des municipalités et communes. Avant la dernière réforme territoriale de 2010 (Réforme Kallikratis), le pays comptait 1033 municipalités et communes. Ce nombre a été ramené à 325.

Pour chaque entité territoriale, nous avons donc :

$$\Delta Population_{2001\text{-}2011} = Population_{2011} - Population_{2001} = SN_{2001\text{-}2011} + SMA_{2001\text{-}2011}$$

Dans un premier temps, nous avons procédé à l'évaluation du solde naturel sur l'ensemble de la période 2001-2010, tant au niveau régional que local. Ce dernier n'est autre que la différence entre les naissances cumulées et les décès cumulés pour les dix années (SN= naissances – décès). Par déduction, nous pouvons évaluer le solde migratoire apparent (SMA) puisque :

$$SN_{2001\text{-}2011} = \sum_{t=2001}^{2010} SN_t = \sum_{t=2001}^{2010} (nais_t - deces_t)$$

Par déduction, nous calculons le solde migratoire apparent (SMA) :

$$SMA_{2001\text{-}2011} = \sum_{t=2001}^{2010} SMA_t = \Delta Population_{2001\text{-}2011} - SN_{2001\text{-}20110}$$

La décomposition du nombre de décès par tranche d'âge quinquennal pour les 10 années étudiées, nous a permis de procéder à une estimation des soldes migratoires cumulés pour chaque tranche d'âge de 2011. Il s'agit d'une estimation car il nous a fallu supposer une répartition équiprobable des décès au sein de chaque tranche d'âge, hormis les âges de 0 à 4 ans pour lesquels nous disposons de données détaillées. Ainsi, pour toute tranche d'âge [n, n+4] en 2011 telle par exemple la tranche [25-29], le solde migratoire n'est autre que :

$$SM[25-29]_{2011} = Population[25-29]_{2001} - Population\ Vivante[15-19]_{2001}$$

avec PopulationVivante$[15\text{-}19]_{2001}$ = population âgée de 15-19 ans en 2001 et vivante en 2011.

Rapportés à la population initiale de 2001, les soldes migratoires traduisent le degré d'attractivité d'un territoire puisqu'ils permettent d'évaluer le poids relatif de l'installation nette de nouveaux résidents. Quant aux estimations par tranche d'âge, elles permettent de détecter, au niveau de chaque unité territoriale, les populations (jeunes, âgées) participant le plus fortement aux mouvements migratoires lorsque ces derniers présentent d'importantes inflexions.

Disposant de l'ensemble des données à l'échelle des régions et des municipalités telles qu'en vigueur avant la Réforme Kallikratis, il est ainsi possible (i) de mettre en évidence les collectivités locales qui se démarquent par une réelle croissance démographique (respectivement déclin) et (ii) d'examiner les composantes de cette croissance et plus particulièrement, la contribution relative du solde migratoire apparent à la variation de population observée entre les deux recensements tout comme les âges plus fortement concernés par les mouvements de population.

Au travers du traitement statistique de ces données, nous tenterons de fournir des éléments de réponse aux questions suivantes: dans quelle mesure les grandes villes du pays continuent-elles d'être attractives, alors même que la période examinée a été bouleversée par l'avènement de la crise économique ? Paradoxalement, la crise ne pourrait-elle pas être « bénéfique », en termes démographiques, aux petites et moyennes villes – voire même à certaines zones rurales ? On ne manquera pas de souligner que l'analyse, en couvrant la période 2001-2011, ne peut évaluer le véritable impact de la crise dans la mesure où les effets socio-économiques de cette dernière se sont très fortement amplifiés à partir de 2011, comme le montrent l'évolution du taux de chômage depuis 2008 de même que les indicateurs de pauvreté ou d'exclusion sociale[3]. En d'autres termes, les résultats que nous obtenons ne sont qu'une première indication de ce que pourrait être l'impact de la crise sur la répartition spatiale de la population et l'opportunité pour certaines régions de bénéficier d'une véritable croissance démographique. Plus encore, du fait que les deux types de phénomènes mis en relation (comportements démographiques et évolutions économiques) répondent à des unités de temps différentes (Montenay, 2011), les principales inflexions que nous pouvons dégager à l'échelle nationale ou régionale, ne représentent qu'une évaluation partielle des effets de la crise.

4. LE PROBLÈME DÉMOGRAPHIQUE RENFORCÉ PAR LA CRISE

Au cours de la dernière décennie, le nombre de résidents en Grèce aurait diminué de 1,1%, soit une perte de 118.900 habitants alors que durant la période 1991-2001, la Grèce avait gagné plus de 710.000 habitants (+7,0%) et ce, en grande partie grâce à des flux soutenus d'immigration en provenance essentiellement des pays limitrophes (Albanie, Bulgarie). Depuis 1951, c'est donc la première fois que le pays présenterait un renversement de tendance.

Tableau 1 : Variation de population en Grèce, 2001-2011

Dates de recensement	Population		
	Totale	Nationaux	Étrangers
2001	10 934 087	10 172 274	761 813
2011	10 815 197	9 903 268	911 929
2011(a)	11 130 181	10 161 367	968 814
Variation intercensitaire (%)			
2001-2011	-1,1	-2,6	19,7
2001-2011[a]	1,8	-0,1	27,2

[a] Données corrigées des erreurs de couverture selon nos propres calculs.
Source : EL.Stat.

Tenant compte des taux d'erreur de couverture du recensement (EL.STAT, 2013b) – conduisant à une sous-estimation de la population recensée de l'ordre de 2,84% – on peut admettre qu'il n'y a pas de réel renversement de tendance mais plus une stagnation qui pourrait être annonciatrice d'un futur renversement

[3]En moyenne mensuelle, le taux de chômage passe de 8,6% en décembre 2008 à 14,6% pour le même mois en 2010 pour atteindre 21,4% en 2011 et finalement 26,3% et 27,5% respectivement en 2012 et 2013.

(Tableau 1). Dès lors, la population aurait légèrement augmenté (+1,8%) et ce, exclusivement grâce à l'installation de nouveaux ressortissants étrangers dont le nombre s'est accru en l'espace de 10 ans de plus de 27%.

L'absence de véritable dynamique démographique est la conséquence d'un problème endémique au pays, lié au faible taux de fécondité accompagné d'une hausse de la mortalité (Duquenne et Kotzamanis, 2012). Lors de la décennie 2001-2011, le solde naturel, à l'échelle nationale, reste légèrement positif (+3,4‰) tandis que le solde migratoire est de l'ordre de +14,5‰.

Tableau 2 : Les composantes de la variation de population

Population		Variation nette de population	Solde naturel cumulé	Solde migratoire cumulé
2001	2011[(a)]	2001-2011[(a)]	2001-2010	2001-2010
10 934 087	11 130 181	196 094	37 647	158 447
Taux rapportés à la population de 2001 (‰)		17,9	3,4	14,5

[(a)] Données corrigées des erreurs de couverture selon nos propres calculs
Source : EL.STAT, Recensements de population 2001 et 2011 et données sur mouvement naturel.

Depuis le début de la crise, la tendance au déclin du mouvement naturel ne fait que s'amplifier, pour finalement devenir négatif. Si en 2008, les naissances étaient supérieures aux décès (+10 300), à partir de 2011, le nombre de décès dépasse les naissances, mettant en évidence une facette souvent négligée de la crise. Cette diminution du taux de natalité, dès 2009-2010, reflèterait bien, conformément à l'approche d'Easterlin (1978), les inquiétudes des ménages quant à l'évolution future de leur niveau de vie et plus particulièrement celui de leurs enfants. Il semble que le climat d'inquiétude et le manque de confiance dans l'avenir aient eu un impact sur les comportements démographiques et plus particulièrement sur la natalité. En perdurant, ce pessimisme pourrait à terme, être lourd de conséquences pour le renouvellement de la population et pour la prise en charge des personnes âgées dont le nombre augmente rapidement, plaçant d'ailleurs le pays parmi les quatre Etats membres de l'UE présentant le plus fort taux de vieillissement, juste avant la Bulgarie, l'Italie et l'Allemagne.

Le solde migratoire nettement positif (Tableau 2) ne peut néanmoins cacher un risque réel d'émigration de certains grecs. La décomposition du solde migratoire selon les deux groupes de population: ressortissants grecs et étrangers fait apparaitre un solde migratoire pour la population étrangère de l'ordre de + 205 000 et un solde migratoire négatif (environ - 46 500) pour les nationaux. Notons que ne disposant pas de données permettant de calculer le solde naturel selon la nationalité, nous avons appliqué pour la population étrangère qui est en moyenne nettement plus jeune que la population grecque, un taux de mouvement naturel légèrement supérieur à la moyenne nationale.

Les mutations en cours ont des conséquences importantes sur la structure par âge de la population et donc sur les capacités futures à prendre en charge les personnes âgées. Entre 2001 et 2011, on observe (i) un rétrécissement marqué de la pyramide pour les tranches d'âges de 15 à 29 ans (Figure 1), confirmant que les départs vers l'étranger concernent avant tout les jeunes à la recherche d'un emploi et (ii) un net élargissement de la pyramide pour les âges les plus avancés. La Grèce, avec l'Italie et l'Allemagne, fait partie des trois pays de l'UE ayant le plus fort pourcentage de personnes âgées de 65 ans et plus (19,4%, 20,3% et 20,6% respectivement).

Les transformations observées au niveau de la pyramide des âges reflètent clairement le double problème sociodémographique auquel est confrontée la Grèce : au-delà du vieillissement qui est un processus incontournable pour les pays développés, il est clair que la crise économique a contribué au rétrécissement des âges correspondant aux jeunes actifs et alimenté leur désir de s'expatrier, désir spécialement prononcé chez les jeunes fortement qualifiés. C'est donc tout un capital humain qui risque de faire défaut au pays dans les années à venir.

Figure 1 : Pyramides des âges, 2001-2011

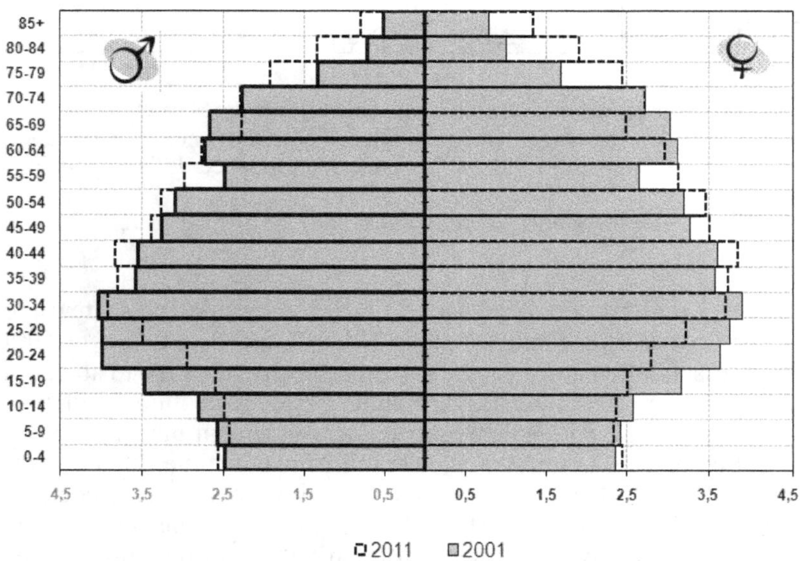

La pyramide des âges pour 2011 a été construite à partir des données de recensement corrigées en fonction des taux d'erreurs de couverture par sexe et âge (EL.STAT, 2013b).

5. QUELLE MUTATION DANS LA DISTRIBUTION SPATIALE DE LA POPULATION GRECQUE ?

En examinant les évolutions au sein du pays, on observe certaines divergences en matière de dynamique démographique. Pour rendre plus lisibles les changements intervenus au cours de la dernière décennie, nous nous proposons d'examiner successivement, l'évolution des régions et grandes aires urbaines puis celles des principales villes de province[4] pour ensuite nous pencher sur l'espace rural en lui-même afin de détecter l'éventualité d'un « certain retour à la campagne».

Tableau 3 : L'évolution démographique des Régions de Grèce, 2001-2011

Régions (NUTS-2)	ΔPOP/POP (%) [(a)]	Excédent naturel	SN/POP (%)	Solde migratoire	SM/POP (%)
Sud de l'Égée	12,4	9 839	3,3	27 177	9,11
Crète	5,7	16 808	2,83	17 230	2,9
Épire	3,4	-7 364	-2,19	18 928	5,63
Macédoine Centrale	2,7	21 605	1,15	29 378	1,57
Attique	2,3	55 945	1,44	35 345	0,91
Macédoine de l'Est – Thrace	1,4	-4 120	-0,68	12 402	2,04
Thessalie	1,1	-7 272	-0,98	15 561	2,1
Grèce Centrale	0,8	-11 338	-2,03	15 889	2,85
Iles Ioniennes	0,3	-3 551	-1,69	4 280	2,04
Nord de l'Égée	-0,8	-6 366	-3,1	4 740	2,31
Péloponnèse	-0,9	-17 357	-2,9	12 213	2,04
Macédoine de l'Ouest	-2,5	-3 206	-1,09	-4 238	-1,44
Grèce de l'Ouest	-4,4	-5 972	-0,83	-25 911	-3,59

[(a)] Données corrigées des erreurs de couverture selon nos propres calculs.
ΔPOP/POP = taux de croissance démographique ; SN/POP = taux de croissance de la population dû au solde naturel ; SM/POP = taux de croissance de la population dû au solde migratoire.
Source : EL.STAT, Recensements de population 2001 et 2011 et données sur mouvement naturel.

Parmi les 13 régions de Grèce, seules deux d'entre elles présentent globalement un véritable déclin démographique (Macédoine de l'Ouest et Grèce de l'Ouest) dû essentiellement à des flux migratoires négatifs (Tableau 3). A l'inverse, la Crète et surtout les îles du Sud de l'Egée restent non seulement très attractives mais bénéficient également d'un accroissement naturel assez important. Il s'agit de régions pour lesquelles le tourisme constitue l'un des piliers de l'activité économique et sans aucun doute, l'un des rares secteurs économiques qui, malgré la crise, continue d'offrir de l'emploi, au moins saisonnièrement. Les autres régions du pays présentent un bilan nettement plus mitigé, même si elles parviennent au moins à maintenir leur population.

5.1. Mutations au sein de l'espace urbain

Les deux plus grandes agglomérations du pays (Athènes et Salonique) regroupant près de 37% de la population totale, ont perdu des habitants au profit de leur couronne périurbaine (Tableau 4). Comme dans de nombreuses agglomérations urbaines d'Europe, on observe un certain recul de ces deux centres

[4]Il s'agit plus exactement des villes, chefs-lieux des préfectures sous régionales.

villes: l'impact des migrations sur le déclin de population y est important puisque leur solde naturel reste sur l'ensemble de la période positif (Table 4). A l'intérieur de l'Attique, on observe un déplacement de population vers les communes littorales qui présentent des taux de croissance de leur population particulièrement élevés, pouvant même dépasser les 5% par an. Ce sont essentiellement les jeunes ménages mais également les ménages proches ou en âge de la retraite qui contribuent à ce processus. La région d'Attique a finalement gagné près de 94.000 habitants en l'espace de dix ans (+2,5%) car elle reste, même en cette période de crise, la première région d'installation pour les immigrés. A Salonique, c'est également la majeure partie de la couronne périurbaine du centre métropolitain qui présente la plus grande attractivité : ces communes sont en effet caractérisées par un solde migratoire de l'ordre de +23% tandis que les taux de migration sont encore plus élevés pour les populations âgées de 30 à 60 ans.

A la différence d'Athènes et Salonique, la population des cinq autres plus grandes agglomérations du pays[5] augmente très fortement (Larissa en Thessalie: +14%, La Canée: +13% et Eraklio en Crète: +9%) ou se maintient (Patras à l'ouest du pays et Volos en Thessalie) et ce, grâce à la combinaison d'un solde naturel et d'un solde migratoire positifs sur l'ensemble de la période.

Tableau 4 : Les deux agglomérations d'Athènes et Salonique

	Variation de la population [a]		Excédent naturel		Solde migratoire	
	Nombre	Taux	Nombre	Taux	Nombre	Taux
Agglomération d'Athènes	-36 463	-1,1	31 795	1,0	-68 258	-2,0
Reste d'Attique sans iles	130 901	27,3	26 079	5,4	104 822	21,8
Agglomération de Salonique	-7 621	-0,9	24 558	2,9	-32 179	-3,8
Zone périurbaine	64 400	26,1	8 016	3,2	56 384	22,8

[a] Données corrigées des erreurs de couverture selon nos propres calculs.
Source : Elstat, Recensements de population 2001 et 2011 et données sur mouvement naturel.

Pour ce qui est des autres grandes villes de province (au nombre de 44[6]), leurs fortunes sont assez diverses. Un peu plus d'un tiers d'entre elles (16) présentent une forte croissance démographique (supérieure à 10%), faisant apparaître de véritables effets d'agglomération à l'échelle locale. Cette dynamique est systématiquement alimentée par l'arrivée de nouveaux résidents, le solde migratoire représentant de loin la principale composante de l'accroissement de leur population. Ces villes se situent essentiellement dans le Nord et Nord-

[5]Ces cinq agglomérations abritent désormais 7,3% de la population nationale contre 6,8% en 2001.
[6] Ces 44 villes, chefs-lieux, concentrent près de 15% de la population contre 13,3% en 2001.

Ouest de la Grèce à l'exception de certaines villes bénéficiant de la proximité d'Athènes. 18 autres villes situées en grande majorité en Grèce Centrale et dans le Péloponnèse bénéficient d'une relative dynamique démographique mais leurs flux migratoires positifs sont sans commune mesure avec ceux observés dans le premier groupe. Finalement, seules 10 villes dont certaines en milieu insulaire parviennent tout juste à maintenir ou voire même perdent de leur population. En définitif, l'évolution au cours de la dernière décennie met en évidence un contraste entre d'une part, à quelques exceptions près, les villes dynamiques du Nord et Nord-Ouest de la Grèce dont le rôle polarisant semble se confirmer et d'autre part celles du Péloponnèse et de la Grèce Centrale nettement moins attractives.

5.2. Crise et attractivité de l'espace rural ?

L'espace rural, composé des dèmes autres que ceux appartenant aux grandes agglomérations du pays et aux municipalités / chefs-lieux des sous-préfectures, voit dans son ensemble, sa population diminuer (-3,3%) sans bénéficier de flux migratoires significatifs (tableau 5). Ce déclin plus ou moins prononcé (Types 1 et 2) touche plus de la moitié des dèmes ruraux (404), regroupant près de 43% de la population rurale contre plus de 48% en 2001. Ces dèmes dispersés dans tout l'espace rural, souffrent bien souvent d'un certain enclavement ou éloignement aux centres urbains (montagne et zones frontalières). Néanmoins, on ne manquera pas de noter que certains dèmes de plaine, à forte vocation agricole mais également à proximité de grands centres urbains, présentent eux aussi un fort déclin au bénéfice du chef-lieu de la sous-préfecture qui continuent d'exercer, même en période de crise, un effet de polarisation.

A l'inverse, un peu plus d'un dème sur cinq (167) bénéficie d'une croissance démographique suffisamment forte pour être jugée significative (Types 6 et 7). Ces dèmes représentent 30% de la population rurale contre 25% en 2001. Pour la très grande majorité d'entre eux, cette dynamique est la résultante de flux migratoires très positifs (majoritairement des jeunes de 25 à 45 ans) qui compensent largement l'absence de croissance naturelle. Ces dèmes ruraux sont dynamiques parce qu'ils se situent soit à proximité d'un centre urbain ou d'une petite - moyenne ville (exerçant ainsi un effet d'attractivité résidentielle), soit encore en zone littorale et/ou insulaire là où le tourisme est le pilier de l'activité économique (Carte 5). On peut suggérer que la migration vers ces dèmes soit moins commandée par les effets de la crise économique que par des choix liés à la qualité de vie et dans certains cas, à un accès plus facile à la propriété (zones périurbaines). On ne manquera pas de souligner qu'au sein de ce groupe de dèmes bénéficiant d'un solde migratoire très positif, certains d'entre eux se situent dans l'arrière-pays montagneux. Cela laisse donc à penser que, dans le contexte actuel de crise, des territoires ruraux pourraient effectivement bénéficier d'un certain «retour à la campagne», sinon définitif du moins temporel.

C'est ce que l'on peut également envisager pour deux autres groupes de dèmes (Type 3 et 5) qui présentent un solde migratoire très positif, la grande majorité d'entre eux parviennent même à combler leur déficit naturel (Type 5). Cependant, dans ce dernier cas, l'arrivée de nouveaux arrivants correspond essentiellement à l'installation de ménages proches ou en âge de la retraite, contrairement aux dèmes du précédent groupe. Il s'agirait beaucoup plus d'un retour au territoire d'origine lorsque la vie active prend fin, reposant sur une stratégie de recherche de qualité de vie.

Tableau 5 : Les dynamiques démographiques dans l'espace rural

Types de dynamique démographique	Nombre de Dèmes	Population recensée en 2011[(a)]	Taux de variation (%)	SN/POP (%)	SM/POP (%)
1. Déclin très prononcé	234	935 587	-16,9	-5,1	-11,8
2. Relatif déclin	170	633 020	-9,1	-7,6	-1,4
3. Déclin : SM > 0 ne compensant pas le SN < 0	10	23 154	-8,7	-16,4	7,7
4. Évolution incertaine [(b)]	108	649 300	-1,2	-1,4	0,2
5. Maintien dû au SM > 0 compensant le SN < 0	66	305 055	1,8	-6,2	8,0
6. Relative dynamique	13	237 952	7,1	4,8	2,3
7. Dynamique très prononcée	154	855 915	16,0	-1,0	17,0
Espace Rural	755	3 639 983	-3,3	-3,7	0,4

[(a)] Données corrigées des erreurs de couverture selon nos propres calculs.
[(b)] Les inflexions sont trop faibles pour être commentées.
Source : Elstat, Recensements de population 2001 et 2011 et données sur mouvement naturel.

Enfin, pour un certain nombre de territoires ruraux (type 4), la variation intercensitaire de population est trop faible pour se permettre toute sorte d'interprétation. Comme nous l'avons déjà mentionné, il serait hasardeux d'interpréter ce type d'inflexion de faible amplitude.

Il est incontestable que certains territoires ruraux, y compris en zone de montagne, aient bénéficié de l'installation de nouveaux résidents. L'analyse de la structure par âge des soldes migratoires met en évidence la diversité des situations. L'apport de population ne se limite pas aux « jeunes retraités », susceptibles de retourner dans leur territoire d'origine. Il s'agit également de jeunes ménages (30-49 ans), ce qui concorde en grande partie avec les résultats des études préalablement citées. On a par ailleurs observé que les dèmes présentant des soldes migratoires très positifs pour ces tranches d'âge, ont également des soldes positifs pour ce qui est des moins de 10 ans. Il est alors probable que la décision pour ces ménages ayant des enfants en bas âge de s'installer en province ait été facilitée par la détention d'un patrimoine (résidence et/ou terres) de même que l'existence d'un réseau de solidarité (familles et amis) et donc le maintien de liens culturels.

Carte 1 : Les types de dynamique démographique en zone rurale (2001-2011)

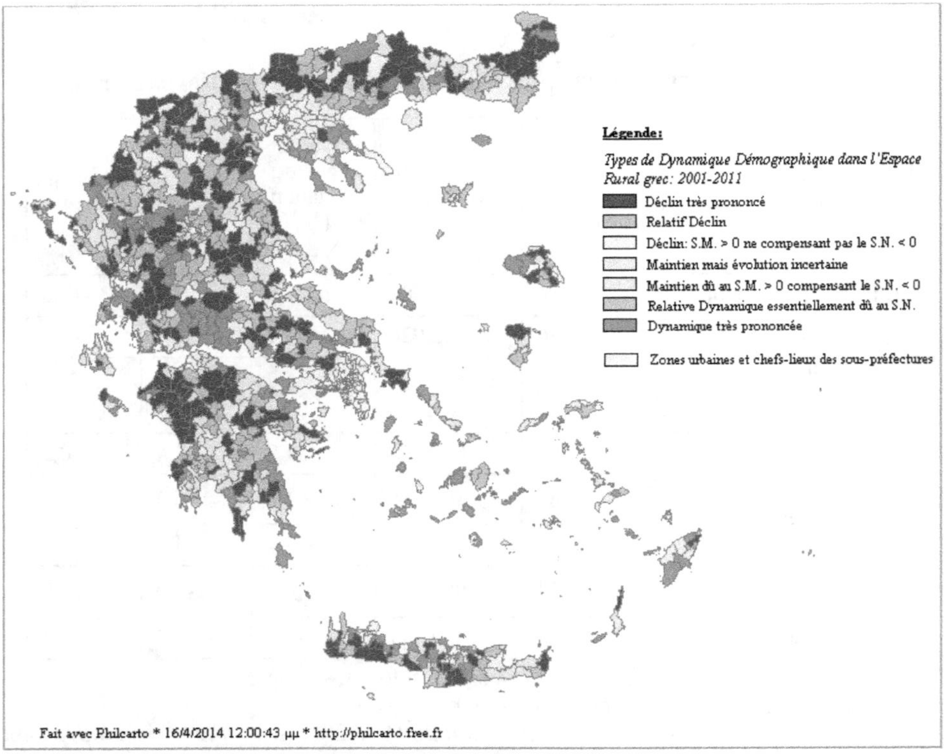

Afin de mieux comprendre ce phénomène, nous avons tenté d'évaluer l'influence de ces facteurs sur les soldes migratoires observés au niveau des dèmes ruraux, les soldes étant exprimés en pourcentage de la population de 2001. Quant au choix des variables explicatives, il est une fois de plus limité par la disponibilité des données, spécialement pour ce qui est des variables relatives à l'emploi. Néanmoins et compte-tenu de notre problématique, nous avons construit 6 variables reflétant :

- le degré relatif d'enclavement du dème (Encla), mesuré par l'altitude moyenne pondérée de ce dème,
- l'intensité des liens culturels traditionnels, estimée au travers de 2 indicateurs : le nombre de personnes présentes au moment du recensement mais ne résidant pas habituellement dans le dème pour 100 résidents permanents (Lien1) ainsi que le pourcentage de personnes habituellement non résidentes mais ayant conservé leur droit civique dans le dème par rapport à la population légale du même dème (Lien2)
- le poids relatif des résidences secondaires (Resec), celles-ci reflétant (spécialement dans les zones de montagne et semi-montagne), la détention d'un patrimoine par des non résidents. Pour les zones de montagne et semi-

montagne, les résidences secondaires correspondent en grande partie à un patrimoine détenu par les originaires.

- L'accroissement du patrimoine bâti (résidences principales) durant la période 1991-2001 (VBat), afin de prendre en compte (au moins indirectement) l'attractivité du dème dans un proche passé. L'accroissement du nombre de résidences principales occupées nous semble un indicateur plus robuste que celui liée à la variation intercensitaire de population, non seulement pour des raisons purement statistiques de comparabilité des données mais également parce qu'il traduit une motivation durable de rester sur le territoire et/ou de s'y installer.
- Enfin, le poids relatif de la Surface Agricole Utilisée (non inclus les pâturages) (SAU) permet de prendre en compte, au moins partiellement, les ressources agricoles et le potentiel de développement d'activités agricoles. Cela nous permet au moins de poser la question du retour en province et/ou à l'agriculture.

Les données portant sur des unités spatiales (dèmes), nous avons été amené à envisager l'existence de phénomènes d'autocorrélation spatiale par la prise en compte aussi bien de variables spatiales décalées que d'une autocorrélation spatiale des erreurs. Pour ce, nous avons construit une matrice de poids, basée sur les k-voisins les plus proches qui est généralement considérée comme la plus appropriée en présence d'unités spatiales insulaires. Le choix du nombre de voisins n'est évidemment pas anodin. Nous avons donc considéré plusieurs solutions alternatives (en posant successivement k=4 à k=8). Les résultats étant suffisamment similaires, nous avons opté pour un nombre limité de voisins (k=4).

Quant à la spécification finale du modèle, nous avons adopté la démarche largement admise, basée sur l'analyse successive des deux types de modèle, en comparant les valeurs respectives des multiplicateurs de Lagrange (LM_{err} et LM_{lag}) et leurs versions robustes. Le modèle robuste est finalement celui avec auto corrélation des erreurs. Quant au problème attendu d'hétéroscedasticité, il a été résolu selon la méthode proposée par Kelejian et Prucha (2010).

Les résultats découlant du modèle (Tableau 6) viennent confirmer aussi bien le rôle des liens culturels traditionnels (Lien1 et Lien2) que la présence d'un patrimoine bâti (Resec), tous ces coefficients étant positifs et statistiquement significatifs ($p < 0,05$). Il n'est pas surprenant que la présence de nombreuses résidences secondaires puissent jouer sur l'installation de nouveaux résidents et ce, pour deux raisons. Dans les zones d'arrière-pays où les attaches au pays sont fortes, les citadins ont conservé leur demeure familiale (Duquenne, Kaklamai, 2008; Goussios, 2011), ce qui peut inciter les ménages à quitter la ville lorsque leurs conditions de vie se sont fortement dégradées, surtout s'ils sont en location. A cet égard, l'enquête réalisée par KAPA Research (2012) montre bien que la détention d'un patrimoine en ville (en particulier de leur habitat) est l'une des raisons qui poussent les personnes à ne pas envisager un départ. Dans les zones littorales et insulaires, la présence de résidences secondaires joue également un rôle important car d'une part celles-ci peuvent se convertir en résidence principale, spécialement pour les ménages en âge de retraite, mais d'autre part, elle reflète aussi la présence d'activités touristiques. Il est largement admis que le tourisme est l'un des principaux piliers de l'économie locale et qu'en continuant d'offrir certaines perspectives d'emploi, il peut inciter à l'installation de personnes à la recherche d'un emploi.

Tableau 6 : Estimation du Modèle avec auto corrélation des erreurs (GMM_HET)

Variable dépendante	TSM	Nombre d'observations	872
		Nombre de variables	7
Pseudo R^2	0,393	Degré de liberté	865

Variables	Coefficient	Ecart-type	z-Statistic	p-value
Constante	-185,025	36,831	-5,024	0,000
Ressources agricoles (SAU)	-1,596	0,340	-4,696	0,000
Lien culturel (Lien1)	+1,164	0,434	2,684	0,007
Lien culturel (Lien2)	+2,580	1,132	2,279	0,023
Résidences secondaires (Resec)	+1,126	0,537	2,098	0,036
Patrimoine bâti (VBat)	+1,909	0,549	3,477	0,001
Enclavement (Encla)	-0,121	0,035	-3,443	0,001
Lambda	+0,248	0,075	3,320	0,001

A l'inverse, le relatif enclavement (altitude pondérée moyenne) reste bien un réel handicap à l'installation de nouveaux résidents. On peut alors envisager que seuls des liens culturels très intenses ainsi qu'une dynamique territoriale déjà en œuvre (ce que pourrait laisser suggérer la variable VBat) pourraient compenser le manque relatif d'accessibilité pour pouvoir envisager l'installation de nouveaux résidents.

Enfin, notre modèle semble montrer que l'installation en province – qu'il s'agisse d'un retour au village d'origine ou non – ne soit pas guidé par des motivations liées à l'exploitation des ressources agricoles disponibles, le coefficient de la variable SAU étant non seulement négatif mais également très significatif. Cette variable est d'ailleurs celle dont l'impact sur le solde migratoire présente la plus forte intensité (z-Statistic). Mais nous devons rester prudents quant à l'interprétation de ce résultat car il est évident que le manque de données relatives au tissu économique des dèmes ruraux biaise en partie l'analyse, ce qui justifie d'ailleurs que le coefficient lambda (auto corrélation des erreurs) soit lui-aussi fortement significatif.

6. EN GUISE DE CONCLUSION

L'examen attentif mais prudent des évolutions démographiques en Grèce durant la dernière décennie semble confirmer que la crise économique ait contribué à faire émerger une nouvelle situation démographique. Le pays, dans son ensemble, est marqué non seulement par un déclin démographique partiellement caché par les flux encore soutenus d'immigrants mais aussi par une réelle modification de la structure par âge de la population, touchant particulièrement les tranches d'âge correspondant aux jeunes actifs. Le déclin de population rend aussi bien le pays que les régions et les municipalités très vulnérables financièrement et économiquement parlant (Geys et al., 2008). C'est en effet tout le système de protection sociale qui est remis en jeu alors que la vulnérabilité est souvent justifiée par le fait qu'il existe un lien réel entre la dynamique démographique (au travers de la taille de la population et de la densité) et la capacité d'entreprendre et d'innover (Jacobs 1969 ; Krugman, 1991 et 1998 ; Glaeser, 1998). La volonté des jeunes diplômés à émigrer ne pourra qu'accentuer ce problème.

Dès les premiers temps de la crise économique, le problème endémique du pays en termes de faible natalité s'est accentué. Il semble bien que les anticipations négatives quant aux conditions futures de vie aient rapidement joué sur le désir de fonder une famille ou de l'agrandir. Parallèlement, le taux de mortalité augmente continuellement et sa croissance semble s'accélérer. Le pays est donc confronté à un sérieux risque en matière de renouvellement de sa population tandis que sont nettement visibles les premiers signes d'un départ à l'étranger de nombreux jeunes, spécialement les plus diplômés et qualifiés. On ne peut en effet expliquer autrement, le rétrécissement en 2001 de la pyramide des âges entre 15 et 29 ans.

Hormis le défi économique, le pays doit faire face à un véritable défi démographique qui n'est pas un phénomène nouveau et ce, du fait même que le pays souffre d'un manque de politique familiale et plus généralement de politique sociale en faveur des ménages. La résolution du problème démographique ne pourra être réalisée sans la mise en place d'un cadre efficace de soutien aux ménages, dépassant le concept traditionnel de la famille. Si cette politique doit prendre en compte les différents types de ménages constituant la société, elle doit également reposer sur le principe de la conciliation entre la vie personnelle – familiale et la vie professionnelle, tout en assurant la solidarité intergénérationnelle. Sans une telle politique, il sera difficile, au cours des années à venir, d'assister à un véritable changement dans les comportements démographiques, la détérioration des conditions de vie et le chômage ne permettant pas aux ménages de modifier leurs anticipations pessimistes.

En définitive, si le contexte actuel génère des «comportements de repli», il ravive également la solidarité familiale. Cela explique que certains ménages (plutôt jeunes et avec des enfants en bas âge) décident de migrer vers des régions où le coût de la vie y est moindre et les conditions de vie plus aisées – en particulier grâce à la solidarité familiale – alors que les jeunes, spécialement les célibataires, semblent préférer opter pour un départ vers l'étranger, même si la décision n'est ni facile ni évidente.

L'étude des soldes migratoires apparents à l'échelle des municipalités, spécialement dans les zones rurales, nous permet d'affirmer que dans le contexte actuel si peu propice, certains de ces territoires parviennent à « résister » face au risque de déclin démographique voire même à être attractifs, et ce spécialement lorsque les liens culturels avec les originaires ont été maintenus, voire même entretenus, assurant ainsi un continuum avec le monde urbain. Dans ce sens, la crise serait une opportunité pour ces territoires car en accueillant de nouveaux habitants même temporairement, c'est toute une dynamique qui pourrait se mettre en œuvre grâce à leur contribution en termes de connaissances, d'idées et de nouveaux projets. Ce n'est alors pas surprenant que la variable que nous avons retenue pour prendre en compte la dynamique d'attractivité déjà mise en œuvre dans un dème, soit particulièrement significative. Cependant cette dynamique ne sera possible que si cette migration vers le rural n'est pas perçue tant par ceux qui la vivent que par ceux qui les accueillent comme un simple comportement de repli et de préservation face à la dégradation des conditions de vie dans les grandes villes. Sans de véritables politiques d'accueil menées par les collectivités locales et autres acteurs locaux, le « retour à la campagne » restera, hormis quelques cas exceptionnels, essentiellement un mythe.

REFERENCES

Alvanides, S. (2006). Geographical Analysis of Population Changes of Communities in Greece: 1940 to 2001.

Burgel, G. (2001). Organisation de l'espace et nouvelles tendances de la ruralité en Grèce, Strates [En ligne], No 10, mis en ligne le 31 janvier 2005,

Confédération Générale des Professionnels, Artisans, Commerçants de Grèce (CGPACG). (2013). Revenus et Dépenses des ménages, Décembre, Athènes.

Duquenne, M-N. (2010). Le regain d'attractivité de la montagne grecque: analyse et tendances", IVème Conférence internationale de Démographie des Balkans : Démographie spatiale des Balkans, Tendances et enjeux, Budva, Monténégro, 13-15 mai,

Duquenne, M-N., Kaklamani, S. (2008). Le va- et- vient culturel entre le lieu de résidence et le lieu d'origine, 15e Colloque de l'AIDELF, Colloque International Démographie et Cultures, Québec, 25-29 Août, In : *Actes des Colloques "Démographie et Cultures"*, Publications de l'AIDELF, 1031-1048.

Duquenne, M-N., Kaklamani, S. (2013). Le nouveau contexte du vieillissement de la population.*DemoNews*No 20, LADS, Université de Thessalie.

Duquenne, M-N., Kotzamanis, B. (2012). La population de Grèce diminue : une première analyse critique des résultats préliminaires du recensement de 2011. *DemoNews*No 17, LADS, Université de Thessalie.

Easterlin, R.A. (1978). The Economics and Sociology of Fertility: a Synthesis, In: Charles Tilly (ed.) *Historical Studies of Changing Fertility*, Princeton, NJ: Princeton University Press.

Geys, B., Heinemann, F., Kalb, A. (2008). Local governments in the wake of demographic change: Evidence from German municipalities, *FinanzArchiv, Public Finance Analysis*, 64(4), 434-457.

Gkartzios, M. (2013).Leaving Athens': Narratives of counterurbanisation in times of crisis. *Journal of Rural Studies*, 32, 158-167.

Glaeser, E.L. (1998). Are cities dying? *Journal of Economic Perspectives*, 12(2) : 139-160.

Goussios, D. (2006). Développement rural dans la petite région rurale de Mouzaki (Grèce) : du territoire identitaire au territoire-réseau, In Chassany J.P. et Pellissier J.-P. (éd.) : *Politiques de développement rural durable en Méditerranée dans le cadre de la politique de voisinage de l'Union Européenne*. Options Méditerranéennes: Série A., Séminaires Méditerranéens; n°71, CIHEAM, 153-167.

Goussios, D. (1999). Rural areas, agricultural space and small towns, In Economou D., Petrakos G. (ed.): *The development of Greek Cities*. Thessaly University Press, Gutenberg, Volos, Greece (en grec).

Goussios, D. (2011). Le regain d'intérêt du secteur agricole en Grèce : tendance lourde ou passagère ? Mission Agrobiosciences.

Goussios, D., Duquenne M-N. (2003). L'exploitation agricole à distance en Grèce: mobilité, pluriactivité et ruralisation, *Recherches récentes en géographie aixoise, Méditerranée, Revue géographique des pays méditerranéens*, Tome 100, n° 1.2, 45-48.

Goussios, D., Duquenne, M-N. (2005). Évolutions démographiques, logiquessocialesetnouvelles territorialisations dans l'espace rural, In Kotzamanis B., Pappas B. (ed.) : *Espace et Population: approches analytiques*, LADS, Université de Thessalie, Volos, 157-169.

Halfacree, K. (2008). To revitalize counterurbanisation research?Recognising an international and fuller picture. *Population, Space and Place*, 14, 479-495.

Hellenic Statistical Authority (EL.STAT). (2013a). Statistics on income and living conditions 2012, Press Release, 29 November, Hellenic Republic, Piraeus.

Hellenic Statistical Authority (EL.STAT).(2013b). Announcement of the demographic and social characteristics of the Resident Population of Greece according to the 2011 Population – Housing Census. Press Release, 23 August, Hellenic Republic, Piraeus.

Jacobs, J. (1969). The *economies of cities*. New York : Random House.

Kasimis, C., Papadopoulos, A.G. (2005). The Multifunctional Role of Migrants in Greek Countryside: Implications for Rural Economy and Society. *Journal of Ethnic and Migration Studies*, Vol. 31(1), 99-127.

Kasimis, C., Papadopoulos, A.G. (2013). Rural transformations and Family farming in contemporary Greece.*Research in Rural Sociology and Development*, 19, 263-293.

Kasimis, C., Zografakis S. (2013). Mobilities within and without : resilience in rural Greece in times of crisis, In: Proceedings of XXVth ESRS Congress, Rural resilience and vulnerability: the rural as locus of solidarity and conflict in times of crisis, 155-156.

Kelejian, H., Prucha, I. (2010). Specification and Estimation of Spatial Autoregressive Models with Autoregressive and Hetersoscedastic Disturbances. Journal of Econometrics, 157, 153-67.

Krugman, P. (1991). Increasing returns and economic geography. *Journal of Political Economy*, 99(3), 483-499.

Krugman, P. (1998). Space: The final frontier. *Journal of Economic Perspectives*, 12(2), 161-174.

Koutsou, S., Anthopoulou, T. (2008). Flux migratoires et systèmes agro-productifs locaux: mutations spatiales et sociales dans l'espace rural, In Zacopoulou E., Kasimis C., Louloudis L. (ed.), *Ruralité, Société et Terriroire*, Plethron, Athènes (en grec).

Lepicier, D., Sencébé, Y. (2007). Migrations résidentielles de l'urbain vers le rural en France: différenciation sociale des profils et ségrégation spatiale, *Espaces-Temps.net*, Travaux, 10.05.2007.

Montenay, Y. (2011). La démographie politique et la crise économique. *Diploweb.com*.

Mitchell, C.J.A. (2004). Making sense of counterurbanisation. *Journal of Rural Studies*, 20, 15-34.

Papadopoulos, A.G. (2011). Transnational Immigration in rural Greece: Analysing the Different Mobilities of Albanian Immigrants, In: Hedberg C. and R.M. do Carmo (eds), *TranslocalRuralism*, Springer, 163-183.

Torre, A., Filippi M. (2005). Les mutations à l'œuvre dans les Mondes Ruraux et leurs impacts sur l'organisation de l'espace, In Torre A. et Filippi M. (eds), *Proximités et Changements socio-économiques dans les Mondes Ruraux*, INRA Editions, collection Un point sur, 1-36.

Verdier, M. (2013). En Grèce, le retour à la terre… des temps modernes, *La Croix, 14-15 Décembre*, Dossier "Face à la violence de la crise économique, bien des Grecs retournent vivre dans les villages d'où sont partis leurs parents et lancent des projets de remise en valeur. Exemple à Ellinopyrgos".

Wilson, G. (2009). The spatiallity of multifunctional agriculture: A human geography perspective. Geoforum, 40(2), 269-280.

Woods, M. (2009). Rural geography: Blurring boundaries and making connections. Progress in Human geography, 33(6), 849-858.

Tsoukalas, K. (1984) Employment structure and the miracle of small and medium size firms, *Anti*, 213, 36.

Wacquant, L. (2008) *Urban Outcasts.A Comparative Sociology of Advanced Marginality,* Cambridge, Polity.

RETURNING IN RURALITY: THE DEMOGRAPHICAL IMPACTS OF THE GREEK CRISIS

Abstract - *Life conditions have strongly deteriorated in the large Greek urban areas and more specifically in Athens and Thessaloniki, after 2008. Poverty, unemployment and exclusion hit an important part of their inhabitants who prefer migrating towards rural areas, less exposed to the economic crisis. This paper aims to examine the changes in the spatial distribution of population between 2001 and 2011, focusing on the impacts of the crisis.*

Key words - REGIONAL MIGRATION, RURALITY, GREECE

COMPTE RENDU

Alain Piveteau, Eric Rougier, Dalila Nicet-Chenaf (dir.), *Emergences capitalistes aux Suds*, Karthala, Paris, 2013, 350 p.

Dans cet ouvrage collectif, A. Piveteau, E. Rougier et D. Nicet-Chenaf regroupent quatorze contributions en quatre parties dont le dénominateur commun est la volonté d'éclairer le concept « d'émergence ». Ce fil conducteur assure une relative homogénéité à la lecture, ce qui n'est pas toujours le cas dans ce type d'ouvrage. Les différents angles d'approche (économique, social, géographique, politique...), les échelles spatiales retenues (macro et micro) et la multiplicité des cas d'études illustrent in fine la diversité des modèles d'émergence dans les pays du Sud.

Une clé possible de lecture de cet ouvrage est de considérer que ces « émergences » ont en commun une intégration croissante à l'économie mondiale. Sur le seul plan des échanges, Michalopoulos et Ng (2013) montrent que les BRICS (Brésil, Russie, Inde, Chine, Afrique du Sud) ont vu leur part dans le commerce mondial passer de 3,7 % à 16,3 % entre 1980 et 2010, quand, dans le même temps, les pays en développement dans leur ensemble (à l'exclusion de la Chine et de l'Inde) voyaient cette part stagner à moins de 30 %. En parallèle, l'OCDE (2010) prévoit que le club des « E7 », les sept plus grandes économies émergentes (BRIC, Indonésie, Mexique, Turquie) dépasseront le G7 dès 2017 en termes de PIB PPA.

Sur ce plan, l'ouvrage permet de battre en brèche un certain nombre d'idées reçues sur la mondialisation, dont deux peuvent être ici particulièrement relevées.

En premier lieu, la mondialisation n'est pas un phénomène homogène : les processus d'émergence actuels, déjà très différents de ceux connus par les pays développés au XIXe siècle, sont peut-être aussi nombreux que les pays qui les expérimentent, et en tout cas ne résultent pas d'un modèle d'ouverture économique unique ; l'émergence, bien que liée à la mondialisation, n'est pas un phénomène « global », elle est au contraire spatialement circonscrite et souvent génératrice d'inégalités.

En second lieu, la mondialisation ne remet pas en cause la capacité d'action des Etats : les différents chapitres de l'ouvrage soulignent la nécessité de politiques publiques adaptées, à la fois dans la première phase de l'émergence pour réussir l'intégration à l'économie mondiale, et dans une deuxième phase pour sortir du « piège » des pays à revenus intermédiaires.

Les « émergences » comme illustration d'une mondialisation hétérogène

Les modèles d'émergence présentent aujourd'hui des trajectoires variées en fonction des pays. Comme le notent A. Piveteau et E. Rougier en introduction, « les émergences capitalistes... sont le résultat provisoire d'une contribution inédite et originale des pays du Sud à la dynamique mondiale du capitalisme ».

L'insertion des émergents dans l'économie mondiale ne résulte pas du calque d'un modèle ultra-libéral unique : « les pays qui ont le plus bénéficié de la mondialisation sont ceux qui ont le moins respecté ses règles et ont mis en place des combinaisons originales d'éléments orthodoxes et d'hérésies locales, c'est-à-dire des variations locales d'expérimentations institutionnelles ».

J. Vercueil revient notamment sur les politiques d'ouverture des BRIC. Alors que la Russie expérimente les errements de la « thérapie de choc » dans les années 1990, le Brésil, l'Inde et bien sûr la Chine adoptent des stratégies d'ouverture plus progressives et plus prudentes qui combinent souvent libéralisation des échanges et protectionnisme. Il aura ainsi fallu 17 ans à la Chine pour conclure son adhésion à l'OMC. En 2010, le niveau moyen de protection tarifaire appliqué par les BRIC est encore le double de celui de l'Union européenne. L'auteur revient également sur d'autres idées reçues, en montrant notamment que l'émergence n'est pas forcément le signe d'un excédent de la balance commerciale (l'Inde et le Brésil s'étant par exemple accommodés d'un déficit courant durable grâce à des flux importants d'investissements directs ou de portefeuille) ou d'une sous-évaluation réelle du taux de change (la Roupie indienne, le Real brésilien ou le Rouble russe ayant plutôt connu une appréciation réelle dans les années 2000).

L. Hasenclever et J. Paranhos proposent également une différenciation des émergents en termes de capacité technologique, à partir d'indicateurs « d'entrée et de sortie » de l'innovation.

P. Hugon, D. Nicet-Chenaf et E. Rougier utilisent le prisme de la crise de 2008-2009 comme révélateur des forces et faiblesses respectives des économies émergentes en fonction notamment de leur degré d'intégration à la mondialisation financière et commerciale. Ainsi, les pays émergents d'Europe vont connaître de fortes turbulences financières du fait de leurs importants liens bancaires avec les pays d'Europe occidentale, alors que les émergents d'Asie seront peu affectés par le canal financier du fait de politiques financières plus prudentes. La transmission de la crise par le canal commercial a davantage impacté l'Amérique du Sud, dont une grande partie des dynamiques de croissance trouvent leurs origines dans celles de l'économie américaine et de l'environnement global, tandis qu'en Asie la plupart des pays réussissent à conserver des rythmes de croissance élevés, en s'appuyant notamment sur des facteurs internes et des coopérations régionales leur permettant de réduire leur dépendance au système global. Les auteurs proposent une typologie des émergents en quatre groupes traduisant des vulnérabilités différentes face à la crise : les grands émergents compétitifs (Chine, Brésil), les pays en voie d'émergence et peu compétitifs, les pays rentiers (Russie...), les petits émergents extravertis faiblement diversifiés et compétitifs (Maroc, Philippines). On peut renvoyer sur ces questions le lecteur à l'ouvrage de Hugon et Salama (2010) dont un compte rendu a été donné dans le n° 31-2010 de *Région et Développement*.

Loin d'être homogène, selon A. Piveteau et E. Rougier, « l'émergence se présente très souvent comme un phénomène partiel, spatialement circonscrit et inégalitaire », posant la question de la soutenabilité sociale de l'essor économique.

L'émergence impacte l'emploi et les marchés du travail. C.A. Vega analyse en détail l'expansion des activités informelles au Mexique, et à Mexico en particulier. L'ouverture économique s'est traduite par de nouvelles formes d'articulation d'un ensemble de micro-activités urbaines avec le marché national et mondial. Dans l'alimentation ou le textile par exemple, les petits ateliers de production ont été frappés par le poids croissant des grands groupes agroalimentaires nationaux ou par la concurrence étrangère, tandis que proliféraient les petits commerces informels distribuant à faible coût des produits importés. Ce poids très important du secteur informel est également souligné par J.C. Verez dans le chapitre consacré à la Turquie. Il affecte les entreprises formelles et ne permet pas de stabiliser l'assiette fiscale nécessaire à la constitution d'un levier durable de croissance.

De manière plus générale, si l'émergence, avec ses phases de croissance rapide, tend à élever le niveau de vie moyen et à réduire la pauvreté, elle génère également des inégalités croissantes au sein des pays. Comme le note J. Ruet à propos de l'Inde et de la Chine, l'intégration de l'Asie dans le système productif mondial a conduit à un rattrapage en termes de PIB/habitant. Les différences entre monde développé et monde émergent sont traduites par un « écart », exprimé en parité moyenne de pouvoir d'achat, qui se résorbe, « mais des phénomènes « dé-moyennisés », territorialisés, apparaissent pour déplacer les inégalités ».

A l'Ile Maurice, K. Koot souligne la fragmentation sociale et les tendances au ré-appauvrissement, avec une forte composante spatiale : dans les régions côtières se développent les zones résidentielles des « gagnants » de la mondialisation, alors que la pauvreté réapparaît ou s'aggrave dans les régions rurales. Au Brésil, la mondialisation a accentué la concurrence entre territoires pour attirer les investissements. La région du Nordeste, plus particulièrement étudiée dans ce chapitre par J. Filho, M.C. Pereira de Melo et Y.A. Fauré, n'a pas su tirer parti de l'ouverture des années 1990 et 2000. Les incitations fiscales pour attirer les investissements n'ont pas suffi, en l'absence de modèle industriel probant, à induire des avantages structurels permettant de placer la région sur une nouvelle trajectoire de développement. En Chine, C. Bonnefond note que le modèle de croissance spatialement déséquilibré suivi à la fin des années 1980 a favorisé les provinces côtières (qui comptent par exemple pour plus de 90 % des exportations et des investissements étrangers du pays) sans que de véritables effets de diffusion se soient encore manifestés vers l'intérieur du pays. Le coefficient de Gini est ainsi passé de 0.28 en 1981 à 0.447 en 2004. Au-delà de la contribution de l'auteur, on peut ajouter que des articles récents montrent un virage depuis, et qu'un certain processus de diffusion économique inter et inter-provinciale s'est mis en place.

Les « émergences » et le renforcement du rôle des politiques publiques dans la mondialisation

Plutôt que de signer la fin de « l'Etat-nation », la mondialisation redéfinit avant tout ses contours, et, de manière apparemment paradoxale, tend plutôt à renforcer le besoin de politiques adaptées face à de nouvelles contraintes pour réussir l'émergence et l'intégration à l'économie mondiale.

Dans une comparaison entre les trajectoires du Mexique, de l'Argentine et du Brésil, I. Bizberg et B. Théret développement l'idée que la réussite du Brésil « est due à une conformation particulière de son système sociopolitique qui lui a permis de préserver puis capitaliser les acquis de son industrialisation passée. A la différence du reste de l'Amérique latine, le Brésil a pu et su résister à une imposition pure et simple du modèle économique néolibéral qui impliquait [...] la destruction des instruments d'intervention de l'Etat dans l'économie ».

Le cas du Vietnam, présenté par J-R. Chaponnière et J-P. Cling, montre comment la réactivité de la politique économique a permis au pays, au-delà d'aspects plus structurels, d'être peu affecté par la crise de 2008-2009 : programme d'austérité pour réduire le déficit commercial, baisse des taux d'intérêts, politiques de relance au travers de baisses d'impôt et de financement d'investissements productifs...). A plus long terme, l'Etat impulse, avec l'aide de capitaux étrangers, une diversification progressive vers des industries de biens intermédiaires ou entrants dans la division verticale du travail à l'échelle de la région asiatique. Ce chapitre illustre bien également les nouvelles contraintes liées à la mondialisation et plus particulièrement à l'adhésion du pays à l'OMC en 2007, avec l'interdiction des subventions à l'exportation de produits industriels imposant un changement de régime des zones franches, l'accélération du processus de privatisation des entreprises publiques, la nécessité de gérer de forts afflux de capitaux, etc.

Dans la même veine, L. Hasenclever et J. Paranhos analysent les performances du Brésil et de l'Inde dans le secteur pharmaceutique en montrant comment leurs trajectoires respectives ont été influencées par les politiques industrielles et technologiques adoptées par ces deux pays, notamment suite à l'approbation de l'Accord de 1994 sur les Aspects des Droits de Propriété Intellectuelle (ADPIC). La libéralisation (trop) rapide du Brésil conjuguée à une faiblesse de la politique industrielle a eu des effets délétères sur sa balance commerciale pharmaceutique. A l'inverse, la libéralisation plus prudente de l'Inde et sa politique technologique active dans les années 1990 lui ont permis de doubler son marché pharmaceutique entre 1996 et 2006. En Inde toujours, L. Kennedy, K. Robin et D. Zamuner mettent en avant le rôle décisif des politiques économiques infranationales dans les trajectoires de développement de quatre Etats indiens : croissance rapide basée sur l'exploitation de fortes ressources naturelles dans l'Orissa mais où perdurent encore de fortes disparités géographiques et sociales ; Le Kerala bien doté en infrastructures physiques et sociales mais ne parvenant pas à attirer suffisamment les investisseurs du fait de discontinuités dans les politiques industrielles ; révolution verte et forte croissance industrielle dans l'Haryana qui met l'accent sur le développement des infrastructures au moyen de partenariats avec le secteur privé ; orientation de l'investissement vers les secteurs dynamiques de l'économie mondiale dans l'Andhra Pradesh.

Le rôle de l'Etat s'avère également fondamental dans ce qu'on pourrait appeler la « deuxième étape » de l'émergence. Pour schématiser, les pays ayant réussi la première phase d'insertion à l'économie mondiale, souvent sur la base d'une forte compétitivité-prix, doivent ensuite consolider en l'espace d'une ou deux générations leur modèle de développement. Le chapitre de K. Koop sur l'Ile Maurice montre que seulement dix ans après son essor dans les années 1980, la hausse de salaires avait déjà mis à mal la compétitivité des produits manufacturiers mauriciens, et le chômage a ré-augmenté depuis 1991, passant de 2,3 % à 8,5 % en 2007. Plus largement, l'OCDE (2010) note qu'« une nouvelle géographie de la croissance mondiale... fait apparaître l'hétérogénéité du Sud : certains pays en développement commencent à rattraper le niveau de vie des pays riches, tandis que d'autres s'efforcent de percer le « plafond de verre » du revenu intermédiaire et que d'autres encore continuent de souffrir de l'extrême pauvreté ».

Ces réformes de « seconde génération » sont complexes car politiquement difficiles : réforme des finances publiques, restructuration/privatisation des entreprises d'Etat, réforme du droit du travail, réformes et transparence des institutions...

Sur le plan productif, la montée en gamme est fondamentale. Au Vietnam, l'Etat, avec l'aide de capitaux étrangers, impulse de grands projets pour développer une industrie de biens intermédiaires (acier, pétrochimie, électronique...) pour diversifier ses exportations manufacturières qui reposent essentiellement sur le textile-habillement. A Maurice, la diversification s'oriente davantage vers des investissements dans les services (centre financier off-shore, port franc...).

Le chapitre de T. Stieven et L. Bensahel-Perrin, présentant le cas de la Russie sous l'angle du capital humain, soulignent que « la question de la préparation des personnes pour vivre et travailler dans les conditions nouvelles générées par la transition rapide vers le marché n'a pas été suffisamment prise en considération dans les politiques gouvernementales ». En considérant en parallèle l'insuffisance des investissements dans les nouvelles technologies et des spécialisations productives faiblement intensives en qualifications, la Russie peine à transformer son capital humain en réel avantage productif.

Plus largement, la dernière partie de l'ouvrage intitulée « Vers une économie politique de l'émergence » pose la question de l'intervention publique en Inde, en Chine, au Brésil, au Mexique et en l'Argentine (coalitions sociopolitiques dominantes, organisations sociales et capacité de régulation du marché du travail, régime monétaire, système financier, forme de l'Etat...). Elle révèle encore une fois la diversité des capitalismes émergeants au Sud et rappelle l'absence de recette miracle en matière de développement socioéconomique.

En conclusion, un livre peu technique mais qui offre un panorama très riche sur le développement des pays émergents.

Références

Hugon P., Salama P. (dir.), 2010, *Les Suds dans la crise*, Revue Tiers Monde, hors-série.

Michalopoulos C., Ng F., 2013, Trends in developing country trade, 1980-2010, *World Bank PRWP*, n° 6334.

OCDE, 2010, *Perspectives du développement mondial 2010 : Le basculement de la richesse*, OCDE.

Christophe Van Huffel
LEAD, Université de Toulon

OMC, *Rapport sur le commerce mondial 2013. Facteurs déterminant l'avenir du commerce mondial*, Organisation mondiale du commerce, 348 pages.

Même si l'OMC est aujourd'hui en perte de vitesse, son édition du *Rapport sur le commerce mondial* est attendue chaque année avec grand intérêt. Le Rapport 2013 ne déroge pas à la règle avec une première partie qui revient sur la situation du commerce en 2012 et une seconde qui examine les facteurs qui influenceront le commerce mondial dans les années à venir.

Les traits majeurs au cours de ces dernières années sont : 1/ Une participation géographique aux échanges de plus en plus élargie, du fait notamment du dynamisme des économies émergentes. 2/ L'essor de la production dans le cadre des chaînes d'approvisionnement mondiales. 3/ Le rôle croissant de la technologie dont les transports et les communications. 4/ Les forces politiques qui ont permis de gérer, amortir voire de résister aux pressions intégrationnistes. 5/ Une croissance vertigineuse du commerce international au cours des 30 dernières années : + 7 % par an pour les marchandises entre 1980 et 2011, atteignant un record de 18 000 milliards de $ US à la fin de cette période ; +8 % pour les services commerciaux pour atteindre 4 000 milliards de $ US en 2011. 6/ L'apparition de nouveaux acteurs dont certains pays en développement et des économies asiatiques en voie d'industrialisation. 7/ Une plus grande régionalisation depuis 1990, en particulier en Asie, contrebalancée par la stabilité des échanges intra-régionaux en Europe et en Amérique du Nord (due aux effets de la crise ?).

Les questionnements sur l'évolution du commerce mondial sont pluriels, notamment en ce qui concerne *les progrès techniques et la technologie* (lesquels ont constitué l'un des principaux moteurs de l'intégration économique mondiale au cours des 200 dernières années) ; *les transferts de technologie* qui deviennent un enjeu majeur dans les processus de délocalisation et de relocalisation ; *l'évolution démographique* (transition, vieillissement, migrations) qui rejaillit sur la structure des échanges et la demande d'importation ; *l'investissement* dans le capital matériel avec de nouveaux acteurs dans le contexte des chaînes d'approvisionnement et une évolution des avantages comparatifs des pays déjà très engagés dans le commerce international, sans omettre les flux de capitaux étrangers qui peuvent accompagner l'épargne intérieure pour financer les projets ; *l'énergie et les ressources naturelles* : la mise à disposition de ressources en énergie, en terre et en eau aura un effet décisif sur le volume, la structure et la croissance du commerce international, au même titre que la hausse et la volatilité des prix des ressources naturelles ; *les transports* dont les coûts impactent le volume, la répartition géographique et la composition des échanges internationaux ; *les institutions* qui, à l'image de l'OMC prônent l'intégration internationale en essayant de limiter l'impact des frontières politiques lesquelles font plutôt obstacle au commerce international.

Le commerce mondial et l'OMC sont face à des défis majeurs qui n'ont cessé d'opposer partisans et opposants au libre échange. L'intérêt du Rapport est de rappeler entre autres que la libéralisation des échanges a participé à la croissance économique sans oublier qu'il reste des préoccupations sociales (chômage et inégalités), environnementales (développement durable), macroéconomiques et financières (financement du commerce et incidence des taux de change). Au niveau de l'OMC *stricto sensu*, la question de la gouvernance relative au respect du libre échange restera le défi majeur. Les Accords commerciaux régionaux (ACR) ou les Accords commerciaux préférentiels (ACPr) sont des obstacles au multilatéralisme des échanges. Il n'est donc pas inutile de rappeler les contradictions des pays membres de l'OMC qui s'engagent à respecter le libre échange tout en multipliant des accords à vocation bilatérale et non multilatérale. Il n'est pas davantage inutile de rappeler que les règles du libre échange sont d'autant plus acceptables pour un pays que celui-ci est doté d'un avantage historique pour reprendre l'expression de Krugman. Si les récents progrès des économies émergentes montrent que la mondialisation des échanges autorise une évolution des rapports de force et un basculement du centre du monde, le commerce mondial reste concentré autour d'un petit nombre de pays.

Sur le plan méthodologique, les scénarios prospectifs proposés dans ce Rapport reposent dans un premier temps sur le volume des échanges qui dépend du PIB des pays (« ainsi que l'a amplement démontré la littérature sur la gravité », p. 93). L'élaboration des trajectoires de croissance économique s'appuie sur un modèle macroéconomique qui prend en compte la convergence conditionnelle, soit le fait que les pays ayant un PIB par habitant relativement faible ont une croissance plus rapide, sous réserve des facteurs structurels et des politiques qui leur sont propres. Les simulations distinguent trois facteurs de production (travail, capital et énergie) en plus du progrès technologique. En projetant chaque variable à partir d'estimations du comportement passé, le *Rapport* élabore un scénario de référence pour tous les pays/régions du modèle, avec des règles générales de bouclage (par exemple, l'épargne globale doit être égale à l'investissement global) et l'introduction de chocs (soit un écart défini d'une variable individuelle par rapport à sa projection de base, afin de voir ce que cela change en termes de résultats économiques par rapport à la situation initiale). Le cadre macroéconomique théorique permet d'assurer la cohérence des projections de base au niveau national et d'établir un ensemble homogène de projections de croissance pour l'économie mondiale.

Les projections à long terme recourent dans un second temps à la modélisation de la structure future des échanges via un modèle classique d'équilibre général calculable (MEGC) de l'économie mondiale. Les pays se spécialisent dans différents secteurs de biens et de services en tirant avantage de leur dotation factorielle, de leur technologie et de la proximité de la demande. « Les simulations présentées considèrent différents types de coûts commerciaux, liés à la fois à la géographie et aux politiques. Les premiers dépendent des transports et de l'évolution des prix des carburants. Quant aux seconds, ils dépendent à la fois des taxes commerciales et des autres mesures non tarifaires, telles que les frais de dédouanement et d'inspection des marchandises, ainsi que des obstacles à la fourniture de services » (p. 93).

Parmi les projections majeures et sous réserve d'un scénario haut, la Chine dépasserait les États-Unis et l'Union européenne en termes de taille économique au plus tard en 2030. En matière commerciale, toujours sous l'hypothèse d'un scénario haut, la Chine pourrait augmenter sa part des exportations pour atteindre près du quart du commerce mondial, tandis que l'Inde pourrait plus que doubler la sienne, atteignant 5 %. Les parts des grands pays développés diminueraient, mais la valeur absolue de leurs exportations et de leur PIB continuerait à augmenter. Le changement le plus spectaculaire concernerait la composition sectorielle du commerce avec une tendance à une augmentation du commerce des services quels que soient les scénarios. Pour autant, les produits manufacturés continueront de dominer le commerce international, représentant plus des deux tiers des exportations mondiales d'ici 2035. Quant au commerce à l'intérieur des grands blocs régionaux, il devrait diminuer fortement par rapport au commerce multilatéral : le commerce intra-UE passerait de 21 % du commerce mondial en volume à 8 % à peine, celui de l'ALENA verrait sa part diminuer de plus de la moitié tandis que le commerce avec les autres régions passerait de 70 % à plus de 85 % du commerce mondial, témoignant ainsi d'une tendance à une intégration multilatérale accrue.

Le Rapport 2013 pose plusieurs interrogations. S'il fournit assurément de nombreux enseignements à un horizon de moyen terme, ce en quoi il est très utile, on regrette que la dimension prospective s'appuie « dans une large mesure sur des extrapolations des tendances actuelles, pour tenter de prédire l'avenir » (p. 42). Bien qu'il faille reconnaître les difficultés inhérentes à ce type d'exercice, il est toujours délicat de penser l'avenir à partir des scénarios passés. On en veut pour preuve l'explosion des pays émergents et leur part croissante dans les échanges mondiaux. On n'aurait sans doute pas prévu avec exactitude il y a 20 ou 30 ans leurs trajectoires récentes.

Une autre limite, soulignée dans le Rapport, concerne le caractère imprévisible ou difficilement prévisible de certaines variables comme les prix de l'énergie qui dépendent certes des lois économiques de l'offre et de la demande mais aussi de facteurs géopolitiques par définition incertains. On retrouve ces mêmes questionnements à propos des flux migratoires, de la mobilité des capitaux, de l'innovation et des processus de sa diffusion, etc. « Par conséquent, bien que les simulations soient effectuées dans un cadre de modélisation théoriquement rigoureux et complet, nous tenons compte de la marge d'incertitude en développant deux trajectoires extrêmes (haute et basse) pour toutes les variables clés » (p. 98). Le degré d'incertitude relatif aux trajectoires reste toutefois « assez élevé ». Le cas des pays en développement l'illustre parfaitement : leur taux de croissance annuel moyen pendant la période de prévision peut varier dans une proportion allant jusqu'à 2 %, le revenu par habitant pourrait être inferieur d'un tiers ou supérieur de 50 % environ en 2035.

Ces limites ne doivent pas occulter les réflexions que suscite le Rapport et qui sont à même de déboucher sur de ***nouveaux thèmes de recherche tant en économie internationale qu'en économie du développement***. 1/ La tendance à la régionalisation du commerce dans le monde en développement, notamment en Asie à l'inverse du commerce intra-régional européen ou américain (du Nord), est une nouvelle configuration des échanges. Les processus d'intégration économique régionale peuvent être révisés à la lumière des expériences passées et des tendances nouvelles. 2/ Le fait que le commerce dépende de plus en plus de quelques grandes entreprises mondiales (sans frontière) pose l'épineuse question de leur régulation et de la gouvernance en général. 3/ Les pays en développement comme les pays développés sont devenus moins spécialisés ou, dit autrement, leurs exportations se sont diversifiées. Est-ce de nature à pointer davantage les limites de la théorie ricardienne ? 4/ La production est de plus en plus fragmentée, tant entre les pays qu'au sein des pays. N'est-ce pas suffisant pour remettre en question les mesures traditionnelles des flux commerciaux et exiger un nouveau système de mesure apte à déterminer le(s) lieu(x) où la valeur ajoutée est accumulée ? 5/ L'ascension des pays en développement est en marche : certains vont échanger de plus en plus entre eux. Est-ce un facteur favorable au multilatéralisme des échanges ou un facteur apte à renforcer le protectionnisme de la part des pays industrialisés ? 6/ La croissance économique dans les pays émergents et en développement et leur participation accrue aux échanges mondiaux contribuent à la création d'une classe moyenne mondiale. Si on y associe un accès plus facile à l'éducation et une participation croissante des femmes à la vie active, il convient de bien mesurer l'évolution des structures économiques de ces pays mais aussi et peut-être plus des structures institutionnelles, sociales et politiques. 7/ La montée en qualification des emplois et la montée en instruction de la population mondiale vont-elles remodeler les marchés du travail avec, notamment dans les pays en développement, des tensions à la baisse en matière de fuite des cerveaux ? 8/ Les croissances démographique et économique auront certainement pour conséquence d'accroître le prix de l'énergie. Cette tendance pourrait se traduire par une diminution de la part des produits à forte intensité énergétique avec à la clé un impact sur les économies nationales selon qu'elles soient exportatrices ou importatrices de ces produits. De même, de graves pénuries d'eau en Asie du Sud, au Moyen Orient, en Afrique du Nord ou en Chine pourraient entraîner une augmentation des importations de produits alimentaires et agricoles, soit là aussi des tendances aptes à modifier la géographie des échanges mondiaux. Comment ne pas imaginer les incidences de ces évolutions sur les politiques commerciales des différents partenaires ? 9/ La hausse des revenus dans de nombreux pays émergents et en développement rejaillit sur le pouvoir d'achat d'une partie des consommateurs qui, plus riches, se soucient moins de l'accès de base à l'alimentation. Ils peuvent ainsi commencer à accorder plus d'importance à la qualité des aliments de sorte que l'on doit souligner la montée des inquiétudes au sujet de la sécurité sanitaire des produits alimentaires. Si dans plusieurs régions du monde, la question de la sécurité alimentaire reste d'actualité, il s'agit ici davantage d'une volonté de renforcement de la réglementation sanitaire des aliments avec à la clé l'adoption de nouvelles formes de mesures non tarifaires (MNT) ou de programmes d'étiquetage privés.

In fine, le Rapport de l'OMC 2013, au-delà de son intérêt avec la publication de ses nombreux indicateurs statistiques et de son analyse de prospective, suscite autant de débats que de questionnements sur les échanges, les règles commerciales, l'évolution des rapports de force entre pays et blocs régionaux, de quoi alimenter les recherches en économie internationale et du développement.

Jean-Claude Vérez
LEAD, Université de Toulon

Arnaud Bourgain, Jean Brot, Hubert Gérardin (dir.), *L'intégration de l'Afrique dans l'économie mondiale*, Karthala, Paris, 2014, 300 p.

Longtemps marginalisée, l'Afrique est aujourd'hui un des acteurs de l'économie-monde multipolaire mais son insertion dans la mondialisation recouvre des situations nationales contrastées. L'ouvrage s'interroge sur le sens et la portée de cette insertion à partir de quatre thématiques : I- Les dynamiques d'intégration Asie/Afrique. II- Les modalités d'exploitation des matières premières. III- La coopération avec l'espace européen. IV- Les enjeux des migrations africaines.

Le thème I comprend trois articles et s'ouvre ***sur le rôle des puissances émergentes dans les transformations économiques de l'Afrique*** (Hugon). L'auteur, spécialiste reconnu du continent, inscrit sa réflexion dans le temps long : d'une part l'Afrique successivement confrontée à la colonisation, à la post colonisation puis à la mondialisation ; d'autre part l'Occident qui constate que l'histoire s'écrit désormais avec les pays émergents. La Chine et l'Inde deviennent des partenaires privilégiés de l'Afrique de sorte qu'au couplage ancien Nord/Sud se substitue un certain couplage Sud/Sud.

Il reste que l'Afrique est hétérogène. Composée de 54 États, les dynamiques en cours dans les pays anglophones d'Afrique de l'Est ou d'Afrique australe ont peu à voir avec celles observées en Afrique centrale et de l'Ouest francophones tandis que certains pays lusophones décollent. De fait, la « décennie perdue » des années 1990 laisse place à une croissance soutenue mais différenciée selon les pays et à des relations de coopération elles aussi différenciées. L'auteur dissocie les pays pétroliers ou miniers (Algérie, Angola, Nigéria) très convoités par la Chine et à un degré moindre par l'Inde, la puissance régionale semi-industrialisée qu'est l'Afrique du Sud (premier partenaire africain de la Chine et l'Inde), les économies agro-industrielles à forte croissance (Ghana Kenya, Tanzanie, les petits pays émergents (Maroc, Tunisie ou Maurice) avec lesquels les relations sont de moyenne intensité et, enfin, les pays pris dans des trappes à pauvreté qui restent fragiles ou en conflit (Somalie, Mali, Madagascar) mais qui attirent la Chine et l'Inde notamment pour l'accès au foncier.

In fine, les relations économiques croissantes entre l'Afrique et les puissances émergentes d'Asie recouvrent des enjeux multiples. Il existe une réelle volonté de l'Afrique de s'intégrer à l'économie mondiale et tourner ainsi le dos à l'ère postcoloniale. L'Afrique aura dans une vingtaine d'années la plus forte proportion de population active du monde (face à une Chine vieillissante), disposera d'un capital naturel substantiel et représentera un marché porteur comptant pour un quart de la population mondiale en 2050. Les défis sont nombreux : devenir le nouvel atelier du monde ou maintenir des économies de rente ; rechercher l'accumulation productive et la promotion de l'innovation ou maintenir des économies peu diversifiées ; se soucier de la croissance et/ou du développement tant humain que durable ; rechercher le bien-être des consommateurs et ou accroître les inégalités de revenus au profit d'une minorité. L'auteur précise avec raison que les réponses à ces défis dépendront autant des stratégies économiques que des rapports de pouvoir, des luttes sociales et des mouvements de démocratisation.

Le deuxième article analyse ***les performances à l'exportation de l'Afrique sub-saharienne (ASS) et de l'Asie en développement (AD)*** (Diaw, Rieber, And-Dao Tran). Les auteurs utilisent un modèle économétrique pour tester les spécificités du commerce Sud-Sud via le commerce bilatéral entre l'ASS et l'AD. De manière générale, une recomposition géographique du commerce mondial se dessine à partir du développement de plusieurs pays asiatiques et de l'approfondissement du processus d'intégration régionale entre pays du Sud. Le cadre d'analyse de référence est celui de Redding et Venables qui permet d'introduire dans les modèles de commerce international une dimension géographique. La dimension spatiale est abordée à la fois sous l'angle de la géographie interne d'un pays et sous l'angle international en resituant un pays dans son espace régional. L'estimation des paramètres par un modèle gravitationnel permet de décomposer les performances à l'exportation en dissociant ce qui relève de la capacité d'offre (facteur interne) et de l'accès au marché international (facteur externe). L'étude empirique porte sur les exportations de 54 pays du Sud (dont 38 d'ASS) à destination de 175 pays. Les auteurs en concluent que ces pays ont partagé une dynamique commune : leurs performances à l'exportation depuis le début des années 1990 résultent principalement de leur capacité d'offre interne.

Le dernier article du thème 1 porte sur ***la Chine, nouvel investisseur et bailleur de fonds : interactions avec le processus de développement des pays africains – le cas de la Zambie*** (Belligoli). La sécurité d'approvisionnement en matières premières est cruciale pour la croissance chinoise qui, elle-même, est cruciale pour la stabilité politique du pays. La réciprocité vaut-elle ? La présence des chinois en Afrique est-elle un atout pour la croissance et/ou le développement du continent ? L'auteur aborde cette question majeure à partir du cas zambien, pays extracteur et exportateur de quelques matières premières et dont les liens avec la Chine sont anciens. Bien qu'il soit difficile de connaître précisément le montant des investissements chinois, l'Agence zambienne du développement classe la Chine au 3è rang pour les IDE entrants, essentiellement dans le secteur minier et l'industrie extractive. Il y aurait entre 2000 et 20000 chinois en Zambie. En contrepartie, ce dernier importe des produits textiles et en cuir, des machines industrielles, des automobiles, des meubles. Fait plutôt rare en Afrique, la Zambie a une balance commerciale positive. Les retombées des importations chinoises sont à la fois positives (prix compétitifs et hausse du pouvoir d'achat zambien) et négatives (concurrence accrue qui pénalise les entreprises locales). La Chine est le premier créditeur de la Zambie, hors pays membres du club de Paris. Sur le plan de la diversification de son économie, la Zambie ne tire pas d'avantages substantiels de la présence chinoise, ce serait plutôt le contraire. Sur le plan environnemental, les effets externes sont négatifs. Le bilan est donc mitigé.

Le thème II commence par un article sur les ***économies territoriales et l'espace économique mondial – le cas de la sous-traitance dans le secteur textile-habillement au Maroc*** (Khallaf). L'espace, le territoire, l'organisation du travail ou celle des échanges entre les acteurs, les réseaux... sont autant de facteurs cités pour analyser la compétitivité des entreprises. Appliquée au textile-habillement marocain, l'étude révèle les liens entre grandes entreprises et

PME, voire les micro-entreprises, avec, à la clé, une conclusion évidente : plus les firmes sont grandes, moins elles sont vulnérables.

La contribution du secteur de l'or à l'économie malienne (Sega Diallo et Mainguy) n'est pas si facile à mesurer car l'abondance de ressources naturelles ou minières peut s'avérer dans les pays en développement une « malédiction ». Faute d'une gouvernance transparente ou d'une régulation durable, l'exploitation d'un telle ressource est souvent synonyme de conflits et de captation par une minorité affectant le développement du pays. En 2010, l'or représentait plus de 75 % des exportations maliennes tandis que les cours passaient de 284 dollars l'once en janvier 2000 à 1 721 en novembre 2012. Activité artisanale ou simplement de survie dans un cadre traditionnel et très ancien, l'exploitation de l'or est devenue une activité à grande échelle, notamment en raison de l'ouverture aux capitaux étrangers depuis une vingtaine d'années. La contribution croissante au budget malien est plus la conséquence de la hausse du prix de l'or que du volume de la production tiré à la baisse.

Au Niger, c'est l'uranium dont il est question. ***L'uranium et l'instabilité politique au Niger*** (Abba Gana) semblent étroitement liés. L'auteur rappelle dans un premier temps les travaux qui mentionnent que les ressources naturelles peuvent accroître la probabilité des guerres civiles ou aggraver la fragilité des États faute de pouvoir sortir des crises. Il rappelle également l'analyse du *Dutch disease* qui met en relation le faible développement des pays « pauvres » et l'abondance des ressources naturelles dont ils sont nantis de sorte que l'hypothèse ethniciste invoquée pour expliquer les guerres civiles africaines ne lui paraît pas crédible.

L'article analyse ensuite l'exploitation d'uranium à Arlit, situé au Nord du Niger, par la société transnationale Areva. En 2011, l'uranium représentait 61 % des exportations totales, contribuait pour 5 % au PIB et pour 5 % des recettes fiscales. On comprend aisément dans ces conditions le rapport de force et les difficultés pour toute autre firme de pénétrer le marché. Pour reprendre Baumol, le marché de l'uranium au Niger s'apparente à un marché non contestable. Si l'arrivée d'autres acteurs acceptée par l'État nigérien depuis 2007 a engendré des tensions, elle n'a pas bouleversé l'asymétrie des positions et Areva a obtenu de nouvelles exploitations. Sur fond d'instabilité politique, l'auteur rappelle avec force les mauvais choix des gouvernements successifs qui n'ont guère permis d'amorcer un réel développement. Il aurait pu mentionner que la très faible diversification de l'économie nigérienne n'est pas de nature à favoriser son intégration dans l'économie mondiale.

Dans ***la croissance économique africaine et l'ajustement du compte courant des États-Unis*** (Maswana), l'auteur souligne à plusieurs reprises l'impact du déficit des comptes courants américains sur la croissance de quelques pays en développement africains. Il recourt à une version modifiée du modèle de Thirlwall où l'élasticité-revenu des importations est estimée par un modèle autorégressif à effet de seuil. La contrainte extérieure s'ajoute à d'autres contraintes endogènes aux économies des cinq pays étudiés. Les contraintes « jumelles » tendent in fine à se renforcer l'une et l'autre de sorte que si l'on admet que le commerce extérieur stimule la croissance, il ne constitue pas pour autant un moyen efficace pour assurer une croissance pérenne.

Le thème III relatif à l'Afrique et aux coopérations européennes commence par ***le partenariat euro-méditerranéen*** (Montalieu et Trandas-Boboc). Les auteurs cherchent à identifier l'efficacité de l'aide européenne en passant en revue la légitimité puis la réforme de la conditionnalité avant d'analyser la réforme économique dans les pays méditerranéens. Trois études de cas sont proposées : Maroc, Égypte et Liban. Ils soulignent ensuite le besoin d'une coordination renouvelée entre schémas de coopération multilatérale qui permet d'une part, de dépasser le consensus de Washington et, d'autre part, de concevoir une logique d'interaction stratégique où l'UE n'est pas (plus) le seul acteur.

La coopération euro-méditerranéenne en matière de politique énergétique (Nicot et Morer), dix-huit ans après la déclaration de Barcelone, doit être encore confortée tant à propos de l'approvisionnement que des déséquilibres sur les marchés d'hydrocarbures ou de la sécurisation des infrastructures. L'Europe ne parvient pas à couvrir 50 % de ses besoins et sa dépendance est donc bien réelle. Les auteurs suggèrent la création d'une véritable Union euro-méditerranéenne pour desserrer la contrainte énergétique et recourent à un modèle gravitaire pour estimer l'impact du Processus de Barcelone (esquisse d'une Union) sur les échanges énergétiques. La méthodologie repose sur une analyse sectorielle des échanges, privilégie les particularismes locaux des blocs initiaux (UE15, PECO, UE25, Maghreb, Monde arabe), avant d'ajouter un nouveau bloc (pays du Golfe, OPEP), et porte sur les années 1995-2005. L'estimation économétrique du modèle gravitaire montre que le Processus de Barcelone a un effet d'entraînement sur les échanges énergétiques entre l'UE-25 et les pays méditerranéens laissant présager, selon les auteurs, des externalités positives d'une future Union euro-méditerranéenne.

Le dernier article du thème III se demande si ***le nouveau partenariat ACP-UE est un mythe ou une réalité*** (Matala-Tala). Au 1er janvier 2013, sur les 49 PMA, 39 sont dans la zone ACP et souffrent de faiblesse institutionnelle, de dépendance vis-à-vis de l'aide et de la multiplication des conditionnalités de la part des bailleurs de fonds. L'article discute de la nouvelle orientation de la coopération au développement de l'UE en direction des ACP sur fond de nouveaux enjeux comme l'intégration régionale ou l'émergence de l'Union africaine.

Le dernier thème (IV) traite des enjeux des migrations africaines. ***Quelles politiques face à la fuite du personnel médical d'ASS ?*** (Bourgain). La problématique est cruciale pour les pays en développement et pays d'émigration tant la fuite des cerveaux dans un contexte mondial d'économie de la connaissance réduit les *capabilities* pour reprendre l'expression de Sen. Le taux de fuite dans le secteur médical ne régresse pas et affaiblit toujours plus les systèmes locaux. Les travaux économétriques portant sur un panel de 47 pays pour les années 1990-2004 laissent apparaître un lien significativement positif entre le taux de fuite des médecins et le nombre d'adultes décédés du sida (Bhargava et Docquier, 2008). Quelles stratégies pourraient contrecarrer cette tendance ? L'auteur en relève trois : développer des politiques d'aides financières au secteur médical sans privilégier systématiquement les capitales ; passer des accords bilatéraux de partenariat avec, par exemple, des jumelages d'établissements hospitaliers ; substituer à du personnel très qualifié du personnel au départ moins qualifié. Il faut encore compter sur les forces d'attrait (*pull factors*) des secteurs médicaux des pays du Nord qui ne vont pas s'estomper si vite.

Le dernier article du thème IV et de l'ouvrage est écrit en anglais : ***Exploring the Brain Drain Phenomenon in Africa, an interdisciplinary approach*** (Hartmann-Mahmud). L'auteur étudie les facteurs *push-pull* via une approche interdisciplinaire. L'éducation valorisée est une source d'émigration afin de « réussir » à l'étranger, de recevoir des revenus supérieurs, en partie destinés ensuite à aider la famille restée au pays et, *in fine*, d'obtenir un certain prestige. Les explications monétaires ne sont donc pas suffisantes pour comprendre la fuite des cerveaux.

On retiendra de cet ouvrage collectif une pluralité d'approches, de thématiques et d'outils méthodologiques. Dans ce genre d'exercice, outre le fait que les contributions sont souvent voire toujours d'inégale valeur, on regrettera un fil conducteur insuffisamment resserré. Pour autant, l'ouvrage a le mérite de replacer les perspectives du continent africain pris dans sa globalité dans le contexte de la mondialisation. L'Afrique, certes plurielle et contrastée, s'intègre dans cette mondialisation au point où les analyses misérabilistes, de trappe à pauvretés ou de marginalisation ne sont plus suffisantes, bien que toujours nécessaires. Si l'Afrique reste un continent où les défis sont nombreux, notamment en matière de répartition des richesses, de développement humain et durable, de gouvernance, de libertés politiques, de nombreuses dynamiques sont en cours. De ce point de vue, l'ouvrage plutôt optimiste rappelle que l'Afrique est désormais davantage portée vers son avenir qu'arrêtée sur son passé. Rien n'est définitif et les scénarios du futur dépendront autant des contraintes et des atouts de la mondialisation que des forces et des faiblesses du continent lui-même.

Jean-Claude Vérez
LEAD, Université de Toulon

Philippe Hugon, *Mémoires solidaires et solitaires, Trajectoires d'un économiste du développement*, Karthala, Paris, 2013, 304 p.

Philippe Hugon, grand spécialiste de l'économie du développement et de l'Afrique, nous offre ses mémoires. Il aborde les différentes facettes de sa vie – sans séparer les pôles d'intérêt personnels et professionnels, l'intimité du parcours collectif, la quotidienneté de la spiritualité, l'anecdote de l'essentiel. Il empile d'une belle littérature les étagères de son parcours, avec une introduction d'une éclairante lucidité sur sa démarche et une conclusion profonde et émouvante.

Cet ouvrage n'est pas seulement une autobiographie au sens d'un parcours et d'un portrait personnel. Une philosophie de vie se dégage où, si toute écriture est solitaire pour le chercheur, comprendre « soi » est fait de rencontres, suppose participer à différents « je ».

Le lecteur ne trouvera pas un livre de réflexion sur l'économie du développement par l'universitaire et l'expert de terrain qu'il est et ce n'est pas du tout un ouvrage scientifique. Le seul tableau chiffré donné dans le livre est le rappel du « Sceau de Saturne » (p. 224) ! Pour Philippe Hugon d'ailleurs, l'économie et a fortiori l'économie du développement, à l'instar d'A. Hirschman[1], est avant tout une science morale et politique, éclectique, loin d'une conception instrumentale et formalisée et des exigences académiques actuelles.

Les souvenirs et les impressions donnés trouveront écho chez les universitaires – au-delà même de ceux de sa génération – soucieux de réfléchir sur les valeurs fondatrices de leur engagement personnel et chez tous ceux imprégnés d'une culture humaniste et non dénués d'humour au sens de Jules Renard : « l'humour c'est la pudeur, la propreté morale et quotidienne de l'esprit » (cité p. 219).

Maurice Catin
LEAD, Université de Toulon

[1] Dont on appréciera le discours qu'il fit en son honneur en 1993 à Paris X Nanterre pour la remise du diplôme de Docteur Honoris Causa, pp. 94-95.

REVUE RÉGION ET DÉVELOPPEMENT

Site Web : www.regionetdeveloppement.org

Recommandations aux auteurs

La Revue Région et Développement publie en français ou en anglais des articles originaux, des notes et documents et des comptes rendus de lecture. Pour soumission à publication, l'auteur doit adresser à la rédaction de la revue le texte par courrier électronique ou le manuscrit dactylographié en deux exemplaires. La présentation des chapitres, des références bibliographiques et des notes de bas de page doit être conforme à celle de la revue. Les articles doivent être accompagnés d'un résumé en français et en anglais d'une dizaine de lignes, des mots-clés correspondants et de la classification du JEL. Le nom de l'auteur, l'institution à laquelle il appartient et l'adresse complète doivent figurer en page de garde.
Les articles proposés à la revue Région et Développement sont évalués par le Comité de rédaction puis soumis de manière anonyme à un ou deux referees. L'auteur reçoit un rapport d'évaluation, lui aussi anonyme, concluant à publication, révision ou refus.
Après avis favorable à la publication dans la revue, il sera demandé à l'auteur un envoi par mail du texte en Word (y compris figures, tableaux et formules mathématiques compatibles avec Word 2010).

Les propositions d'articles doivent être adressées à la rédaction de la revue :

Professeur Maurice Catin
Revue Région et Développement
LÉAD - Faculté de Sciences Économiques et de Gestion
Université de Toulon
70 Avenue Roger Decouvoux
83 000 Toulon

Tél. : 04 83 36 63 18
Mail : maurice.catin@univ-tln.fr

Secrétaire général de la rédaction : Christophe Van Huffel
Mail : vanhuffel@univ-tln.fr

BULLETIN D'ABONNEMENT

Revue "Région et Développement"

• **Je désire souscrire un abonnement pour l'année 2014 (deux numéros) :**

☐ France, DOM-TOM : 37 € ☐ Étranger : 40 €

• **Règlement :**

☐ CCP ☐ Chèque bancaire ☐ Mandat international

Pour l'étranger, merci d'effectuer un virement en euros sur le ***CCP 23 625 44 N Paris*** ou bien un règlement par chèque bancaire en euros sur une banque domiciliée en France ou par carte de crédit internationale.

N° de la carte : ☐☐☐☐☐☐☐☐☐☐☐☐☐☐☐☐

Date d'expiration : ☐☐☐☐☐☐☐ Banque : ....

Nom et Prénom : ....

Adresse : ....

....

Code Postal : .... Ville : ....

Pays : ....

Date :

Signature :

Ce bulletin d'abonnement à la Revue "Région et Développement" et votre règlement sont à retourner à :

Éditions L'HARMATTAN - 7, rue de l'École-Polytechnique, 75005 PARIS

Tél. : 01 40 46 79 14 - fax : 01 43 29 86 20 - site web : www.librairieharmattan.com

Abonnement annuel : 2 numéros

France, DOM-TOM :	37 €
Étranger :	40 €

L'HARMATTAN ITALIA
Via Degli Artisti 15; 10124 Torino

L'HARMATTAN HONGRIE
Könyvesbolt ; Kossuth L. u. 14-16
1053 Budapest

L'HARMATTAN KINSHASA
185, avenue Nyangwe
Commune de Lingwala
Kinshasa, R.D. Congo
(00243) 998697603 ou (00243) 999229662

L'HARMATTAN CONGO
67, av. E. P. Lumumba
Bât. – Congo Pharmacie (Bib. Nat.)
BP2874 Brazzaville
harmattan.congo@yahoo.fr

L'HARMATTAN GUINÉE
Almamya Rue KA 028, en face
du restaurant Le Cèdre
OKB agency BP 3470 Conakry
(00224) 657 20 85 08 / 664 28 91 96
harmattanguinee@yahoo.fr

L'HARMATTAN MALI
Rue 73, Porte 536, Niamakoro,
Cité Unicef, Bamako
Tél. 00 (223) 20205724 / +(223) 76378082
poudiougopaul@yahoo.fr
pp.harmattan@gmail.com

L'HARMATTAN CAMEROUN
BP 11486
Face à la SNI, immeuble Don Bosco
Yaoundé
(00237) 99 76 61 66
harmattancam@yahoo.fr

L'HARMATTAN CÔTE D'IVOIRE
Résidence Karl / cité des arts
Abidjan-Cocody 03 BP 1588 Abidjan 03
(00225) 05 77 87 31
etien_nda@yahoo.fr

L'HARMATTAN BURKINA
Penou Achille Some
Ouagadougou
(+226) 70 26 88 27

L'HARMATTAN SÉNÉGAL
10 VDN en face Mermoz, après le pont de Fann
BP 45034 Dakar Fann
33 825 98 58 / 33 860 9858
senharmattan@gmail.com / senlibraire@gmail.com
www.harmattansenegal.com

L'HARMATTAN BÉNIN
ISOR-BENIN
01 BP 359 COTONOU-RP
Quartier Gbèdjromèdé,
Rue Agbélenco, Lot 1247 I
Tél : 00 229 21 32 53 79
christian_dablaka123@yahoo.fr

Achevé d'imprimer par Corlet Numérique - 14110 Condé-sur-Noireau
N° d'Imprimeur : 114250 - Dépôt légal : décembre 2014 - *Imprimé en France*

www.ingramcontent.com/pod-product-compliance
Lightning Source LLC
LaVergne TN
LVHW011011061026
849535LV00006B/1826
* 9 7 8 2 3 4 3 0 5 1 3 2 1 *